BOOKS AND THEIR READERS IN EIGHTEENTH-CENTURY ENGLAND: NEW ESSAYS

Edited by

Isabel Rivers

continuum
LONDON • NEW YORK

Continuum

The Tower Building, 11 York Road, London SE1 7NX
15 East 26th Street, New York 10010, USA
www.continuumbooks.com

First published in 2001
Reprinted 2003

British Library Cataloguing-in-Publication Data
A catalogue record for this book is available from the British Library.

ISBN 0-8264-7194-3 (hardback)
ISBN 0-8264-6717-2 (paperback)

Library of Congress Cataloging-in-Publication Data
Books and their readers in eighteenth-century England : new essays / edited by Isabel Rivers.
    p. cm.
    Includes bibliographical references and index.
    1. English literature—18th century—History and criticism. 2. Book industries and trade—England—History—18th century. 3. Books and reading—England—History—18th century. 4. Popular culture—England—History—18th century. 5. England—Intellectual life—18th century. I. Rivers, Isabel.

PR442.B57 2001
028′.0942′09033—dc21   00–054586

Typeset by CentraServe Ltd, Saffron Walden, Essex
Printed and bound in Great Britain by Biddles Ltd, *www.biddles.co.uk*

CONTENTS

NOTES ON CONTRIBUTORS   vii

PREFACE   ix

1 The Book Trades   1
  James Raven

2 The English Bible and its Readers in the Eighteenth Century   35
  Scott Mandelbrote

3 Theological Books from *The Naked Gospel* to *Nemesis of Faith*   79
  Brian Young

4 The History Market in Eighteenth-Century England   105
  Karen O'Brien

5 Biographical Dictionaries and their Uses from Bayle to Chalmers   135
  Isabel Rivers

6 Review Journals and the Reading Public   171
  Antonia Forster

7 Literary Scholarship and the Life of Editing   191
  Marcus Walsh

8 The Production and Consumption of the Eighteenth-Century
  Poetic Miscellany   217
  Michael F. Suarez SJ

SELECT BIBLIOGRAPHY   253

INDEX   283

NOTES ON CONTRIBUTORS

Antonia Forster, BA, MA (Flinders University), PhD (University of Melbourne), is Professor of English at the University of Akron. She is the author of *Index to Book Reviews in England 1749–1774* (1990), *Index to Book Reviews in England 1775–1800* (1997) and, with James Raven, Vol. 1 (1770–99) of *English Novels 1770–1829: A Bibliographical Survey of Prose Fiction Published in the British Isles* (2000). She has published a number of articles on early book reviewing and is preparing an edition of the correspondence of Ralph Griffiths.

Scott Mandelbrote, MA (Oxford), is Official Fellow and Director of Studies in History at Peterhouse, Cambridge, and Fellow of All Souls College, Oxford. His publications include *The Garden, the Ark, the Tower, the Temple: Biblical Metaphors of Knowledge in Early Modern Europe* (1998), written with Jim Bennett. He is currently working on a study of the knowledge and use of the Bible, and in particular the Book of Genesis, in early modern Britain. He is one of the editorial directors of a project to publish the theological, alchemical and administrative papers of Isaac Newton.

Karen O'Brien, MA, DPhil (Oxford), is Reader in English and American Literature at the University of Warwick. Her publications include *Narratives of Enlightenment: Cosmopolitan History from Voltaire to Gibbon* (1997), and a number of articles on historical writing and on literature and the British Empire in the eighteenth century. Her second book, *Feminist Debate in Eighteenth-Century Britain*, is forthcoming from Cambridge University Press.

James Raven, MA, PhD (Cambridge), is Reader in Social and Cultural History at the University of Oxford. He has written widely on the history of printing, publishing and reading practices in eighteenth-century Britain, Europe and the colonies. He is co-editor of *The Practice and Representation of Reading in England* (Cambridge University Press, 1996), and editor of *Free Print and Non-Commercial Publishing since 1700* (Ashgate Press, 2000). His most recent book is *London Booksellers and American Customers* (University of South Carolina Press, 2001).

Isabel Rivers, MA (Cambridge), MA, PhD (Columbia), is Professor of English Language and Literature at the University of Oxford and Fellow and Tutor in English at St Hugh's College, Oxford. Her publications include *The Poetry of Conservatism, 1600–1745* (1973), *Classical and Christian Ideas in English Renaissance Poetry* (2nd edn, 1994), and *Reason, Grace, and Sentiment: A Study of the Language of Religion and Ethics in England, 1660–1780*, 2 vols (1991, 2000). She is currently working on *The Literary Culture of Evangelicalism and Dissent, 1720–1800*.

Michael F. Suarez SJ, BA (Bucknell), MDiv, ThM (Weston Jesuit School of Theology), MA, MSt, DPhil (Oxford), is Associate Professor of English at Fordham University in New York. A Jesuit priest, his scholarly interests include bibliography and publishing history, the so-called 'sister arts', and literature and the history of ideas. In addition to having produced a study of Robert Dodsley's *Collection of Poems* (1997), he is co-editor (with Peter D. McDonald) of *Making Meaning: Selected Essays of D. F. McKenzie* (2001) and (with Michael Turner) of *The Cambridge History of the Book in Britain, Volume V, 1695–1830* (forthcoming). His current project is a study of mock-biblical satire from 1660 to 1832.

Marcus Walsh, MA, BPhil (Oxford), PhD (Toronto), is Professor of English Literature at the University of Birmingham. He edited with Karina Williamson the Oxford University Press *Poetical Works of Christopher Smart*. He has written extensively on Smart, Swift, Johnson and Sterne, on the history and theory of editing, and on biblical interpretation and scholarship in the seventeenth and eighteenth centuries. His study of *Shakespeare, Milton, and Eighteenth-Century Literary Editing* was published in 1997 by Cambridge University Press.

Brian Young, BA (Durham), DPhil (Oxford), is Reader in Intellectual History at the University of Sussex. He is the author of *Religion and Enlightenment in Eighteenth-Century England* (Oxford, 1998), and a co-editor with Stefan Collini and Richard Whatmore of *History, Religion, and Culture*, and *Economy, Polity, and Society* (Cambridge, 2000). He is at work on studies of the contexts of eighteenth-century scholarship, and the intellectual history of the British Empire in India.

PREFACE

When, as young lecturers at the University of Leicester in 1976, the late Ian Hilson and I thought up what was to become the first volume of *Books and their Readers in Eighteenth-Century England*, we were innocently unaware that we were striding as pioneers into a new world. *The Eighteenth Century Short Title Catalogue* was only in the planning stage, there were no electronic library catalogues, and a discipline called 'the history of the book' had not yet been widely recognized. *Books and their Readers* was published by Leicester University Press in 1982; it was a very successful and influential study, is much cited and has long been out of print. In the past twenty years there has been a revolution in the academic study of the history of the book, and I decided to bring together a new collection of essays by several younger scholars, all of whom have already made a considerable contribution to the subject. Both collections are concerned with the writing, editing, making, distributing, reading and interpreting of books in England, with some reference to Scotland and Ireland. The original collection contained essays by Terry Belanger on 'Publishers and writers', Pat Rogers on 'Classics and chapbooks', W. A. Speck on 'Politicians, peers, and publication by subscription', Penelope Wilson on 'Classical poetry', Thomas R. Preston on 'Biblical criticism', myself on 'Dissenting and Methodist books', John Valdimir Price on 'Philosophical literature' and G. S. Rousseau on 'Science books'. The new collection complements the original and adds much important new material. James Raven's account of the book trades builds on and considerably extends Belanger's survey. Religious literature, the largest area in eighteenth-century publishing, was well represented in the original collection; here Scott Mandelbrote gives a richly documented account of how the English Bible was regarded and disseminated, and Brian Young shows, through a series of case studies, how complex the role of the theological writer was. The remaining chapters explore topics that were untouched in the previous collection. Karen O'Brien surveys the development of the market in historical writing throughout the century, and Marcus Walsh explores the changes in the role of the literary scholar and editor. The other contributors focus from different points of view on specific kinds of eighteenth-century publication: Antonia Forster on review journals, Michael Suarez on poetic miscellanies, and myself on biographical dictionaries. The making of this book has been greatly assisted by *The Eighteenth Century Short Title Catalogue* (now subsumed in *The English Short Title Catalogue*), but, however valuable, it remains only an enabling tool: the history of the book is in the hands of individual readers and interpreters of individual books.

Isabel Rivers
Oxford, October 2000

CHAPTER 1

THE BOOK TRADES

JAMES RAVEN

Introduction

In the opening chapter to the first volume of *Books and their Readers* Terry Belanger reviewed the history of publishing in the eighteenth century. His account offered an important outline of the shifting contours of the book industry during a period of extraordinary transformation. Since the publication of that survey — written very much in recognition of the want of a general up-to-date publishing history of the period — many others have laboured on our often rough-hewn profile of eighteenth-century bibliographical change. The result is a more sharply focused history of the sort called for by Belanger. Although the general features of his original survey are largely retained, much is also more clearly defined.[1]

The fundamental story remains that of the complex penetration of print through eighteenth-century English society. In the early 1690s, shackled by post-Restoration licensing laws, printing was a restricted medium confined to London, Cambridge, Oxford and York; by 1800 print issued from hundreds of presses operating in London and almost every small town in the country. In 1700 a handful of double-sided weekly or twice-weekly news-sheets served London; by 1800 dozens of daily and weekly newspapers were published in London and the major provincial towns. London and country booksellers now sold a range of literature, still mostly printed and published in London, but available in unprecedented variety and, according to their type, in unprecedented quantity and quality. In the final decades before the introduction of steam-driven mechanized printing in 1814, English bookseller-publishers brought out an immense diversity of books, pamphlets, newspapers, general and specialist magazines, periodicals and part-issues that could reach almost every town in the three kingdoms. As will be given particular emphasis in this account, the eighteenth-century English book trade might be more precisely understood as the book *trades*, a set of distinctive crafts and employments supporting each other, but also linked to other occupations, and with their own particular constraints and rates of change.

During the eighteenth century the pace of most book trades development was startling, even in comparison with many other eighteenth-century domestic industries. After vigorous growth from the late 1690s, publication rates mushroomed between the late 1740s and the end of the century. Major bibliographical projects, headed by *The English Short Title Catalogue*, have charted more accurately than ever before the increases in eighteenth-century publication and the sale of print. Prior to 1700 up to about 1800 different printed titles were produced annually; by 1800 this had risen to over 6000. The surviving printed items are very disparate, ranging from locally printed ephemera, handbills, ballads, sale catalogues, petitions, and, in the words of the *ESTC* editors, 'oddities which defy classification'.[2] By edition title count alone (and this is obviously a crude gauge, taking no account of the varying size of editions), a particularly sharp take-off in book and magazine production can be identified in the final decades of the eighteenth century. The average rate of growth in publication as measured by numbers of titles (including different editions) was just over 2 per cent per annum for the years between 1740 and 1800. From 1740 to 1780 the average annual growth rate was 1.5 per cent, but from 1780 to the end of the century this rate increased to nearly 3.5 per cent. The challenge is to explain this revolution in printed output. Certain basics have long been identified: new entrants to both the London and provincial trade, the challenge to and relaxation of official and unofficial restrictive practices, the expansion of the country newspaper and book distribution network, a much increased individual and institutional demand, financial and organizational innovation, and (perhaps less generally recognized) improved productivity and flexibility advanced by new and greater capitalization. As fresh evidence provides more detail, the exact mix and timing of these features will be subject to continuing debate.

Economic and demographic inducements

The rapid growth of many market towns and new settlements offered a critical stimulus to the national book trade of the period. Throughout the eighteenth century over one-tenth of the population lived in London, but this was also the century of the British 'urban renaissance' and the growth of the 'leisure town'.[3] By 1750 London's population matched that of all country towns put together, but by 1801 this combined total was almost double that of the capital. Excluding London, nineteen towns had populations greater than 10,000 in 1750. Five of these – Bristol, Norwich, Liverpool, Newcastle and Birmingham – claimed populations greater than 20,000. By the first census returns of 1801, forty-eight towns had populations of over 10,000, fifteen of which exceeded 20,000. Recruits to the urban first rank included the growing ports of Portsmouth, Plymouth and Hull, the resort of Bath, and the new manufacturing towns of Manchester, Sheffield and Leeds.[4] In response to the demographic changes, one of the most striking features of the different book trades of this period was the advance first of regional printing (but not, until much later, of regional book publishing). In the location of printing the 1690s proved the watershed decade, although printers moving out of London remained fearful of the reimposition of legal restrictions and expansion was relatively modest prior to the 1740s. From the mid-eighteenth century, however, with growth in population, the economy, and in confidence that the newly accepted (if still circumscribed) freedoms of the press were to continue, bookselling and newspaper publishing increased sharply in the country towns. It was a development which was to underpin the publishing and business strategies of booksellers in London for the next hundred and fifty years.

The importance of London needs particular emphasis. In 1700 the population of the capital had reached about 675,000, but rebuilding after the 1666 Fire had not spread much further than a mile beyond the medieval city walls. Migration to the capital continued, but this was offset by higher mortality rates than in the rest of the country, and after fifty years the population of the capital had not increased by much more than 3000. In the second half of the eighteenth century, however, London was transformed. By 1800 its population had reached 900,000. Its main rival, Paris, boasted the largest urban population in Christian Europe at the beginning of the eighteenth century; a hundred years later, London was at least one-third larger than the French capital and dwarfed all other European cities. New London squares devoured fields to the west of the City and property speculators launched vast rebuilding schemes in Westminster and the northern villages. Commerce and financial activities intensified, and most of London's great markets, wharves and trading areas were reorganized. Within the tumult of the city the book trades flourished. London, now the site of hundreds of trades and industries, was also a vast consumer's market which dominated the British economy. The book trade, always centred in London, responded to demand led by the metropolitan population and institutions, and swollen by fast advancing country custom. Relocational factors, namely the pursuit of raw materials and new sources of power, did not directly affect the production of books, magazines and newspapers. This offers a sharp contrast with many other developing industries of the period.

Overly linear explanations will not do, however. New histories of the book in Britain will have to avoid simplistic accounts of an onward and upward march of print that led directly to social and political improvement.[5] Not everyone associated with the book trades prospered and the impact of print was complex and unexpected, but these features are easily neglected in broad assessments of the eighteenth century.[6] Any comparison of the technological limitations of the press with its remarkable eighteenth-century output curve encourages a certain triumphalism in cultural histories. At the very least, it devalues eighteenth-century protests against change and the exactments it brought. In pursuing a history of the book from production and circulation to collection and reception, attention should be given to the specific conse- quences of new commercial practices. Such a history should include consider- ation of contradictions and resistances as well as compliance and development. It must not ignore deficiencies in production and distribution, nor the ambiguities and diversities of reception.

One obvious problem is that our relatively fragmentary evidence provides a 'top-down' perspective on the changes, inclining to the perception of the creation and response to a certain demand. Investigation of the entrepreneurial activities of individual operators brings questions of demand and response into new light, but few records can reveal broader business limitations or the failure of individual operators to exploit particular options. The difficulty is that with so few book trades business records surviving for this period, many important questions can rarely be pursued in detail. All too often the absence of comparative case studies thwarts our understanding of the attempts of pub- lishers (booksellers or self-financing authors) to supply and encourage demand. Particularly elusive are the printers, their business methods and even their identities, especially when employed by many of the bookseller-publishers or authors putting work out. Certain other features of the trades can also be overlooked, notably the continuing circulation of manuscript editions and their relationship (especially in antiquarian circles) to printed books.[7]

What is at least clear is that our understanding of the business structures of the eighteenth-century book trades – so fundamental to reconstructing the broader framework of cultural transformation – remains problematic. At the most basic level, literary production and patronage flourishes or declines according to the economic resources of the land, its population and the derivative wealth of particular individuals. The response of the book trades to changes in economic conditions and market profiles is further determined by technological capabilities, and by the cultural, religious and political cast of its operatives. All the book trades were reliant on demand, distribution, trade regulation and material supplies (largely of paper, type, and increasingly towards the end of the period, binding papers and leathers). The supply of books to readers required transactions involving different manufacturers, processors, finishers, wholesale and retail distributors, circulation agents, and contractual and open market consumers. Such issues were reviewed in the Belanger essay, but they have also greatly benefited from the attention of more recent scholarship. Several important printing, publishing and bookselling records have been recovered and analysed, notably the Bowyer and Murray business ledgers and letters. These have been accompanied by fresh inspections of the Dodsley letters, the Strahan ledgers, and the archives of Longmans and the Stationers' Company, as well as the results of major bibliographical reconstructions of particular genres, the output of particular bookseller-publishers and even of bookselling districts.[8]

Not all the conclusions are obvious. Increased output was not necessarily propelled by the pursuit of more efficient production, especially when publishing was driven by investment opportunity as well as by the possibility of immediate returns on work in hand. Historically, publishing organization, developed for both long-term investment purposes and flexibility, had ranged from the groups of bookseller–stationer collaborators that flourished in the late sixteenth century through to the publishing congers of the late seventeenth century and beyond. Even where copyright purchase could count as a form of speculation, however, the rate of sale of the products obviously remained a crucial determinant in the economic development of book and allied trades. Very few writers were beneficiaries of this boom, at least in financial terms, although the print avalanche did encourage many more to write and publish. It was increasingly easy to rant against the world, while book trades activity only fuelled delusions of reaping easy profits.

Even more remarkably, technological development in the book trades before the early decades of the nineteenth century was largely limited to advances in paper manufacture and type founding and design. Although the rolling press, used for the printing of metal engravings, was improved and became an important adjunct to the arts of the pressman, the basic design of the printing press remained almost unchanged. Caxton, if transported to the printshops of Samuel Richardson or Luke Hansard, would have felt quite at home.

Technological development: paper, type and engraving

The earliest of the technological changes concerned the making of paper.
Beginning with the establishment of new Scottish paper mills in the seventeenth century, innovation in paper manufacture began to reduce British and
especially English dependence on the import of quality paper from the
Continent. In Scotland, where twelve mills had been established before 1700,
output increased massively from an annual production of board and paper of
some 100,000 lbs in 1750 to over two million lbs by 1800.[9] English home
production of paper increased from some 2000 tons in 1700 to about 15,000
tons *per annum* in 1800. In 1700 nearly two hundred paper mills, scattered
across the country, were supplying regional stationers and feeding an increasing demand for paper for wrapping, writing and printing.[10] In 1785 381
licences were issued to paper-makers in England and Wales, although the
great majority of these manufactured coarse papers only. By 1800 the number
of licences issued had risen to 417.[11]

   The supply of paper was now transformed. Many bales of paper were sent
along newly opened trading routes, and many of the suppliers of paper were
local. Throughout the century, the greatest concentration of paper mills
remained in south Buckinghamshire, Hertfordshire and Middlesex, with a
further large scattering of mills throughout Kent. Large numbers of regional
mills were established before the mid-eighteenth century, and many local
dealers prospered in nearby large towns within a few years of the founding of
each mill. In order to ensure a sufficient and constant supply of paper,
however, it was often necessary for the regional stationer to open commercial
negotiations with a London wholesaler rather than with a local manufacturer.
In London, where the manufacture of paper had moved largely to the
surrounding villages even by 1700, a complex system of paper warehousing
and distribution developed. After the imposition of Stamp Duty in 1712 the
importance of supply from the metropolis increased, and after the first Act to
impose an excise tax on home-produced paper (1711), some twenty-six
further Acts were passed during the next 150 years. Subsequently, the only
legal source of supply for newspaper stamped paper was the warehouse of the
Commissioners of Stamps in Serle Court, Lincoln's Inn, to which unsold
papers also had to be returned in order to claim a rebate.[12]

   Technological change in the paper industry must not be exaggerated,
however. Labour remained manual. All early papers were laid papers made by
hand from a pulp of linen rags with a wire screen mould and strengthening

frame. A paper mill driven by a Boulton and Watt steam-engine was set up at Wilmington near Hull in 1786, but it proved to be a short-lived experiment. The first successful paper-making machines, established by Henry and Sealy Fourdrinier, and separately by John Gamble in 1803, introduced a continuous process of paper manufacture from a belt of wire mesh over which the pulp flowed to felt rollers and steam-heated drying drums. Yet by 1810, in the year the Fourdriniers were declared bankrupt, only a handful of paper mills had adopted power-driven machinery.[13]

Of the technological changes in the eighteenth-century book trades, the most significant were those concerned with engraving and with the design and manufacture of type. Until at least the 1720s most of the type used in Britain was of a poor standard. The majority of type and all of the quality founts were imported from the Low Countries and from Germany. In 1674 Thomas Grover set up his London type foundry in Aldersgate Street. It produced the dramatic script type used by Ichabod Dawks in his *News-Letter* from 1696 until at least 1716. The type was also employed by Hugh Meere, the printer of the Sun Fire Office's *British Mercury*. In the *Observator* of 1708 Meere advertised 'Scriptographia; or Written Print Hand (which can't be imitated by any other printer) fit for bills of lading, Bills of Sale, Bonds of all Sorts . . . or any other blank Law forms'.[14] By the time of William Caslon's first work in the early 1720s, the older firms of English founders had been absorbed by the business of Thomas James which continued after 1736 under the direction of James' son Thomas. It is their type and that of their predecessors which still largely appears in the matrices of the few surviving detailed inventories of the English jobbing printing firm.[15]

From the 1730s substantial printers, and especially those engaged in book work, experimented with new type. Most prized was that made by Caslon and his successors, while in Birmingham John Baskerville (1706–75) set new standards in the manufacture of both type and paper. The Baskerville founts, cast for their maker's own book printing, were not widely adopted during his lifetime, but they were of particular importance in influencing the development of letterpress type. Alexander Wilson's first Edinburgh specimen book, not issued until 1772, included large types heavily modelled on Baskerville. In the final quarter of the century the specimen books of Joseph and Edmund Fry rivalled those of the Caslons, and the Frys competed with six or more other English firms in producing fine and exotic founts. Many of the London printers swiftly adopted the technical innovations in typography. Founders sent out specimen sheets to the printers, and printers circulated specimens of printing with newly purchased type to show book and newspaper syndicates what was possible. For the simple conveyance of information, many of the new founts and ornaments were clearly an embellishment rather than a necessity. Their value in attracting customers and satisfying clients was swiftly appreciated, however. As well as begging attention, finely printed decoration became a status symbol, much in the manner of modern letter-heads and printed logos.[16]

Almost all new typefaces remained within the conventions of book type. Despite experiments with head and tail pieces and the 'flowers' used for border decoration, familiar proportions were continued in the cutting of letters. For most of the century, the absence of type of a height greater than about three-quarters of an inch was a serious limitation to display printing. Decorative founts from the Low Countries were expensive to import and not obviously suitable for many new forms of jobbing. In 1765 Thomas Cottrell, founder at Nevil's Court, Fetter Lane, between 1758 and his death in 1785, issued a twelve-line pica (nearly two inches high), but other typefounders were slow to follow. Surviving examples of jobbing work from the 1770s and 1780s rarely contain large display type. Joseph Fry's castings were among the earliest of the large typefaces available for poster work. For jobbing printing Fry's ornaments and large founts, such as his five-line pica, were therefore especially prized. *The Specimen of Printing-Types, made by Joseph Fry and Sons*, issued in 1785, went through annual editions with numerous type and flower additions to each.

For much of the eighteenth century the development of printing techniques outside London should not be exaggerated. Printers setting up in the country and specializing in jobbing printing or the publication of weekly newspapers were often too poor to buy the most modern type or ornaments. In letterpress printing veteran type continued to be used. Decorative printing remained a modest and London-based craft at the end of the century, even though it was practised increasingly widely. Difficult or embarrassing editorial decisions were often presented to clients by printers working with incomplete sets or limited sizes and styles of founts. The conservatism and crudity of regional jobbing printing contrasted with examples of regionally sold printing from London, although the common availability of London material probably continued to provide encouragement to many over-ambitious requests from country customers.

The advance of engraving and copperplate-making, particularly from the mid-eighteenth century (when the artist-engraver George Vertue listed fifty-five London engravers), was associated with the development of specialist craftsmen, adopting intaglio techniques to produce copperplate engravings and etchings. Both engraving and etching flourished as a result of the greater availability of working materials. Of the two, etchings were both cheaper and faster to turn out, but engraved plates produced a more elegant and versatile illustration, if one requiring retouching or complete recutting after heavy use. Printed both by conventional and rolling-press, the copperplate was of a quality far superior both to the wood-block 'cut' (with its negative impression) and its finer form, the wood engraving, itself revived from the early decades of the century. Many producers of popular print, like John Cluer and William and Cluer Dicey, increasingly mixed letterpress and rolling-press in their texts and advertisements.

Particularly noticeable is what has been called the 'open-access character' of the engraving trade, involving men and women from various crafts.[17] Picture-sellers, print-sellers, mapmakers, printers and booksellers worked closely together, and some notable booksellers, including the Knaptons, claimed regular involvement with the prints and picture trade.[18] The history of the engraving trades and of book and pamphlet illustration has more to tell us about new associations and collaborations and about new types of trading and working practices than about fundamental technological change. The most obvious advance in techniques from the mid-eighteenth century was the greater use of stipple, a combination of engraved dots and etching (where acid was used to create the ink-holding grooves) and, a decade or so later, of aquatint (based on the application of resin to craze the copperplate surface). With increased demand for prints and book illustrations, the reworking of heavily used plates became more common, and although still rare, a few more coloured prints and illustrations were attempted. Similarly, the mezzotint, demanding more updating and a relatively expensive procedure, increased in popularity as a consequence of the rising status of English painting (a popular subject for mezzotint reproductions).[19]

New money and new markets

Technological advance, restricted to typefounding and design, and to a lesser extent to paper manufacture and experiments with intaglio techniques and the rolling-press, was therefore a limited force in the book trades revolution of this period. A more concrete basis for the expansion of printing and publishing is to be found in the greater capitalization of the industry over the century, although we again have to be aware of certain cautions and limitations. The injection of capital (from diverse sources) into the book trades transformed their business activities and potential – as well as encouraging greater risks and inducing greater failures.

The importance of the broader financing of the book trades is apparent from many of the new studies of individual printers and publisher-booksellers operating in the second half of the eighteenth century. It is becoming increasingly clear that book trades' profits and monies reinvested in publishing resulted not only from greater diversification of trading practices, but also from the deepening of money markets and the financial infrastructure available. Capital was drawn from new sources, but, even more significantly, readier circulation and more flexible use of assets were ensured by new means of accessing capital and limiting risk. Inflows of capital from increased mercantile activity backed the expanding London money market, enabling credit to go further and extending credit chains. By the early nineteenth century the London money market was effectively based on the ready discounting of bills of exchange, whereby third parties bought debts to redeem them at maturity, enabling the freer availability of monies to trading partners. The effect of this on the book trades was clear by the final quarter of the eighteenth century, while the development of the insurance market reduced risk on stock, buildings, shipping and other transportation (although fire insurance remained the most valued safeguard).[20]

In these ways, credit and insurance availability lowered book trades' transaction costs, but such development was not even. In what has been accurately termed a 'face-to-face society', in which individual trust was still at a premium in credit and debt relations, banking operations remained primarily based on the relative respectability and credit reputation of the operators. This meant that those in the book trades who benefited most from new financial mechanisms and opportunities were such individuals as Strahan, Cadell, Robinson and the Rivingtons, all able to demonstrate the respect and trust of a far-flung commercial élite. More provocative booksellers like Trusler, Lane and Bell were able to avail themselves of the broader developments, but did not benefit from the sort of reductions in long-term capital tie-up and risk acceptance available to the richest and most eminent in their profession. One result, therefore, of mechanisms and structures that were rapidly developing but still based more on personal reputations than on impersonal institutional management was to extend differences between the book traders. The humblest operators struggled to cope with credit and risk conveyance, while the grandest book merchants diversified investments into property, annuities, and a broader range of commercial and banking activities. None, however, could escape one other result of this development – that credit broking, insurance services and economic confidence were made even more sensitive to external commercial pressures. The crisis years of the American war in the 1770s, for example, can be clearly identified in charts of book trades' output and bankruptcies.

The introduction of new money into the trades, and its more versatile deployment, is the more striking given the broader resource limitations that had continued to constrain business expansion and technological advances. Across all trades most fixed capital had been invested in ways that produced only indirect gain. In most cases circulating capital – namely raw materials and goods – comprised whatever long-term business investment there was. In some respects, trades were also handicapped by the relatively inefficient deployment of resources that economists now term 'path dependency'; that is, the continuation of particular (but in theory not inflexible) working practices because of a cultural inertia to change. By modern standards the overall regime allowed a very low productivity rate, with particularly high labour-intensity, and, in the economy at large, a vast reservoir of under-employed labour. This created very little inducement for cost-reducing innovations in all trades and industries. The book trades were certainly not exceptional in this state of affairs, and the publishing sector was especially handicapped by the requirement to have so much capital tied up in a particular item of production (an edition) before any part of this could be sold to realize returns.

In addition to start-up costs (workplace, press, type and other permanent necessities), the overall economics of publication included job-specific costs of paper, the labour involved at all stages of printing, and, much more rarely, whatever might have been paid to the author or begetter of the text. However, these factors alone cannot explain the price structure adopted by particular publishers. The most successful among them made investments in the long-term value of published titles by the ownership of shares in copyright, while at the same time, and related to these stored (if not immediately realizable) assets, the pricing of the printed products was based on particular additional decisions made by the publisher – whether that publisher (that is, the financial backer) were the bookseller or the author. Both the material and design considerations crucially rested upon an assessment of changes in market structures, and thus the evaluation of the changing market became a vital consideration.

Booksellers and printers had courted growing consumer demand from the late sixteenth century, and particularly so from the 1660s onwards when retailing and allied services more obviously expanded according to the changing commercial potential of the audience. Direct retailing of books and pamphlets was nothing new, of course, but since the earliest commerce in print, off-the-shelf trading had coexisted with a client economy of producers in service to closed patronage. Elite support for specialist literature had been nurtured most recently by subscription collection and by specialist publishers directing their output to specific clients, professions, interest groups and even regions. Much of the direct retailing centred on the active (but often overlooked) second-hand market as well as on the sales of smaller productions, notably the thousands of almanacks, pamphlets and chapbooks peddled by chapmen and general traders. The early auctioneers usually acted as middlemen in the sense that they were agents who had usually not bought outright the libraries that they sold. With set times for sale, the auctions also boosted the crucial second-hand market.[21] Particular attractions intended to entice custom for a sale also increased. At the end of the seventeenth century, for example, William Cooper introduced artificial lighting to illuminate winter evening sales of his books, and the Thames ice fairs offered exotic retail environments complete with printed mementoes of a person's visit to a print stall. Summer spa resort sales were also flourishing by the mid-eighteenth century. Sales promoted as events and entertainments in themselves gained new prominence, and outings to bookshops (whether the new fixed sites or the regular features of fairs and markets) became frequent subjects for diarists and travel writers.[22]

The changes in the methods of retailing books resulted from increased custom from the propertied classes. Provincial sales outlets were extended, and London booksellers launched new titles of both religious and 'entertaining and instructive' literature with no advanced assured custom. For the majority of metropolitan booksellers, the sales of open market publications became the basis for survival. The first-generation commercial circulating libraries of the 1740s also developed from the *ad hoc* lending services of London retailing booksellers. Almost all these pioneer libraries closed after a few years, but their publishing, stocking and lending arrangements became the framework for the establishments of Lowndes, the Nobles (both firms were survivors of the early days), Lane, Hookham and Carpenter, Bell, and many others. Publisher-booksellers operating circulating libraries set aside a major portion of their own editions to supply their libraries and those of counterparts.[23] For both bookshops and commercial libraries, regional variation was marked, and although interest in the expanding country market was important, the London market must again be emphasized. As noted earlier, London dominated the economy and, more importantly, grew disproportionately faster than other established towns during the period, its population fed by immigration from the regions. Here was a market close to the centres of production, with fewer distribution problems and with affluent and fashionable custom, particularly in the parliamentary and social season. In support, choice products of the London booksellers offered very particular (and almost always highly exaggerated) textual and visual representations of their shops, reading-rooms and customers.[24]

The further evaluation of market structures (and hence pricing decisions) depended largely on changes in the potential for onward selling. With transport costs consistently high in the first centuries of print, the transformation in the economics of distribution over this period very obviously affected marketing strategies and calculations for text and edition production. In particular, improvements in transport routes and distance times encouraged the development of discount systems to promote greater retail distribution in the country. Distribution costs had always been a significant add-on, and with booksellers' margins so tight, allowing very little scope for the major tie-up of capital in printed and warehoused stock, the efficiency of transportation was critical, and underpinned the urgency of selling editions in which so much was usually invested. Nor was cheap print excluded from this assessment. Where carriage costs were paid for by the bookseller-publishers, these contributed significantly to production costings. Questions about delivery expenses feature persistently in the new studies of some of the most important (and diverse) booksellers of the period, including John Murray, the printer, Bowyer, the Nobles, and Robert Dodsley, with his reliance on Thomas and Mary Cooper and other trade publishers to provide a marketing network.[25]

In this face-to-face society where little institutional support existed, family and kinship support structures were vital. Neighbourhoods played an important role, and we have to understand both the importance of trust and obligation and how this was policed. This is particularly so given that the devolution of economic and policing functions by the state remained a crucial feature of English (and later British) book trades development. Until the close of the eighteenth century, the Stationers' Company dominated the regulation and restrictive practices of the trade. The establishment of the joint-stock of the Company also created a financial corporation with arrangements for the successive distribution of dividends to members. Under legal protection refined and extended by successive injunctions, the members of the Company operated a trading cartel, regulating not only the products and the manner of trade, but access to trading and the instruments of production. By the control of their own property, members prepared the way for the emergence of a

particular group heading the control of the English stock. By means of
association, control and self-regulation, the Company came to offer welfare
and guardianship, but it was thereby very rarely a force for innovation and
seemed increasingly obdurate. The Company did establish a corporate identity
and forged both business and social links between members, including some
shared warehousing, but the most flamboyant innovators of the century came
from outside the ranks of the Stationers. Nevertheless, the Company largely
maintained its role as financial protector and disperser of dividends, as well as
controlling official apprenticeship, entry to trade, and its own office-holding
(and dividend-rich) hierarchy. Throughout the period Stationers' Hall also
continued to attempt to regulate the quality of work and wage levels,
upholding monopolies and exclusion in the art and mystery of printing and
publishing.[26]

Investments, profits and sales

We therefore return to the question of the relationship between investment
in printing rights and the publication and sale of books, all of which might be
undertaken independently or in association with other booksellers. It is clear
that the greatest profits in eighteenth-century book publication in England
(but less so in Scotland) derived from the ownership of copyrights to successful
works. The fundamental division between the different booksellers of the
period remained between those who invested and dealt in the ownership of
the copyright to publication (whether by independent or collaborative financing of a new copyrighted work or by purchase of an existing copyright
share), and those who either printed, sold or distributed books for existing
copyright-owners or who traded entirely outside the bounds of copyright
materials.

Any analysis confronts the much-discussed distinction between bookseller
and publisher. The appellation 'bookseller' in the eighteenth century was a
conveniently broad job description, while 'publication', as in making a book
public, might also be applied to its dissemination in the broadest (and often
deliberately ambiguous) terms. In this sense, 'publication' might further
represent a continuous process, offering an explanation (other than as a canny
commercial ploy) for the frequent repetition over several days or weeks of the
advertisement for books and pamphlets 'this day published'. The vagueness of
the term 'bookseller' also meant that many more traders were involved in
selling and publishing books than is suggested by many modern estimates.

Dozens of small-time operators, highly mobile and with fluctuating fortunes, moved in and out of bookselling, often combining this with other trades.

What we also have to note is how distinct trades were described more indeterminately than in the previous two centuries – at the very time of increased separation between the crafts. By the beginning of the eighteenth century a 'bookseller' could, in common parlance, be a publisher and retailer of books, or a retailer acting as an agent for a wholesale publisher. As publishers, booksellers might rely on contracted printers, rather than operate their own press. The 'topping' bookseller undertook the financing, printing and distribution of books to other booksellers or directly to the public, while the term 'publisher' – to create still more confusion for later readers – was sometimes retained to describe those issuing rather than financing publications.[27] Alternatively, a retailing but (in modern terms) non-publishing bookseller – often the owner of a general store – might also run a press for local jobbing printing. Retailing booksellers could be categorized in various ways. Collier's *Parents and Guardians Directory*, published in 1761 (and now usefully reused in many publishing histories of the period), advised that booksellers might be divided into the following classes:

> 1. The wholesale dealer, who subsists by his country trade, and by serving some of our plantations. 2. Those who deal only or principally in bibles, common prayers, almanacks, &c. who are also wholesale dealers. 3. The retale dealers, who generally deal in new books. 4. Those who deal chiefly in foreign books. 5. And those who sell old books.[28]

The right to reproduce a book was almost always bought outright by the bookseller-publisher or consortium of booksellers. Most authors surrendered all claims to subsequent entitlement; most copyrights were then divided into shares between several combining booksellers. Such division was made according to the booksellers' stake in the original financing of the publication. Part-shares formed the staple investments to be bought at the London trade auctions, and commerce was brisk. Another contemporary commentator, Thomas Mortimer, in his *Universal Director* of 1763, despaired of calculating ownership of shares because they were so greatly divided and exchanged hands so rapidly. Although the history of the associations of booksellers is well known, the surviving series of marked-up trade sale catalogues, covering both copy and stock transactions, continue to provide valuable information about the course of transactions by different booksellers, of prices and share divisions, and the comparative worth and long-term investment potential of different types of publication or even of individual titles.[29] The greatest accumulator of the second half of the eighteenth century was probably George Robinson, who was a keen rival to the established literary investors by the early 1770s, and before 1780 had, according to John Nichols, 'the largest wholesale trade that was ever carried on by an individual'.[30] By 1800 the businesses of Cadell and of Longman and Rees surpassed all others in the extent of their literary holdings.

Two further critical features stand out in this changing production history. First, with some very notable exceptions, most books had little intrinsic value. Copyrights to most publications fetched relatively little at sale, and authors were paid paltry sums for their initial surrender of rights to works which booksellers knew were very unlikely to be reprinted or to return much profit in their own right. The second critical issue is that reprints of popular book titles were to feature significantly in new market development and were a key encouragement to new booksellers (as well as a key temptation to overreach). Most conspicuously, the book trades were transformed by the successful assault on the publishing monopoly maintained by the leading booksellers' associations for most of the century until 1774. As a caution against too great an obsession with the 1774 contest, however, we have to accept that the framework for the protection of sale and investment in rights to *new* works remained intact in the final decades of the century. Clarified rather than undermined by the earlier legal battles, the copyright laws brought new riches to those with the skill to favour the right authors and publications.

The value of all copyright shares clearly depended on their remaining exclusive rights to publish. Under the Copyright Act of 1710 copyright to existing publications had been limited to twenty-one years for books already in print and fourteen years for new books. After expiration of the fourteen-year term, copyright was to remain with the author for a second fourteen-year term, if living, even though the author's rights were more technical than actual, and ones apparently not previously greatly considered by those passing the legislation. In invoking authorial rights, in fact, the Act introduced uncertainty about the validity of Common Law claims by the booksellers, who, far more than authors, submitted testing injunctions in subsequent decades. Immediately following the mid-eighteenth-century technical expiration of rights to older works and works first protected under this statute, the booksellers' associations seemed successful in arguing that its spirit sanctioned perpetual copyright under Common Law. The 1768–69 King's Bench decision followed by the injunction by the Court of Chancery, prohibiting Alexander Donaldson from continuing his cut-price reissues of the works of Thomson and others, marked the high point of the efforts by closed associations of booksellers to control copyright. In 1774 a ruling of the House of Lords, overturning the 1768 restraining injunction and confirming the limitations of the 1710 Act, ended the booksellers' invocation of Common Law to sanction perpetual copyright, and a Bill to quash the Lords' verdict failed in the following year.[31] This opened the way for those without ownership of share-copies and outside the charmed circle of leading booksellers to publish cheap reprint editions of classic works. Dozens of new, modestly resourced publishers were the clear beneficiaries of the syndicates' loss of control over copyright. From the mid-1770s the reprinting of popular texts rejuvenated the market, and most notably the advancing provincial market. At first, these ventures were led by London booksellers taking advantage of the loss of control by the booksellers' associations, but by the end of the century a regrouping of copyright-owners re-established familiar methods of sharing the financing of publication.

Change and conflict

Although the basic structure continued, the battle over copyright transformed the market in popular publishing. This was clear both in terms of the literary investments by bookseller-publishers and the availability of well-known texts, but the consequences for first-time book publication were more indirect. Few new titles were to enjoy commercial benefit from new opportunities to reprint old favourites. Rather, the efforts of many booksellers, based on new promotional techniques, advertising, and more adventurous retail and distribution, continued to erode the power of closed booksellers' associations, and many of the new books published by the new booksellers benefited from the changed market and marketing activities. Although Donaldson and his brother John are rightly credited with the initial actions which baited and finally defeated the bookseller consortiums, it was John Bell who seized the initiative in cheaper, part-issued and reprinted popular literature. Early Bell editions proved highly competitive and sent shock-waves through the trade. Many publishers deliberately imitated Bell, while 'Robin Hood' Donaldson, as Dr Johnson called him,[32] together with many others, both launched and revived collaborative reprints and part-issues. In cheap editions and serial numbers, however, the clear rivals to Bell were first James Harrison and then John Cooke and Alexander Hogg. None of these were significant publishers of new book titles, despite their republishing activity. By the end of the century popular reprint series were being issued by a wide range of booksellers, from the confident newcomer acting on his own to groups of more established members of the Stationers' or other livery companies, sharing publication expenses and shadowing earlier, more exclusive collaborative practice. Of the 1000 books published by John Murray between 1768 and his death in 1793, nearly 40 per cent were co-published, some on his own initiative before inviting others to join in the financing, some after similar invitations to join others, and some resulting from the purchase of copyright shares in the trade auctions.[33]

At the same time, interest in these developments was rivalled by the attention given to Irish piracies and Scottish reprints, not least by the London booksellers themselves. Cheap imported piracies from Dublin but also reprints from Edinburgh (many of which might well have been legally published within the limits of the 1710 Act) had long been condemned by the London trade. Many Irish reprints were half the price of the London originals. Cheaper paper was used, as well as closer printing, and sometimes hidden abridgement enabled two- or three-volume works to be issued in a single volume. Despite vociferous protests made in the mid-eighteenth century, however, the threat from Ireland was either largely illusory or a trumped-up promotional gambit. As now seems clear, Dublin reprints were never imported in sufficient numbers nor aimed at the right targets to pose an effective direct challenge to the London booksellers, even if the effect on the Scottish trade, and Scots incursions in England, is more debatable. At least until the problems of the 1790s, Dublin publishers appear to have concentrated on an expanding and potentially valuable Irish market. They had more to fear from London booksellers than London booksellers had to fear from them. Scottish competition was more complicated, with the costs and likely ineffectiveness of prosecution deterring actions against the efforts of the Edinburgh and Glasgow presses. In the early 1780s Scots booksellers were themselves under threat from Irish piracies smuggled in and bearing false imprints. In all of this, title-page assertions of being printed in London cannot always be taken at face value.[34]

Another material feature of the system for publishing and marketing books was the involved relationship between booksellers, both financing bookseller-publishers and their retailing, usually bookseller, agents. As Murray, but also Cadell, the Robinsons, the Longmans, and even the Rivingtons found, cooperation in some form was essential to most operations. The weakening of the share book system also increased the risk for all, and rewards resulted from many gambles in the late eighteenth-century book trades expansion. The increasing number of bankruptcies after 1774 is testimony to the new adventuring. Unprecedented turnover in books was matched by unprecedented turnover in booksellers, many quickly returning to the battle to secure a cut of the new literary marketplace. Although some London traders continued joint ventures and *ad hoc* partnerships, a new vulnerability and rivalry was introduced into the trade. Hundreds of small firms, many of them engaged in additional trades, attempted to make their fortunes from publishing or selling books. For every ostentatious success story, from the eminence of Cadell to the audacity of Lane's Minerva Press and Lackington's Temple of the Muses, there were dozens with miserable or wildly fluctuating returns. Eventually – although this was far from obvious in the final decades of the century – all these considerations pointed towards the primacy of what John Murray called the 'simple publisher';[35] that is, the bookseller, risking all (and often failing), and acting on his own in negotiations with the author and the rest of the trade. The further consequence was that many of the most successful operators had raised their start-up capital from assorted outside sources and entered the trade with practical and financial expertise learned from a previous profession.

Recovering these trading relationships is not easy. Many distribution agents are unspecified, and, in the absence of most business records, we usually have little idea of the different financial apportionments in the publication of a new book. The information offered about the connections between booksellers in the imprint line on almost all title-pages is difficult to interpret. Some booksellers (and some authors, wholly or partly) acted as the publisher; that is, as the entrepreneur accepting the risk of financing publication. Others remained as manufacturers of the product, already assured of payment even if the book sold badly, while still others (including many general traders) served in various distribution and retailing capacities, also identified at the time as the 'publishers' or issuers of books to a wider audience. Single names of booksellers might appear to be the simplest indicators to publication, but it cannot be taken for granted that a book 'printed for' a particular bookseller was entirely paid for by that bookseller. Moreover, where a book was sold by a consortium of booksellers, some or all might contribute to the financing of its publication (in proportions usually unknown), and it was not always the case that all those listed had contributed directly to publication costs. Arrangements between booksellers listed as the principal financing publishers ('printed for', etc.) and first-level associates ('also sold by', etc.) usually, but not always, implied an agreement to share costs approximately in proportion to the number of copies to be taken by the participating shops. Newspaper advertisements for these titles extend the problem further, often including additional names of 'sold by' booksellers to those listed on the title-page or advertisements at the end of the book.

Despite these reservations, we can at least be certain that in most cases inclusion of a name in an imprint line indicates some sort of financial involvement. This is particularly the case where the author is mentioned (almost always as 'printed for the author'). Where a bookseller was unwilling to take the risk of publishing a book, he might nevertheless print or enable the printing of the work on the understanding that the author advanced the costs. In some cases the provision of the actual paper, not merely its costs, was expected. Here, with the author as publisher, the bookseller often acted as little more than a vanity press, although in some cases authorial risk-taking did pay off. To most booksellers, the acceptance of such a commission must have seemed like simple jobbing printing. Many title-pages hide known commission agreements 'on account of the author', where the publisher-writer assumed responsibility for any loss.

For some authors the only option was to fund the costs of publication from their own resources, although subscription schemes might also be launched. Booksellers often acted as collecting agents for such support, but where a project looked particularly uncertain the authors, their friends or patrons organized subscription themselves. Nevertheless – and circumstantial evidence is scarce – it seems that a bookseller rarely turned down a book if financing were available. It is simply not known how many manuscripts of authors looking for booksellers' support were refused. Negotiations over publication where the bookseller acted wholly or even in part as financing publisher are obscure. Few letters survive between first-time or even popular writers and booksellers, and refusals are rarely glimpsed. One admittedly self-interested commentator, the popular publisher John Trusler, even suggested that the more underhand booksellers might agree to print a book at the author's expense and then print half as many again, selling, moreover, the booksellers' portion first and then claiming unsold copies as entirely from the number paid for by the author.[36]

What this did was to put heavy responsibility upon authors to choose, in what was largely a buyer's not a seller's manuscript market, the best option for having their work published. They usually risked heavily if they wished to avoid the easy but disappointing option of a meagre outright sale of the copyright. Before the early nineteenth century few writers – and certainly very few first-time writers – could avoid the sale of the copyright, full self-financing (and thus acting as publisher themselves) or deals in which the author bore liability for all losses.[37] Commission agreements whereby the bookseller put up the capital for printing an edition, on the understanding that the author would bear any loss, seem to have been very rare. Most booksellers appear to have interpreted commissions as between 7.5 and 10 per cent of the wholesale price, although few agreements have survived. Profit-sharing arrangements, as favoured by Longmans in the early nineteenth century, seem to have been even rarer. Although better than having to find all the capital or walking away from the shop with a few guineas for outright sale of the copyright, a commission agreement could nevertheless bring financial loss as well as reward.

Material consequences: constraints and risks

The basis of any analysis of the economics of British publishing in this period is therefore that copyright was cheap, that most authors had very weak bargaining positions, and that, where financed, a book was published either in the slim hope of future returns if it proved popular and worthy of a subsequent edition, or, more likely, to supply a relatively closed system based – in the case most obviously of the popular novel – on the stocking of circulating libraries, or, for most other works, on high mark-ups in direct sales to the public. Where booksellers acted as real publishers, taking on the full financial risk, key factors were the costs of paper, labour and wear on type or new type requirements. These, however, were not the sole determinants of profits, given that the choice of a particular price structure seems to have been based on more than the factor costs of manufacture, encompassing considerations of design and market profile. The idea that a title might yet prove a surprise success must have encouraged some booksellers, and was certainly a spur to new marketing and promotional enterprise. More realistically, a commercial strategy based on maximum variety and novelty in the library, but supporting wholesale backlists for a decade or more, required a particular balance between printing sufficient copies of an edition to maximize the unit costs of the press work, but limited enough to avoid tying up capital in unsold stock and the burden of long-term storage space.

The main result of these considerations was the printing of a relatively small number of copies of each edition and the encouragement of favoured formats and styles of presentation to maximize pricing advantage, most notably the publication of books in two or more volumes. In most cases, the labour costs of composition and presswork made it unviable to print very small editions, while the risks of high capital expenditure and storage made it unwise to print large editions. Most book editions therefore remained at about 750 copies. The clear exceptions to this were the monster editions of popular titles reprinted over and over again, such as school books, hymn-books and the like. Playbooks might reach editions of 2000 copies or more, and histories might in some cases, where proven sellers, be issued in 4000-copy editions; but these pale before the huge print runs commissioned by Longmans (our best surviving evidence) for staple titles such as Watts's *Hymns*, Johnson's *Dictionary* and numerous school books, including an 18,000-copy edition of Fenning's spelling manual. Even so, the question of risk had to be measured carefully. All remembered the sorry history of Andrew Millar's first 1751–52 edition of Fielding's *Amelia* of 8000 copies in two impressions. Millar had hoped to emulate the runaway success of *Tom Jones* (10,000 copies printed between 1749 and 1750), but was left embarrassed, with copies still for sale ten years later.

The high return expected on the publication of such books is confirmed by the surviving evidence of production costings. For much of the century the greatest production expense appears to have resulted from composition and presswork, but in the Longman accounts of book publication from the late 1790s paper costs are almost always greater than printing costs. The proportion of both to total production costs varied greatly, however, and depended upon the additional contribution of advertising, copyright and incidental costs. The ledger entries for pre-1800 books in the surviving Longman accounts suggest that paper costs ranged between just over a quarter and just a half of total production costs. Printing expenses, always less than those of paper, ranged from between one-fifth to one-third of total costs. Bills for printing sent to Longmans were calculated at rates per sheet, with additional labour charges for the corrections made to the presswork before the sheets left the printing house.[38]

Comparisons between cost and retail prices can also be derived from such evidence. Everything points to high potential returns, even if against extreme risks in a market where even an edition of 500 copies might prove a slow earner. In almost all cases of London book publication, however, potential profit calculations must be reduced for whatever allowance was made for discount to the retailing booksellers buying within the trade. In sales from the bookshop we also have to take into account the vagaries of payment and credit arrangements to both individual and trade customers. The trade discount offered to other booksellers, some of whom were library managers, was especially important for provincial retailers developing local markets for new literature. A large proportion of trade offers in the final quarter of the

eighteenth century were advertised as bound; earlier discounts often specified
sheets. The novel and *belles-lettres* specialist, Thomas Hookham, allowed his
trade customers a free copy for every twenty-five bought.[39] From their earliest
years, the even more populist Nobles offered a trade discount of 14 per cent
on twenty-five volumes of the same title. If country booksellers were able to
sell their volumes for, say, the metropolitan price of three shillings, the
potential for profit appears large. In practice, however, the largest profits were
taken by the London wholesalers.

The one outstanding complication, however, remained the continuing
problem of securing payments. The credit terms allowed by booksellers to
both trade and direct customers were, by modern standards, extraordinarily
generous. An allowance of six months seems to have been quite normal, and
some overseas customers expected eighteen months or even two years' grace
between order and the payment of an invoice. Reliance on credit and the
uncertainty of many credit notes added to the overheads carried by all types
of booksellers and to the niceties of calculations in pricing and sizing an
edition. One drastic solution, James Lackington's discounting of remaindered
and second-hand books for cash only, was condemned by rival booksellers as
unfair practice, given that they could not, like Lackington with his large one-
off emporium, break free of the retailing and newspaper-led advertising
structure that customers now expected. The retail specialization of the book
trades by the end of the century, allowing booksellers like Hogg, Bell and
Lackington to develop innovative services, left many booksellers tied to older
practices and relatively inflexible trading relationships.

In the popular market, and particularly in the publication of novels where
high risk was moderated by high retail pricing, other production decisions
followed during the final third of the century. The most conspicuous of these
was the distribution of the text over more than one volume, attempting to
ensure, at standard pricing per volume, greater returns from retail and, for
some, from library-lending receipts. By the end of the century it was quite
common for novels to be issued in five or more volumes in a set, and three
came to be regarded as a norm. Duodecimo was the favoured format for
popular book production throughout this period, although the alternative
octavo was adopted in particular cases. Library shelving arrangements and the
order of sales and library catalogues were dictated by the size of a book,
recognizably described according to its physical composition. The association
of the novel, in particular, with the 'twelve' was reinforced by the listings of
collections, sale descriptions, and advertising and review notices. Octavo, by
contrast, was usually adopted in the popular market when booksellers aimed

to give publications a certain distinction. In some cases it promoted more efficient as well as more elegant composition when, in difficult times, the amount of text per page was increased. Towards the end of the period more volumes seem to have been sold already bound (titles were often marketed as 'sold, bound, unless otherwise stated'), but by far the most common advertised price remained that of the volume sewn in paper or boards. This left the buyer with the option of having a book bound according to his or her choice, with the binding undertaken either by the retailing bookseller or independently.[40]

Advertising and the genius of newspapers

The final consideration here is the support given to the selling of books and print by newspaper publication. Total sales of all newspapers in England amounted to some 7.3 million in 1750, 9.4 million in 1760, 12.6 million in 1775 and over 16 million in 1790. In addition, unstamped weekly newspapers, probably exceeding 50,000 by 1730, were also distributed in the London area. Estimates from the late 1730s put the weekly total at between 50,000 and 80,000 copies. In 1781 some seventy-six newspapers and periodicals were published in England and Wales; by 1821 this total had reached 267. The greatly increased production of newspapers was the most impressive feature of printing history in the final two decades of the eighteenth century. It also demonstrated the transformation in the means of distribution. In 1760 London boasted four daily newspapers and five or six tri-weeklies, and by 1770 at least five dailies, eight tri-weeklies and four weeklies. By 1783 the total had risen to nine dailies and ten bi- or tri-weeklies; by 1790 to thirteen morning, one evening, seven tri-weeklies, and two bi-weeklies. In 1793 sixteen London dailies were published, and in 1811 a total of fifty-two different newspapers were published in the capital. In 1782 the Post Office despatched just over three million London newspapers to the country. Ten years later the volume had doubled, and by 1796 the annual postal distribution of London newspapers stood at 8.6 million copies.[41]

The combination of road improvement and the activity of postmasters proved crucial to newspaper distribution. The turnpike mania beginning in the 1750s resulted in some 20,000 miles of road maintained by trusts by the end of the third decade of the nineteenth century. Meanwhile, the Post Office, no longer in 'grant and farm', was placed under Treasury control after 1688. During the eighteenth century the effective cost of newspaper distribution was lowered by groups with Post Office franking privileges. At first the clerks to the Secretaries of State and then the Post Office Clerks of the Road served as retailers of newspapers to all parts of England. By 1782 some 60,000 newspapers were said to be distributed by the Post Office in London alone. Five years later John Palmer established a separate office for newspapers in the Post Office to ease the burden of distribution. A staff of eighteen supervised the receipt, sorting and distribution of news-sheets. In 1785 mail coaches were exempt from tolls and in 1792 franking requirements for newspapers were finally abandoned, largely because of the ease with which the nominal stamps could be forged. What developed was a tiered newspaper market, with a free delivery service available to stamped and post-day publications, and with other kinds of unstamped and non-post-day newspapers confined to circulation within London.[42]

Across the country the maintenance of newspaper circuits secured the solvency of the main book distributors for the London publishers. Newspapers became the mainstay of many printer-booksellers, most notably in the fastest growing of the towns outside the capitals. Between 1750 and 1780 dozens of presses were set up in Manchester, Liverpool and Birmingham. Among the most active of the regional stationer-printers were William and Cluer Dicey of Northampton, John Binns of Leeds, Thomas Saint of Newcastle, and, in the south, the Farleys of Exeter and Bristol, Samuel Hazard of Bath, Benjamin Collins of Salisbury, and Robert Goadby of Sherborne.[43] In many of the rapidly enlarging towns of the final third of the century there was a further major increase in the number of book trades firms. In Newcastle, for example, where there had been two firms in 1700 and about fifteen between 1730 and 1770, there were twenty-six in 1776, thirty in 1782 and thirty-five in 1790.

In all this development the role of commercial advertising was crucial. Advertisements had provided income for publishers of news-sheets as early as 1640, and by 1710 advertising brought additional revenue to a dozen or more newspapers from London, Dublin and Edinburgh. Although the potential for printed advertising was clear to the newspaper proprietors, the first examples of free news-sheets supported entirely by advertising revenue were financial disasters. The limited circulation of the papers was probably the main reason for trade advertisers failing to support the ventures. With the notable exception of price currents and other lists serving trade and finance, the advertising-only journals did not flourish. The key to future advertising was its incorporation into newspapers. Advertisers were willing to pay higher charges for notices guaranteed to appear in multi-purpose publications enjoying wide circulation. By the mid-eighteenth century advertising was a financial mainstay for most newspapers published. In long-running newspapers from both the country towns and the capitals, an increasing proportion of the total space was devoted to advertising. This increase in newspaper advertising was not evenly paced, however. Many have noted the effect of the Stamp Act on the circulation of newspapers, but the Act was also an abrupt disincentive for advertisers, applying a shilling duty to each advertisement. Pressures eased thereafter, with the advertising tax remaining at one shilling for over forty years. In 1757 this tax was doubled. It was further raised to two shillings and sixpence in 1776, and advanced to three shillings in 1789.[44]

Over the century aggregate financial returns from such newspaper advertising increased sharply. The total payments of advertising duty, even allowing for duty increases, rose from the £912 collected in 1713 to £3158 in 1734, £7915 in 1754, £33,662 in 1774, £46,284 in 1784, £69,943 in 1794 and £98,241 in 1798 (the last year for which gross figures are available). The Treasury's exactions did not jeopardize the health of the most popular newspapers, however. In 1746 the *London Daily Post* carried 12,254 advertisements which brought a post-tax profit of £753.10s. In 1771 the *Public Advertiser* carried 24,613 advertisements which brought in £2303.17s.[45] Assuming a three-shilling duty on each advertisement, the total number of advertisements placed in British newspapers (excluding Ireland) in 1798 totalled 654,946. The increasing proportion of advertising duty paid by provincial newspapers is still the most striking feature of the duty returns for England and Wales in the final two decades of the century. Country newspapers paid half the total duty levied in the 1760s, two-thirds by the late 1770s, and overtook the total payment made by London newspapers in 1796.[46]

Winners and losers

Boosted by newspaper advertising, the greatly expanded number of titles and volume of print clearly resulted in more extensive distribution, and evidently a wider readership. Yet given the doubts about the extent to which increased book production in this period indicates a greatly increased number of book readers (given that demand from institutions and from those already in the habit of acquiring books was more obvious than that from working men and women), the extension of cheap print by means of newspaper circulation represents the most pointed evidence for expanded literacy and for a broader audience for new literature. These changes also brought revisions to the physical appearance of books, print and newspapers, enabled by advances in fount design, engraving and other typographical techniques.

All this resulted from a business development that was not without costs and high risks, and where new production and distribution methods were not uniform across the country. Bankruptcies were common, especially in the 1790s (and again later in the 1820s), and a very large proportion of new magazine and newspaper titles ceased publication within a few years of their launch. Similarly, changing styles and types of readership should not be exaggerated in this period. For all the extraordinary increase in the volume of print, literacy rates appear not to have greatly increased until the early nineteenth century, and then with great regional differentiation. For most semi-literate artisans and labourers, the humble chapbook and broadside continued to be the most immediate contact with print. What did change, however, were the contexts in which books and newspapers were read, read aloud, or provided the best available source for oral dissemination of infor- mation, entertainment, news (and rumour).[47]

As the financial base of English book production changed, the industry also reacted more speedily and effectively to market demands, publishing specialist works in response to new professional interests as well as to new fashions in entertainment and instruction. By the end of the eighteenth century support- ing agencies ranged from commercial libraries and subscription book-clubs to private debating societies and the solemn recommendations of the periodical reviews. Publication rates soared, and for those who could afford it access to print was easier and more diverse. The Post Office handled a massively increased volume of print, while many more publications were available from much expanded retail operations, including new methods of street vending. By the beginning of the nineteenth century the literate were engaged with a sophisticated, expansive and highly commercial print culture, and yet the most remarkable thing was that all this was achieved within the technological constraints of the hand press.

The real winners in this struggle were the successful bookseller-publishers, many of whom had arrived in London from the country (or from Scotland) with almost no capital and little or no previous knowledge of the trade. One of the most striking things to emerge from the many new studies of the eighteenth-century book trades is an awareness of how little professional training was required to take part – and succeed – in the increasingly diverse world of publishing and bookselling (thereby offering a sharp contrast with printers, compositors and other apprenticed labourers of the printshop). There remained in the trades many family alliances and interconnections, and for many printers and booksellers these provided the requisite introductions and capital. Many bookshops were also of recent foundation, however, established by men with few or no connections with book trades families and older institutions.

The beneficiaries of this cut-and-thrust world were very wealthy but also very few. Many booksellers died in obscurity and with precious little in the coffers. Henry Dell, bookseller and a lively recorder of the trade in 1766 (in a poem rescued by Terry Belanger), apparently died shortly after in great poverty.[48] The German bookseller Carl Heydinger, who traded in the Strand in the same year as Dell's poem was published, died in penury in 1778.[49] In his nineteenth-century history of the trades, Timperley loftily rejoiced that Stanley Crowder, bookman of Paternoster Row, managed, when his business fell on hard times, to gain employment as clerk to the commissioners of the commutation house and window tax, which 'afforded him a comfortable asylum in his old age'.[50]

At the other end of the scale, the meteoric rise of a few self-made booksellers became the stuff of legend: Robert Dodsley the footman, Thomas and James Harrison the sons of a Reading basket-weaver, Thomas Wright the son of a Wolverhampton buckle-maker, Ralph Griffiths the watchmaker, and William Lane the poultryman's son. Many of these first- or second-generation traders attained great civic distinction. John Boydell rose to be not only Master of the Stationers' Company but also Lord Mayor of London in 1790. Thomas Cadell became an alderman in 1798 and sheriff in 1800, ostentatiously presenting the great west window to Stationers' Hall in 1801. By the turn of the century the sons of booksellers sat in the House of Commons. George, second son of Thomas Longman II, was both wholesale stationer and MP for Maidstone. Andrew, son of William Strahan, followed his father into Parliament.

The wealth gained by a successful bookselling career was also spectacular. Jacob Tonson set new standards when he died in 1736 worth in excess of £40,000. In the mid-1760s Thomas Osborne claimed to be worth more than £40,000, and John Hinton 'died very rich' in 1781. For the successful bookseller the purchase of an estate (however modest) was an obvious attraction, and by the end of the century far fewer of the great booksellers lived over the shop. Tonson led the way, giving up business in 1720 for 'The Hazells' in Ledbury, Herefordshire. Alexander Donaldson retired from London in 1786, returning to Scotland to his newly bought Broughton Hall near Edinburgh. George Robinson took up a fashionable villa at Streatham, 'a snug retreat . . . with diamond latticed cottage windows', and a frequent resort for

Holcroft, Godwin and other writers in his circle. William Strahan, MP, left
an advowson to an Essex rectory and an estate in Norfolk at his death in
1785, in addition to £95,000 in personalty.[51]

Several of the more notorious bookmen also prospered. The heir to the
first children's bookseller, Francis Newbery, bought Heathfield Park in Sussex
in 1795. In about 1789 John Cooke, the publisher of jest books, novels and
crime chronicles, retired to a country estate with a 'handsome' fortune. At his
death in 1814, William Lane, circulating librarian-publisher, left a fortune of
'something under £17,000'. Joseph Johnson, famed for his radical publishing
and his imprisonment in the early 1790s, became, it now seems, something of
a literary and a bricks-and-mortar property speculator, and on his death in
1809 left about £60,000 in addition to a country house at Purser's Cross,
Fulham. James Dodsley, heir and brother of Robert, left over £70,000 and a
landed estate near Chislehurst.[52]

Johnson's and Dodsley's fortunes, like those of many of their successful
fellow bookseller-publishers, were clearly augmented by shrewd investments
quite outside the publishing trade. It is now impossible to decide what
proportion of most of the various fortunes came directly from book trades'
profits, but given that the literary stock of John Murray on his death in 1793
comprised some £9000 from total assets of about £12,000, it would seem
that the business of the book trades was far from an indulgence by rich men;
publishing and bookselling certainly created the fortunes in the first place and
the continuance of the trade in these tumultuous years added further substantial wealth. By the end of the century the profits seemed unprecedented.
Thomas Longman II, nephew to the founder of the house, left over £60,000
at his death in 1797. Charles Dilly bequeathed over £80,000 to his heirs in
1807. In 1793 Thomas Cadell, the richest copyright owner of his generation,
relinquished his trade with 'an ample fortune'. At his death in 1802 he was
estimated to have been worth at least £150,000. Together, the great stationers
Thomas Wright and his partner William Gill, who both died in 1798, left
over £600,000, including a £2000 legacy by Wright to the Stationers'
Company.[53]

How such men made their wealth – or lost it – was the subject of much
contemporary interest and debate. Some booksellers were congratulated upon
their achievement, but many more were not. A few laudatory Victorian
accounts of booksellers-made-gentlemen stressed their philanthropy and generous spirit (rather than their profits), but, like so many practitioners of other
trades, self-made booksellers were often vilified in both popular and learned
literature. Thomas Osborne, whose sale of great libraries from his Gray's Inn

shop provided him with his fortune, was belittled by Dibdin fifty years later as 'short and thick; and, to his inferiors, generally spoke in an authoritative and insolent manner'.[54] John Cooke and his son Charles, like Lane and Dodsley, were denounced as *nouveaux riches* profiteers. Cooke's rural villa, known as 'Cooke's folly' and 'expensively fitted up and furnished', was, according to Rees, 'wholly devoid of the elegancies of high life, and exhibited more ostentatious finery than classical or simple beauty'.[55] It is as a consequence of the new studies in the history of English books and publishing in the eighteenth century that we are at last beginning to understand more about these men – and a few women – and to appreciate the fuller context of the commercial challenges and environment in which they worked.

Notes

1. Terry Belanger, 'Publishers and writers in eighteenth-century England,' in Isabel Rivers (ed.), *Books and their Readers in Eighteenth-Century England* (Leicester: Leicester University Press and St Martin's Press, 1982), pp. 5–25. Important source references that have not been superseded are not repeated here. Revisionist studies are cited in appropriate footnotes below and include Michael Treadwell, 'London trade publishers, 1675–1750', *The Library*, 6th ser., 4 (1982): 99–134; Michael Harris, *London Newspapers in the Age of Walpole: A Study of the Origins of the Modern English Press* (London: Associated University Press, 1987); James E. Tierney (ed.), *The Correspondence of Robert Dodsley 1733–1764* (Cambridge: Cambridge University Press, 1988); M. Pollard, *Dublin's Trade in Books 1550–1800* (Oxford: Clarendon Press, 1989); David Foxon and James McLaverty, *Pope and the Early Eighteenth-Century Book Trade* (Oxford: Clarendon Press, 1991); Harry M. Solomon, *The Rise of Robert Dodsley: Creating the New Age of Print* (Carbondale and Edwardsville: Southern Illinois University Press, 1996); Arnold Hunt *et al.* (eds), *The Book Trade and Its Customers 1450–1900* (Winchester and New Castle, DE: St Paul's Bibliographies and Oak Knoll Press, 1997); Paula McDowell, *The Women of Grub Street: Press Politics and Gender in the London Literary Marketplace 1678–1730* (Oxford: Oxford University Press, 1998); William Zachs, *The First John Murray and the Late Eighteenth-Century Book Trade* (London: British Academy and Oxford University Press, 1998); and James Raven and Antonia Forster, *The English Novel 1770–1799: A Bibliographical Survey of Prose Fiction Published in the British Isles: Volume 1* (Oxford: Oxford University Press, 2000).

2. *The Eighteenth Century Short Title Catalogue*, now subsumed within *The English Short Title Catalogue* (in progress); Michael Crump and Michael Harris (eds), *Searching the Eighteenth Century* (London: British Library, 1983).

3. Peter Borsay, 'The English urban renaissance: the development of a provincial urban culture *c.* 1680 – *c.* 1760', *Social History*, 2 (1977): 581–603; Angus McInnes, 'The emergence of a leisure town: Shrewsbury, 1660–1760', *Past and Present*, 120 (August 1988): 53–87; Peter Borsay and Angus McInnes, 'Debate: leisure town or urban renaissance?', *Past and Present*, 126 (February 1990): 189–202; Rosemary Sweet, *The English Town 1680–1840: Government, Society and Culture* (London: Longman, 1999).

4. P. J. Corfield, *The Impact of English Towns, 1700–1800* (Oxford: Oxford University Press, 1982).

5. The continuing Histories of the Book in Britain (and in the United States, Canada, Ireland and Scotland) will provide standards for the future, building upon the pioneering example of *L'histoire de l'édition Française*. A particular challenge is offered by incorporating literary and historical scholarship beyond the normal ambit of bibliography.

6. Many older studies, themselves pioneering histories, and including A. S. Collins, *Authorship in the Days of Johnson: Being a Study of the Relation Between Author, Patron, Publisher, and Public, 1726–1780* (London: R. Holden and Co, 1927); Collins, *The Profession of Letters: A Study of the Relation of Author to Patron, Publisher, and Public, 1780–1832* (New York: Dutton, 1929); Frank Arthur Mumby, *Publishing and Bookselling* (London: Jonathan Cape, 1934); and Richard D. Altick, *The English Common Reader: A Social History of the Mass Reading Public 1800–1900* (Chicago and London: University of Chicago Press, 1957) are particularly prone to Whiggish perspectives. For comment on the broader debate see Joanna Innes, 'Jonathan Clark, social history and England's "ancien régime"', *Past and Present*, 115 (May 1987): 165–200.

7. See Harold Love, *Scribal Publication in Seventeenth-Century England* (Oxford: Clarendon Press, 1993); and David McKitterick, *Set in Print: The Fortunes of an Idea, 1450–1800: The Lyell Lectures, 2000* (Oxford, forthcoming, 2001).

8. Including Tierney (ed.), *Correspondence of Robert Dodsley*; John Murray I, Account Ledger, Daybook, Booksellers' Book and other records, John Murray Archive, 50 Albemarle Street, London, examined in Zachs, *First John Murray*; K. I. D. Maslen and John Lancaster, *The Bowyer Ledgers: The Printing Accounts of William Bowyer, Father and Son* (London and New York: Bibliographical Society and Bibliographical Society of America, 1991); and Raven and Forster, *English Novel 1770–1799*. The location and history of the trade in the churchyard before the Fire is charted in Peter W. M. Blayney, *The Bookshops in Paul's Cross Churchyard* (Occasional Papers of the Bibliographical Society, No. 5, London, 1990), a project continued by James Raven, Nigel Hall *et al.*, *Mapping the Print Culture of Eighteenth-Century London* (http://members.tripod.co.uk/bookhistory/1999–).

9. Alistair G. Thomson, *The Paper Industry in Scotland, 1590–1861* (Edinburgh and London: Scottish Academic Press, 1974), p. 74.

10. The standard account remains D. C. Coleman, *The British Paper Industry, 1495–1860* (Oxford: Clarendon Press, 1958).

11. Alfred H. Shorter, *Water Paper Mills in England* (London: Society for the Protection of Ancient Buildings, 1966), p. 10.

12. Stephen Dowell, *A History of Taxation and Taxes in England*, 3rd edn, Vol. 3 (London: Frank Cass, 1965), p. 290.

13. Further details are given in Coleman, *British Paper Industry*, pp. 180–90.

14. *Observator*, 7 February 1708, p. [2].

15. Daniel Berkeley Updike, *Printing Types: Their History, Forms and Use: A Study in Survivals*, Vol. 2 (Cambridge, MA: Belknap Press, 1962), pp. 101–24; and Talbot Baines Reed, rev. edn by A. F. Johnson, *A History of the Development of Old English Letter Foundries* (London: Faber and Faber, 1952).

16. F. E. Pardoe, *John Baskerville of Birmingham: Letter-Founder and Printer* (London: F. Muller, 1975); Johnson Ball, *William Caslon, 1693–1766: The Ancestry, Life and Connections of England's Foremost Letter-Engraver and Type-Founder* (Kineton: Roundwood Press, 1973); and Allen Hutt, *Fournier: The Compleat Typographer* (London: Muller, 1972), pp. 21–41. The Frys' firm is greatly neglected as a subject for eighteenth-century business history. A brief sketch is given in Arthur

Raistrick, *Quakers in Science and Industry*, 2nd edn (Newton Abbot: David and Charles, 1968), pp. 214–16.

17. Michael Harris, 'Scratching the surface: engravers, printsellers and the London book trade in the mid-eighteenth century', in Hunt *et al.*, *Book Trade and its Customers*, pp. 95–114.

18. Louise Lippincott, *Selling Art in Georgian London: The Rise of Arthur Pond* (New Haven and London: Yale University Press, 1983).

19. See Timothy Clayton, *The English Print 1688–1802* (New Haven and London: Yale University Press, 1997); and Sven H. A. Bruntjen, *John Boydell, 1719–1804: A Study of Art Patronage and Publishing in Georgian London* (New York and London: Garland Press, 1985).

20. Further references are given in James Raven, 'Establishing and maintaining credit lines overseas: the case of the export book trade from London in the eighteenth century, mechanisms and personnel', in Laurence Fontaine and Gilles Postel-Vinay (eds), *Des Personnes aux institutions: Réseaux et culture du crédit du XVIe au XXe siècle en Europe* (Louvain-la-Neuve: Bruylant-Academia, 1997), pp. 144–62.

21. Book auctions had been regular events since at least 1666; see Robin Myers, 'Sale by auction: the rise of auctioneering exemplified', in Robin Myers and Michael Harris (eds), *Sale and Distribution of Books from 1700* (Oxford: Oxford Polytechnic Press, 1982), pp. 126–63. See also H. G. Pollard and A. Ehrman, *The Distribution of Books by Catalogue* (Cambridge: Roxburghe Club, 1965).

22. Among many examples, see Pierre Jean Grosley, *A Tour to London: or, New Observations on England and its Inhabitants*, trans. Thomas Nugent, 2 vols (London, 1772); Clare Williams (ed.), *Sophie in London, 1786 Being the Diary of Sophie von la Roche* (London: Batsford, 1933); Reginald Nettel (ed.), *Journeys of a German* [Carl Philip Moritz] *in England in 1782* (London: Jonathan Cape, 1965). A long list is given in James Raven, *Judging New Wealth: Popular Publishing and Responses to Commerce in England, 1750–1800* (Oxford: Clarendon Press, 1992), pp. 274–6.

23. For further references see Raven and Forster, *English Novel*, pp. 71–103, 110–13; and Robin Alston, *Library History Database* (http://www.r-alston.co.uk/contents.html, 1998–) with listings (October 1999) of 3071 libraries (of all types) founded between 1700 and 1799.

24. Illustrations and a brief discussion are offered in James Raven, 'From promotion to proscription: arrangements for reading and eighteenth-century libraries', in James Raven, Helen Small and Naomi Tadmor (eds), *The Practice and Representation of Reading in England* (Cambridge: Cambridge University Press, 1996), pp. 181–8.

25. Zachs, *First John Murray*, ch. 2; Maslen and Lancaster, *Bowyer Ledgers*; James Raven, 'The Noble brothers and popular publishing', *The Library*, 6th ser., 12 (1990): 293–345; Tierney, *Correspondence of Robert Dodsley*, p. 42.

26. The most recent surveys are offered in Robin Myers, *The Stationers' Company Archive, 1551–1984* (Winchester and Detroit: St Paul's Bibliographies, 1990); and Robin Myers and Michael Harris (eds), *The Stationers' Company and the Book Trade, 1550–1990* (Winchester and New Castle, DE: St Paul's Bibliographies and Oak Knoll Press, 1997).

27. On the distinction between booksellers and trade publishers see also Treadwell, 'London trade publishers'.

28. J. Collier, *The Parents and Guardians Directory* (London, 1761), p. 69.

29. Cyprian Blagden, 'Booksellers' trade sales 1718–1768', *The Library*, 5th ser., 5 (1951): 243–57; Terry Belanger, 'Booksellers' trade sales 1718–1768', *The Library*, 5th ser., 30 (1975), 281–302; Terry Belanger, 'Booksellers' sales of copyright: aspects of the London book trades, 1718–1768', unpublished PhD dissertation, Columbia University, 1970. Belanger also warns of the dangers of 'promiscuous isolation of individual literary copyrights' when the sale price of individual shares was tied to the fluctuating value of the total share market. For the origins of

the eighteenth-century fragmentation of copies, see Giles Mandelbrote, 'Richard Bentley's copies: the ownership of copyrights in the late 17th century', in Hunt et al., *Book Trade and its Customers*, pp. 55–94.

30. Collection of Literary Assignments of George Robinson, Manchester Central Library MS F 091.A2; John Nichols, *Literary Anecdotes of the Eighteenth Century*, Vol. 3 (London, 1812), pp. 445–6.

31. See Mark Rose, *Authors and Owners: The Invention of Copyright* (Cambridge, MA and London: Harvard University Press, 1993); and Gwyn Walters, 'The booksellers in 1759 and 1774: the battle for literary property', *The Library*, 5th ser., 29 (1974): 287–311.

32. *Boswell's Life of Johnson*, ed. G. B. Hill and L. F. Powell, 2nd edn, Vol. 1 (Oxford: Clarendon Press, 1964), p. 438.

33. Zachs, *First John Murray*, ch. 5.

34. See Warren MacDougall, 'Smugglers, reprinters and hot pursuers: the Irish-Scottish book trade and copyright prosecution in the late eighteenth century', in Myers and Harris (eds), *Stationers' Company*, pp. 151–83.

35. Murray to Gilbert Stuart, 25 September 1775, cited in Zachs, *First John Murray*, p. 61.

36. John Trusler, *Modern Times: Or the Adventures of Gabriel Outcast*, Vol. 3 (London: 'Printed for the Author', 1785), p. 39.

37. See the discussion in Jan Fergus and Janice Farrar Thaddeus, 'Women, publishers, and money, 1790–1820', *Studies in Eighteenth-Century Culture*, 17 (1988): 191–207.

38. Reading University Library, Longman Impression Book H4 (1794–1801), reproduced in *The House of Longman 1794–1914*, microfilm edn (Cambridge: Chadwyck Healey, 1978), reel 37.

39. PRO, Chancery Masters' List, Ledgers of Hookham and Carpenter, 1791–98.

40. This discussion is based on the introductory essay to Raven and Forster, *English Novel 1770–1799*.

41. 'Report on reform and improvement of the Post Office', *Parliamentary Papers* (1807), Vol. 2, p. 219; PRO, A.0.3/950 ff.; Harris, *London Newspapers*, pp. 28, 200, n. 60.

42. See Michael Harris, 'The structure, ownership and control of the press, 1620–1780', in George Boyce, James Curran and Pauline Wingate (eds), *Newspaper History from the Seventeenth Century to the Present Day* (London and Beverly Hills, CA: Constable and Sage, 1978), pp. 82–97.

43. See C. Y. Ferdinand, *Benjamin Collins and the Provincial Newspaper Trade in the Eighteenth Century* (Oxford: Clarendon Press, 1997).

44. See G. A. Cranfield, *The Development of the Provincial Newspaper, 1700–1760* (Oxford: Oxford University Press, 1962); James Sutherland, *The Restoration Newspaper and its Development* (Cambridge: Cambridge University Press, 1986); and R. B. Walker, 'Advertising in London newspapers, 1650–1750', *Business History*, 15 (1973): 112–30.

45. Full tables are provided in A. Aspinall, 'Statistical accounts of the London newspapers in the eighteenth century', *English Historical Review*, 63 (1948): 201–32.

46. PRO, Audit Office Papers, A.O. 3/950 ff., cited in Aspinall, 'Statistical accounts', p. 204.

47. See James Raven, 'New reading histories, print culture, and the identification of change: the case of eighteenth-century England', *Social History*, 23 (1998): 268–87.

48. [Henry Dell], *The Booksellers: A Poem* (London, 1766); Terry Belanger, 'A directory of the London book trade, 1766', *Publishing History*, 1 (1977): 7–48.

49. Nichols, *Literary Anecdotes*, Vol. 3, p. 665.

50. C. H. Timperley, *Encyclopaedia of Literary and Typographical Anecdote* (London, 1842), p. 787.

51. William West, *Fifty Years' Recollections of an Old Bookseller* (London, 1837), p. 93.

52. Thomas Rees and John Britton, *Reminiscences of Literary London from 1779 to 1853* (London, 1896), p. 26; marginal note in Lane's will, cited in Dorothy Blakey, *The Minerva Press 1790–1820* (London, 1939), p. 23; Phyllis G. Mann, 'Death of a London Bookseller', *Keats-Shelley Memorial Bulletin* 15 (1964): 11; Nichols, *Literary Anecdotes*, Vol. 6, p. 438; and E. Marston, *Sketches of Booksellers of Other Days* (London, 1901), pp. 85–6.

53. Nichols, *Literary Anecdotes*, Vol. 3, pp. 401, 441, 442, 649; Philip Wallis, *At the Sign of the Ship: Notes on the House of Longman, 1724–1974* (London, private edn, 1974), p. 14; William Granger, *New Wonderful Museum and Entertaining Magazine*, 6: 3135, cited in Belanger, 'Directory of the London book trade', p. 48; fortune of Cadell noted in *Gentleman's Magazine* (1802), pt. 2: 1173–222; Theodore Besterman (ed.), *The Publishing Firm of Cadell and Davies: Select Correspondence and Accounts, 1783–1836* (London, 1938), pp. viii–ix; *The Farington Diary: By Joseph Farington, R.A.*, ed. James Greig (London, 1922–28), Vol. 2, p. 79; copies of wills, Stationers' Hall, Supplementary Documents, box N, folder 2, iv, x.

54. Thomas Frognall Dibdin, *Bibliomania; or Book Madness: A Bibliographical Romance* (London, 1811), p. 470.

55. Rees and Britton, *Reminiscences*, p. 28.

CHAPTER 2

THE ENGLISH BIBLE AND ITS READERS IN THE EIGHTEENTH CENTURY

SCOTT MANDELBROTE

Introduction: An argument about faith and Scripture

In 1922, the Belfast professor of medicine, Member of Parliament and former president of the British Medical Association, Sir William Whitla (1851–1933), published an edition of Sir Isaac Newton's *Observations upon the Prophecies of Daniel and the Apocalypse of St. John* (1733), in which he commented, 'when this antique volume was written, the destructive German critic had not appeared above the horizon'.[1] Dedicated to the General of the Salvation Army, William Bramwell Booth, this work commended Newton's 'simple childlike faith that has never been excelled' and attempted to apply his writings in order to demonstrate that contemporary events in Palestine, notably the establishment of the British mandate, represented the fulfilment of Daniel's prophecies.[2] By writing in this way, Whitla was perhaps seeking to co-opt Britain's most famous scientist to the defence of tradition that Bramwell Booth had undertaken in his attacks on the evolutionary theory and theological Modernism of Ernest William Barnes, then Canon of Westminster, in 1920.[3] He certainly showed no awareness of the complexity that had in fact characterized Newton's view of Scripture nor of the anti-trinitarian theology that Newton had espoused.[4] Unlike many contemporary evangelicals, Whitla, who was himself a Methodist, displayed a determined conviction not only in the personal appeal of Christ to the believer but also in the inerrant truth of the Old Testament and in particular of biblical prophecy.[5]

In taking this intellectual and religious position, Whitla aligned himself with a developing tradition among British and American premillennialists, who, in addition to expecting the imminent return of Christ, formulated a view of the absolute and literal truth of Scripture that later came to be known as fundamentalism.[6] The shadow cast by fundamentalism still continues to darken present-day understanding of eighteenth-century readers of the Bible. This chapter will consider its effects on interpretation, together with those of other modern attitudes. It will then discuss the standing of the English Bible among eighteenth-century readers and critics, some of the ways in which the Bible was printed and distributed, and the debate which surrounded attempts to revise its translation.

For many modern writers who regard the influence of the 'destructive' German critic in a positive light, the eighteenth century marks a turning point in scholarship, in which awkward questions of history and authority posed by the humanists and reformers of the sixteenth century and their successors were transformed into a new critical freedom. This cast doubt on the accuracy and historicity of the Bible, undermined its claim to present a single, coherent narrative of past, present and future events, and suggested that its human scribes might have played a greater role in its composition than its divine author.[7] Recently, this interpretation has come under an assault of increasing scholarly sophistication, mounted by authors for whom the establishment of a long history for current evangelical beliefs about biblical inerrancy provides a doctrinal bulwark behind which to shelter from the storm of modern science and critical theology. In the words of one of their number, 'it is instructive to learn that many Christians in centuries far removed from us affirmed a belief in the utter truthfulness of God's Word.'[8] As well as arguing that most Christians in the past have shared their view of the divine inspiration of the Bible, these historians suggest that the key change in the eighteenth century was that the number of critics of inerrancy increased and that it thus became necessary for the orthodox to stress its fundamental importance with greater stridency.[9]

Despite the emphasis that British and Continental reformers placed on the primacy of Scripture and the longevity of scholastic methods of interpretation among Protestants, the prominence now given to the doctrine of inerrancy seems misplaced. According to David Durell (1729–75), Principal of Hertford College, Oxford, 'The Idea [tha]t every Word in the sacred Writings was suggested by the H[oly] Spirit is too extravagant I suppose to find many Abbetors in the eighteenth Century.'[10] Durell's dismissive comments formed part of a reply to Thomas Randolph (1701–83), President of Corpus Christi College, Oxford, which was later extended by Durell's friend and client Benjamin Blayney (1728–1801).[11] Randolph was a steadfast defender of doctrinal orthodoxy and opponent of the spread of anti-trinitarian ideas, who, at this time, was prominently involved in defending the university's right to impose subscription to the Thirty-Nine articles of the Church of England on its members.[12] He was unsympathetic to Durell's doubts about the divine inspiration of curses in the Old Testament and, like many of his contemporaries, was convinced of the providential preservation of the text of Scripture over time.[13] Yet Randolph's concerns were principally with the stability of the received version of the Bible and with its reliability as a basis for the interpretation of prophecy. Neither he nor his opponents were especially concerned with the concept of inerrancy itself. Despite the originality of some of their ideas, however, they saw themselves as defenders of ecclesiastical orthodoxy rather than proponents of critical novelty. As Blayney remarked, nothing was so prejudicial to Christian belief and its foundations in prophecy as 'the many vain and idle attempts that have been made to multiply the number of prophetic predictions without any reasonable foundation'.[14]

The significance of the Authorized Version

One important feature of the attitude of conservative evangelicals of the late nineteenth and early twentieth centuries was their loyalty to the Authorized Version of the Bible. To a large extent, this had its origins in contemporary debates over new English translations of the Bible, but it was also a product of decisions that were made in the eighteenth century.[15] Published for the first time in 1611, the Authorized Version itself resulted from dissatisfaction with earlier English translations. Translated by committees of scholars based in Cambridge, Oxford and Westminster as a result of decisions made at the Hampton Court conference of 1604 about the desirability of a revision of the English Bible, the Authorized Version was intended from the start to be the Bible for use by the Church of England.[16] Its initial success was limited, although editions of high quality and accuracy were available by the late 1620s, and in the following decade it rivalled the Geneva Bible as the easiest English translation to obtain.[17] Both the Irish Canons of 1634 and the Scottish Canons of 1636 enjoined its use.[18] During the 1640s and 1650s it was the target of considerable criticism, but attempts to produce a more correct translation foundered in the early 1650s.[19] After 1660, the Authorized Version was virtually without competition as the only edition of the English Bible that was readily available for purchase. Throughout this period, it was also the only version of the English Bible to be printed in the largest formats, suitable for use in church worship.[20] Changes in habits of buying and reading may have contributed to the relative rise in the number of editions of the whole Bible published during the second half of the seventeenth century.[21] A significant factor in that rise, however, was growing rivalry in the marketplace, particularly in the 1670s and 1680s, when the University of Oxford attempted to assert its right to print Bibles in order to provide the financial basis for a learned press.[22] Competition between the King's Printers, who claimed to have the sole privilege to print Bibles in the smallest and cheapest sizes, and the Oxford University Press and its London partners, flooded the market and led eventually to the disposal of surplus stock at knockdown prices.[23] By the end of the seventeenth century, attention had again focused on inaccuracies in the printed text of many Bibles and on the intellectual and linguistic shortcomings of the Authorized Version: 'the daily complaints of Commentators and Preachers against the present Translations, with several other things I could mention, do shew, that there is an indispensable Necessity of revising and correcting them.'[24]

The most vocal critics of the shortcomings of the Authorized Version at this time were Catholics, seeking to undermine the Protestant claim that the Bible could provide a rule of faith for believers, or radical Protestants who were disturbed by discrepancies between the Authorized Version and the received texts of the Hebrew or Greek Bibles.[25] Faced with the criticisms of the radical Huguenot, Charles Le Cène, one contemporary English reader commented 'As to [his] Objections . . . [they] are most frivolous . . . so [tha]t we need not debase [th]e Grandeur of [th]e Scripture style to render it intelligible'.[26] More threatening concerns about the state of the Authorized Version were raised by the Lower House of Convocation in 1703, which censured the printing errors to be found in recent editions of the Bible.[27] In the years that followed, however, a group of prominent churchmen, notably the Whig bishops Edmund Gibson of London and White Kennett of Peterborough, together with their low church allies, sought to restore the status of the Authorized Version. Partly as a result of their actions, the Authorized Version was eventually to become both a bulwark of royal and episcopal authority within the Church and a symbol of pride in the English Reformation. Gibson was instrumental in obtaining an order from George I, dated 24 April 1724, which regulated the quality and price of Bibles printed by the King's Printers in London.[28] Kennett encouraged two clerical authors, John Russell (c.1693–1762), prebendary of Peterborough from 1720, and John Lewis (1675–1747), rector of Margate in Kent and a friend of Russell's father, to work on the life and writings of John Wyclif, in particular on

Wycliffite translations of the New Testament.[29] Russell never completed his edition of the Wycliffite Bible, but Lewis published first a life of Wyclif and then an edition of his translation of the New Testament which he prefaced with a history of the translation of the Bible into English. This was enlarged and published separately in 1739.[30]

Although Lewis complained that he, like Russell, had 'had but poor encouragem[en]t', his enterprise was strongly supported by the leading Whig divine Daniel Waterland, and his fellow Cambridge antiquarian, the broad-minded non-juror Thomas Baker.[31] Along with others, these men supplied Lewis with transcripts of manuscripts and information on printed books. From Waterland, Lewis acquired a fifteenth-century manuscript of the Wycliffite New Testament which he used in the preparation of his edition.[32] Through Waterland and Baker, he came into contact with the work of John Bagford, who at one stage had been one of Baker's book-scouts, and of Humfrey Wanley, librarian to two generations of the great Harley family. Both Bagford's extensive collections about the history of printing and Wanley's notes about early editions of the Bible seem to have provided information for Lewis' history.[33] Whereas some of those who knew Wanley's work had suggested that, despite the 'general Consent and Approbation' of the Author-ized Version, 'it has many considerable Faults, and very much needs another Review', Lewis was far more positive.[34] Although he chronicled with pains-taking care the criticisms which had been levelled against the Authorized Version, he did so largely to reject them as products of the excessive zeal of dissenters or of the wily deceit of Roman Catholics. Against such criticism, he quoted John Selden's remarks that 'the *English Translation* of the Bible is the best Translation in the world' and that 'the Translators in K. *James*'s time took an excellent way'.[35]

Lewis' defence of the Authorized Version needs to be set in the context of his broader polemical activity against all kinds of detractors of the Church of England. His history of English translations of the Bible might have concluded gloomily that 'whatever Reputation the Holy Bible *has* been had in, it is *now* treated with the utmost Slight and Neglect, and is scarce any where read but in our Churches', but it did so in order to admonish its readers.[36] In the dedication to Waterland, Lewis vindicated an earlier generation of Anglican historians who had claimed that the original Scriptures of the Church had always been written in the mother tongue of its people. Throughout the work, the narrative is a positive one of the triumph of the vernacular Bible.[37] Like many low churchmen, Lewis regarded the English Bible as a providential benefit of the Reformation, whose broader characteristics he sought to defend

from attack. Willing to accommodate Presbyterians, he bemoaned failures to
revise the liturgy to enable their inclusion within the Church and the
maintenance of the 'ancient sobriety of the Nation'.[38] However, while he
ridiculed the alleged claims of the non-jurors that the English liturgy had
initially been 'compiled *by the aid of the Holy Ghost*', he was equally scathing
about contemporary attacks on the integrity of Scripture and about the licence
exercised by some dissenters 'not only to *read* but to *interpret* the Scriptures
according to their particular Fancies'.[39] Lewis' charity towards moderate
nonconformity was not echoed by his rival in the writing of the history of the
English translation of the Bible and fellow advocate of the Authorized Version,
Anthony Johnson, who upbraided the Presbyterians for 'complain[ing] that
they could not see into the sense of the Scriptures, for the lack of those
Geneva Annotations'.[40] Despite such criticisms, the Scottish Presbyterian
minister and historian Robert Wodrow (1679–1734) expressed sentiments
that were remarkably close to those of Lewis and his low church allies:

> I am not among those who Think our Translation cannot be Bettered, It may
> have some fe[w] Imperfections, which cleave To all Human uninspired perform-
> ances, But these are fe[w] and of no Great Importance and are very far from
> being a Just Foundation for the Cry raised by some, for a Ne[w] Translation of
> the Bible. The Amendments proposed, By some Essayes of that nature, will be
> found, perversions many of them, Rather than Just versions of the text. And
> notwithstanding all the Advances In Light and Learning since [th]e Time of our
> Translation, no[w] about 130 years, I see very little mat[e]riall proposed To be
> altered, and we have Reason To be Thankfull To providence that hath sent us
> so excellent a version.[41]

The debate over the English Bible

The work of Lewis and his allies provided both historical and intellectual
justification for pride in the Authorized Version, but it also underlined the
political and doctrinal reasons for resisting attempts to rewrite the English
Bible. The last major work of translation to be considered by Lewis was
Daniel Mace's attempted revision of the New Testament 'from the Authority
of the most Authentic Manuscripts'.[42] Mace was a Presbyterian minister who,
like so many of his brethren at this time, had begun to have doubts about the
scriptural witness to the doctrine of the Trinity and to question the divinity
of Christ and the Holy Ghost. His parallel text of the Greek New Testament
alongside a new English version explored at length the difficulties with the

manuscript tradition of the two texts that provided the strongest biblical support for the Trinity, I Timothy 3:16 and I John 5:7.[43] Mace drew on a long tradition of humanist scholarship concerning the transmission of the text of the New Testament. This stretched from Erasmus via the editors of the great polyglot Bibles of the sixteenth and seventeenth centuries to the French Oratorian critic Richard Simon, whose controversial French translation and edition of the Vulgate New Testament was published in English in 1730.[44] In particular, Mace based himself on the survey of variant readings in manuscript and printed texts of the New Testament conducted by the Oxford divine, John Mill.[45] The revision of Mill's work had formed the basis of the abortive edition of the Greek New Testament that the Cambridge critic Richard Bentley had planned in the years around 1720.[46] Bentley hoped to clear the Greek text of the New Testament of errors and interpolations and to restore it 'exactly as it was in [th]e best Exemplars at [th]e time of [th]e Council of Nice' (that is, before disagreements over the doctrine of the Trinity had divided the Church).[47]

Debate over the doctrine of the Trinity formed the background for much of the discussion about revising the Bible in the middle and later years of the eighteenth century. There were a number of positions that individuals might adopt, depending in part upon their view of the Church. High churchmen in general were suspicious of the scholarship that questioned the foundations of traditional Christian teachings. This was particularly true of the minority of high churchmen who followed the teachings of John Hutchinson (1674–1737), who nevertheless had their own reasons to offer new versions of Scripture. Hutchinsonians believed that the Jews had corrupted the text of the Old Testament and obscured the true meaning of Hebrew by the introduction of vowel points and other changes to their language. They advocated a novel translation of many of the Hebrew roots, which, among other things, introduced many unexpected references to the Trinity into the Old Testament.[48] According to the editor of the most sustained of these translations, the intention was to be 'very intelligible and highly improving to the unlearned'.[49] George Horne (1730–92), President of Magdalen College, Oxford, and later Bishop of Norwich, contended:

The H[utchinsonian]s . . . have published their notion fairly & openly to the world – their design & intention plainly is to vindicate & establish the bible against all imaginations of men – They make no sect or schism – contradict none of the articles of faith but are fast & firm freinds to the church of england in opposition to all Jesuits whether popish or protestant.[50]

Sadly, James Bate (1703–75), parson of Deptford, responded to Hutchinsonian efforts at biblical interpretation and translation with the scorn that elder siblings usually reserve for the achievements of their younger brothers. He defended himself from the slur of association with the work of Julius Bate (1711–71), who had become rector of Sutton through his friendship with Hutchinson, by remarking:

> I being the elder Branch, and so – having a right to think for myself, can assure you, that Hutchinsonianism does not run in the blood of the whole Family. For, upon a carefull Examination of their Scheme, I found it to be, in general, an arrant Peice of Nonsense; – diametrically opposite to the real System of the World, – as well as to all the Rules of true Oriental Criticism.[51]

Although it might seem that the conclusions and methods of Hutchinson and his followers were almost a parody of orthodox scholarship, they were in fact quite close to views that predominated among contemporary low church critics. Gregory Sharpe (1713–71), chaplain to Frederick, Prince of Wales, for example, suggested that it would be better to teach Hebrew without vowel points. For this, he was praised by Thomas Hunt (1696–1774), Laudian Professor of Arabic and Regius Professor of Hebrew at the University of Oxford, who argued that 'I was always inclin'd to think that the 22 Alphabetical Letters contain'd the Vowels, as well as the Consonants, and that what we commonly call the Vowels were superinduced by the Jewish Rabbis, ignorant of their own Language'.[52] However, the Hutchinsonians themselves were keen to demonstrate the differences between their interpretations and those of more orthodox scholars, in particular rejecting the use of other Oriental languages, especially Arabic, as a key to the meaning of Hebrew roots.[53]

Many of those who were not high churchmen saw critical and Oriental scholarship as a way out of the difficulties posed for doctrine by ambiguities in Scripture or uncertainties about the text of the Bible. In the end, even so resolute a defender of orthodoxy as Waterland was willing to allow doubts about some of the more controversial passages, notably I John 5:7, but he nevertheless maintained that they did not alter the content of doctrine. This flexibility helped to prolong the possibility that the Church of England might one day be reunited with some of its more moderate dissenting cousins, especially from among the Presbyterians. The avoidance of doctrinal conflict also minimized the pressure for major changes from within the Church itself.[54] Further study might determine controversial points without necessarily compromising the identity of the Church.[55] Thus, although most low churchmen held a positive view of the Authorized Version, others accepted that some form of revision might be in the interests of their Church. An extreme example was Edmund Law, Master of Peterhouse, Cambridge and later Bishop of Carlisle, who, in 1757, compared the Authorized Version unfavourably with the Geneva Bible as he collected 'Materials towards a more perfect Edition, as well as a more accurate Translation, w[hi]ch is extremely wanted'.[56] These efforts bore fruit in the work of Edward Harwood (1729–94) and Gilbert Wakefield (1756–1801), both of whom were associated with anti-trinitarian dissenters, in particular through their contacts with Joseph Priestley and with the Warrington Academy.[57] Less exalted in his position in the Church of England than Edmund Law, although perhaps even more contro-versial through his pioneering of an altered, Arian form of worship 'upon what he judged to be the gospel plan', William Hopkins (1706–86), vicar of Bolney in Sussex, hoped that 'king and parliament' might 'issue out a proper commission' for a new translation of the Bible 'as learned persons and many intelligent Christians of all denominations, seem convinced of the necessity of it'.[58]

Throughout the second half of the eighteenth century there were Protestant dissenting authors who followed in the footsteps of Daniel Mace in criticizing the existing English translations of the Bible. In the vanguard were anti-trinitarians like Harwood, who corresponded with many contemporary critics, both orthodox and heterodox, and who attacked with vigour what he called 'the bald and barbarous language of the old vulgar version'. Given the pedantic but often florid style that Harwood himself displayed, one might question whether the 'young and gay' readership that he sought was likely to judge his work the equal of that of secular authors such as Hume, Robertson or Samuel Johnson, whose tone he attempted to emulate.[59] Less conspicuous than Harwood were earlier heterodox critics of the Authorized Version. Although she was probably not as learned as Mace or Harwood, Mrs Elizabeth Ginn, a widow of Newington Butts, near London, displayed remarkable ingenuity in her study of the Authorized Version. The founder of an independent Baptist congregation in Southwark, and friend of the alleged unitarian Sayer Rudd, Mrs Ginn spent much of the years 1735 and 1736 in copying out the New Testament from an early sixteenth-century edition of William Tyndale's translation for critical comparison with the Authorized Version, which she also transcribed.[60]

Although many dissenting critics were inspired by the spread of Arian or Socinian ideas, others were orthodox trinitarians. Thus in the mid-1760s, Samuel Palmer could comment adversely on the antiquity of the Authorized

Version and be encouraged by signs that the governors of the Church of England might soon sanction a new translation, arguing that 'Till this is undertaken under the patronage of supreme authority, it will be an useful attempt in private Divines to supply the defect'.[61] The bookseller Nathaniel Scarlett and his friends in the Artillery Lane chapel in London in the 1790s engaged in theological discussions which highlighted the extent to which genuine curiosity about the meaning of the Bible was a concern as much of tradesmen and artisans as it was of critics and divines. One result of their debates was an estimate of the time that it took to read the whole of the New Testament (fourteen hours); another was the translation of it published by Scarlett in 1798. Like so many of his predecessors, Scarlett justified his undertaking because of the obscurity of some of the language of the Authorized Version, otherwise a translation that he judged to be good, and on which he was often reliant.[62]

In the eyes of early eighteenth-century churchmen at least, two categories of dissenters were particularly irreverent in their attitude to the Bible – Quakers and Catholics – yet neither of these communities was immune to the growth of private translation of the Bible that represented one characteristic of late eighteenth-century responses to Scripture. Nor were they necessarily insensitive to the possibilities created for criticism of the doctrines of the Church of England by contemporary concern about the accuracy or currency of the Authorized Version. From the time of the Rheims and Douai translators of the late sixteenth and early seventeenth centuries, Catholic critics had pointed to the instability of vernacular translations as a reason for preferring the text of the Vulgate as sanctioned by the traditions of the Church. These arguments had been reinforced by the findings of seventeenth-century textual scholars, notably Richard Simon, and formed the basis for the cautious attitude taken towards Scripture by early eighteenth-century English Catholic writers.[63] However, just as Anglican critics came increasingly to see the positive aspects of Simon's work, so the Catholic hierarchy began to realize the usefulness of a translation of the Vulgate which would take into account changes made by its late sixteenth-century Roman editors and reflect more contemporary developments in language and taste.[64] The prime mover in this development was Richard Challoner (1691–1781), who perhaps did more to bring English Catholics back into the mainstream of contemporary life than any of his co-religionists. A paradox of Challoner's success was the fact that in his translation, Roman Catholics were reading work which was at times much closer to the spirit of the Authorized Version than its contemporary the original Douai translation had been.[65]

The Scottish Catholic priest Alexander Geddes (1737–1802) was perhaps the most serious and acute of all those who attempted private revisions of the Bible in the late eighteenth century.[66] Although at first he intended little more than an extension of Challoner's work, Geddes was well acquainted with both British and Continental scholarship at a time when the latter was falling out of favour in Britain as a consequence, in part, of reactions to the French Revolution.[67] By 1782, he was 'determined to translate from the Originals; as I find it impossible to make a tolerable one of the Vulgat'.[68] Geddes, however, remained critical of Protestant attachment to the idea of the literal translation of Scripture, but eventually formulated plans for a rational version that might have more than sectarian appeal. He hoped that 'the day may come, when the translator of the Bible will be as little shackled as the translator of any other ancient book.'[69] He was conscious of the extent to which Catholic attitudes to the Bible had changed during the eighteenth century, and was aware that the textual criticism that had seemed an ally to a traditional faith in the seventeenth century was now felt by Catholics as much as by Protestants to be a challenge to it.[70] Despite his self-proclaimed moderation, which had already led to censure from his bishop when he was serving as a missionary priest on the Gordon estates near Aberdeen, Geddes' translation foundered and was left substantially incomplete at his death.[71] In this, it was somewhat less successful than the work of the Quaker shoemaker and schoolteacher Anthony Purver (1702–77), whose often idiosyncratic version of the Bible appeared in 1764.[72] Purver's interest in critical scholarship had been awakened by reading the works of the mid-seventeenth-century Quaker Samuel Fisher, who had engaged in polemic with the Independent divine John Owen about the reliability of the literal meaning of Scripture.[73] However, unlike the Quakers of Fisher's generation, Purver preferred to use his own painstakingly acquired knowledge of Oriental languages to present the Bible in what he hoped was a more comprehensible and contemporary form, rather than to denigrate the written word for being spiritually dead.[74] Like the work of Challoner and Geddes, Purver's translation testified to the difficulty of ignoring or deriding the importance of lay readership of Scripture in eighteenth-century polite culture. Yet, in common with many other private translations, it also suggested that the linguistic standards of a refined and newspaper-reading public were too exacting for the antique style of the Authorized Version.

Readership of the English Bible

Writing of his experiences as a child growing up in the Scottish Highlands, Geddes remarked:

> Although my parents were Roman Catholics, they were not bigots; and the Bible was the principal book in their scanty library. They taught me to read it with reverence and attention; and before I had reached my eleventh year, I knew all its history by heart.[75]

His comments suggest a number of essential points that need to be made about popular readership of the Bible and about the provision of Bibles for ordinary people. The Bible was increasingly the focus of early education and rudimentary learning during the eighteenth century. Both charity schools and Sunday schools concentrated extensively on conveying the fundamentals of a Christian education through knowledge of the catechism, the Book of Common Prayer and simple biblical texts.[76] Scriptural material also played an important role in dame-schools and, most importantly, in the teaching of reading at home.[77] Children were taught to read the Bible in particular ways. To some extent, this varied with denomination, and it was certainly the case that the Church of England was most prescriptive in urging that certain parts of the Bible, notably prophecy, were unsuitable reading for ordinary people.[78] Near to home, at least, some of this clerical teaching and exhortation seems to have sunk in. Jane Johnson (1706–59), wife of a Buckinghamshire vicar and an enthusiastic teacher of both her sons and her daughter, commented:

> the scriptures are not set forth as a Riddle for every one to guess at, but every thing that is necessary for any one to Believe, & Practice, is so Plain, that those that Run may Read it, & a Way-Faring man tho' a Fool shall not Err therein. Therefore those parts that are mysterious to any one, don't relate to them, but were wrote for different Persons, or different Times, & by those Persons, & at those Times were, or will be, well understood.[79]

It was, however, possible to take excessive care to prevent the abuse of Scripture by unwary readers. One can only wonder what Edmund Gibson, Bishop of London, must have made of the deposition he received against Richard Peters, concerning a sermon preached at Christ Church, Philadelphia on 3 April 1737, in which it was alleged that Peters had 'gravely exhorted parents & Teachers of youth to discontinue [tha]t Custom [of teaching children to read the Bible], nay insisted [tha]t the Bible ought not to be promiscuously used in Families, but should be kept as a Sacred Deposition by Masters of Families, & ought not to be read, unless [th]e usefulness & excellency of [th]e portion read should be at [th]e same time opend and explaind.' Certainly, it seems safe to say that Peters' opinion that 'the little regard paid to the Scriptures, was chiefly owing to Childrens being taught to read by putting them into their hands' also found few sympathizers on the other side of the Atlantic.[80]

Many printed works were available to guide parents, teachers and children in their reading of the Bible. On the one hand, there were works by learned authors aimed at a popular audience, like those of the Swiss divine, J. F. Ostervald, which were widely distributed by the Society for Promoting Christian Knowledge throughout the century. Ostervald instructed his readers to follow the programme of beginning with the narrative works of the Old Testament that was later adopted by the young Geddes along with many other children, arguing that 'the first instruction God was pleased to give his church, was by history'.[81] But the number of books written specifically to aid children to learn about the Bible was also increasing. These varied from picture-books conveying the essence of biblical stories, to heavily abridged retellings of the most famous parts of the Bible, often accompanied by pictures, to verse paraphrases of passages of Scripture, or to moral lessons drawn from the stories of the New Testament.[82] They included miniature Bibles and other curiosities such as hieroglyphic Bibles, in which the narrative was partly composed of pictures which stood for the words they represented, and biblical prints for placing on the nursery wall.[83] The intention of such books was to make reading the Bible enjoyable as well as instructive for young people, thus avoiding the problem that 'the accustomed mode of putting the *Bible* into the hands of children, and causing them to read difficult and obscure passages, before they can have the least conception of what they are doing . . . naturally creates a dislike to the book.'[84]

Despite these innovations, it seems to be the case that English authors lagged behind both German and, to some extent, French writers in producing biblical literature tailored to the needs of children.[85] Such lack of enterprise was less apparent in the English response to the problem of distributing the Bible to the deserving poor and their families. Throughout the eighteenth century, a number of voluntary organizations concentrated on the distribution of Bibles or of biblical and religious literature to poor children, widows and other objects of charity. The most famous and largest of these was the Society for Promoting Christian Knowledge (SPCK) founded in 1698, which was firmly associated with the Church of England and increasingly patronized by its hierarchy as well as by many wealthy divines and gentlemen, and a growing and significant number of ladies. During the eighteenth century, the SPCK collected subscriptions for and handled the distribution of several editions of the Bible in Welsh and a version of the Bible in the language of the Isle of Man. The Society distributed Bibles largely through its charity schools and through sales to members for charitable gifts 'for the use of the poor'. Bibles were among the most expensive books that the SPCK gave away, although the majority of their distributions were of cheap, small-format Bibles, many of which came from editions that were effectively produced on their behalf by the King's Printers and later by the university presses at Oxford and Cambridge. That the Society was able to support even this level of charity was very largely due to a single donation of land in Romney Marsh and of South Sea stock by Edwin Belke, a gentleman from Kent, in 1735. Most of the Bibles and New Testaments that the SPCK distributed were charged to Mr Belke's charity.[86] Nevertheless, in many years, the annual total of Bibles and New Testaments given out by the Society was rather modest. In the 1720s and early 1730s, the SPCK seems to have distributed slightly fewer than 1000 Bibles, together with a couple of hundred New Testaments, each year.[87] Between 1736 and 1745, the Society increased the number of Bibles it gave away to an average of 1188 per year but began to distribute more than double the previous number of cheaper New Testaments. As the Society increased in size in the latter part of the eighteenth century, so its levels of giving also rose. In the 1750s and 1760s it was not uncommon for the SPCK to distribute over 3000 Bibles in a year, together with between 1500 and 2000 New Testaments. These figures continued to rise throughout the 1770s and 1780s. In a particularly generous year (1784–85), the Society gave away 6896 Bibles and 15,545 New Testaments; that year, together with 1786–87, represented the peak of the SPCK's donation. By 1787, the Society was complaining of the 'prodigious' increase in its distributions and was forced to limit members to applying 'for *their own* distribution, or for Charity-Schools, with which they are *personally* connected'.[88] Whereas the prices charged by the SPCK's booksellers, and available both to the Society and to its members, had remained almost constant between the 1740s and the early 1780s, they had risen significantly in 1783 and were to rise by a larger amount in 1800. By then, the Society had already absorbed charges for increased paper and labour costs at the university presses which were the product of the higher levels of duty and the inflation of the years of war following the French Revolution. During the 1790s, the Society distributed around 5000 Bibles and 9000 New Testaments each year.

While the SPCK responded positively to a number of social trends that generated an increase in demand for cheap Bibles, its resources were insufficient to allow it to keep pace with population growth and increased urbanization or to enable it to ride out protracted periods of economic dislocation. Nevertheless, the volume of its distributions, particularly in the middle years of the century, was significant since the Society generally avoided making more than one gift per household. At least until the late 1780s, the SPCK seems to have sought out deserving categories of recipient with zeal, making special donations to regiments of soldiers and the militia, to naval vessels, the convicts embarking for Botany Bay, 'the Negroes in and about London', and even to some Sunday schools associated with its members. These gifts supplemented those to the more regular targets of poor families, poor servant maids, orphans and poor boys, old men and widows.[89] After May 1787, however, the Society's worries about costs and also about the religious benefit of some of its donations led to a scaling back of activity. As early as November 1780, the Society had decided to curtail donations to the army and the militia, which it judged to have been expensive and ineffective. Several requests for Bibles and other books for urban Sunday schools were rejected ostensibly on grounds of cost, but perhaps also because of concern about competition with the Society's own charity schools and about the evangelicalism that often inspired the new ventures. An exception to the SPCK's reduction in its distribution was its supplying of naval vessels with Bibles and religious literature on an increased scale during the Revolutionary and Napoleonic Wars. The upheaval generated by these conflicts did much to rekindle millenarian zeal among dissenters, but the SPCK was in the vanguard of attempting to ensure that the men of the Royal Navy were supplied with Bibles, prayer-books and moral tracts that might divert them from dangerous, prophetic speculations. Following the mutinies at Spithead and the Nore in the spring of 1797 and the brief establishment of a 'floating republic' at the Nore, the Society responded by raising the proportion of Bibles, prayer-books and works of piety that it distributed to ships so that there might be one Bible available for every seven seamen. Among the ships to which it gave books were several stationed at the Nore.[90] For this work, the SPCK was thanked by, among others, Admiral Sir Horatio Nelson, who observed with a perhaps disingenuous moral tone that

when he went out in the Agamemnon in the Year 1793, he had been supplied by the Society with a quantity of Common Prayers & religious tracts, which he flatters himself answer'd the good purposes they were intended for; & requests that he may be favor'd with as many Bible & Prayer Books [as the Society's rules allow] for the use of such of H.M. Ships, as he may hoist his flag in.[91]

The successes and failures of the SPCK in the distribution of English and also Welsh Bibles have been largely eclipsed by the later work of the British and Foreign Bible Society in the nineteenth century. A similar fate has befallen the work of smaller charities such as the fund set up by Philip, Lord Wharton in 1692, originally to pay for gifts of Bibles as rewards to children from dissenting ministers in Westmorland, Cumberland, Yorkshire and Buckinghamshire, but later under the trusteeship of members of the Church of England, or that established by the Hoare family of bankers, creators of Stourhead and frequent servants of the SPCK, again to distribute Bibles.[92] All these organizations participated in contemporary attempts not just to discipline but to improve the poor through philanthropy. The evangelical, and perhaps even millenarian, ambitions of the Bible Society seemed almost threatening by contrast in the first decade of the nineteenth century.[93]

Printing and publishing the Bible

Almost all the Bibles that the SPCK distributed as charity were small duodecimo volumes printed in nonpareil type. Up until 1760, the Society's principal supplier had been the King's Printer, either from presses in London or, more frequently, from the Oxford University Press, which was leased by him from 1712 to 1765. From 1744, however, the Society also began to advertise similar Bibles printed by the Cambridge University Press, where Joseph Bentham had resumed publication of Bibles in 1743, although at first it did so only at higher prices.[94] In 1760, the Society advertised both Oxford and Cambridge nonpareil Bibles at a price of 1s 10d, selling duodecimos in the larger minion character at 2s 9d, and octavo Bibles at 5s 6d. These prices compared well with those of the Bibles that the SPCK had offered for sale in 1733, when a duodecimo in minion type would have cost 3s, or 2s in nonpareil. By 1783, rising duties on insurance and paper had forced the university presses to raise their prices, and the Society offered Oxford or Cambridge octavo Bibles at 6s, a smaller Cambridge octavo without marginal references at 4s, duodecimos in minion at 3s and those in nonpareil at 2s. They briefly supplied an octavo Bible from the King's Printers in London, now no longer linked to either university press, at the former price of 5s 6d.[95] Following complaints from the Vice-Chancellor of the University of Oxford, the SPCK advertised from 1787 a small Oxford octavo Bible without references also priced at 4s.[96] By 1800, the Society's charges had risen again – despite growing subsidy – to 7s for larger octavo Bibles and 4s 5d for smaller ones and to 3s 6d for duodecimos in minion and 2s 4d in nonpareil.

The prices charged by the SPCK reveal more than the pattern of inflation in paper and labour costs over the century. They also demonstrate the efficient working of the monopoly on printing and publishing Bibles in England held by the King's Printer and the two university presses. The dominance of the Bible trade established by the great monopolist John Baskett at the beginning of the second decade of the eighteenth century, in which he came to control both the King's Printing House and the presses at Oxford, bought into a share of the Scottish Bible patent, and reached an agreement with the lessee of Cambridge University Press that it would not print Bibles, effectively established the pattern of a system that would survive the expiry of the patents and contracts of Baskett's heirs in the 1760s.[97] Even after the breaking of Baskett's monopoly by Joseph Bentham at Cambridge University Press (whose first duodecimo Bible, published in 1743, sold for 2s unbound), there was little real competition on either price or quality.[98] This remained true once the partnership of Eyre and Strahan had taken over the King's Printing House in 1770, without having obtained the lease on printing at Oxford University Press which was bought by Wright and Gill in 1765.[99] Indeed, the relationship between the SPCK and Cambridge University Press formed a sub-species of monopoly, since the Society's own bookseller, John Rivington, was one of the London distributors for the publications of the Press from 1765.[100]

The monopoly on printing the Authorized Version was in many ways a consequence of the nature of publishing at the time. The high costs of paper, type and presses made the undertaking of bulky and repetitive jobs such as that required to keep the Bible in print in various sizes both difficult and expensive. The monopoly was also supposed to protect the integrity of the text, adding higher proof-reading charges to those already mentioned. Thus, although the operation of the Bible patent probably stood in the way of innovation and helped to perpetuate poor standards of work, particularly at the cheaper end of the market, it also ensured a regular and relatively dependable supply of affordable Bibles while guaranteeing a good return for the printers involved.[101] In two important ways, however, the Bible patent and the practices that it encouraged worked against the interests of readers, especially in the later eighteenth century.

The poor paper, inking and presswork of cheap Bibles was a constant complaint of members of the SPCK. This criticism was levelled particularly frequently at Bibles produced by the Baskett family. In the early 1720s, the SPCK explored a number of options for dispensing with Baskett's services. Concern about the maintenance of his monopoly may well have been behind Baskett's agreement to print the prices of Bibles on their title-pages in 1724.[102] Similar exasperation with the quality of publications from the King's Printing House and Oxford University Press resurfaced in 1744, when Thomas Baskett was required to give assurances to the Archbishop of Canterbury about proof corrections and, in a brief moment of competition, it was threatened that 'none but Cambridge Bibles & Com[mon] Prayers be sent for the future to the Members of the Society'.[103] It was in this context that the Society decided to quote Cambridge Bibles in its catalogues and to place the contract for printing a new edition of the Welsh Bible in the hands of Joseph Bentham. Complaints about Baskett's work continued, however, and he was again called to account for poor paper and unclear, uneven printing in an edition of the New Testament published in 1757.[104] Unfortunately, the effects of inferior printing and, indeed, binding were hard to remedy. Their main impact was on poor readers, the very people who most depended on cheap Bibles or charitable distribution for their knowledge of Scripture. These were the people of whom John Wilson, a Rutland priest, observed that 'when I have taught their little Ones to read the Scriptures they cannot (most of them) purchase Bibles for them'.[105] In November 1719, one of the SPCK's correspondents, Maurice Wheeler, suggested that the letters in which cheap Bibles were printed 'need to be decipher'd even to some of the Learned, except Printers or Scholars that have been conversant with the Press'.[106] The following year, Henry Darby remarked that 'the badness of Paper together with the Blindness & Falsities in print . . . have been . . . the greatest cause of Ignorance among the meaner sort.'[107] The appearance in the Society's catalogues of expensive octavo and even quarto editions by the end of the century need not necessarily imply concern for well-to-do subscribers rather than for recipients of charity. The Oxford quarto Bible that was introduced into the SPCK's list in 1798 responded to a request for a Bible in large and clear type 'suitable for old Persons, with weak Eyes'.[108] The indigent needed large sizes of Bible as well as the smallest, and they needed them to last. There were therefore frequent complaints about the quality of the bindings that the Society used for its books. The temptation to cut costs in this expensive area of book production and presentation meant that the instructions issued by the SPCK to its binders in October 1765 'to take Care in particular, that Bibles, the New Testaments and Common Prayers be bound in a stronger Manner than is commonly done for the Shops' were rarely carried out.[109]

More surprising, perhaps, than the monopolists' lack of interest in the needs of poorer readers was their neglect of readers who wanted to purchase Bibles with illustrations or commentaries. In the eyes of the Bible patentees, the task of the publisher was, at best, to produce an accurate reprinting of the Authorized Version as it had stood in 1611. For all sorts of reasons, including changing canons of taste as well as print shop practice, this proved impossible. Thus the activities of learned correctors could be used to proclaim the benefits of editions restored to a new standard, such as that published by Cambridge University Press in 1762.[110] Similarly, when they took over the Oxford Bible Press in 1743, Thomas and Robert Baskett were eager to make amends for their father's errors in one edition at least and, in so doing, to set a high level of competition for Bibles that were beginning to be printed again at Cambridge.[111] However, most editions of the Bible contained innumerable minor errors of the kind that occasionally exercised members of the SPCK.

The variety of English Bibles

What editions of the Authorized Version produced by the Bible patentees often did not contain was the full range of additional material that some readers sought in order to help them understand the text of Scripture. According to Alexander Fortescu,

> 'Tis well known that the *common* Bibles, used in most Families, abound with innumerable Errors, and literal Mistakes, chiefly owing to the great negligence in the Common *method* of Printing them, and the inattention of the Publishers; and having no Illustrations to explain the dark and obscure Texts of Scripture, they certainly fall short of the intended Design, of dispensing Christian Knowledge to those of *weaker Capacities*.[112]

Although large-format Bibles, especially folios and quartos, but also some octavos, often contained chronological information and almost always had extensive marginal notes identifying parallel texts of Scripture, many late eighteenth-century readers sought more coherent and comprehensive aids to understanding. Many works claiming to be of such assistance were available, especially for the New Testament.[113]

Other readers, perhaps put off by the relatively high cost of the larger Bibles, looked to new developments in subscription publishing and part books to enable them to buy the substantial and visually impressive tomes of Scripture that they coveted.[114] Although weighty, many of these works were bulked out with general learning rather than critical scholarship that might have tired their aspiring purchasers.[115] These readers were clearly not put off by puffs such as Fortescu's: 'It may seem Presumptuous, in an Age when so many Bibles are daily publishing, to offer any Thing of the Kind with an *Original* degree of Merit and Utility.'[116] Provincial publishers who strove to meet these new markets were aware of the opportunities that loopholes in the Bible patent provided. Bibles dressed up as works of biblical commentary were immune from seizure by the patentees, and by 1800 several booksellers had stretched the principle that Bibles might be published outside the patent if they included substantial notes. They produced pocket editions with exaggerated lower margins, at the bottom of which on occasional pages lurked a single line of trite comment or cross-reference, awaiting the binder's knife to turn the book into an ordinary duodecimo Bible.[117]

In response to these practices, the King's Printers and the university presses frequently sought legal rulings to defend their monopoly. The principal target of these actions remained the King's Printer in Scotland, the importation of whose publications into England posed the biggest threat to the monopolists throughout the century. However, steps were also taken to prevent such obvious flouting of the patent as the publication of the Bible with notes that were clearly intended to be cut off by the binder. The lead in this case was taken by the University of Oxford, which by the 1790s was the main publisher of the small-format Bibles whose market was threatened by this practice. Recourse to law was a double-edged sword, however, as the monopolists would find in the 1830s when, under pressure from the Bible Society, Parliament began to investigate their practices and the rather feeble legal justifications that underlay them. Since the university presses in particular, and to a lesser extent the King's Printers, published very few Bibles in large formats, it was easier for their competitors to expand into this market. Indeed, almost the entire growth in the number of editions of the Bible published after 1760 can be explained by the rise in production of more expensive editions.[118]

Those who entered this market were often not reticent about the justifications for doing so. The works of Simon and Le Cène influenced some of the first critics of the layout of the Authorized Version.[119] For others, critical scholarship had exposed as a particular obstacle to comprehension the haphazard division of the Bible into chapters and verses.[120] Several were concerned that the Authorized Version was in places little better than a paraphrase and wanted to improve it by following a more literal manner of translation, though few of these were as extreme as the Scottish translator John Callender of Craigforth, who wrote that 'those who love to search the SCRIPTURES, and to read them divested of every human gloss, will not perhaps be displeased to see a version so *entirely literal* as to abandon the English idiom altogether, that the genius of the Greek language may be every where preserved, and even the unlearned reader made to feel the energy of the divine original.'[121] However, the most telling criticism remained the following:

> the English Translation of the BIBLE in the Reign of King James I. is, no doubt, a very good one; and justly so esteemed to this day; though it be above a hundred and fifty years old; but it is not to be wondered at if some words and phrases, then in use and well understood, should by this time become obsolete and almost unintelligible to common readers.

John Worsley, the author of this passage, went on to urge the benefit for private readers of access to new translations of Scripture, but others, while recognizing some of the problems, were less ambitious in their conclusions.[122] Thus John Wesley argued:

> there is, to my Apprehension, I know not what peculiarly solemn and venerable in the Old Language of our Translation. And suppose this to be a mistaken Apprehension and an instance of human Infirmity, yet is it not an excusable Infirmity, to be unwilling to part with what we have been long accustomed to, and to love the very Words, by which GOD has often conveyed Strength or Comfort to our Souls?[123]

Clement Cruttwell, the editor of the biblical notes of Thomas Wilson, Bishop of Sodor and Man and instigator of a Manx translation of the Bible, suggested that his contemporaries had gone too far in altering the language of the Authorized Version, sacrificing dignity in the process. Cruttwell's views, as well as the history of the English Bible that he summarized, owed much to those disseminated by John Lewis earlier in the century.[124] Yet, despite widespread acknowledgement of the value of the Authorized Version, eighteenth-century critics remained prepared to undertake its revision.

Revising the Authorized Version

Among no group of authors and scholars was willingness to undertake the work of revision more apparent than in the circle of Thomas Secker

(1693–1768), successively Bishop of Bristol and Oxford and later Archbishop of Canterbury. Secker had been brought up as a dissenter, but from 1714 had gradually conformed to the Church of England during a long education that included wide theological reading and extensive study of the Bible in its original languages. He was ordained priest in 1723. As a young man, Secker initially shared the doubts that Samuel Clarke and others had expressed about the doctrine of the Trinity, but he was persuaded of the divine inspiration of Scripture, in part by reading criticism of the work of Richard Simon.[125] Throughout his career, Secker displayed an active interest in biblical scholarship and in the possibility that a revision of the Authorized Version, undertaken with the sanction of authority, might increase the standing and appeal of the established Church. For much of his life, he annotated the margins of a Hebrew Bible with conjectures, alternative readings and translations based on wide critical study. Many of these comments were eventually transferred by Secker to a copy of the Authorized Version in which he marked unsatisfactory passages in the English translation.[126] As Bishop of Oxford, Secker patronized several notable biblical critics, particularly the young Benjamin Kennicott (1718–83), who was already making a name for himself as a Hebrew scholar.[127] He also took a close interest in the administration of his diocese, being careful among other things to enquire about the provision of suitable copies of the Bible for parochial worship.[128] When Thomas Herring (1693–1757) succeeded John Potter as Archbishop of Canterbury in 1747, he soon consulted Secker as part of a programme of enquiry to discover whether there was support for further reformation in the Church. Among the queries that Herring put to his correspondents was the question 'whether there sh[oul]d not be a better translation of the Bible'.[129]

Like many of his contemporaries, Herring was concerned that minor errors in the Authorized Version might detract from its authority and from the standing of the Church of England. Many of those errors were in fact due to the shortcomings of the printers rather than the translators of the Bible. They related to the apparatus provided to support the text, not to the English version itself. The 'Proposals drawn up by dutiful sons of the Church' that Herring distributed therefore remarked:

the want of a better translation is confessed. Intimations that may be of service for one[:] Some parts of Scripture supposed to be out of due place, may be better arranged. A more commodious Division may be made. Contents of chapters neither accurate clear nor full. Short notes sh[oul]d be added where principaly wanted.

Secker was, however, sceptical about some of these suggestions.[130] For low churchmen who had cut their teeth on the debates of the 1720s and 1730s, these criticisms of the Authorized Version perhaps seemed to concede too much to its detractors. Rather than concentrating on faults in the language or style of the English Bible, Secker and those whom he patronized generally sought the improvement of the Authorized Version through the introduction of the findings of contemporary, orthodox critics. The revision of the Authorized Version was to be contemplated not because of the carping of private individuals but as a result of the linguistic and theological achievements of members of the established Church.

Once he had himself succeeded to Canterbury, Secker therefore warned the clergy of his diocese about their preaching, arguing that 'giving a New Translation or Sense of a Text, unless the present hath considerable Inconveniences, will only puzzle your Audience, and tempt them to doubt, whether they understand the rest of their Bible.'[131] Yet he also continued to encourage the leading contemporary English critics, taking a close interest in the work of Kennicott and Robert Lowth (1710–87), whom he recommended for preferment. As Professor of Poetry at Oxford in the 1740s, Lowth argued for the importance of a correct understanding of Hebrew poetry in order to translate the wide range of biblical literature, including many of the prophetic writings, that he identified as being composed in verse. He rejected contemporary typologies of Hebrew poetry based on classical or English schemes of metre, suggesting instead that the structure of biblical verse was provided by a system of verbal echoes and repetitions known as parallelism. The difference between Lowth and those whom he criticized was particularly apparent in their treatment of the acrostic poetry of some of the psalms, although Lowth later made it explicit by showing that the metrical divisions advocated by his opponents could be applied to Hebrew prose as effectively as they could to verse.[132] Lowth's work was particularly important in the context of contemporary debate over the translation of the Psalter and over the role of metrical psalms in worship. Together with other eighteenth-century critics, Lowth also helped to promote the reputation of Hebrew literature, particularly in comparison with the Greek and Latin classics, through his demonstration of the poetic quality of Hebrew verse.[133] Lowth greeted Secker's promotion to the see of Canterbury by telling Kennicott that 'we sh[oul]d now have the finest opportunity that can be desir'd or expected for procuring a New Translation of the Bible.'[134] With the help of Secker's patronage and the support of the University of Oxford, Kennicott embarked in 1760 on the collation of the extant manuscripts of the Hebrew Old Testament in order to identify variant readings and to establish the text that might be used in a new translation.[135]

The work of both Kennicott and Lowth drew on the teaching and encouragement of Thomas Hunt, which was also apparent in the scholarly publications of other Oxford critics such as David Durell or Benjamin Blayney, all of whom were known to Secker.[136] When he was Oxford's Vice-Chancellor between 1765 and 1768, Durell presided over the bidding process in which the Baskett family lost control of Oxford University Press. He then sought Secker's advice about printed editions of the English Bible on which to base future copies printed at Oxford. Secker's reply demonstrated the interest in the history of the printing and production of the English Bible that underpinned orthodox attempts at revision.[137] Blayney was chosen by the delegates of Oxford University Press to make a collation of the three editions of the Bible that had been selected. Eventually, in 1769, a corrected edition of the Authorized Version was published which aimed to be 'a standard of purity' in its English text and to follow some of Secker's suggestions for improvements to the marginal references while avoiding 'mere fanciful allusions'.[138]

Secker's encouragement of a standard edition of the Authorized Version was intended to be a step in a process of revision that would respect the achievements of the early seventeenth-century English translators. The Archbishop himself prepared extensive commentaries and notes on the Bible, some of which he allowed to slip into print in the compilations of other Anglican critics who were in favour of reform.[139] His belief that the application of orthodox scholarship to the translation of the Bible might help achieve the resolution of conflict in the Church was especially apparent in the address he composed for the abortive meeting of Convocation in 1761, but which was never delivered. Raising the question of contemporary debate about the articles and liturgy of the Church, Secker argued:

> Indeed, many believe that, whatever is decided about these matters, a new version of Scripture at least is required; so that Christian people may profit from that light which the continual industry of learned men, with the help of the Godhead, has uncovered in the divine oracles during the last 150 years that have elapsed since the English Vulgate was produced.

He attacked the pernicious effect of the multiplication of private interpretations of Scripture:

> Many interpreters come forward daily to compete with one another: but either they are people of effectively no learning or their unnecessary diligence has

made us even less certain than we were before ... if we want to do anything worthwhile, [we will have to wait] until ... the heat of coming up with new meanings, as well as this recent ... frenzy of emending, by which good and not uneducated men are spurred on imprudently to cram the sacred codex with errors ... will have cooled down.

In their place, he extolled the importance of the hierarchy in supervising the necessary work of translation:

And who will resist this most legitimate petition? But once this multi-faceted apparatus of erudition has been acquired, this work will certainly have to be undertaken. And many men will have to collaborate on it for a long time in the most friendly way and with the utmost piety, caution, industry, and care.[140]

In 1761, Secker's principal reservation about the work of revising the English translation of the Bible concerned the current state of Hebrew scholarship, in response to which he had offered encouragement to many of the leading English Hebraists of the time. However, his comments about the dangers inherent in scholarly emendations that changed the received text of the Bible might have been aimed at the very individuals whom he nevertheless patronized. Kennicott remarked:

if our present Eng[lish] Translations shall appear, in some places, nearly the same with what is suppos'd here to be the true Sense, tho' founded upon the Corrections of the Text: the reason is, that our Translators have frequently given the Sense, not of that which *is*, but of that which seem'd to them *necessary to be*, in the Heb[rew] Bible. It is therefore very happy to find, in fact, that in *some* places, our Heb[rew] M[anuscript]s confirm their Conjectures; and that, in *others*, these M[anuscript]s have preserv'd, and are ready to communicate, good Sense, where former Translators have necessarily fail'd for want of such Assistance.[141]

Lowth similarly argued that his own translations were essentially conservative in nature and denied that changes might be necessary because of the antiquity of the Authorized Version: 'nothing has so much offended me in some late translations of parts of Scripture, as the use of words & phrases of too modern a cast. This therefore I have not only intentionaly but even studiously avoided.'[142] Thus many of those who were working towards a new translation of the Bible within the Church of England did so without jettisoning their respect for the Authorized Version and regardless of many of the criticisms that had been levelled against it by more heterodox commentators. An awareness of linguistic archaism and the romantic, poetic character that it might lend to their writings therefore formed part of the armoury deployed by these innovative biblical scholars.

'By a new & judicious arrangement of Isaiah, you have made it much more intelligible than it was before; and, although the sublimity of many parts was well supported by the translation, to which we have been accustomed, the additional beauty and dignity, which the whole has received from your pen, are conspicuous in every page.'[143] Despite such approval for Lowth and his contemporaries, official sanction for the public revision of the Authorized Version never came. A codicil added to Secker's will in October 1765 ensured that the manuscript materials he had prepared were deposited in the Archbishop's library at Lambeth, where they continued to be consulted by scholars.[144] To some extent, Secker's mantle as a patron fell on Lowth, and on Shute Barrington (1734–1826), Bishop of Llandaff, Salisbury and, from 1791, Durham. In his translations, Lowth drew extensively on the ideas of Kennicott and Durell, both of whom were friends of Barrington.[145] Durell himself encouraged Blayney, whose translations of the prophetic books of Scripture followed on from Lowth's and who in due course also came under Barrington's wing.[146] William Newcome (1729–1800), who rose through the hierarchy of the Church of Ireland to become Archbishop of Armagh in 1795, joined Blayney in translating the prophets and hoped that this work would 'facilitate, an improved English version of the scriptures; than which nothing could be more beneficial to the cause of religion, or more honourable to the reign and age in which it was patronised and executed.'[147] Lowth and Barrington both encouraged Robert Holmes (1748–1805), whose collation of the manuscripts of the Septuagint (the ancient Greek translation of the Old Testament) was supported by Oxford University and mirrored the work of Kennicott.[148]

The failure of revision

By the 1780s and 1790s, however, the pursuit of a new translation began to appear less like an undertaking that might favour the Church of England and more like a challenge to its reputation and authority. A massive annotated Bible published in Birmingham in 1788 noted all the variant readings uncovered by Kennicott and others as well as the conjectures of Lowth and his allies. It even inserted passages found only in the Samaritan Pentateuch for 'those who wish to read the five Books of Moses as they came from the hands of the Author'. Yet it named not a single Anglican bishop or university professor among its subscribers, who numbered well in excess of a thousand individuals.[149] Joseph Priestley, who had contributed to this work, soon argued that 'the learned friends of free enquiry' should take on the work of improving the English translation of the Bible.[150] Priestley's Unitarian disciples, rather than the bishops of the Church of England, sponsored an edition of the Bible in 1808 based on Newcome's ideas.[151] By this time, the project of revision had largely slipped out of the hands of churchmen. Their efforts had withered before the resurgence of anti-trinitarianism and the scepticism epitomized by the writings of Tom Paine.[152] The attacks by Paine and others forced churchmen to adopt more conservative and defensive attitudes to the Bible, not least to protect themselves from sectarian assault. Despite this, they faced the charge that 'to defend the Bible in this year 1798 would cost a man his life'.[153] The orthodoxy and heroism of George Travis, Archdeacon of Chester (1741–97), mattered more to his readers than the shortcomings of his scholarship. Travis had set off for Paris at the height of the French Revolution in 1791 in order to consult manuscripts that he hoped would support his defence of the authenticity of I John 5:7 against the aspersions cast by Edward Gibbon. Not surprisingly, his steadfastness in the face of an adversary who 'stands so fully convicted of plagiarism, misrepresentation, second hand quotation, vanity, malevolence to the truth, partiality to vice and irreligion' weighed far more heavily in the balance than his inability to identify manuscripts or to follow critical reasoning.[154] Similarly, the excessive claims made for the authority of one particular manuscript of the Greek New Testament by its editor Thomas Kipling, deputy to the Regius Professor of Divinity at Cambridge, were more than compensated for by his role 'as a Theological Dictator' in the university's persecution of the anti-trinitarian William Frend.[155]

There were exceptions to this trend, for example in the work of the high church bishop and critic of Priestley, Samuel Horsley (1733–1806), who drew extensively on Blayney's ideas in his own treatment of prophecy and was cautiously complimentary about the publications of Geddes.[156] Nevertheless, the arguments of the proponents of a revised translation were themselves becoming less palatable by the 1780s and 1790s. The achievements of Geddes were praised in an attempt to shame the Church of England into action: 'Even the English Roman Catholics, – few in number and dispersed, – votaries of a Religion averse to every change, – labouring under restraints and unpopularity ... are not blind to the advantages which will attend a better Translation of the Scriptures.'[157] Although the orthodox critics of the Authorized Version in general maintained their respect for its excellence as a translation, Newcome also began to agree with Geddes that 'no English version has yet surpassed' the early sixteenth-century private translation by William Tyndale, on which all later English Bibles had drawn.[158] The reputation of Tyndale had risen in part because of the activities of Joseph Ames (1689–1759), the friend and executor of Lewis, whose own records on the history of the English Bible had attracted the attention of the hierarchy of the Church of England in the 1770s, but perhaps a more important factor was that 'the collecting of Black Letter Books is become fashionable.'[159] Nevertheless, the suggestion that better English translations than the Authorized Version might already exist ran counter to both contemporary sentiment and the weight of historical opinion that had built up during the eighteenth century.

The idea of sponsoring a new edition of the Authorized Version had always been politically contentious. Its supporters had been a group of irenic low churchmen, several of whom, including both Secker and Newcome, came from dissenting backgrounds. The success of the scheme depended on there being a change in the political climate that might allow a meeting of Convocation or some other body with the power to commission a new English translation of the Bible and perhaps even to alter the liturgy and articles of the Church, for revision of the Bible was one part of a programme designed to counter the spread of Socinianism within the Church of England. In an astonishing attack on the 'old debased Coin' of the Authorized Version, Durell argued that Parliament should consider 'the Petitions of serious and well disposed Men . . . with becoming Humility'. He did not rule out the possibility that a new translation might be only a first step in the reformation of the Church.[160] As the controversy over subscription to the Thirty-Nine Articles gained ground in 1772, Kennicott reminded Lowth that he had suggested that 'some Concession is expected, & must be made' and pointed out that, while his own loyalty to the Church was not in doubt, 'yet, [he] was not without a possibility of being more zealous, in case of a further Reformation'.[161] Although the scheme of revising the Bible did not expire in the early 1770s, it was severely weakened by the subscription controversy, the spread of critical scholarship among dissenters, and the political crises that began with the American war.

There were, however, intellectual as well as political reasons for the failure of revision. Many of the proponents of reform belonged to a generation of Oxford men for whom the defining political moment had been the Oxfordshire Election of 1754.[162] For several of them, in particular Durell, Hunt and Kennicott, triumph in that contest set the seal on political and intellectual victory over the Hutchinsonians within the university and particularly within its newest foundation, Hertford College.[163] In terms of both ecclesiastical and university politics, this success was short-lived. Although more durable intellectually, it was still unsure. Most of the reformers were at one time or another disciples of Hunt. Their approach to biblical studies was marked by an exceptional distrust of both Jewish learning and the reliability of the Jews as guardians of the ancient text of Scripture. It was this suspicion that provided the excuse for their study of Oriental languages other than Hebrew and for the use of that study to emend the received text of the Bible. Doubts about that text, supposedly confirmed by the discovery of numerous variant readings in the recent manuscript tradition, justified the conjectures that demonstrated the need for a new English translation of the Bible. Lowth's discovery of parallelism similarly established a structure for ancient Hebrew poetry independent of the pronunciation used by contemporary Jews.[164] The work of Hunt and Lowth frequently depended on the ideas of controversial foreign scholars, especially those of Charles Houbigant or of members of the Schultens family.[165] Although popular with conservative German critics, Lowth's writings were viewed less favourably on the Continent by the end of the eighteenth century.[166] By then, the project of collecting variant readings had also begun to seem flawed as critics realized the inconsequential nature of much of the material being compiled.[167]

More seriously, the work of revision was concentrated disproportionately on the poetical books of the Old Testament and lacked a similar intellectual foundation in its approach to the other parts of the Bible.[168] Furthermore, the attack mounted by Lowth on William Warburton (1698–1779), Bishop of Gloucester, over the style, dating and meaning of the book of Job seemed to set men of the same party against one another.[169] Long after the criticisms of Warburton's allegorical interpretation had been forgotten, his allies were still carping about the 'narrow' scholarship of Lowth, Kennicott and even Secker, and running down the project of a new translation of the Bible.[170] The intellectual argument for reform was weakened by the appearance of arrogance and mean-spiritedness, and by doubts about the linguistic and codicological assumptions that underpinned it. Yet undoubtedly its most dangerous flaw was that it appeared to give hope to anti-trinitarianism.

Into the nineteenth century

The controversies of the 1790s changed the nature of the readership of the Bible. The success of the Bible Society after 1800 transformed popular ownership of the Bible, reaching out through networks of local association that largely ignored denominational differences to fresh audiences, above all in urban Britain. Attempts were made to provide for poor readers by new methods of production, especially the use of stereotyping. When these initially failed, the new power of a mass market was brought self-righteously to bear on the monopoly practices that helped to maintain high prices for Bibles in England.[171] Although other voluntary societies attempted to promote a critical attitude to text and translation among readers of the Bible, their efforts were necessarily less widely successful.[172] The anxieties that had been created about the enthusiastic, not to say revolutionary consequences of an excess of private reason served to limit the effect of such ventures both in the 1790s and thereafter. To some extent, however, those fears also acted as a brake on the progress of the Bible Society. Thus some prominent churchmen and scholars, such as Herbert Marsh (1757–1839), who had spent much of the 1790s in Germany but who ended his career as Bishop of Peterborough, did continue to stress the need for a new translation. In their eyes, the evangelical zeal of the Bible Society represented a possible threat to the structure and even the establishment of the Church of England, which might be countered by a critical approach to the text of Scripture.[173] However, it was more common for those whose vested interests were under attack to take refuge in the reputation of the Authorized Version, the power of monopoly, and invective against the denominational identity of their opponents.[174]

Although, in a curious way, the Authorized Version had somehow become a touchstone of whose power almost everyone was convinced, there remained some dissenting critics who attempted new translations. Their ideas, and by implication those of low churchmen, from Secker and Lowth to Marsh, who supported the revision of the Bible, were greeted with increasing disdain. As the Regius Professor of Hebrew at Oxford put it in 1820, 'the language of our present version has the full tide of popular opinion strongly in its favour; it exhibits a style appropriately biblical, and is distinguished by a general simplicity of expression, which the most uncultivated mind may comprehend, and the most cultivated admire.'[175] Critical scholarship and linguistic modernity alike were forced to give way to antiquarian affection and affectation, fear of disorder and panic about the consequences of change. The loyalist myth that the Authorized Version was the 'sole property of the King' was trotted out to shame sectarian proponents of revision.[176] Behind the debate lurked the continuing fear that to give ground might be to open the gates to the Trojan Horse of heterodoxy. Henry John Todd, the biographer of the great seventeenth-century critic Brian Walton, dismissed Blayney's work, and with it that of the leading scholars of a later period, as 'a new text for Socinianism'.[177] Increasingly conservative English scholars, worried by developments in Continental criticism, rejected outright the scholarly principles on which Lowth and his followers had based their suggestions for changes to the Authorized Version. So it was concluded that 'no *actual* alteration of the Hebrew text ought to be made from conjecture alone'.[178]

By the second quarter of the nineteenth century, the Authorized Version had achieved a position of respect and admiration that defied changes in readership and crossed denominations. It was supported most strongly by the hierarchy of the Church of England and its allies, but it commanded an increasingly uncritical devotion from ordinary individuals who no longer necessarily understood its archaic language. It achieved this brief dominance despite the efforts of many eighteenth-century readers of the Bible, although with the assistance of one or two influential writers.[179] However, just over the horizon, the destructive German critic was gathering some English allies.

Acknowledgements

I am extremely grateful to Mrs D. V. Durell for giving me access to papers in her possession. I would also like to thank Toby Barnard, Neil Hitchin, Colin Kidd, Tabitta van Nouhuys and Steven Tomlinson for the assistance they have given me.

Notes

1. Sir William Whitla, *Sir Isaac Newton's Daniel and the Apocalypse* (London: John Murray, 1922), p. x.

2. Whitla, *Newton's Daniel*, pp. 8 and 121–2; Richard H. Popkin, 'Newton and fundamentalism, II', in James E. Force and Richard H. Popkin, *Essays on the Context, Nature, and Influence of Isaac Newton's Theology* (Dordrecht: Kluwer, 1990), pp. 172–4.

3. Peter J. Bowler, 'Evolution and the Eucharist: Bishop E. W. Barnes on science and religion in the 1920s and 1930s', *British Journal for the History of Science*, 31 (1998): 456–61; D. W. Bebbington, *Evangelicalism in Modern Britain* (London: Unwin Hyman, 1989), p. 208; cf. Whitla, *Newton's Daniel*, pp. 15–16.

4. For which see H. W. Turnbull (ed.), *The Correspondence of Isaac Newton*, Vol. 3 (Cambridge: Cambridge University Press, 1961), pp. 83–146. The standard biography of Newton at the time, Sir David Brewster's *Memoirs of the Life, Writings, and Discoveries of Sir Isaac Newton*, Vol. 2 (Edinburgh: Thomas Constable, 1855), pp. 301–55, contained extensive discussion of theology and biblical criticism. Newton's Arianism had largely been concealed, however,

in Brewster's earlier *The Life of Sir Isaac Newton* (London, 1831), frequent reprints of which were issued from British and American presses throughout the nineteenth and early twentieth centuries.

5. Whitla, *Newton's Daniel*, pp. 13–14, 57–69; cf. Dale A. Johnson, *The Changing Shape of English Nonconformity, 1825–1925* (New York: Oxford University Press, 1999), pp. 109–12, 125–62. For Whitla's Methodism, see R. Lee Cole, *History of Methodism in Ireland 1860–1960* (Belfast: Irish Methodist Publishing Co, 1960), pp. 99, 129, 167; Katie Newmann, *Dictionary of Ulster Biography* (Belfast: Institute of Irish Studies, 1993), p. 266.

6. Harriet A. Harris, *Fundamentalism and Evangelicals* (Oxford: Clarendon Press, 1998), pp. 21–5. For Whitla's premillenarianism, see *Newton's Daniel*, p. 122; for Newton's, see his 'The Synchronisms of the Three Parts of the Prophetick Interpretation', in Frank E. Manuel, *The Religion of Isaac Newton* (Oxford: Clarendon Press, 1974), pp. 126–36.

7. The standard treatments of these themes are Hans W. Frei, *The Eclipse of Biblical Narrative* (New Haven: Yale University Press, 1974); Henning Graf Reventlow, *The Authority of the Bible and the Rise of the Modern World*, trans. John Bowden (London: SCM Press, 1984); John Drury (ed.), *Critics of the Bible 1724–1873* (Cambridge: Cambridge University Press, 1989).

8. John D. Woodbridge, 'Some misconceptions of the impact of the "Enlightenment" on the doctrine of Scripture', in D. A. Carson and John D. Woodbridge (eds), *Hermeneutics, Authority, and Canon*, new edn (Grand Rapids: Baker Books, 1995), p. 269.

9. Woodbridge, 'Some misconceptions', p. 257; see also W. Robert Godfrey, 'Biblical authority in the sixteenth and seventeenth centuries: a question of transition', in D. A. Carson and John D. Woodbridge (eds), *Scripture and Truth*, new edn (Grand Rapids: Baker Books, 1992), pp. 225–43; Richard A. Muller, *Post-Reformation Reformed Dogmatics*, Vol. 2 (Grand Rapids: Baker Books, 1993).

10. 'On the Imprecations in Holy Scripture', p. 13 (unpublished manuscript, private collection); for details of Durell's biography, see G. R. Balleine, *A Biographical Dictionary of Jersey* (London: Staples Press, [1949]), pp. 454–5, where it is erroneously stated that he became 'Regius Professor of Greek'.

11. Thomas Randolph, *The Excellency of the Jewish Law Vindicated* (Oxford, 1773), pp. 69–79; [Benjamin Blayney], *An Expostulatory Letter to the Reverend Dr. Randolph* (Oxford, 1773).

12. See L. G. Mitchell, 'Politics and revolution 1772–1800', in L. S. Sutherland and L. G. Mitchell (eds), *The History of the University of Oxford. Volume V: The Eighteenth Century* (Oxford: Clarendon Press, 1986), pp. 167–77. Earlier in his career, Randolph had been attracted by Hutchinsonian ideas; see [Thomas Randolph], *Four Letters concerning the Study of the Hebrew Scriptures* (London, 1755). By the 1770s, however, his views seem to have become more conventional.

13. Thomas Randolph, *The Prophecies and other Texts, cited in the New Testament, compared with the Hebrew Original, and with the Septuagint Version* (Oxford, [1782]), pp. 52–4; cf. David Durell, *Critical Remarks on the Books of Job, Proverbs, Psalms, Ecclesiastes, and Canticles* (Oxford, 1772).

14. [Blayney], *Expostulatory Letter*, p. 17.

15. James Barr, *Fundamentalism*, 2nd edn (London: SCM Press, 1981), pp. 209–14; Peter J. Thuesen, *In Discordance with the Scriptures. American Protestant Battles over Translating the Bible* (New York: Oxford University Press, 1999).

16. See Alfred W. Pollard (ed.), *Records of the English Bible* (London: Henry Frowde, 1911), pp. 331–4, 336–77; Ward Allen (ed.), *Translating for King James* (n.p.: Vanderbilt University Press, 1969); Ward S. Allen and Edward C. Jacobs, *The Coming of the King James Gospels*

(Fayetteville: University of Arkansas Press, 1995); Christopher Hill, *The English Bible and the Seventeenth-Century Revolution* (London: Allen Lane, 1993), pp. 63–5.

17. David McKitterick, 'Customer, reader and bookbinder: buying a Bible in 1630', *The Book Collector*, 40 (1991): 382–406.

18. Gerald Bray (ed.), *The Anglican Canons, 1529–1947* (Woodbridge: Boydell Press, 1998), pp. 528, 546–7.

19. See in particular [Edward Whiston], *The Life and Death of Mr. Henry Jessey* ([London], 1671), pp. 41–60; Robert Gell, *An Essay toward the Amendment of the Last English-Translation of the Bible* (London, 1659), sig. A2r–4v, a1r–e1r; Public Record Office, Kew, Ms. State Papers 18/26, ff. 199r–200r.

20. For editions of the English Bible, see T. H. Darlow and H. F. Moule, *Historical Catalogue of Printed Editions of the English Bible 1525–1961*, revised and expanded by A. S. Herbert (London: British and Foreign Bible Society, 1968) (hereafter DMH). Examples of the purchase or gift of the Authorized Version for use in church may be found in M. J. Ockenden, 'Churchwardens' accounts for Ormskirk Parish, 1692–1730', *Transactions of the Historic Society of Lancashire and Cheshire*, 144 (1995): 105; Peter du Moulin, *A Sermon Preached in the Metropolitical Church of Canterbury, October 17. MDCLXXII. At the Funeral of the Very Reverend Thomas Turner* (London, 1672), pp. 23–4; 'Mrs Elizabeth Freke, her Diary, 1671 to 1714', *Journal of the Cork Historical and Archaeological Society*, 2nd ser., 19 (1913): 142.

21. Ian Green, 'Développement et déclin de la production des Bibles en Angleterre entre 1530 et 1730', in Bertram Eugene Schwarzbach (ed.), *La Bible imprimée dans l'Europe moderne* (Paris: Bibliothèque nationale de France, 1999), pp. 336–49.

22. Bodleian Library, Oxford (hereafter Bodleian), Ms. Rawlinson Letters 93, ff. 99–100; John Johnson and Strickland Gibson, *Print and Privilege at Oxford to the Year 1700* (London: Oxford University Press, 1946).

23. Oxford University Archives, SP/D/2, SEP/P/10, SEP/P/15–16; John Lawler, *Book Auctions in England in the Seventeenth Century (1676–1700)* (London: Elliot Stock, 1898), pp. 81–4.

24. [Charles Le Cène], *An Essay for a New Translation of the Bible*, trans. H[ugh] R[oss], part 1 (London, 1701), sig. A3r. Le Cène's own comments were directed mainly at French translations, but Ross applied them to the Authorized Version.

25. T[homas] W[ard], *The Errata to the Protestant Bible, or the Truth of their English Translations Examin'd* (London, 1688); [Le Cène], *An Essay*, trans. R[oss], 2 parts (London, 1701–2); Ross was 'a *Scotchman* and Sea-Chaplain', according to John Lewis, *A Complete History of the Several Translations of the Holy Bible, and New Testament, into English*, 2nd edn (London, 1739), p. 338.

26. Charles Le Cène, *Projet d'une Nouvelle Version Françoise de la Bible* (Rotterdam, 1696), annotated copy at Bodleian shelfmark 8° K.261 B.S., p. 29; for Le Cène's Huguenot background and sympathies with Socinianism, see Jeroom Vercruysse, 'La Bible hérétique de Charles Le Cène', in Yvon Belaval and Dominique Bourel (eds), *Le Siècle des Lumières et la Bible* (Paris: Beauchesne, 1986), pp. 649–56.

27. Lewis, *Complete History*, p. 350.

28. *The London Gazette*, 21–25 April 1724; Lewis, *Complete History*, pp. 350–1; Lambeth Palace Library, Ms. 1741, ff. 28–9, 38–9.

29. For Russell's career, see Bodleian, Mss. Rawlinson J fol. 4, ff. 236r, 333–4; Rawlinson J fol. 7, f. 93r; Rawlinson J 4° 1, f. 214v. For Lewis' links with Kennett, see British Library, London (hereafter BL), Add. Ms. 28, 651, f. 27v; Bodleian, Ms. Eng. Misc. c. 273, p. 42a.

30. John Russell, *Proposals for Printing by Subscription, the Holy Bible, Containing the Old*

Testament and the New Translated in English by John Wicleffe ([London], 1719); John Lewis, *The History of the Life and Sufferings of the Reverend and Learned John Wicliffe* (London, 1720). Lewis' corrected copy and the manuscript of his work may be found at Bodleian shelfmark Don. e. 151, and Ms. Rawlinson C 979 respectively. John Lewis (ed.), *The New Testament*, trans. John Wyclif (London, 1731), of which the author's corrected copy is Bodleian shelfmark N.T. Eng. 1731 b.1. Lewis, *Complete History*; the author's collections for this work may be found at Bodleian Mss. Rawlinson C 155, esp. ff. 137–246, and Rawlinson D 787; Lambeth Palace Library, Ms. 3017, ff. 221–37.

31. Cambridge University Library, Add. Ms. 103, letter 20 (Lewis to Samuel Knight); cf. Bodleian, Ms. Rawlinson D 376, which includes correspondence between Lewis and both Baker and Waterland; see also Frans Korsten, *A Catalogue of the Library of Thomas Baker* (Cambridge: Cambridge University Press, 1990), pp. xix–xxiv, on Baker's antiquarian circle.

32. Bodleian, Ms. Gough Eccl. Top. 5.

33. Cambridge University Library, Ms. Dd X 56 (John Bagford's collections on the history of typography); BL, Sloane Ms. 1378, ff. 150–79 (notes by Bagford on the history of the English Bible); Harleian Mss. 5908–9 (collections made by Bagford and Wanley on the history of the English Bible); Harleian Ms. 5958 (Bagford's collections on the history of the English Bible); cf. 'An essay upon the English translation of the Bible', *Bibliotheca Literaria*, 4 (1723): 1–23, which referred to Wanley's work. For evidence of Lewis' knowledge of these collections, see Bodleian, Ms. Rawlinson D 376, ff. 42r, 54r, 100r.

34. 'Essay upon the English translation', p. 22.

35. Lewis, *Complete History*, pp. 328–76, quotations at pp. 353–4.

36. *Ibid.*, p. 376.

37. Lewis defends James Ussher, *Historia dogmatica controversiae inter orthodoxos & pontificos de scripturis et sacris vernaculis*, ed. Henry Wharton (London, 1690).

38. Dr Williams's Library, London, Ms. 12.8, p. 310.

39. John Rylands University Library, Manchester, Mss. 47, f. 24r, and 49, ff. 23–4.

40. Anthony Johnson, *An Historical Account of the several English Translations of the Bible and the Opposition they met with from the Church of Rome* (London, 1730), p. 98.

41. Glasgow University Library, Ms. Gen. 1214, f. 75r.

42. Lewis, *Complete History*, pp. 365–71; cf. [Daniel Mace], *The New Testament in Greek and English*, 2 vols (London, 1729).

43. [Mace], *New Testament*, Vol. 2, pp. 772–3, 921–35; on Mace, see H. McLachlan, 'An almost forgotten pioneer in New Testament Criticism', *The Hibbert Journal*, 37 (1938–39): 617–25.

44. Richard Simon (ed.), *The New Testament*, trans. William Webster, 2 vols (London, 1730); cf. Lewis, *Complete History*, pp. 372–5.

45. John Mill (ed.), Ἡ Καινὴ Διαθήκη. *Novum Testamentum cum lectionibus variantibus* (Oxford, 1707).

46. Richard Bentley, Ἡ Καινὴ Διαθήκη *Graece. Proposals for Printing* (n.p., [1720]); the relationship between the work of Mill and Bentley is described by Adam Fox, *John Mill and Richard Bentley* (Oxford: Blackwell, 1954).

47. Christ Church, Oxford, Ms. Wake Letters 20, ff. 76r–7v (Bentley to William Wake, 15 April 1716), at f. 76r.

48. For example, Julius Bate, *An Essay towards Explaining the Third Chapter of Genesis, and the Spiritual Sense of the Law* (London, 1741), pp. 3–5; John C. English, 'John Hutchinson's critique of Newtonian heterodoxy', *Church History*, 68 (1999): 581–97.

49. Julius Bate, *A New and Literal Translation from the Original Hebrew, of the Pentateuch of*

Moses, and of the Historical Books of the Old Testament, to the End of the Second Book of Kings (London, 1773), sig. A2r (editor's advertisement to the reader).

50. Cambridge University Library, Ms. Add. 8134 B/1, f. 2v; see also Nigel Aston, 'Horne and heterodoxy: the defence of Anglican beliefs in the late Enlightenment', *English Historical Review*, 108 (1993): 895–919.

51. Bodleian, Ms. Kennicott c. 12, ff. 9–10 (James Bate to Benjamin Kennicott, 22 January 1761), at f. 9r. Compare the earlier, more positive assessment of Thomas Brett, a friend and distant relation of the Bate family, that 'though I cannot altogether approve some of Julius's Hutchinsonian Nostrums, yet I do not find that they affect any Article of Faith': Lambeth Palace Library, Ms. 2219, ff. 7–8 (Brett to Mr Gordoun, 22 October 1741).

52. Gregory Sharpe, *Two Dissertations: I. Upon the Origin, Construction, Division, and Relation of Languages. II. Upon the Original Power of Letters; wherein is proved . . . that the Hebrew ought to be read without Points* (London, 1751); Bodleian, Ms. Eng. Lett. d. 145, ff. 8–9 (Hunt to Sharpe, 21 July 1750); cf. Richard Grey, *A New and Easy Method of Learning Hebrew without Points* (London, 1738).

53. Julius Bate, *Micah v.2 and Mat. ii.6 Reconciled; with some Remarks on Dr. Hunt's Latin Oration at Oxford 1748* (London, 1749); Benjamin Holloway, *The Primaevity and Preeminence of the Sacred Hebrew, above all other Languages, Vindicated from the Repeated Attempts of the Reverend Dr. Hunt to Level it with the Arabic* (Oxford, 1754); cf. Thomas Hunt, *De usu dialectorum Orientalium ac praecipue Arabicae, in Hebraico codice interpretando, oratio* (Oxford, 1748).

54. Daniel Waterland, *The Works of the Rev. Daniel Waterland, D.D.*, ed. William van Mildert, Vol. 10 (Oxford, 1823), pp. 410–11.

55. For example, Waterland seems to have encouraged both John Berriman, ΘΕΟΣ ἐφανερώθη ἐν σαρχί. Or, a Critical Dissertation upon I Tim. iii. 16 (London, 1741), which defended the integrity of the text, and [John Mawer], *Letters in Answer to some Queries sent to the Author, concerning the Genuine Reading of the Greek Text, I Tim. iii. 16* (York, 1758), which questioned it.

56. *The Bible* (London, 1606), BL shelfmark C. 45. g. 13, bound in three volumes and interleaved with comments by Law, dated 1757, Vol. 1, f. 1r; on Law, see B. W. Young, *Religion and Enlightenment in Eighteenth-Century England* (Oxford: Clarendon Press, 1998), pp. 53–5.

57. On Harwood, see John Nichols, *Literary Anecdotes of the Eighteenth Century*, Vol. 4 (London, 1812), pp. 350–62; Vol. 9 (London, 1815), pp. 579–80. Gilbert Wakefield, *A New Translation of the Gospel of Matthew* (Warrington, 1782), p. iv, records the loan of Law's interleaved New Testament (now Vol. 3 of the Bible described above) to Wakefield in 1781.

58. J[ohn] D[isney], *A Short Memoir of the late William Hopkins* (Leeds, 1815 [1st edn, 1787]), p. 13; William Hopkins, *Exodus. A Corrected Translation with Notes, Critical and Explanatory* (London, 1784), p. vii.

59. Edward Harwood, *A Liberal Translation of the New Testament*, Vol. 1 (London, 1768), pp. iv–v; cf. Edward Harwood, *Five Dissertations* (London, 1772).

60. British and Foreign Bible Society's Library (on deposit in Cambridge University Library), Ms. DMH 1035(a).

61. Samuel Palmer (ed.), *A New Translation of the New Testament of our Lord and Saviour Jesus Christ. Extracted from the Paraphrase of the late Philip Doddridge*, Vol. 1 (London, 1765), sig. A4r.

62. Nathaniel Scarlett, *A Translation of the New Testament from the Original Greek* (London, 1798). On Scarlett and his circle, see Neil W. Hitchin, 'The politics of English Bible translation in Georgian Britain', *Transactions of the Royal Historical Society*, 6th ser., 9 (1999): 89–91. For an

assessment of the contemporary London religious milieu, see Iain McCalman, 'New Jerusalems: prophecy, dissent and radical culture in England, 1786–1830', in Knud Haakonssen (ed.), *Enlightenment and Religion* (Cambridge: Cambridge University Press, 1996), pp. 312–35, and for the role of consciousness about linguistic change in forming radical attitudes to literature, including Scripture, see Olivia Smith, *The Politics of Language 1791–1819* (Oxford: Clarendon Press, 1984).

63. For example, R[obert] W[itham], *Annotations on the New Testament of Jesus Christ*, 2 vols ([Douai], 1730); cf. the controversial new translation of the Dublin parish priest Cornelius Nary, *The New Testament of our Lord and Saviour Jesus Christ* ([Dublin], 1718), which was criticized by Witham and other members of the Catholic hierarchy. See Patrick Fagan, *Dublin's Turbulent Priest. Cornelius Nary (1658–1738)* (Dublin: Royal Irish Academy, 1991), pp. 79–91.

64. Some arguments in favour of Simon are presented by William Webster's dedicatory preface to Simon (ed.), *The New Testament*, Vol. 1, sig. A2r–3r.

65. *The New Testament* ([Douai], 1738) [DMH, No. 1041]; *The Holy Bible*, 4 vols ([Dublin], 1750) [DMH, No. 1089]; *The New Testament* ([Dublin], 1750) [DMH, No. 1090]; Edwin H. Burton, *The Life and Times of Bishop Challoner (1691–1781)*, Vol. 1 (London: Longmans, 1909), pp. 270–89; Hugh Pope, OP, *English Versions of the Bible*, revised and amplified by Sebastian Bullough (St Louis: Herder, 1952), pp. 346–71; see also Eamon Duffy (ed.), *Challoner and his Church* (London; Darton, Longman & Todd, 1981).

66. See Reginald C. Fuller, *Alexander Geddes* (Sheffield: Almond Press, 1984); Mark Goldie, 'The Scottish Catholic Enlightenment', *Journal of British Studies*, 30 (1991): 20–62; William McKane, *Selected Christian Hebraists* (Cambridge: Cambridge University Press, 1989), pp. 151–90.

67. Alexander Geddes, *Idea of a New English Edition of the Holy Bible for the Use of the Roman Catholics of Great Britain and Ireland* ([London], [1782]); Scottish Catholic Archives, Edinburgh, Ms. BL 3/355/10 (Alexander Geddes to John Geddes, 26 January 1782).

68. Scottish Catholic Archives, Edinburgh, Ms. BL 3/355/15 (Alexander Geddes to John Geddes, 17 November 1782).

69. Alexander Geddes, *The Holy Bible, or the Books accounted sacred by Jews and Christians, otherwise called the Books of the Old and New Covenants*, Vol. 1 (London, 1792) [DMH, No. 1416], p. xxii; Scottish Catholic Archives, Edinburgh, Mss. BL 3/375/9–10 (Alexander Geddes to John Geddes, 9 January and 14 February 1783); cf. Alexander Geddes, *Critical Remarks on the Hebrew Scriptures: Corresponding with a New Translation of the Bible* (London, 1800), p. v.

70. Alexander Geddes, *Prospectus of a New Translation of the Holy Bible* (Glasgow, 1786), p. 11; Scottish Catholic Archives, Edinburgh, Ms. BL 3/438/5 (Alexander Geddes to John Geddes, 3 March 1785). For the increasing conservatism of much Catholic debate about the inspiration of Scripture, see James Tunstead Burtchaell, CSC, *Catholic Theories of Biblical Inspiration since 1810* (Cambridge: Cambridge University Press, 1969).

71. Scottish Catholic Archives, Edinburgh, Mss. PAG 6/1–4 and BL 3/327/6; Geddes, *Prospectus*, p. 147. Only two out of a projected six large quarto volumes of the Bible appeared: see Alexander Geddes, *Proposals for Publishing by Subscription a New Translation of the Holy Bible* (London, 1788), sig. a3r.

72. Anthony Purver, *A New and Literal Translation of All the Books of the Old and New Testament*, 2 vols (London, 1764).

73. Samuel Fisher, *Rusticus ad academicos in exercitationibus expostulatoriis apologeticis quatuor. The Rustick's Alarm to the Rabbies* (London, 1660); Kathleen L. Cottrell, *Anthony Purver. Quaker* (Bath: Fyson, n.d.), pp. 3–4; Friends House, London, Ms. Facsimile Box L.9.

74. Purver, *A New and Literal Translation*, Vol. 1, pp. i–vii; cf. Friends House, London, Ms. S212, pp. 469–77; at the other end of the scale of the growing Quaker respect for Scripture lay

works like John Fothergill, *A Short Account of the Several Books of the New Testament. For the Use of Ackworth School* (London, 1780).

75. Alexander Geddes, *Dr Geddes's General Answer to the Queries, Counsils and Criticisms that have been communicated to him since the Publication of his Proposals for Printing a New Translation of the Bible* (London, 1790), pp. 2–3.

76. See M. G. Jones, *The Charity School Movement* (London: Frank Cass, 1964 [1st edn, 1938]), pp. 73–84; Thomas Walter Laqueur, *Religion and Respectability. Sunday Schools and Working Class Culture 1780–1850* (New Haven: Yale University Press, 1976), pp. 107–46, 160–9; see also K. D. M. Snell, 'The Sunday-school movement in England and Wales: child labour, denominational control and working-class culture', *Past and Present*, 164 (1999): 122–68, for the importance of Sunday schools in rural Anglican parishes.

77. See Shirley Brice Heath, 'Child's play or finding the ephemera of home', and Margaret Spufford, 'Women teaching reading to poor children in the sixteenth and seventeenth centuries', both in Mary Hilton, Morag Styles and Victor Watson (eds), *Opening the Nursery Door* (London: Routledge, 1997), pp. 17–30 and 47–62.

78. Marcus Walsh, 'Profession and authority: the interpretation of the Bible in the seventeenth and eighteenth centuries', *Literature and Theology*, 9 (1995): 383–98.

79. Bodleian, Ms. Don. c. 190, f. 99v.

80. Lambeth Palace Library, Ms. Fulham Papers, Vol. VII, No. 187, deposition of William Currie with additions by Archibald Cummings.

81. J. F. Ostervald, *The Necessity and Usefulness of Reading the Holy Scriptures*, trans. John Moore, new edn (London, 1770), p. 16.

82. For example, *A Compendious History of the Old and New Testament, Extracted from the Holy Bible* (London, 1726), of which there were at least five editions by 1750; John Newbery, *The Holy Bible Abridged*, 4th edn (London, 1762 [1st edn, 1757]), which became the subject of a copyright battle involving Newbery's heirs and another bookseller, also called Newbery, by the time of the 1772 edition; Carl Heinrich von Bogatzky, *A Golden Treasury for the Children of God* (London, [c. 1760]), which appeared in many further editions both before and after 1800; Sarah Trimmer, *An Abridgment of the New Testament, consisting of Lessons Composed from the Writings of the Four Evangelists* ([London], [1793]); for which there was also an accompanying Old Testament volume; on these books see Sydney Roscoe, *John Newbery and his Successors, 1740–1814* (Wormley: Five Owls Press, 1973); and Ruth B. Bottigheimer, *The Bible for Children from the Age of Gutenberg to the Present* (New Haven: Yale University Press, 1996), esp. pp. 43–5.

83. For example, *Biblia or a Practical Summary of [th]e Old & New Testaments* (London, 1727); *A Curious Hieroglyphick Bible* (London, 1783), which was published in twenty editions by 1812; Sarah Trimmer, *A Series of Prints of Scripture History, Designed as Ornaments for those Apartments in which Children receive the first Rudiments of their Education* (London, [1786]); see also W. A. Clouston, *Hieroglyphic Bibles* (Glasgow: David Bryce & Son, 1894).

84. W[illiam] S[ellon], *An Abridgement of the Holy Scriptures* (London, 1781), pp. xvi–xvii. This work was published by J. F. and C. Rivington, long-standing booksellers to the Society for Promoting Christian Knowledge. It went through at least twelve editions by 1803.

85. Bottigheimer, *Bible for Children*, pp. 39–43.

86. These comments and those that follow relating to the SPCK derive from study of the complete run of eighteenth-century Minute Books, Annual Reports, and Letter Books of the Society for Promoting Christian Knowledge, now on deposit in Cambridge University Library. The best introduction to the work of the Society remains W. O. B. Allen and Edmund McClure, *Two Hundred Years: The History of the Society for Promoting Christian Knowledge, 1698–1898* (London: SPCK, 1898).

87. Figures based on those given in the Annual Reports; for the earlier years, see the circular letters in Christ Church, Oxford, Ms. Wake 27.

88. SPCK Annual Report, 1787, p. 120.

89. Examples of all these types of giving are recorded in the Society's Minute Books, esp. Vol. 28 (1776–81) and Vol. 29 (1782–87).

90. SPCK Minute Books, Vol. 32 (1796–9), pp. 149–250, esp. pp. 238–9. Iain McCalman, *Radical Underworld*, 2nd edn (Oxford: Clarendon Press, 1998), pp. 50–72, presents evidence for millenarian sentiment among some disaffected sailors and soldiers; see also Albert Goodwin, *The Friends of Liberty* (London: Hutchinson, 1979), pp. 406–11.

91. SPCK Minute Books, Vol. 32, p. 259, from a letter dated 6 February 1798.

92. See K. W. Wadsworth, 'Philip, Lord Wharton – revolutionary aristocrat?', *Journal of the United Reformed Church History Society*, 4 (1987–92): 474–5; C. G. A. Clay, 'Henry Hoare, banker, his family, and the Stourhead Estate', in F. M. L. Thompson (ed.), *Landowners, Capitalists, and Entrepreneurs: Essays for Sir John Habakkuk* (Oxford: Clarendon Press, 1994), pp. 113–38, which, however, neglects their charitable activity.

93. Roger H. Martin, 'The Bible Society and the French connection', *Journal of the United Reformed Church History Society*, 3 (1983–7): 278–90.

94. SPCK Annual Reports, 1744 and 1745. Between 1744 and 1749, although the Society's offers allowed London or Oxford Bibles in the smallest format to undercut Cambridge Bibles by 2d, they nevertheless represented a cheaper price for Cambridge Bibles than that allowed to the university's London agent: see David McKitterick, *A History of Cambridge University Press*, Vol. 2 (Cambridge: Cambridge University Press, 1998), p. 183.

95. All these figures come from the relevant Annual Reports.

96. SPCK Annual Report, 1787, p. 83; cf. Minute Books, Vol. 29, pp. 417–18.

97. On the arrangements made by Baskett and his heirs, see Harry Carter, *A History of Oxford University Press, Volume I: To the Year 1780* (Oxford: Clarendon Press, 1975), pp. 168–9, 352–4; Robert L. Haig, 'New light on the King's Printing Office 1680–1730', *Studies in Bibliography*, 8 (1956): 157–67; A. F. Johnson, *Selected Essays on Books and Printing*, ed. Percy H. Muir (Amsterdam: Van Gendt, 1970), pp. 381–5; Archives of the Stationers' Company, London, Court Book G, f. 204r, and Baskett Papers; Bodleian, Ms. Gough Gen. Top. 28, ff. 305–6; S. C. Roberts, *A History of Cambridge University Press 1521–1921* (Cambridge: Cambridge University Press, 1921), p. 95.

98. DMH, No. 1063; McKitterick, *Cambridge University Press*, Vol. 2, pp. 175–94, 224–5.

99. Carter, *Oxford University Press*, pp. 352–4; R. A. Austen-Leigh, *The Story of a Printing House*, 2nd edn (London: Spottiswoode, 1912), pp. 10–12.

100. McKitterick, *Cambridge University Press*, Vol. 2, p. 194; H. R. Plomer, G. H. Bushnell, E. R. McC. Dix, *A Dictionary of the Printers and Booksellers who were at Work in England, Scotland and Ireland from 1726 to 1775* (London: The Bibliographical Society, 1932), p. 214.

101. Jim Mitchell, 'Bible publishing in eighteenth-century Britain', *Factotum*, 20 (1985): 17.

102. Christ Church, Oxford, Ms. Wake 22, No. 276 (John Baskett to William Wake, 9 March 1724); SPCK Minute Books, Vol. 10 (1722–24), pp. 102, 140, 202.

103. SPCK Minute Books, Vol. 20 (1743–46), pp. 127, 139, 147, 149, 156, 173, 174, 203, 219, 221–2, quotation at p. 131; cf. Letter Book (CR1/25), pp. 93–4 (Thomas Baskett to the Society, 12 February 1745).

104. SPCK Minute Books, Vol. 23 (1756–62), pp. 133, 136, 145.

105. SPCK Letter Book (CR1/25), pp. 113–14 (dated 25 July 1755).

106. SPCK Abstract Letter Book 9 (1718–19), No. 6171.

107. SPCK Abstract Letter Book 10 (1719–21), No. 6298.

108. SPCK Minute Books, Vol. 32, pp. 140–1.

109. SPCK Minute Books, Vol. 25 (1765–9), p. 26; cf. Vol. 30 (1787–91), p. 16.

110. DMH, No. 1142.

111. B. J. McMullin, 'Creating a good impression at the Oxford Bible Press in 1743', *Studies in Bibliography*, 51 (1998): 205–12.

112. Alexander Fortescu, *The Holy Family Bible* (Winchester, 1774), sig. A2r. The author claimed to have based his own text on a Cambridge Bible of 1659 which he naively believed to be '*correct*': see also DMH, Nos 666 and 1237.

113. For example, Francis Fox, *The New Testament, With References set under the Text in Words at Length: So That the Parallel Text may be Seen at one View*, 2 vols (London, 1722); Daniel Fox, *A New Version of St. Matthew's Gospel: With Select Notes* (London, 1741); John Wesley, *Explanatory Notes upon the New Testament* (London, 1755); Joseph Brown, *The Family Testament and Scholar's Assistant*, 2nd edn (1767); John Worsley, *The New Testament or New Covenant* (London, 1770); *The Holy Bible . . . With Notes . . . Selected from the Works of Several Eminent Divines* (London, 1776); John Herries, *The Royal Universal Family Bible*, 2 vols (London, 1780); *The Holy Bible . . . With Annotations*, 2 vols (Birmingham, 1788).

114. For example, *Divers Parts of the Holy Scriptures done into English* (London, 1761–2); Francis Fawkes, *The Complete Family Bible*, 2 vols (London, 1769); Henry Southwell [and Robert Sanders], *The Universal Family Bible* (London, 1773) [see DMH, No. 1225]; Thomas Sisson, *The Complete Family Bible; or, the Christian Treasury* (London, 1785); Thomas Scott, *The Holy Bible . . . with Original Notes*, 4 vols (London, 1788–92); *The Holy Bible Ornamented with Engravings by James Fittler from Celebrated Pictures by Old Masters* (London, 1791–4); see also R. M. Wiles, *Serial Publication in England before 1750* (Cambridge: Cambridge University Press, 1957), esp. pp. 112–13, 296, 301, 306–7, 313, 317, 320, 330.

115. For example, Fawkes, *Complete Family Bible*.

116. Fortescu, *The Holy Family Bible*, sig. A2r.

117. Clear examples of this practice are *The Holy Bible . . . with Notes* (London, 1776) [DMH, No. 1249]; *The Holy Bible* (London, 1796) [DMH, No. 1405]. More respectable use of additional notes was made by *A Commentary on the Holy Bible* (Bristol, 1774).

118. G. E. Bentley, Jr., 'The holy pirates: legal enforcement in England of the patent in the Authorized Version of the Bible ca. 1800', *Studies in Bibliography*, 50 (1997): 372–89; *Report from Select Committee on King's Printers' Patents* (London, 1832); Mitchell, 'Bible Publishing', pp. 16–17.

119. Fox, *The New Testament*, p. xii.

120. Richard Wynne, *The New Testament: Carefully Collated with the Greek*, Vol. 1 (London, 1764), p. iii; Palmer (ed.), *A New Translation of the New Testament*, Vol. 1, sig. A5r.

121. [John Callender], *An Essay towards a Literal English Version of the New Testament, in the Epistle of the Apostle Paul directed to the Ephesians* (Glasgow, 1779), sig. [A2r]; cf. Worsley, *The New Testament*; Thomas Haweis, *A Translation of the New Testament from the Original Greek* (London, 1795), p. iv.

122. Worsley, *The New Testament*, sig. A3v–4r.

123. Wesley, *Explanatory Notes*, p. iv.

124. Thomas Wilson, *The Holy Bible . . . With Notes*, ed. Clement Cruttwell, Vol. 1 (Bath, 1785), sig. a1v.

125. John S. Macauley and R. W. Greaves (eds), *The Autobiography of Thomas Secker Archbishop of Canterbury* (Lawrence: University of Kansas Libraries, 1988), pp. 3–5. Secker had been reading [Jean Le Clerc], *Sentimens de quelques theologiens de Hollande sur l'histoire critique du Vieux Testament, composée par le P. Richard Simon* (Amsterdam, 1685), esp. pp. 219–86.

126. Lambeth Palace Library, Mss. 2578 (Secker's copy of Johan Heinrich Michaelis (ed.), *Biblia Hebraica* (Halle, 1720)); 2559–62 (Secker's copy of *The Holy Bible* (London, 1723) [DMH, No. 965]); see also some of Secker's notes on and translations of particular biblical passages: Mss. 2564–9, 2590–4, 2596–7.

127. Bodleian, Ms. Rawlinson J fol. 3, f. 372.

128. A. P. Jenkins (ed.), *The Correspondence of Bishop Secker*, Oxfordshire Record Society 57 (1991), pp. 36, 102, 173.

129. Lambeth Palace Library, Ms. Secker Papers, Vol. 2, ff. 158–82 ('Abstracts of papers put into my hands by the A[rch]B[isho]p of Canterbury Nov[ember] 4 1748'), at f. 161.

130. Lambeth Palace Library, Ms. Secker Papers, Vol. 2, ff. 164–9, quotations at ff. 164–5; cf. Secker's comments, f. 182.

131. Thomas Secker, *Eight Charges Delivered to the Clergy of the Dioceses of Oxford and Canterbury*, ed. Beilby Porteus and George Stinton (London, 1769), p. 293; Secker's concern for the pastoral side of his ministry as Archbishop is made explicit in Jeremy Gregory (ed.), *The Speculum of Archbishop Thomas Secker* (Woodbridge: Boydell Press, 1995).

132. Robert Lowth, *De sacra poesi Hebraeorum* (Oxford, 1753), esp. pp. 347–51; Robert Lowth, *Lectures on the Sacred Poetry of the Hebrews*, trans. G. Gregory with notes by J. D. Michaelis, Vol. 2 (London, 1787), pp. 436–46; cf. Francis Hare (ed.), *Psalmorum liber in versiculos metrice divisus*, 2 vols (London, 1736); Thomas Edwards, *Prolegomena in libros veteris testamenti poeticos* (Cambridge, 1762); Robert Lowth, *A Larger Confutation of Bishop Hare's System of Hebrew Metre* (London, 1766). On this debate see James L. Kugel, *The Idea of Biblical Poetry* (Baltimore: Johns Hopkins University Press, 1981), pp. 12–15, 204–86; for Secker's interest in Lowth's work, see Macauley and Greaves (eds), *Autobiography of Secker*, pp. 33, 50; Bodleian, Ms. Eng. Lett. c. 574, ff. 67–74; Lambeth Palace Library, Mss. 2559, 2569, 2596; see also the extensive discussion of the deficiencies of Hare's work in Ms. 2260.

133. Anthony Blackwell, *The Sacred Classics Defended and Illustrated*, 3rd edn, 2 vols (London, 1737); [John Johnson], *Holy David and his Old English Translators Clear'd* (London, 1706); David Norton, *A History of the Bible as Literature*, Vol. 2 (Cambridge: Cambridge University Press, 1993), pp. 59–73; Murray Roston, *Prophet and Poet. The Bible and the Growth of Romanticism* (London: Faber and Faber, 1965).

134. Bodleian, Ms. Kennicott c. 12, f. 92v (letter of 23 May 1758).

135. Lambeth Palace Library, Mss. Secker Papers, Vol. 2, ff. 10, 18–19, 38–40; 1720–1; Benjamin Kennicott, *The State of the Printed Hebrew Text of the Old Testament Considered*, 2 parts (Oxford, 1753–9); Benjamin Kennicott, *Proposals for Collating the Hebrew Manuscripts* (Oxford, 1760); Benjamin Kennicott, *A Sermon Preached before the University of Oxford* (Oxford, 1765); Benjamin Kennicott (ed.), *Vetus testamentum Hebraicum cum variis lectionibus*, 2 vols (Oxford, 1776–80); cf. Matthew Pilkington, *Remarks upon Several Passages of Scripture* (Cambridge, 1759); William Worthington, *The Use, Value, and Improvement of Various Readings Shewn and Illustrated* (Oxford, 1761); William McKane, 'Benjamin Kennicott: an eighteenth-century researcher', *Journal of Theological Studies*, NS 28 (1977): 445–63; David S. Katz, 'The Chinese Jews and the problem of biblical authority in eighteenth- and nineteenth-century England', *English Historical Review*, 105 (1990): 893–919.

136. See Thomas Hunt, *Observations on Several Passages in the Book of Proverbs*, ed. Benjamin Kennicott (Oxford, 1775). Secker successfully recommended that Durell become a prebend of Canterbury in 1766 (Macauley and Greaves (eds), *Autobiography of Secker*, p. 55); he may also have had access to Durell's unpublished notes on the biblical prophets (Lambeth Palace Library, Ms. 2580).

137. 'Diary of David Durell, 1765–8' (unpublished manuscript, private collection), entries

for 4 December 1765, 12 June 1766, 28 June 1766; Macauley and Greaves (eds), *Autobiography of Secker*, p. 53; Durell, *Critical Remarks*, p. vii.

138. Letter from Benjamin Blayney to the Vice-Chancellor and delegates of the Clarendon Press, 25 October 1769, printed in *The Gentleman's Magazine*, 39 (1769): 517–19. See also DMH, Nos 1194 and 1196. The Bibles used by Blayney for his work were DMH, Nos 309 (London, 1611); 868 (London, 1701); 1131 (Cambridge, 1760); 1143 (Cambridge, 1762). The last two of these contained corrections prepared by F. S. Parris for the first Bible printed in Cambridge by Joseph Bentham in 1743 (DMH, No. 1063). Secker had suggested using the 1611 and 1701 London Bibles and the 1743 and 1760 Cambridge Bibles; cf. Ronald Mansbridge, 'The Bentham Folio Bible', *The Book Collector*, 45 (1996): 24–8; B. J. McMullin, 'Extinguishing the fire at Dod's warehouse in 1762', *The Book Collector*, 45 (1996): 476–84.

139. See James Merrick, *Annotations on the Psalms* (Reading, 1768), in which notes by Secker appear anonymously; cf. [Gregory Sharpe], *A Letter to the Right Reverend the Lord Bishop of Oxford, from the Master of the Temple. Containing Remarks upon some Strictures made by His Grace the Late Archbishop of Canterbury in the Revd. Mr. Merrick's Annotations on the Psalms* (London, 1769). Merrick also acknowledged Secker's help with the provision of works of Continental scholarship in *The Psalms, Translated or Paraphrased in English Verse* (Reading, 1765).

140. Secker, *Eight Charges*, ed. Porteus and Stinton, pp. 363–4 (my translation). Secker's comments recall those of Robert Lowth, *A Sermon Preached at the Visitation of the Honourable and Right Reverend Richard Lord Bishop of Durham* (London, 1758).

141. [Benjamin Kennicott], *Remarks on the Forty Second and Forty Third Psalms* (n.p., [1763]), p. 7.

142. National Library of Scotland, Edinburgh, Ms. 25299, ff. 43–4 (Robert Lowth to David Dalrymple, Lord Hailes, 7 June 1779); cf. Robert Lowth, *Isaiah. A New Translation*, 2nd edn (London, 1779 [1st edn, 1778]).

143. Bodleian, Ms. Eng. Lett. c. 574, ff. 1–2 (Sir G. Baker to Robert Lowth, 18 December 1778).

144. Lambeth Palace Library, Ms. 1373, ff. 28–9. Lowth, for example, acknowledged the use of Ms. 2578 in the preparation of his *Isaiah*, p. lxix.

145. Lowth, *Isaiah*, pp. lxx–xxi; Bodleian, Ms. Eng. Th. c. 94, ff. 18, 29–36; David Durell, '[Critic]al Remarks on passages in the Old Testament' (Bodleian, uncatalogued manuscript). After Kennicott's death, Barrington helped to care for his wife: see Magdalen College, Oxford, Ms. 471, ff. 97–8, 114–15, 119–20, 123–4. Durell is said to have saved Barrington from drowning; it is certain that after Durell's death, Barrington became the patron of a younger member of his family (unpublished correspondence, private collection).

146. Benjamin Blayney, *Jeremiah and Lamentations. A New Translation* (Oxford, 1784); Benjamin Blayney, *Zechariah. A New Translation* (Oxford, 1797); in 1802, Barrington was responsible for the deposit of Blayney's papers at Lambeth Palace Library 'to be there kept in the like manner and for the like purposes as the manuscripts of Archbishop Secker': see Mss. 2577, 2579, 2581–8.

147. William Newcome, *An Attempt Towards an Improved Version, a Metrical Arrangement, and an Explanation of the Twelve Minor Prophets* (Dublin, 1785), p. xvi; William Newcome, *An Attempt Towards an Improved Version, a Metrical Arrangement, and an Explanation of the Prophet Ezekiel* (Dublin, 1788).

148. See Robert Holmes, *The First Annual Account of the Collation of the Mss. of the Septuagint-Version* (Oxford, 1789). The undertaking of this parallel to Kennicott's labours had been urged by Henry Owen, *A Brief Account, Historical and Critical, of the Septuagint Version of the Old Testament* (London, 1787), which was dedicated to Barrington; Joseph White, *A Letter to the*

Right Reverend the Lord Bishop of London, Suggesting a Plan for a New Edition of the LXX (Oxford, 1779), which was addressed to Lowth, and by Alexander Geddes in conversations with Lowth and Kennicott in September 1782 (see Scottish Catholic Archives, Edinburgh, Ms. BL 3/355/14).

149. DMH, No. 1324, preface and list of subscribers.

150. Quoted in Marilyn Brooks, 'Priestley's plan for a "continually improving" translation of the Bible', *Enlightenment and Dissent*, 15 (1996): 103.

151. Brooks, 'Priestley's plan', 101; Newcome had deposited his interleaved and annotated copy of *The Holy Bible* (Oxford, 1772) at Lambeth Palace Library in 1799: see Mss. 2570–3.

152. For example, the first part of *The Age of Reason* (1794), see Thomas Paine, *Political Writings*, revised edn, ed. Bruce Kuklick (Cambridge: Cambridge University Press, 2000), esp. pp. 276–90.

153. William Blake, *Annotations to Richard Watson*, ed. G. Ingli James (Cardiff: University College Cardiff Press, 1984), title-page verso; Blake's own view of the Bible was hardly orthodox: here he was attacking Richard Watson, *An Apology for the Bible*, 8th edn (London, 1797).

154. See the letters from John Butler, Bishop of Oxford, to David Dalrymple, Lord Hailes, National Library of Scotland, Edinburgh, Ms. 25299, ff. 84–112, quotation from ff. 101–2 (23 November 1786). George Travis, *Letters to Edward Gibbon* (Chester, 1784), the third edition of which (London, 1794) contains the account of Travis' journey to Paris; cf. Richard Porson, *Letters to Mr. Archdeacon Travis* (London, 1790); Henry Richards Luard (ed.), *The Correspondence of Richard Porson, M.A.* (Cambridge: Cambridge Antiquarian Society, 1867), pp. 23–59; [Herbert Marsh], *Letters to Mr. Archdeacon Travis* (Leipzig, 1795). See also Joseph M. Levine, *The Autonomy of History* (Chicago: University of Chicago Press, 1999), pp. 157–240.

155. Thomas Edwards, *Remarks on Dr Kipling's Preface to Beza*, Part 1 (Cambridge, 1793), p. vii; cf. Thomas Kipling (ed.), *Codex Theodori Bezae Cantabrigiensis Evangelia et Apostolorum Acta Complectens*, 2 vols (Cambridge, 1793); David McKitterick, *Cambridge University Library. A History. The Eighteenth and Nineteenth Centuries* (Cambridge: Cambridge University Press, 1986), pp. 337–42.

156. Lambeth Palace Library, Ms. 2810, pp. 113–17, 119–39, 141–5, 257–75.

157. *The Reasons for Revising by Authority our Present Version of the Bible* (Cambridge, 1788), p. 59; the sentiments of this anonymous work were echoed by William Newcome, *An Historical View of the English Biblical Translations* (Dublin, 1792), pp. 187–209.

158. Newcome, *An Historical View*, p. 25; cf. Geddes, *General Answer*, p. 4.

159. Lambeth Palace Library, Ms. 1140 (Andrew Coltee Ducarel to Archbishop Frederick Cornwallis, 30 March 1776); cf. Joseph Ames, *A List of Various Editions of the Bible and Parts Thereof, in English from the Year 1526 to 1776*, ed. M. C. Tutet (London, 1778), which was printed at the expense of the Archbishop of Canterbury. Ames had been the owner of the then only known copy of the first edition of Tyndale's translation of the New Testament ([Worms, 1526] [DMH, No. 2]), now BL, shelfmark C. 188. a. 17. By 1784, the book had been purchased by the Baptists of Bristol.

160. Durell, *Critical Remarks*, p. ix.

161. Bodleian, Ms. Eng. Lett. c. 574, ff. 25–6 (Benjamin Kennicott to Robert Lowth, 23 February 1772).

162. R. J. Robson, *The Oxfordshire Election of 1754* (London: Oxford University Press, 1949); David Durell to Thomas Durell, 27 April 1754 (unpublished correspondence, private collection).

163. W. R. Ward, *Georgian Oxford. University Politics in the Eighteenth Century* (Oxford:

Clarendon Press, 1958), pp. 196–7, 205–6; Exeter College, Oxford, Ms. L.IV.7, esp. folders B, C, F; *Jackson's Oxford Journal*, 7 (16 June 1753); *London Evening Post*, 3584 (29–31 May 1753); Bodleian, Ms. Rawlinson J fol. 2, ff. 412–16; [Fowler Comings], *The Printed Hebrew Text of the Old Testament Vindicated. An Answer to Mr. Kennicott's Dissertation* (Oxford, 1753).

164. For these points, see in particular the works of Hunt, Lowth and Kennicott referred to above; Alun Morris David, 'Christopher Smart and the Hebrew Bible: poetry and biblical criticism in England (1682–1771)', unpublished Cambridge University PhD thesis (1994), pp. 80–97.

165. Charles Houbigant, *Prolegomena in Scripturam Sacram* (Paris, 1753), which summarized the critical material included in Houbigant's version of the Bible. The manuscripts of Houbigant's work may be found in the Archives de l'Oratoire, Paris, Mss. Fol. 10–14. Cf. Bodleian, Mss. Eng. Lett. d. 146, ff. 91–4; Eng. Th. c. 94, ff. 39–45. See also Françoise Deconinck-Brossard, 'England and France in the eighteenth century', in Stephen Prickett (ed.), *Reading the Text. Biblical Criticism and Literary Theory* (Oxford: Blackwell, 1991), pp. 136–81; Mireille Hadas-Lebel, 'Le P. Houbigant et la critique textuelle', in Belaval and Bourel (eds), *Le Siècle des Lumières et la Bible*, pp. 103–112; J. van den Berg, 'The Leiden professors of the Schultens family and their contacts with British scholars', *Durham University Journal*, 75 (1982–3): 1–14; Jan Nat, *De Studie van de Oostersche Talen in Nederland in de 18e en de 19e Eeuw* (Purmerend: J. Muusses, 1929), pp. 37–103.

166. For some discussion of the reception of Lowth's work, see Christoph Bultmann, *Die biblische Urgeschichte in der Aufklärung* (Tübingen: Mohr Siebeck, 1999), pp. 75–85; Edward Breuer, *The Limits of Enlightenment* (Cambridge, MA: Harvard University Center for Jewish Studies, 1996), pp. 86–101.

167. An early, partisan but nevertheless devastating example can be found in Bodleian, Ms. Kennicott e. 43 (Ignatius Adolphus Dumay's observations on Kennicott's work).

168. A major exception to this claim is the work of Henry Owen, in particular *Observations on the Four Gospels* (London, 1764); see also William Bowyer (ed.), *Critical Conjectures and Observations on the New Testament*, 3rd edn, ed. J. Nichols (London, 1782); James MacKnight, *A Harmony of the Four Gospels*, 2nd edn, 2 vols (London, 1763); Abraham Dawson, *A New English Translation, from the Original Hebrew, of the Three First Chapters of Genesis* (London, 1763); Abraham Dawson, *A Fourth and Fifth Chapter of Genesis, Translated from the Original Hebrew* (London, 1772).

169. [Robert Lowth], *A Letter to the Right Reverend Author of* The Divine Legation of Moses Demonstrated (Oxford, 1765) and 4th edn (London, 1766); [John Towne (ed.)], *Remarks on Dr Lowth's Letter to the Bishop of Gloucester* (London, 1766); [J. Brown], *A Letter to the Rev. Dr. Lowth* (Newcastle-upon-Tyne, 1766); Bodleian, Mss. Eng. Lett. c. 572, ff. 128–89; Eng. Lett. c. 574, ff. 74–89; Eng. Misc. c. 817, ff. 17d–e, 22; BL, Ms. Add. 42560, ff. 1452154; National Library of Scotland, Edinburgh, Mss. 962, f. 159r–v; 1002, ff. 165–6; Young, *Religion and Enlightenment*, p. 199.

170. [Thomas Wintle], *A Letter to the Lord Bishop of Worcester Occasioned by his Strictures on Archbishop Secker and Bishop Lowth*, 2nd edn (Oxford, 1796), quotation on p. 27; see also Jonathan Lamb, *The Rhetoric of Suffering. Reading the Book of Job in the Eighteenth Century* (Oxford: Clarendon Press, 1995), pp. 110–27.

171. Leslie Howsam, *Cheap Bibles. Nineteenth-Century Publishing and the British and Foreign Bible Society* (Cambridge: Cambridge University Press, 1991), pp. 1–120; *Report from Select Committee*, pp. 41–64.

172. *Commentaries and Essays Published by the Society for Promoting the Knowledge of the Scriptures*, 2 vols (London, n.d.).

173. Robert Kendall Braine, 'The life and writings of Herbert Marsh (1757–1839)', unpublished Cambridge University PhD thesis (1989), pp. 197–232.

174. [Edward Cardwell], *Oxford Bibles: Mr Curtis' Misrepresentations Exposed* ([Oxford, 1833)]; Thomas Turton, *The Text of the English Bible as Now Printed by the Universities Considered with Reference to a Report by a Sub-Committee of Dissenting Ministers* (Cambridge, 1833); cf. Thomas Curtis, *The Existing Monopoly, An Inadequate Protection, of the Authorised Version of Scripture* (London, 1833).

175. [Richard Laurence], *Remarks upon the Critical Principles, and the Practical Application of those Principles, Adopted by Writers, who have at Various Periods Recommended a New Translation of the Bible as Expedient and Necessary* (Oxford, 1820), p. 161.

176. John William Whittaker, *An Historical and Critical Enquiry into the Interpretation of the Hebrew Scriptures* (Cambridge, 1819), p. ix.

177. Henry John Todd, *A Vindication of our Authorized Translation and Translators of the Bible* (London, 1819), p. iv.

178. J. Rogers, *Remarks on the Principles Adopted by Bishop Lowth in Correcting the Text of the Hebrew Bible* (Oxford, 1832), p. 10.

179. Several of the writings of John Lewis were reprinted in the early nineteenth century, including *A Complete History of the Several Translations of the Holy Bible and New Testament into English*, 3rd edn (London, 1818).

CHAPTER 3

THEOLOGICAL BOOKS FROM *THE NAKED GOSPEL* TO *NEMESIS OF FAITH*

BRIAN YOUNG

[F]or what has this book done more than the Legation of Moses, or the Tale of a Tub, that it may not swim down the gutter of Time along with them?

Laurence Sterne, *The Life and Opinions of Tristram Shandy, Gentleman*[1]

'The Fire's continued at Oxford'

On 19 August 1690, the Convocation of the University of Oxford judged that a recently published book by Arthur Bury, the Rector of Exeter College, was heretical, and that it should be burned. Accordingly, the following day, *The Naked Gospel* was put to the flame in the schools quadrangle of the Bodleian Library.[2] In 1849, William Sewell, the Senior Tutor of Exeter College, having just finished a condemnatory lecture on the work of a colleague to his undergraduates in Hall, consigned a copy of James Anthony Froude's recently published novel, *Nemesis of Faith*, to the flames. Froude's was the only publicly burned English book of the nineteenth century; the result was notoriety and a second edition, to which he was able to prefix an even more effective apologia than that contained in the novel itself.[3] Much of the theological literature produced in England between the seventeenth and nineteenth centuries was written by dons such as Bury and Froude, and it was the attempts of the learned at internal policing which often led to printed controversies, or to such extreme instances of book-burning as those which adversely affected two senior members of Exeter College some 150 years apart. The universities and the dissenting academies provided the major engines of the controversial culture in which theological reflection flourished, with the result that the Victorian 'crisis of faith' was at least as much a crisis of vocation as it was anything so abstract as a war between science and faith. Whereas able young men in the 1690s onwards might have seen it as their duty (as well as in their long-term interest) to denounce, or even occasionally to defend, the likes of Bury in early forays into print, young clerical fellows from the 1840s to the 1880s were announcing their defections from organized religion in learned magazine articles and, less often but more celebratedly, in novels and poems.[4] This, then, was a notably academic culture which maintained itself over two centuries, and which produced theological literature across a variety of genres, including fiction and poetry. The productive competition between orthodoxy and heresy, between doxa and allodoxia, which Pierre Bourdieu has analysed in modern culture, has a long history.[5]

Rather more than in the 1840s, the imagery of book-burning in the 1690s had unfortunate associations in a country which had just resoundingly rid itself of 'Popery' and its supposed commitment to censorship and heresy-hunting. A not disinterested Oxford writer, James Parkinson, recently ejected from a fellowship at Lincoln College for whiggery, defended Bury anonymously, emphasizing (in a manner which was to become typical among self-consciously Protestant writers) the usefulness of their supposedly pacific and inherently simple creed when opposed to the intricacies of priest-ridden Catholicism:

> The Design and Tendency of the Book, I will presume to whisper to you (out of hearing of the Convocation) is . . . to turn Men's Minds from the study of Opinions, and Speculations, to Practical Piety, Devotion toward God and Christ, and Love toward all Christians of all *Persuasions*; in the Mean Time making Rents and Divisions, Heats and Animosities about Matters hardly determinable, to be dangerous and unbecoming sincere Christians.

In a tract unsubtly but effectively entitled *The Fire's continued at Oxford* (economically rekindling Foxe's heated depictions of Protestant martyrdoms in his ever popular *Acts and Monuments*), Parkinson contrasted the laudable ambitions for Protestant purity which he attributed to Bury with the altogether different ends of 'these Gentlemen-burners', a sarcasm he continued in a deliberately unsettling reference to 'the Learned Assembly of Burners'.[6] Not that the learned burners were without their defenders; one anonymous writer celebrated the actions of the university as a dignified means of seeing off a Socinian threat against Trinitarian orthodoxy, of which Bury was but a mouthpiece, reminding Bury's readers that 'never any more Decree was more unanimously sign'd, nor more willingly assented to by the Right Reverend, and Reverend the Heads, and the worthy Members of the whole University'.[7]

Apologists for *The Naked Gospel* insisted that it had not been designed as an incendiary device, but that the times had made it much more combustible than its author suspected:

> If the Rector ordered this book to be Printed, he never ordered it to be Published. If he intended to have presented it to the Convocation, it was to have been done, not openly, but within doors; that so from the Principles of the Gospel, they might be induced to indulge their Charity, at a time when all the Christian World expected it from them. If he made Alterations, it was to remove Offences, which might be taken by some of the Vulgar, for whom it was not calculated.[8]

It was, paradoxically, Convocation's very desire to destroy the privately printed book that gave it the attention it might not otherwise have gained, thereby allowing Bury, in a 1691 edition of the work, to insinuate that high church orthodoxy was but a variant of Catholicism, and that its promoters were Jacobites in all but name. The Bible itself was presented as a sufferer at the hands of an uncomprehending inquisition, as a very Protestant rhetoric promoted the glorious 'Plainness' which torturing divines blasphemously denied:

> No sentence, hardly any word in the New Testament escapeth the rack, that they may be forced to confess what they never thought of: They are put to many Questions, and every Question is stretched by many Articles, and every Article vext with many Objections, and all this in a New rude Language unknown to any civil Nation.

Such difficulties, Bury argued, were designed to deter 'free and generous Minds' from undertaking Biblical study, and to give it up entirely to monks and to a papacy which thereby assumed the role of 'Oracle'.[9] None of this could save Bury from pious answerers. Thomas Long, a clergyman in Exeter (the see of Jonathan Trelawny, who had censured Bury in his role as Visitor of Exeter College), congratulated his bishop on having 'mortified' the 'Gangrene' of Bury's heresies, thus preventing him 'from infecting the Members of that Famous College'. For Long, Bury's politico-theological self-defence was so much persiflage adopted in order to disguise the vehemence of his heresies, allowing him to amend Bury's solicitous questioning of the fidelity of Jacobites over that of Williamites:

> Which are the truer Church of England men, those who dread the growth and success of the Arian and Socinian Heresies; or those who adhere to the established Doctrine of the Trinity and Incarnation of our blessed Saviour? Those who would erect a *Natural Religion*, a Jewish or Turkish *Faith*, on the Ruines of that which is truly Christian, Ancient and Catholick? or those who live in the Communion of the Church of England, where this Christian Religion is established? Every good Protestant will readily answer these Queries.[10]

Not all Protestants were agreed, however, and Jean Le Clerc, one of the leading lights of the Huguenot diaspora which proved so important in the formation of a cosmopolitan republic of letters in the closing decades of the seventeenth century,[11] defended *The Naked Gospel* with some alacrity in a short, anonymous tract which he published in 1690. Le Clerc pointed to the paradox which Protestant purists detected in the destruction of a work that had been designed 'to discover the *Naked Truth*, as far as 'tis possible, after the Destruction of such infinite Numbers of Volumes by the Barbarity of former Ages':[12] the learned burners were reverting to a past which progressive theologians were determined to overcome. Anthony Wood, the Oxford antiquarian, likewise expressed an amused but deeply felt disdain for the burning ordered by 'the valiant Sanchapancas [*sic*]' in Oxford's Convocation.[13] If it was, then, by implication, quixotic to burn the book in an age of print, when Bury was so quickly able to bring out a new edition of his work, the burning nevertheless had devastating consequences for him. Despite attempts at ingratiating himself through preaching a university sermon and promoting theological latitude in the Church, Bury's career was effectively destroyed by Trelawny and the action of Convocation, and he ended his life a broken man, his portrait all too appropriately exiled to a West Country workhouse.[14] Writing theological books could never in itself lead the penurious to riches, though it might secure them a comfortable benefice; it could, however, as the case of Bury shows, lead even the comfortably beneficed to penury.

'Sermons & plays & novels': theology as literature

Parson Adams, the quixotic and penurious clergyman whose innocently bookish temperament acts as the source of much of the humour of Fielding's *Joseph Andrews*, optimistically undertakes his part of the novel's picaresque journey in answer to an advertisement for speculative publication put out by booksellers, with no fewer than nine volumes of manuscript sermons packed into his saddlebags. His encounter with a fellow clergyman proved discouraging, however, as he was confidently told that 'The Age was so wicked, that no body read Sermons'. A bookseller similarly lamented that, unless written by Whitefield or Wesley, or else when taking the form of occasional sermons, such as those commemorating the execution of Charles I on 30 January, sermons, unlike plays, simply would not sell, a matter which he devoutly regretted.[15] Not for nothing then does Fielding assert at the beginning of his mock biography that 'A good Man therefore is a standing Lesson to all his Acquaintance, and of far greater use in that narrow circle than a book'.[16] The fictional experience of Parson Adams, long since removed from the encouragement and expectations of the university world, could thus be viewed as a guiding metaphor for the problematic situation of theological books in the eighteenth-century literary landscape.

In a highly self-conscious invocation to genius in *Tom Jones*, Fielding alluded to William Warburton's reputation for extensive learning.[17] Warburton, the would-be dictator of literary taste in mid-eighteenth-century England, was an autodidact who was perennially conscious of not having attended university; he was more realistic than his fictional colleague Adams in seeking to promote a series of sermons which he had delivered in his capacity as preacher to Lincoln's Inn. His reputation as a dogmatic theologian already established, Warburton was able to write to his publisher, John Knapton, in quietly assertive terms in December 1751:

> I intend to print a small Vol of Sermons ab[ou]t 16 or 17 with this title *The Principles of Religion natural and revealed* ... and I would have as small an impression as can possibly be printed. For I know the difference between Sermons & plays & novels.[18]

Warburton was himself later almost to appear as a character in a work of fiction: Laurence Sterne had threatened to make him Tristram Shandy's tutor, a position which Warburton was understandably loath to accept, and which he successfully prevented.[19] Richard Hurd, Warburton's closest disciple, was likewise critical of 'our Yorkshire Novelist', preferring the 'sensibility of passionate poets' which informed Rousseau's *La Nouvelle Héloïse*.[20]

Warburton's experience of the literary world, and Fielding's use of the novel as a species of secular sermon, make plain two centrally important matters. First, theological books were increasingly being composed with a strong sense of the competing attractions offered by novels, poems and plays, a situation to which writers reacted in different ways. Second, it is often difficult to make any ready separation between the world of fiction and that of theological books in this period. Although long interpreted as an inherently secularizing genre, the eighteenth-century novel was also frequently a form of theological literature. The interpenetration of the fictional and the religious informed much literary engagement in this period. The dominant figure of Warburton provides a signal instance of the importance of these matters, since his own career displays their impact on his literary as much as his theological labours, further complicating any ready distinction between theological and non-theological literature in a life which, beginning in 1698 and ending in 1779, encompasses the greater part of the eighteenth century.

The first characteristic of theological literature in this period, namely the competition it faced from creative literature, is well exemplified in the admittedly extreme but telling case of William Law, a prominent nonjuror who was committed to opposing the worldliness of Walpolean England through a series of influential devotional writings. As a central part of this self-imposed mission, Law rigorously condemned the reading of all '*corrupt, impertinent*, and *unedifying* Books', a very wide and severe categorization, since it comprised 'Books of *Wit* and *Humour*, *Romances*, Plays, and other Productions of the Poets'.[21] This condemnation was made in *A Practical Treatise upon Christian Perfection* (1726), a model of Augustan devotional prose, and a work very explicitly directed to ascetic ends but which could easily also be read for pleasure; its successor volume, *A Serious Call to a Devout and Holy Life* (1729), contains even greater literary rewards for its readers, and its sharp pen-portraits of both exemplary and decidedly sinful figures invite comparisons with the very best caricatures delineated in the fictions of his contemporaries.[22] Edward Gibbon, the son of Law's pupil, plainly enjoyed extolling the specifically literary qualities of these and allied works, noticing in his *Autobiographies* that 'his satire is sharp, but it is drawn from the knowledge of human life; and many of his portraits are not unworthy of the pen of La Bruyère'. In Gibbon's opinion it was only Law's pronouncedly otherworldly piety which compromised his stylistic achievement, as he provocatively opined that 'had not his vigorous mind been clouded by enthusiasm, he might be ranked with the most agreeable and ingenious writers of the times'.[23]

What would Law have made, then, of Richard Hurd's essay on romance and chivalry, or of Warburton's editorial devotion to Pope and Shakespeare, literary labours which he would surely have denounced as going entirely against the grain of a serious Christian life? Hurd's praise of Spenser and Milton, and Warburton's of Pope and Shakespeare, proved to be of enormous

significance in the formation of an English canon by literary historians, not a
few of whom were clergymen whose critical skills had been honed both on
Scriptural study and in editions of the classics.[24] Such directly literary labours
were not without their religious element. While Warburton lamented Shakespeare's 'licentious Phraseology', he nevertheless found in his work an
unparalleled dedication to 'The Truth', and he therefore defended himself
against those who would have dismissed his editorial work as being incompatible with his clerical duties. He noted that St Chrysostom had been devoted
to Aristophanes, whose work was 'buffonery' when compared with Shakespeare, and whose freedoms were so gross that, in comparison, 'Shakespeare
writes with the purity of a Vestal'. Similarly, he regretted that a learned
colleague had been put off preparing an edition of Spenser by friends who
ought to have known better.[25] Hurd, who encouraged the promotion of
Spenser's reputation, also made much of Milton's rejecting pagan gods and
gothic fairies in favour of angels and devils:

> And this, no doubt, was the main reason of his relinquishing his long-projected
> design of Prince Arthur, at last, for that of the Paradise Lost; where, instead of
> Giants and Magicians, he had Angels and Devils to supply him with the
> *marvellous*, with greater probability.[26]

Warburton and Hurd were also avid readers of Samuel Richardson,
Warburton even going so far as to provide a rather unsatisfactory preface to
Clarissa, and the two clerics were forever recommending his work to their
correspondents.[27] Richard Graves, a clergyman and former Fellow of All
Souls, produced in *The Spiritual Quixote* (1773) an Anglican 'comic romance',
which combined the picaresque with the tradition of learned wit; it was one
of only two novels (the other being Burney's *Evelina*) which the devoutly
Anglican Anna Larpent recommended as reading for her younger sister in
1778.[28] Graves' novel appreciatively alluded to Warburton's strong attack on
Methodism, *The Doctrine of Grace* (1763), which he praised as an instructive
entertainment written 'with exquisite humour, by one of the first writers of
the age for genius and learning'.[29] He also firmly defended his work from
charges of the sort earlier made anonymously in the *Monthly Review* by the
barrister Owen Ruffhead and the rational dissenter William Rose against what
they considered to be the frivolous nature of Sterne's publication of the
Sermons of Parson Yorick (1760). Sterne's character as a clergyman, the reviewers
had argued, was such that he ought not to have published sermons under the
name of a fictional priest in a morally dubious novel.[30] In contrast, Graves
noted that Heliodorus, who was himself a bishop, had written the first

'Romance', and he saw this as having instituted a tradition of priests writing improving novels. Again, the allied purposes of fiction and theology (especially moral theology) were affirmed, as Graves made plain:

> Nay, I am convinced that Don Quixote or Gil Blas, Clarissa or Sir Charles Grandison, will furnish more hints for correcting the morals of young persons, and impress them more forcibly on their minds, than volumes of severe precepts seriously delivered and dogmatically inforced.[31]

Again, the contribution of Warburton is quietly to the fore in Graves' reckoning: not only had he contributed to *Clarissa*, but he had also provided introductory material to Charles Jarvis' translation of *Don Quixote* (1742).[32]

This broadening of the generic scope of theological literature also applies to much eighteenth-century poetry. Warburton, whose intellectual ambitions were as much literary as theological in nature, first made his way into Alexander Pope's affections by publicly asserting the theological orthodoxy of *An Essay on Man* after a disapproving critic had identified it as a religiously heterodox work, and he continued to supply Pope with suitably orthodox theological glosses up to and beyond the poet's death.[33] Warburton, Pope's literary executor, is as strong a presence in the elucidatory notes to the 1743 edition of the *Dunciad* as is Pope himself, and as a consequence they are (especially as expanded in the 1751 edition) a mine of theological as much as literary reflection.[34] If Pope, once a close friend of Warburton's enemy Bolingbroke, clearly stood in need of theological defences, other poets piously embodied their own conceptions of orthodoxy in their verse. Edward Young's *Night Thoughts* (1743) is a doctrinally effective repository of eschatological commonplaces by a cleric, although this former Fellow of All Souls was dismissed by Warburton with some acerbity in 1759, when he described Young as 'the finest writer of nonsense, of any of this age'.[35] The dissenting divine Philip Doddridge, whose correspondence with Warburton and other clergy contained much discussion of books, was less critical of Young, revealing himself, in 1742, to be prophetic of what others would later make of his work: 'Dr Young is too obscure, but they must be very foolish wits & shallow Thinkers who call it Nonsense.'[36] Divines, both Anglican and dissenting, were often as sharp with one another as they were with free-thinkers, the one enemy against whom they could be guaranteed occasionally to unite.[37]

Odium theologicum

The controversies with free-thinkers which so preoccupied most clerical writers in the first half of the eighteenth century, and which produced a great deal of ephemera as well as one theological masterpiece, Joseph Butler's *The Analogy of Religion, Natural and Revealed* (1736), were paralleled by internal squabbles which continued to inspire writings well into the 1800s, and which had their origin in such crises as those generated by the burning of *The Naked Gospel*. The debates so encouraged were frequently venomous and spiteful, providing an opportunity for David Hume to remark that 'The *Odium Theologicum*, or Theological Hatred, is noted even to a proverb, and means that degree of rancour, which is the most furious and implacable'.[38] This was to provide the spirit in which Gibbon descanted on the trials of heresy and orthodoxy in the early ages of the Church, sometimes subtly, sometimes not so subtly, drawing parallels with the animosities which characterized so much eighteenth-century divinity, the published products of which litter his learnedly facetious footnotes.[39] Believers as well as sceptics regretted this aspect of theology, and Sterne elegantly voiced this in *Tristram Shandy*: 'I wish there was not a polemic divine, said Yorick, in the Kingdom; – one ounce of practical divinity – is worth a painted ship load of all their reverences have imported these fifty years.'[40]

Dissent prospered largely through its contributions to theological writing, and such nonconformist ministers as Isaac Watts and Philip Doddridge enjoyed high reputations beyond their own denominations. The works most admired by Anglicans were, however, either those in which common cause was made against free-thinking and unbelief (hence the importance of such works as Nathaniel Lardner's *Credibility of the Gospel History* (1730)), or else in devotional prose promoting 'affectionate religion', hence the success of Doddridge's work on the Bible, *The Family Expositor* (1739–56), which was praised by Warburton among others.[41] The Unitarians would continue this self-conscious bookishness, and it was typically the writings as well as the character of Joseph Priestley which John Disney praised in a memorial sermon in 1804, a bias later reflected in Thomas Jervis' memorial sermon for Disney, preached in 1817. Unitarians were keen to distance themselves from the charge of polemicism, and Disney insisted on Priestley's pure biblicism as the source of his intellectual success, while Jervis likewise delivered an encomium to Disney which explicitly promoted the image of an apologetically successful rational piety as opposed to the blundering ineffectiveness of polemical

Anglican divinity. Disney's controversial writings were, Jervis observed, remarkable for 'that manly liberality, candour, and moderation, which reflect honour on the cause which he espoused, and at once distinctly mark the character of the scholar, the gentleman, and the christian'.[42] Celebrating the literary and intellectual achievements of the eighteenth century at its close, Jervis had singled out the liberating influence of his denomination for particular praise:

> But nothing has contributed so much, by a slow, yet sure, process, to promote the rights of human nature, as the liberal and enlightened spirit of christianity, divested of all human corruptions.[43]

Polemical divinity, however, had many practitioners in the eighteenth century, and their labours are best appreciated by detailing the controversial writings of some representative divines. Daniel Waterland (1683–1740), William Warburton (1698–1779), Francis Blackburne (1705–87) and Richard Watson (1737–1816) will usefully serve their turns in this respect, although a large number of other clergymen, including dissenters, could equally well have been drawn upon. All these writers could also have been denounced as polemical divines, and on occasion most were, even if, as in the case of Watson, they presented themselves as eirenic critics of polemicism, the disinterested guardians of gentlemanly mores and pacific Christianity against its dangerous opponents. Acerbity, in one form or other, was a prominent note in their writings, but it was an element which they felt necessary in promoting the truth as they saw it. Above all, it was a comprehensive perspective which they sought as they rebutted the arguments of opponents and defined their own positions, a perspective mildly ridiculed by Sterne through Shandy's citation of one of Yorick's notes to his sermons:

> This sermon upon the jewish dispensation – I don't like it at all; – Though I own there is a world of WATER-LANDISH knowlege in it, – but 'tis all tritical, and most tritically put together. – This is but a flimsy kind of a compilation; what was in my mind when I made it?[44]

Waterland was an omnivorous reader of theological writings, both ancient and contemporary: hence the power of the adjective 'Water-landish'. One of Waterland's self-imposed tasks as Master of Magdalene College, Cambridge was the preparation of a reading programme for undergraduates, an ambitious piece of work which he penned in the 1710s and had published by Cambridge University Press in 1730; a revised edition appeared posthumously at Oxford in 1755. Waterland noted that it had not originally been intended for publication since it would always be changing, 'according as new and better Books should come out'. It was nevertheless published to make up for the problems of the tutorial system, and to encourage a proper sense of the purpose of study in a Christian culture:

> You are to consider, that you are sent to the University, to be train'd up for God's Glory, and to do Good in the World. . . . Endeavour then first to be *religious*, next to be *learned*: It is something to be a good Scholar; but it is much more to be a good Christian.[45]

Plainly intended for candidates for the priesthood, Waterland's *Advice to a Young Student* emphasized that his first four years of study ought to be devoted to philosophy and classics, 'for they are the Foundation, without which a Man cannot be a learned Divine'. These preparatory studies were to take up all the student's time, apart from Sundays and holidays, which would be given over to the private study of divinity. The transition to theological study was to be undertaken by reading English sermons, which would not only supply the young with hints about style, accuracy and judgement, but were also 'the easiest, plainest, and most entertaining of Books of Divinity; and therefore fittest for young Beginners'. Anglican chauvinism also accounted for this preference, as Waterland insisted they contained 'as much and as good Divinity as any other Discourses whatever, and might be digested into a better *Body of Divinity* than any that is yet extant'. Supreme among the sermonizers recommended was John Tillotson, although even this classic exemplar was pulled up for his erroneous teaching on the nature of Hell's torments; Waterland recommended two confutations of Tillotson on the matter. Dogmatic didacticism would out, especially when doctrine was under consideration, and Waterland was therefore concerned, when recommending John Locke's *Essay concerning Human Understanding* for study, to note that Locke was 'faulty' in other writings.[46] It was the emerging canon of worthy seventeenth-century divines which Waterland most strongly approved, and such hints for reading as the one he provided played their part in creating and sustaining this body of orthodox writings, comprising works by latitudinarians (in addition to Tillotson, he promoted the work of Edward Stillingfleet, Gilbert Burnet and Thomas Sprat), as well as by more consciously orthodox theologians, such as Robert South, George Bull, Robert Nelson, Henry Hammond and John Cosin. Among contemporaries, Waterland instanced the work of Francis Atterbury and Samuel Clarke (with whose metaphysical writings he profoundly disagreed); surprisingly for so orthodox a writer, he also singled out for praise the sermons of Benjamin Hoadly, widely denounced by contemporaries as a heretic, but whose sense and style Waterland judged to be 'very exact and judicious . . . just, close, and clear'.[47] His second edition was primarily concerned with updating philosophical works, although he added such new books in divinity as William Wollaston's celebrated *Religion of Nature* (1722) and Butler's *Analogy of Religion*, along with an important work by a dissenter, Watts' *Scripture History* (1736). His list of approved preachers also contained fresh, largely contemporary names, including his own (added, most probably, by another hand to a work which appeared posthumously).[48] The editor of his sermons drew a distinction between Waterland the polemical and Waterland the '*practical*' divine, seeking to prove that 'He understood *Men* as well as He did *Books*'.[49]

Waterland's recommendations imply a great deal about his own reading practices; something of his actual mode of reading can also be inferred from the presence in the Bodleian Library of books which contain his often detailed annotations. He seems to have been in the habit of annotating those books which he planned to answer, or the reading of which simply led him to such anger that he felt a need to confute the arguments of the opponents so discovered. His contributions to polemical divinity were not inconsiderable, and something of their force can be traced in his annotations to his copy of Matthew Tindal's *Christianity as Old as the Creation*; they constitute the raw materials of his published reply *Scripture Vindicated* (1731). Most of his marginalia are moderate and judicious, but his ire was never far from the surface, as in his observations regarding Tindal's central claim:

> The Gospel has all that ye Law of Nature has, and great Improvements besides. If therefore the Law of Nature is a Thing so valuable and precious, how much more ye Gospel? This writer seems not to know what every Idiot knows, that the *whole* is greater than the *part*.[50]

Sarcasm about the intelligence of this particular Fellow of All Souls permeates Waterland's notes, as in his observations, contra Tindal, on perfection over time as a necessary and essential part of the Gospel dispensation:

> No, but it is *wise* and *good* to bring Things to their perfection by *degrees*. Plants do not grow up to Trees in a night-Time. Children do not grow up to be men but in a course of years: And yet infinite Wisdom orders all these things. Why was not our Writer born a Philosopher? Many years has he lived, and scarce arrived to any perfection, yet.[51]

Arguments *ad hominem* were a favourite device of Waterland when annotating books, as in his observations on Tindal's celebration of 'the blessed Revolution' of 1688; Tindal had turned Catholic during the reign of James II, and his peculiar standing in the Oxford which saw the furore over *The Naked Gospel* was easily adverted to: 'And this writer has a mind to disturb this happy settlement, by throwing us into confusions, in order, perhaps, to bring in Popery again to which he may still retain some Affection, having once embraced it.'[52] In the privacy of his study, Waterland seriously entertained the common fantasy of the apparent promotion of unbelief acting as a means for Catholicism to overwhelm the Protestant settlement: 'Popery in disguise.' Waterland's Anglican militancy left him open to any number of interpretations of Tindal's heterodoxy; thus references to the light of reason led him to conclude that 'This Writer's Religion is most like Quakerism, of any. The *Light Within* is the whole of it.'[53] When Tindal accuses 'Dr. W——d' of the Trinitarian heresy of Sabellianism, Waterland reacts in similar tones, referring to himself in the third person in the proper style of eighteenth-century religious controversy: 'A calumny. For Dr.W: never asserts 3 minds, nor Spirits, but one mind, and one Spirit.'[54] Waterland's use of such very public discourse in the private moment of reading is revealing: it demonstrates the inherently controversial nature of so much divinity in this period.

For a polemical divine, all reading would seem to be a potential occasion of argumentative engagement.[55] Waterland's annotations to a reply to his *Scripture Vindicated* by Conyers Middleton, a Cambridge rival whose claims to theological orthodoxy were decidedly tenuous, reveal an even stronger desire to refute an opponent's arguments than do those in his copy of *Christianity as Old as the Creation*.[56] At Waterland's premature death, Middleton wrote to Warburton that their mutual enemy had bequeathed to Magdalene College 'such of his printed Books, as they find scribbled by his own Hand, for such, I hear, is his own Description of them'.[57] Resolutely orthodox though Waterland may have been in his writings, whether published or in the form of anxious annotations, the reports regarding them of another Cambridge don, Thomas Gray, which he made to the sceptical Horace Walpole, were far from favourable. Central to this distaste for Waterland's polemical industry was Gray's own admiration for Middleton, especially his *Life of Cicero* (1741): for Gray, literary concerns prevailed over any desire for theological orthodoxy. This accounts for his devastating reference to Colley Cibber's criticism of Middleton's *Cicero*, in which, Gray asserted, 'there are whole Pages of Common-Place Stuff, that for Stupidity might have been wrote by Dr Waterland or any other grave Divine'; in 1751, Gray detailed his reading of some unpublished papers by the recently deceased Middleton, and again he is depicted as Waterland's superior, demonstrating that, contra Waterland's claims, 'the primitive Ages of the Church, in w[hi]ch Tradition had its Rise were (even by Confession of the best Scholars & most orthodox Writers) the *Aera of Nonsense and Absurdity*'.[58] In the privacy of letters, the reading of controversial divinity becomes an occasion for amused disdain; literature and literary judgements were considered by Gray and his circle to be a good deal more conducive to rewarding reading than the outpourings of combatively orthodox divines. This division of intellectual labour is very apparent in Gray's references to Warburton, whose praise of his poetry he greatly valued, but whose discomfiture when attacked by Robert Lowth, on the reading of Job, he also much enjoyed (though he avoided any mention of it when visited by Hurd).[59]

Warburton had sought out clerical subscribers, including an archbishop, for the expensive publication of Middleton's *Life of Cicero*, a task which, as Middleton noted, could have caused him problems as the openly concerned friend of an allegedly insincere priest:

> I am obliged to you for my Rt. Revd. Subscriber, and the more so, for the Pains that it cost you to draw them in. Episcopal Gold, like that from the Royal hand, may help to cure the Evil, with which I am said to be infected. I have now got fifteen of that Bench, one or two of whom were ever my Solicitors, but cou'd not persuade some of the rest, that my Work was not levell'd against Religion.[60]

Once acquired, a reputation for unorthodoxy was difficult to dislodge, and in an age of subscription lists it was not a useful reputation to have gained. Warburton himself had a somewhat less damaging reputation for theological experimentation, and such was its force that Middleton could not resist passing on a story involving Waterland to Warburton, assuming his friend to be as fiercely opposed to the champion of orthodoxy as he was. Middleton strongly implied that it was an unholy mixture of authorial jealousy and the passion for orthodoxy that had effectively killed Waterland. Journeying during his last illness, Waterland had been attended by a surgeon who mistook him for the author of the *Divine Legation*, Warburton's recently completed masterpiece, which provoked him into

> a violent Passion, he call'd the poor Fellow a Puppy, and Blockhead, who must needs be ignorant in his Profession, and unfit to administer anything to him, and might possibly poyson his Bowels; and notwithstanding Dr. P-e's endeavours to moderate his Displeasure, by representing the Expediency of the Operation, and the Man's Capacity to perform it, he wou'd hear nothing in his Favour, but

order'd him to be discharg'd, and postpon'd the benefit of the Clyster till he reached his next Stage. With such wretched Passions and Prejudices did this poor Man march to his Grave, which might deserve to be laugh'd at, rather than lamented, if we did not see what pernicious Influence they have in the Church, to defame and depress Men of Sense and Virtue who had had the Courage to despise them.[61]

Warburton himself was quickly to acquire a reputation for being at least as prickly as Waterland, and his public falling out with Middleton over a critique of one of the arguments of the *Divine Legation* contained in a fifth edition of Middleton's *Letter from Rome* (1742) was of a piece with the behaviour attributed to their erstwhile opponent.[62] Warburton, like Waterland, was to turn into a frequent writer against free-thinkers and unorthodox clergy, although he constantly assured his correspondents that he would not reply to such tired free-thinkers as Thomas Morgan, since 'It is that indiscreet conduct of our defenders of Religion, that conveys so many worthless books from hand to hand'.[63] It was not advice which he always followed; he worried that replying to Hume might bring the philosopher more attention than he deserved, so he co-wrote a reply which he attributed to Hurd, his disciple and collaborator.[64] When he did reply to opponents he did so in tones of presumed rectitude, as in his claim that his defence of miracles in a tract on Julian the apostate was something that should interest not only all clergymen but also 'every Christian in England, as much as myself'.[65] Profane and licentious writers, Hurd declared, were fit objects of Warburton's rebuke, and it was 'literary chastisement' rather than civil punishment which served as his weapon in this struggle.[66] It was not, however, as a critic of free-thinkers that Warburton earned his reputation as a literary dictator (albeit one who played a major liberating role for authors in the emergence of literary copyright),[67] but rather as a denouncer of his fellow clergy for failing to fall in with his style of apologetic. None the less, Warburton's achievement was considerable: Montesquieu was charmed by *Julian* (1750), though it also raised Voltaire's ire, and Rousseau was similarly minded to condemn the civil theology of *The Alliance of Church and State* (1736) in *The Social Contract* (1762); Warburton's pioneering work on the deciphering of hieroglyphics in *The Divine Legation of Moses Demonstrated* (1738–41) inspired Condillac.[68] Despite the field day which contemporary critics had with the excesses of the *Divine Legation* (an encyclopaedic if infuriatingly digressive reply to free-thinking), Hurd was not too wide of the mark when he claimed that 'in the whole compass of modern or antient theology, there is nothing equal or similar to this extraordinary performance'.[69] As in France, so elsewhere, laymen read the work with varying degrees of approbation. The Governor of Virginia wrote to Warburton to congratulate him on a work which was effective against infidelity there, citing the testimony of a friend that it had 'made him ten times more a Christian, than he had ever been'.[70] It was the Solicitor General, Charles Yorke, who persuaded Warburton to keep to the task of attempting to complete his work on the *Divine Legation* when criticism from his fellow clergy had all but defeated him.[71] Even abstruse works of apologetic could make their way into the reading of a piously engaged laity.

Warburton was also very much concerned with the reading undertaken by the clergy. In an unpublished 'Charge on the study of theology' he had recommended a reading of works by Ralph Cudworth, Samuel Clarke, Locke and the popularizers of Isaac Newton, all necessary to combat the assaults made by unbelievers on the basic elements of Christian doctrine.[72] In another unpublished tract, 'The true Methodist, or Christian in earnest', he had recommended that students of theology acquaint themselves with 'heathen' classics only as a necessary preparation for true knowledge of the Bible; such reading was to furnish the means of an improving clerical conversation which would further perfect the grounds of 'polemical divinity' in defending the faith in a 'corrupt & captious Age'.[73] This tract was completely revised as *The Doctrine of Grace*, and it elicited predictably hurt replies from both John Wesley and George Whitefield, to whom replies were made in turn.[74] Attacks on Warburton's reading of the functions of the Holy Ghost and the nature of Scripture language also came from such altogether less pastorally exposed divines as John Andrews, a clergyman in Warburton's own diocese, and Thomas Leland of Trinity College, Dublin:[75] as ever, Warburton had managed to alienate his fellow clergy as much as the supposed enemies of 'reasonable Christianity' whom he had hoped to confute.

One of Warburton's most effective clerical critics was Francis Blackburne, a theologian of decidedly progressive opinions, who denounced Warburton's bullying in a tract published in 1756, where he wryly noted that his critics would probably find their way into future editions of the *Dunciad*.[76] Blackburne was to emerge as a leading opponent of the subscription to the Thirty-Nine Articles enforced on undergraduates at the English universities and on clergy when taking up preferment, a cause which he spearheaded in a historical apologetic, *The Confessional*, first published in 1767, and which reached a third, much enlarged edition in 1770. This work was to become a *cause célèbre*, and it encouraged close relations between its clerical author and his sponsor Thomas Hollis, a bibliophile and eighteenth-century Commonwealthman.[77] Blackburne was to compile a two-volume commemoration, *Memoirs of Thomas Hollis* (1780), which also served as a repository of the English Commonwealth tradition, filled as it was with encomia to its heroes, engravings of whom graced its handsome pages. Blackburne also received the tidy sum of £1000 for his labours, a gift from Hollis' heir, Thomas Brand Hollis.[78] Blackburne's very Protestant perspective is evident in his admiration for the work of the dissenting minister Richard Baron on Milton's antiprelatical tracts, which he defended against the disparaging of Milton's politico-theology to be found in the entry on Milton in the *Biographia Britannica*.[79] In this entry Sir Philip Nichols had mildly criticized both *Eikonoklastes* and the *Defence of the People of England*, criticisms which he developed into an explicit rebuke of Milton's politics at its close:

> Hitherto he is admirably excellent, and in many respects without an equal; an honour to his country, and even to human nature. But we must not suffer ourselves to be dazzled by these brilliances, so as not to see and acknowledge his failings; we may wish there had been no such lament, but they are too notorious to deny or disguise: and when we find his principles guilded with the specious name of the love of absolute liberty, and dislike of the trappings and expence of Kingly Majesty, it only serves to bring to our minds his contemporary John Lilburne and his rabble, who were for ever swelling their throats with the same cry. But to leave this irksome (though to an historian indispensible task), of uttering disagreeable truths, we shall be inclined to forgive this, for the sake of the other, part of his moral and religious character; for it was agreed on all sides, that he was a zealous follower of moral beauty and virtue, with a thorough contempt for the opinion of the meer vulgar.[80]

In his *Life* of Milton, Samuel Johnson had been much more critical of Milton's religion. This provoked Blackburne to attack Johnson's own religious prejudices in his *Remarks on Johnson's Life of Milton* (1780), a pendant derived from the pages devoted to the celebration of a Commonwealth pantheon which constitutes so much of the biography of Hollis.[81]

Blackburne also praised Baron in the Hollis biography for his edition of Locke's tracts on toleration, a project financed by Hollis. He further singled out the dissenter Lardner's work on Christian history as a source book of Protestant liberty, as well as that of Jonathan Mayhew, a champion of religious and political dissent in America. Protestant vigilance involved not only the celebration of a canon, whose volumes Hollis reprinted and promoted both in England and America (where he was especially generous to the library at Harvard), but it also affirmed the need for new works and new champions who would write against the defenders of established orthodoxies, whom Blackburne willingly identified for his readers:

> Hence so much work was cut out at one period for John Milton and Andrew Marvel[l]; at another, for John Locke; at a third, for Benjamin Hoadly; and hence more is preparing for some future friends to the civil and religious liberty of English protestants, by the industry of our present Johnsons, Shebbeares, Balguys, Randolphs, &c. &c.[82]

Hollis also had an eye to futurity, and to the educative uses of new institutions, when he bound up ten volumes of defences of and replies to Blackburne's *Confessional*, which he deposited in the British Museum. Hollis' politics were not fashionable, and he had had to indemnify his publishers against the losses they incurred in promoting Commonwealthman politico-theology in both its seventeenth- and eighteenth-century incarnations.[83]

Indeed, Blackburne had acquired a very sharp eye for the wiles of booksellers and printers. A rabid anti-Catholic, he was especially wary of the allegedly dubious influences of Catholic booksellers and printers; not such a peculiar claim when one considers that it was through a Catholic bookseller that the young Gibbon was introduced to the priest who received him into the Catholic communion.[84] It was Gibbon's publisher Thomas Cadell, a future Unitarian, who published *The Confessional*, a work to which Archbishop Secker encouraged replies, as did 'Warburtonian' authors, and it was another publisher, John Rivington, who revealed to Secker the name of the author of *The Confessional*. Blackburne dramatically alleged that it was a habit of the dogmatically assertive Secker to trace out the anonymity of the writers of 'what he called obnoxious books; and [he] sometimes used means to gratify this passion which would not have passed for allowable practice among horse-dealers in Smithfield'.[85]

It was as a consciously disinterested promoter of good divinity that Richard Watson, Regius Professor of Divinity at Cambridge and a distant member of the circles which intersected around Blackburne, produced a six–volume compilation of theological writings in 1785. This undertaking was complementary to that made half a century earlier by Waterland; it was designed for clergy who had not been to university, and for those who had not studied there beyond the completion of their BA degree. It was also to be read by 'young men of rank and fortune' as a preservative against infidelity, 'which is the disgrace of the age'.[86] Watson was also, however, somewhat removed from the polemical concerns of Waterland, noting, without apparent concern, that 'the taste of the present age is not calculated for making great exertions in Theological Criticism and Philology'. Nor was he yet concerned to build up a storehouse of orthodoxy (of which as a theological progressive he was deeply suspicious); his intentions were practical rather than theological:

> I do not consider the Tracts which are here published as sufficient to make what is called a deep divine, but they will go a great way towards making, what is of more worth – a well-informed Christian.[87]

Watson believed that 'the aera is approaching very fast, when Theological Acrimony shall be swallowed up in Evangelical Charity, and a liberal tolera-tion become the distinguishing feature of every church in Christendom.' The very ecumenism of his chosen tracts was a demonstration of this belief, as he noted when defending his choice of writings by dissenters (such as Lardner): 'it was a circumstance of utter indifference to me, whether it was out of Paul, or Apollos, or Cephas, provided it was of Christ.'[88] A thousand copies of the tracts were sold within three months; some bishops remained unhappy at Watson's inclusion of works by dissenters.[89] In his artless memoirs, Watson admitted that it was only after he had secured the Regius Chair of Divinity at the age of 34 that he applied himself 'with great eagerness to the study of divinity'. His decision to concentrate on what he found for himself in Scripture meant that he refused to engage with 'bulky systems of German divinity' which slept unconsulted in university libraries; he reduced the study of divinity so as to preclude 'the opinions of councils, fathers, churches, bishops, and other men, as little inspired as myself'. This assertive anti-dogmatism stood him in good stead on occasions of theological controversy:

> I never troubled myself with answering any arguments which the opponents in the divinity schools brought against the articles of the church, nor ever admitted their authority as decisive of a difficulty; but I used on such occasions to say to them, holding the *New Testament* in my hand, *En sacrum codicem!* [Behold the sacred book][90]

Such evasiveness disappeared in the face of attacks on Christianity from unbelievers, and Watson replied both to Gibbon in 1776 (thus swelling the ranks of a clerical cottage industry), and, more testily, to Thomas Paine's *Age of Reason* in 1796. He even considered replying to allegedly unchristian elements in Thomas Malthus' *Essay on Population*, while admitting that he had not read the work in question.[91] Replies to the writings of supposed enemies of the faith remained a staple of theological writing throughout the eighteenth century, and there could be no doubt that the prospect of preferment sometimes determined both the tone and the very appearance of such works:

a decided enemy of Watson thought this the only reason for his jousting against Gibbon and Paine, since self-interest motivated him in all his ventures. To his critic, Watson was plainly another Warburton, his memoirs constituting 'one of the most revolting effusions of egotism which the literary history of this country can boast'.[92]

Both the reading and, more especially, the writing of theological books was thus a highly competitive business, and one in which it was possible to lose everything, including one's reputation, as Bury had discovered. Equally, as both Warburton and Watson found, it was no guarantee of preferment beyond the indifferently beneficed sees of Gloucester and Llandaff. Even sermonizing could serve as an opportunity to exercise rivalrous rancour, the pulpit frequently acting as a site for political posturing; small wonder that connoisseurs of the *odium theologicum* should have hit upon Warburton with such ill-disguised glee. A letter from Gray to Walpole typifies the intense theatricality of texts which were designed to be spoken as well as read, something which the modern reader has to bear in mind when reading them in the very different discursive realms of a pronouncedly secular age:

> now I am talking of Bishops, I must tell you, that not long ago B[p] Warburton in a sermon at Court asserted, that all preferments were bestow'd on the most illiterate & worthless objects, & in speaking turn'd himself about & stared directly at the B[p.] of London. he added, that if any one arose distinguish'd for merit & learning, there was a combination of dunces to keep him down. I need not tell you, that he expected the B[k] of London himself, when Terrick got it. so ends my ecclesiastical history.[93]

Notes

1. Ed. Melvyn and Joan New (Gainesville: University Press of Florida, 1978), Vol. 2, p. 754 (Book IX, ch. viii).

2. For useful discussion, see John Redwood, *Reason, Ridicule and Religion: The Age of Enlightenment in England, 1660–1750* (London: Thames and Hudson, 1976), pp. 156–61; Nicholas Tyacke, 'Religious controversy' in Tyacke (ed.), *The History of the University of Oxford*, Vol. 4: *Seventeenth-Century Oxford* (Oxford: Clarendon Press, 1997), pp. 569–619, at pp. 616–17.

3. James Anthony Froude, *Nemesis of Faith*, 2nd edn (London, 1849); C. J. Walsh, 'A critical study of the works of J. A. Froude with special reference to the novels, the essays, and the biography of Carlyle', unpublished DPhil dissertation, Oxford (1982), pp. 69–72, 101–3.

4. See Jeffrey von Arx, 'The Victorian crisis of faith as a crisis of vocation'; Bernard Lightman, '*Robert Elsmere* and the agnostic crises of faith', in Richard J. Helmstadter and Bernard Lightman (eds), *Victorian Faith in Crisis: Essays on Continuity and Change in Nineteenth-Century*

Religious Belief (Basingstoke: Macmillan, 1990), pp. 262–82, 283–311; Rosemary Ashton, 'Doubting clerics: from James Anthony Froude to *Robert Elsmere* via George Eliot', in David Jasper and T. R. Wright (eds), *The Critical Spirit and the Will to Believe: Essays in Nineteenth-Century Literature and Religion* (Basingstoke: Macmillan, 1989), pp. 69–87; P. G. Scott, 'A. H. Clough: a case study in Victorian doubt', in Derek Baker (ed.), *Schism, Heresy, and Religious Protest, Studies in Church History*, 9 (1972): 383–89.

5. Pierre Bourdieu, 'The field of cultural production, or: the economic world reversed' and 'The production of belief: contribution to an economy of symbolic goods', in *The Field of Cultural Production: Essays on Art and Literature* (Cambridge: Polity Press, 1993), pp. 29–73, 74–111.

6. James Parkinson, *The Fire's Continued at Oxford: Or, The Decree of the Convocation for Burning the Naked Gospel, Considered* (n. pl., 1690), pp. 2, 3, 11. On Parkinson, see Anthony Wood, *Athenae Oxonienses*, ed. Philip Bliss (London, 1813–20), Vol. 4, p. 571.

7. Anon., *A Defence of the Proceedings of the Right Reverend the Visitor and Fellows of Exeter College in Oxford* (London, 1690), pp. 46, 48.

8. James Colmer, *The Account Examined: Or, A Vindication of Dr. Arthur Bury, Rector of Exeter College* (London, 1690), p. 7.

9. Arthur Bury, *The Naked Gospel* (London, 1690), preface (unpaginated).

10. Thomas Long, *An Answer to a Socinian Treatise, Call'd The Naked Gospel* (London, 1691), preface (unpaginated), and p. 158.

11. Anne Goldgar, *Impolite Learning: Conduct and Community in the Republic of Letters, 1680–1750* (New Haven, CT: Yale University Press, 1995).

12. Jean Le Clerc, *An Historical Vindication of the Naked Gospel, Recommended to the University of Oxford* (n. pl., 1690), 'The preface to the reader' (unpaginated).

13. Wood, *Athenae Oxonienses*, Vol. 1, p. 4, and Vol. 4, pp. 482–85.

14. Arthur Bury, *The Danger of Delaying Repentance; Set forth in a Sermon Preached to the University, at St. Mary's Church in Oxford, On New Year's Day, 1691/2* (London, 1692); Bury, *Latitudinarius Orthodox* (London, 1697). As late as 1725, Henry Felton, Principal of St Edmund Hall, felt it his duty to attack Bury's heterodoxy: *The Resurrection of the Same Numerical Body, and its Reunion to the Same Soul; Asserted in a Sermon Preached Before the University of Oxford, at St. Mary's On Easter-Monday, 1725. In Which Mr Locke's Notions of Personality and Identity are Confuted. And the Author of the Naked Gospel is Answered* (Oxford, 1725).

15. Henry Fielding, *Joseph Andrews*, ed. Martin C. Battestin (Oxford: Clarendon Press, 1967), Book I, chs xv, p. 67; xvi, pp. 73, 75; xvii, pp. 79–80.

16. *Ibid.*, ch. i, p. 17.

17. Henry Fielding, *The History of Tom Jones, a Foundling*, ed. Martin C. Battestin and Fredson Bowers (Oxford: Clarendon Press, 1975), Vol. 2, p. 687 (Book XIII, ch. i).

18. Warburton to Knapton, 9 December 1751, in Donald W. Nichol (ed.), *Pope's Literary Legacy: The Book-Trade Correspondence of William Warburton and John Knapton With Other Letters and Documents 1744–1780* (Oxford: Oxford Bibliographical Society, 1991), p. 50.

19. *Ibid.*, pp. 134–7 (Warburton to Garrick, 7 March and 16 June 1760); Arthur H. Cash, *Laurence Sterne: The Later Years* (London: Methuen, 1986), pp. 5–7, 23; A. W. Evans, *Warburton and the Warburtonians: A Study in Some Eighteenth-Century Controversies* (London: Oxford University Press, 1932), pp. 226–32; F. M. Doherty, 'Sterne and Warburton: another look', *British Journal for Eighteenth-Century Studies*, 1 (1978): 20–30; Melvyn New, 'Sterne, Warburton, and the burden of exuberant wit', *Eighteenth-Century Studies*, 15 (1981–2): 245–74.

20. Hurd to Warburton, 18 March 1761, in Sarah Brewer (ed.), *The Early Letters of Bishop Richard Hurd 1739–1762* (Woodbridge: Boydell Press, 1995), pp. 365–9. He was equally critical

of Sterne when again praising the 'incomparable' *Hèloïse* in a letter to Thomas Balguy, 1 May 1761, pp. 373–4.

21. William Law, *A Practical Treatise upon Christian Perfection* (London, 1726), pp. 329, 349.

22. For a more negative assessment of Law's achievement in this respect, see Peter Malekin, 'The character-sketches in the *Serious Call*', *Studia Neophilologica*, 38 (1966): 245–60.

23. *The Autobiographies of Edward Gibbon*, ed. John Murray (London: John Murray, 1896), pp. 23–7. For an interesting reading of Law, see John Sitter, *Literary Loneliness in Mid-Eighteenth-Century England* (Ithaca, NY: Cornell University Press, 1982), pp. 50–73.

24. Peter Seary, *Lewis Theobald and the Editing of Shakespeare* (Oxford: Clarendon Press, 1990), pp. 102–30; Simon Jarvis, *Scholars and Gentlemen: Shakespearian Textual Criticism and Representations of Scholarly Labour, 1725–1765* (Oxford: Clarendon Press, 1995), pp. 13, 83–7, 107–28, 160–4, 175–80; Marcus Walsh, *Shakespeare, Milton and Eighteenth-Century Literary Editing: The Beginnings of Interpretative Scholarship* (Cambridge: Cambridge University Press, 1997), pp. 149–54 and *passim*; Jonathan Brody Kramnick, *Making the English Canon: Print Capitalism and the Cultural Past, 1700–1770* (Cambridge: Cambridge University Press, 1998), pp. 88–100, 168–89.

25. William Warburton, 'Preface' to *The Works of Shakespeare* (London, 1747), Vol. 1, pp. vii–xxviii, at pp. ix, xv–xvi, xxi, xxii–xxiii, xxvi.

26. Richard Hurd, *Letters on Chivalry and Romance* (London, 1762), pp. 102, 117–18.

27. Tom Keymer, *Richardson's* Clarissa *and the Eighteenth-Century Reader* (Cambridge: Cambridge University Press, 1992), pp. 63, 211–12. On 7 November 1742, Hurd effusively thanked a friend, Cox Macro, for inducing him to read *Pamela*: *Early Letters*, pp. 91–2.

28. John Brewer, 'Reconstructing the reader: prescriptions, texts and strategies in Anna Larpent's reading', in James Raven, Helen Small and Naomi Tadmor (eds), *The Practice and Representation of Reading in England* (Cambridge: Cambridge University Press, 1996), pp. 226–45, at p. 233. On the religious context of the novel, see Nicholas Lyons, 'Satiric technique in *The Spiritual Quixote*: some comments', *Durham University Journal*, 66 (1973–74): 266–77.

29. Richard Graves, *The Spiritual Quixote*, ed. Clarence Tracy (London: Oxford University Press, 1967), p. 4.

30. *The Monthly Review*, 22 (1760): 422–31. For discussion, see Frank M. Donoghue, *The Fame-Machine: Book-Reviewing and Eighteenth-Century Literary Careers* (Stanford, CA: Stanford University Press, 1996), pp. 72–3, 75–6, 81, 85. The first part of the review was written by Ruffhead, and the second half by Rose, on whom see Benjamin Christie Nangle, *The Monthly Review First Series 1749–1789: Indexes of Contributors and Articles* (Oxford: Clarendon Press, 1934), pp. 37, 39, 203.

31. Graves, *The Spiritual Quixote*, p. 3.

32. Warburton's anonymous contribution forms a large part of the translator's preface, and can be found in Charles Jarvis, translator, *The Life and Exploits of the Ingenious Gentleman Don Quixote de la Mancha* (London, 1742), Vol. 1, pp. vii–xxiii.

33. Alexander Pope, *Essay on Man*, ed. Maynard Mack, *The Twickenham Edition of the Works of Alexander Pope*, Vol. 3, Part 1 (London: Methuen, 1950); Mark Pattison, 'Pope and his editors', in Henry Nettleship (ed.) *Essays* (Oxford: Clarendon Press, 1889), Vol. 2, pp. 350–95; Evans, *Warburton and the Warburtonians*, ch. 5. When John Wilkes chose to libel Warburton in 1763 he did so by making him the verbose and dubiously erudite editor of a pornographic parody, the *Essay on Woman*.

34. Pope, *The Dunciad*, ed. Valerie Rumbold (Harlow: Longman, 1999); Arthur Friedman, 'Pope and Deism (*The Dunciad* IV, 459–92)', in James L. Clifford and Louis A. Landa (eds), *Pope and his Contemporaries: Essays Presented to George Sherburn* (Oxford: Clarendon Press, 1949),

pp. 89–95; B. W. Young, '"See *Mystery* to *Mathematics* fly!"': Pope's *Dunciad* and the critique of religious rationalism', *Eighteenth-Century Studies*, 26 (1993): 435–48.

35. *Letters from a Late Eminent Prelate to One of His Friends* (2nd edn, London, 1809), Letter CXXIX (17 May 1759), p. 285; Edward Young, *Night Thoughts*, ed. Stephen Cornford (Cambridge: Cambridge University Press, 1989).

36. Doddridge to Mercy Doddridge, 21/22 December 1742, in Geoffrey F. Nuttall (ed.), *Calendar of the Correspondence of Philip Doddridge DD (1702–1751)* (London: Historical Manuscripts Commission, for the Northamptonshire Record Society, 1979), p. 165.

37. Isabel Rivers, *Reason, Grace, and Sentiment: A Study of the Language of Religion and Ethics in England, 1660–1780*, Vol. 2: *Shaftesbury to Hume* (Cambridge: Cambridge University Press, 2000), p. 15.

38. David Hume, 'Of national characters', in Eugene F. Miller (ed.), *Essays, Moral, Political and Literary*, rev. edn (Indianapolis: The Liberty Fund Press, 1987), p. 199n.

39. B. W. Young, '"Scepticism in Excess"': Gibbon and eighteenth-century Christianity', *Historical Journal*, 42 (1998): 79–99.

40. Sterne, *Tristram Shandy*, Vol. 1, p. 462 (Book V, ch. xxviii).

41. Isabel Rivers, *Reason, Grace, and Sentiment*, Vol. 1: *Whichcote to Wesley* (Cambridge: Cambridge University Press, 1992), pp. 173–85.

42. John Disney, *A Sermon Preached in the Unitarian Chapel, in Essex Street, London, on Occasion of the Death of the Rev. Joseph Priestley, L.L.D. F.R.S. &c.&c.* (London, 1804), pp. 8–9, 16–18; Thomas Jervis, *The Memorial of the Just* (London, 1817), p. 37.

43. Thomas Jervis, *Reflections on the State of Religion and Knowledge, at the Close of the Eighteenth Century: A Discourse Delivered on that Occasion in the Chapel of Princes-Street, Westminster* (London, 1801), p. 27.

44. Sterne, *Tristram Shandy*, Vol. 2, p. 514 (Book VI, ch. xi).

45. Daniel Waterland, *Advice to a Young Student, With a Method of Study for the Four First Years* (Cambridge, 1730), 'Advertisement by the author', and pp. 1 and 3.

46. *Ibid.*, pp. 7, 12, 13–14, 24, 23.

47. *Ibid.*, pp. 22–32.

48. Waterland, *Advice to a Young Student*, 2nd edn (Oxford, 1755), pp. 33–4.

49. 'Preface' to Waterland, *Sermons on Several Important Subjects of Religion and Morality* (London, 1742), Vol. 2, pp. ii–lxviii, at p. vii.

50. Waterland's annotation to Matthew Tindal, *Christianity as Old as the Creation: Or, the Gospel, a Republication of the Religion of Nature* (London, 1730), Bodleian Shelfmark Rawl. 4° 92, at p. 59.

51. *Ibid.*, Waterland's annotation at p. 60.

52. *Ibid.*, Waterland's annotation at p. 139.

53. *Ibid.*, Waterland's annotation at p. 292.

54. *Ibid.*, Waterland's annotation at p. 321.

55. On the deeply ideological nature of much early modern marginalia, see Steven Zwicker, 'Reading the margins: politics and the habits of appropriation', in Kevin Sharpe and Steven N. Zwicker (eds), *Refiguring Revolutions: Aesthetics and Politics from the English Revolution to the Romantic Revolution* (Berkeley, CA: University of California Press, 1998), pp. 101–15.

56. The annotations are to be found in Conyers Middleton, *A Letter to Dr. Waterland; Containing Some Remarks on his Vindication of Scripture* (1731), Bodleian Shelfmark Rawl. 8° 437.

57. Middleton to Warburton, 8 January 1741, in *The Miscellaneous Works of the Late Reverend and Learned Conyers Middleton, D.D. Principal Librarian of the University of Cambridge* (London, 1752), vol. 2, p. 484.

58. Paget Toynbee and Leonard Whibley (eds), *Correspondence of Thomas Gray* (Oxford: Clarendon Press, 1935), Vol. 1, letters 131, 161, at pp. 264, 348.

59. *Ibid.*, Vol. 2, letters 251, 256, 262, at pp. 532, 538, 551.

60. Middleton to Warburton, 4 September 1739, in *The Miscellaneous Works*, Vol. 2, p. 479.

61. Middleton to Warburton, 8 January 1741, in *ibid.*, Vol. 2, p. 485.

62. Middleton, 'Post-script, in which Mr. Warburton's opinion concerning the paganism of Rome is particularly considered', in *A Letter from Rome*, 5th edn (London, 1742), pp. 225–48.

63. Letter to Thomas Birch in 1741, cited in John Nichols, *Literary Anecdotes of the Eighteenth Century* (London, 1812), Vol. 5, p. 570.

64. *Ibid.*, letter to Doddridge, 15 June 1750, p. 601n; *Letters From the Reverend Dr. Warburton, Bishop of Gloucester, to the Hon Charles Yorke, From 1752 to 1770* (London, 1812), letter of 31 December 1757, p. 31; Richard Hurd, *A Discourse By Way of General Preface to the Quarto Edition of Bishop Warburton's Works, Containing Some Account of the Life, Writings, and Character of the Author*, (London, 1794), pp. 77–82.

65. Warburton, *Julian* (London, 1750); letter to Balguy, 17 January 1753, cited in Nichols, *Literary Anecdotes*, Vol. 5, pp. 601–2.

66. Hurd, *A Discourse*, p. 113.

67. Mark Rose, *Authors and Owners: The Invention of Copyright* (Cambridge, MA: Harvard University Press, 1993), esp. pp. 68–74.

68. Hurd, *A Discourse*, pp. 65–6; B. W. Young, *Religion and Enlightenment in Eighteenth-Century England: Theological Debate from Locke to Burke* (Oxford: Clarendon Press, 1998), pp. 170, 192–3; Nicholas Hudson, *Writing and European Thought 1600–1830* (Cambridge: Cambridge University Press, 1994), pp. 55–71, 76–83.

69. Hurd, *A Discourse*, p. 36.

70. *Ibid.*, pp. 48–9.

71. *Letters from Warburton*, letter of 11 September 1768, p. 94.

72. *A Selection From Unpublished Papers of The Right Reverend William Warburton, D.D. Late Bishop of Gloucester*, ed. Francis Kilvert (London, 1841), pp. 358–68.

73. Warburton, 'The true Methodist, or Christian in earnest', John Rylands Library, Manchester, Mss. 253 AB, fos.50r–69r, 93r–94r, 103r–105r.

74. John Wesley, *A Letter to the Right Reverend The Lord Bishop of Gloucester: Occasioned by His Tract, On the Office and Operations of the Holy Spirit* (London, 1763); George Whitefield, *Observations On Some Fatal Mistakes, In A Book Lately Published, and Intitled, The Doctrine of Grace* (Edinburgh, 1763); Samuel Charndler, *An Answer to the Rev. Mr. John Wesley's Letter to William, Lord Bishop of Gloucester* (London, 1763).

75. John Andrews, *The Scripture-Doctrine of Grace. In Answer to a Treatise on the Doctrine of Grace, by William Lord Bishop of Gloucester* (London, 1763); Thomas Leland, *A Dissertation On The Principles Of Human Eloquence: With Particular Regard to the Style and Composition of the New Testament* (Dublin, 1764).

76. Francis Blackburne, *Remarks on Dr Warburton's Account of the Sentiments of the Early Jews Concerning the Soul* (1756), in *The Works Theological and Miscellaneous of the Revd. Francis Blackburne, Archdeacon of Cleveland*, ed. Francis Blackburne, LLB (Cambridge, 1804–5), Vol. 2, pp. 261–338, at p. 268.

77. On the Blackburne–Hollis circle, see Annabel Patterson, *Early Modern Liberalism* (Cambridge: Cambridge University Press, 1997), pp. 27–61; and Caroline Robbins, 'The strenuous Whig: Thomas Hollis of Lincoln's Inn', in Barbara Taft (ed.), *Absolute Liberty: A Selection of the Articles and Papers of Caroline Robbins* (Hamden, CT, 1982), pp. 168–205. More broadly, see Robbins' classic study, *The Eighteenth-Century Commonwealthman: Studies in the Transmission,*

Development and Circumstance of English Liberal Thought from the Restoration of Charles II until the War with the Thirteen Colonies (Cambridge, MA: Harvard University Press, 1959).

78. Francis Blackburne, *Memoirs of Thomas Hollis, Esq.* (London, 1780), Vol. 1, pp. 307, 371; John Disney, *Memoirs of Thomas Brand Hollis, Esq.* (London, 1808), pp. 8–10.

79. Blackburne, *Memoirs of Hollis*, Vol. 1, pp. 61, 93–5, 137–45.

80. Sir Philip Nichols, 'John Milton', in *Biographia Britannica: Or, The Lives of the Most Eminent Persons Who Have Flourished in Great Britain and Ireland, From the Earliest Ages Down to the Present Times* (London, 1747–66), Vol. 5, pp. 3106–19, at pp. 3115 and 3118. For the identification of the authors of these biographies, see the second edition of the *Biographia*, ed. Andrew Kippis, Vol. 1 (London, 1778), p. xx, and Vol. 2 (London, 1780), p. viii. On the early republican endorsement of Milton's politics, see Nicholas von Maltzahn, 'The Whig Milton, 1667–1700', in David Armitage, Armand Himy and Quentin Skinner (eds), *Milton and Republicanism* (Cambridge, 1995), pp. 229–53.

81. W. H. Bond, 'Thomas Hollis and Samuel Johnson', in James Engell (ed.), *Johnson and His Age* (Cambridge, MA: Harvard University Press, 1984), pp. 83–105. For Johnson's notably prejudiced account, see 'Milton' in *The Lives of the English Poets*, ed. George Birkbeck Hill (Oxford: Clarendon Press, 1905), Vol. 1, pp. 84–194.

82. Blackburne, *Memoirs of Hollis*, Vol. 1, pp. 81–2, 224, 253, 259–61, 353. Dr Johnson's name was often allied with that of the political writer John Shebbeare in Whig polemic, especially in the wake of the war with the thirteen colonies. In *An Answer to the Queries, Contained in a Letter to Dr Shebbeare* (London, 1775), Shebbeare had ill-advisedly attacked the memory of William III and the actions of the Presbyterians in the seventeenth century, for which he was roundly reprimanded by the prominent lawyer Hugh Baillie in *A Letter to Dr. Shebbeare: Containing A Refutation of His Arguments Concerning the Boston and Quebec Acts of Parliament: And His Aspersions Upon the Memory of King William, and the Protestant Dissenters* (London, 1775). Thomas Balguy, Archdeacon of Winchester, was denounced by Blackburne for his defences of subscription to the Thirty-Nine Articles as a guarantee of what he saw as church order, and what Blackburne identified as clerical tyranny: particular vituperation was heaped on Balguy's sermon *On Church Authority* (London, 1769), the argument of which he had extended in *A Charge Delivered to the Clergy of the Archdeaconry of Winchester, in the Year 1772* (London, 1772). Thomas Randolph, President of Corpus Christi College, Oxford, had argued vehemently against Blackburne and his fellow anti-subscription petitioners in a strongly worded tract: *The Reasonableness of Requiring Subscription to Articles of Religion From Persons to be Admitted to Holy Orders, or a Cure of Souls, Vindicated in a Charge Delivered to the Clergy of the Diocese of Oxford in the Year 1771* (Oxford, 1771). On Hollis' gifts to Harvard, see Caroline Robbins, 'Library of liberty – assembled for Harvard College by Thomas Hollis of Lincoln's Inn', in *Absolute Liberty*, pp. 206–29.

83. Blackburne, *Memoirs of Hollis*, Vol. 1, pp. 371–2, 399–400.

84. Colin Haydon, *Anti-Catholicism in Eighteenth-Century England, c. 1714–80* (Manchester: Manchester University Press, 1993), pp. 184–92; Blackburne, *Memoirs of Hollis*, Vol. 1, p. 315; Patricia B. Craddock, *Young Edward Gibbon, Gentleman of Letters* (Baltimore, MD: Johns Hopkins University Press, 1982), pp. 50–2.

85. Blackburne, *Memoirs of Hollis*, Vol. 1, pp. 326, 406.

86. Richard Watson, 'Preface' to *A Collection of Theological Tracts* (Cambridge, 1785), Vol. 1, pp. v–xx, at pp. vii–ix.

87. *Ibid.*, Vol. 1, p. v.

88. *Ibid.*, Vol. 1, pp. xviii–xix.

89. Richard Watson, *Anecdotes of the Life of Richard Watson, Bishop of Landaff* (London, 1817), p. 136.

90. *Ibid.*, pp. 33, 38–9.

91. *Ibid.*, pp. 60–1, 475–8; Watson, *An Apology for Christianity, in a Series of Letters Addressed to Edward Gibbon, Esq., Author of The Decline and Fall of the Roman Empire* (London, 1776); Watson, *An Apology for the Bible, in a Series of Letters Addressed to Thomas Paine* (London, 1796).

92. Anon., *A Critical Examination of the Bishop of Landaff's Posthumous Volume, Entitled 'Anecdotes of his Life'* (London, 1818), p. 90.

93. *Correspondence of Gray*, Vol. 2, letter 401, at p. 872.

CHAPTER 4

THE HISTORY MARKET IN EIGHTEENTH-CENTURY ENGLAND

KAREN O'BRIEN

Introduction

Surveying the enormous range and quantity of historical writings in eighteenth-century England, it seems almost impossible to hazard any definition which would distinguish such works from biographies, memoirs, annals, antiquarian surveys or fictional narratives since all described themselves as 'histories'. Yet eighteenth-century readers had a clear sense of what constituted proper, narrative history; it was a well-established genre of good, classical pedigree, and its orientation towards élite, educated audiences was usually underscored by expensive, multi-volume, folio formats, dedications to aristocratic or royal personages, and other para-textual material such as appendices, indexes and endnotes. Even in the case of relatively cheap, octavo editions of histories shipped over from Dublin, or produced by English printers to recoup losses made on folio issues, purchasers felt that they were buying something that was, by its very nature, part of a sophisticated culture of readership. Narrative history, particularly political history, had traditionally played an important role in the education of gentlemen and men of affairs. To acquire and read works of history was, in part, to enter into that world of political seriousness.

There were those, excluded by social position or gender from the political sphere, who found it hard to see the relevance of history to their lives. The early eighteenth-century feminist writer Mary Astell complained that male writers

> recommend history; tho' with submission, history can only serve us for amusement and a subject of discourse. For tho' it may be of use to the men who

govern affairs, to know how their fore-fathers acted, yet what is this to us, who have nothing to do with such business?[1]

But there were many more, within and outside the country's political classes, who found more than just 'amusement' in history, and who helped to sustain the modest but growing market for such works. The achievement of eighteenth-century publishers and booksellers was to attract a broader, more diverse readership for history without fatally compromising its prestigious image. Historians followed suit, adopting a traditional, classical rhetoric to describe their historical practice (history teaches prudence and wisdom to statesmen, history is philosophy teaching by examples, and so on), even as they broadened the generic and thematic scope of their works to reflect the new kinds of audience.

The staple audience for narrative histories remained, throughout this period, the élite, professional and clerical acquirers of personal libraries. Print runs were mainly in the thousands rather than in the tens of thousands, and costs were likely to deter poorer readers. James Tyrrell's three-volume *General History of England* (1696–1704), for instance, cost 30 shillings when it came out, a figure amounting to around 1.5 per cent of an average gentleman's annual income.[2] There was nevertheless a steady growth in the readership for demanding, lengthy histories, indicated by the success of such works as David Hume's *History of England* (in its later editions) or William Robertson's *History of Charles V*. This corresponded with a general increase in the demand for works of 'polite' literature, but it also reflected public support for history as a genre: more than other kinds of literature, history was perceived to be bound up with national prestige, and an increasingly prestige-conscious English public was eager to foster internationally famous English historical productions. As we shall see, publishers and entrepreneurial historians exploited public commitment to history as a nationally important form of writing, regularly falling back on patriotic rhetoric to attract donations for research, subscribers and buyers. Periodicals such as the *Gentleman's Magazine* and the *Critical Review* played a significant role in bolstering this national demand for good histories, with some historians, such as Tobias Smollett, reviewing and publicizing their own works in patriotic terms.

Whether histories were read or simply displayed on library shelves, their increasing popularity with consumers was also part of a more general transformation in the historical awareness of the English people, leading to an enhanced sense of imaginative participation in the great currents of history. This had commercial and generic consequences for narrative history; historians paid greater attention to the social and artistic dimensions of life in the past, and, by the end of the century, produced many more specific studies of particular periods, regions or persons, or topics such as literary history, histories of costume, chivalry and sport. The particularist cultural or biographical turns which history took in the later eighteenth century did not spell the end of grand narratives of nations or empires, but they did reflect an audience engagement with history that was as much imaginative as moral or prudential.

Given the high cost of producing historical works, reader demand and publisher initiative inevitably played a significant role in determining what kinds of works were printed. The clearest example of market-led historical writing, discussed in greater detail below, was the production of the numerous histories of England commissioned, compiled, translated or stitched together by firms and consortia of printers. For the first time in England, history became a commercial venture, with publishers appointing general editors to oversee multi-volume projects and translations. Publication of works other than small, local histories was almost exclusively London-based, albeit with some stiff competition from 'pirated' imports from Dublin. Scottish-based publishers, such as Balfour, Hamilton and Neil, who published the first volume of Hume's *History of Great Britain* (1754) (as it was originally entitled) but who relinquished the project to London houses after poor English sales, were generally unable to compete in terms of distribution, sales and copyright fees.[3] Owing to the costs and risks involved, many histories were produced by consortia of booksellers. Serial publication of histories in small, affordable units was common for multi-volume projects, with subscribers signing up for weekly or monthly instalments in the (sometimes misplaced) trust that their purchases would eventually build into a complete work. The most spectacular of these ventures was the forty-four-volume, serially published 'Ancient Part' of *The Universal History* (1730–44), produced and sold by a shifting confederation of booksellers, and compiled from a variety of English and translated sources.

There were numerous other such ventures on a lesser scale, and there was also the increasingly common practice of commissioning a 'continuation' of an existing history, and then either marketing it as a job-lot with the first history, or, at least, encouraging readers to buy and see it in the reflected glory of the original. Hume's publisher, William Strahan, tried to persuade him to bring his *History of England* up to the present day, instead of stopping at 1688, warning him that otherwise 'we shall be pestered with continuations from some of our hackney writers'.[4] This was an accurate prediction, and Hume's decision to leave his history as it was effectively condemned the existing volumes to appear, throughout the late eighteenth and nineteenth centuries, with the works of Smollett and various other writers attached as 'continuations'. Cadell and Baldwin even produced an edition of Smollett's *Continuation* harmonized, in terms of typographical presentation, with the latest edition of Hume, 'so that any gentleman, possessed of the latter, may take up [Smollett's] History of the Revolution, where Hume breaks off, and find a regular connexion in his complete History given by Smollet'.[5]

Despite the entrepreneurial aspects of much history publication, the commercialization of history and the rise of the authoritative historian were, paradoxically, mutually reinforcing events. Without investment from the publishing industry, history would have had few other means of support. The professionalization of the discipline did not get underway in England until after this period. Chairs in history at Oxford and Cambridge were created in the early part of the century, but, with the exception of Robert Brady at Cambridge, and Joseph Priestley at the Warrington Academy, very few historians of the period were based in English educational institutions. Oxford University made its most substantial contribution by bearing the whole burden of publishing the Earl of Clarendon's *History of the Rebellion* (a copyright which, by statute, the university retains to this day), but generally it was publishers and booksellers who provided the research expenses and copying fees necessary to historians, and promoted history as a worthwhile, scholarly endeavour. Certainly there were other sources of financial patronage, although few benefited from them. Laurence Echard, a clergyman of limited means, received £300 from George I towards his *History of England* (1707–18), and, in the late 1730s, Thomas Carte was granted £50 a year for seven years by the City of London to write a history on the same subject (he also, more discreetly, accepted funds from the mainly Jacobite Society for a History of England).[6]

In general, the tendency was for history to become less institutionalized, and less closely affiliated with Crown, Church and university. The case was very different in Scotland where history had long been part of the university curriculum, and where many of the country's most important historians, such as Robertson and John Millar, held university posts. English historians were not professionals, and they were no longer men of affairs, as historians such as Francis Bacon or Clarendon had been; they adopted instead the personae of studious, reflective gentlemen of letters. Edward Gibbon, an independent gentleman scholar, liked to refer to himself as having assumed the 'name' and 'character' of a 'Historian'.[7] It was a name and character largely inaccessible to women writers, who generally lacked either the personal wealth (Gibbon spent a great deal of his resources acquiring a working library) or the backing of publishers or patrons necessary to embark on ambitious historical projects. The conspicuous exception was Catharine Macaulay, who had used her moderate means and leisure to carry out primary research in the British Library for her eight-volume *History of England* (1763–83).[8] Macaulay felt obliged to invent her own 'character' as a historian, and commissioned portraits of herself as variously Clio or a Roman matron which appeared as frontispiece engravings in her volumes; but she clearly benefited as a female historian from the respectability which others had gained for narrative history.

For the purposes of this chapter, the eighteenth century will be subdivided into three partly chronological, partly generic phases of historical production: (1) the first five decades, including the publication of Clarendon's *History of the Rebellion* and of numerous party political histories of England up to and including the successful works of Hume, Smollett and Macaulay; (2) the period of the 'high' Enlightenment from the 1750s to the 1780s, including the great works of Robertson and Gibbon; and (3) the later eighteenth century, during which time history was transformed into a more diverse practice, leading to the birth of what will be called 'cultural antiquarianism'. This periodization is, of course, inadequate for such a large and complex field, but it gives some idea of the main preoccupations of the history market, as well as the generic evolution of history from political narrative to civil history, and then to a novelized kind of history incorporating biographical elements, anecdotes, and epistolary and other fictional formats. The overall generic identity of history as a branch of literature remained constant throughout this period, and historians continued to pay homage to classical models and ideals. Even so, the thematic range of history increased enormously, with Scottish historians, in particular, introducing such subjects as modes of economic organization, the evolution of legal systems, the development of technology and the history of the family, including the position of women. Society, rather than the political realm, became the primary object of historical enquiry, reflecting and instigating changes in the composition of the readership for historical works.

Clarendon and the search for a viable history of England

At the beginning of the century, few commentators would have thought thematic breadth and generic flexibility desirable qualities for historical writing. There was also a consensus among men of letters that narrative history had for too long declined in relation to the other kinds of non-narrative historical works produced, for example, by the Anglo-Saxon scholars and classical philologists at Oxford, or by the authors of works of ecclesiastical or regional antiquarianism. The Ancient/Modern debate of the late seventeenth and early eighteenth centuries stimulated interest in the idea of classical English history, unencumbered by 'modern' scholarly apparatus and yet authoritative by virtue of its stylistic polish and philosophical insight. William Temple pointed the way back to classical history with the publication of his elegant and unfootnoted *Introduction to the History of England* in 1695.[9] No contemporary historian followed Temple's lead, but the search for a more rigorously classical model of history continued until well into the century, and with it the attempt to narrow down and separate the genre from other kinds of auxiliary activities, such as chronology, chorography or numismatics. Viscount Bolingbroke's *Letters on the Study and Use of History* (written in the late 1730s but published in 1752) attempted to update the historical enterprise of the 'ancients' by incorporating some of the insights of contemporary French historical theorists. Bolingbroke suggested ways in which linear narrative history, providing a classical account of political events and exemplary characters, could be combined with French-style philosophical reflections on the general properties of human nature, the verifiability of facts and data, and the laws of historical causality.

Following Temple and Bolingbroke, proponents of the classical-philosophical model of history continued to insist upon distinctions between their activity and dusty antiquarianism or elaborately footnoted scholarship. Modern commentators have erred, however, in taking the polarization of antiquarianism and narrative history to be a defining feature of this period. In reality, historical practice was very mixed, with a number of narrative works such as Clarendon's *History of the Rebellion* and Gilbert Burnet's *History of the Reformation* (1679–1715) incorporating massive primary documentation, and many more relying heavily and openly upon anthologies of source material such as the *Foedera* of Thomas Rymer *et al.* (1704–35). Declarations of hostility to the dustier aspects of historical labour were part of the marketing rhetoric of the day, but as the century wore on, readers came to accept that massive endnotes (of the kind used in Robertson's *History of Charles V*, for instance), were not incompatible with polished narrative exposition.

In adverting to the ideal of a commercially disinterested, classical history written by a retired man of affairs, eighteenth-century commentators of the 'ancient' persuasion always had before them the example of Clarendon's *History of the Rebellion and Civil Wars in England*. Clarendon completed the manuscript in 1671, shortly before his death, but it was not until the reign of his granddaughter Queen Anne that his sons and their Oxford associates touched up the work and released it for publication. Philip Hicks, in his study *Neoclassical History and English Culture*, has reconstructed the story of the work's first publication.[10] This was undertaken not for financial but political reasons, to boost the standing of the Tory Party. Oxford University Press printed a total of 2500 luxurious three-volume folio sets from 1702 to 1704, which were individually distributed to the great and the good. This was followed by 2500 six–volume octavo sets at the not inconsiderable price of 30 shillings, with a further 11,000 sets printed during the next thirty years. Thereafter, interest in the work seems to have run its course, and there were no further eighteenth-century printings after 1732 (though the unpublished portion of Clarendon's manuscript appeared in 1759 as *The Life of Edward Earl of Clarendon*). The merits of Clarendon's work, both as a unique source and as a work of literature, were apparent to most, although the perception of the work as highly amenable to a Tory political agenda limited overt appreciation and acknowledgement by other historians (notably in the cases of Echard and Hume, who drew heavily upon Clarendon's work). As a publishing venture, *The History of the Rebellion* was a one-off; the production quality of the first edition folio remained unsurpassed by other eighteenth-century works of history. As a work of highly readable, profoundly philosophical Thucydidean history, however, it was to have many emulators.

The fact that *The History of the Rebellion* seemed to many to be too partial in its political outlook and too limited in its chronological scope to count as a national history only stimulated demand for a more satisfactory history of England. Temple briefly took charge of the widespread aspiration to an English national history on the model of Livy or Tacitus, but he was not successful in prevailing upon Swift or any other member of his circle to deliver the kind of work required. Instead, it was the booksellers who took the initiative, and made successive attempts to find or commission a polished, modern and encompassing work. In 1706, a group of London booksellers put together a compilation, *A Complete History of England*, filling in each different period with works by Samuel Daniel, Bacon, Milton and others, and contracting a cleric named White Kennett to supply the seventeenth-century section and preface. Kennett's preface restated the traditional idea that history is necessary to the education of a man of political action, linking it to the notion that history is necessary to teach English gentlemen the source of their civil and political rights: 'the Original of our Laws and Customs is a part of Knowledge . . . requisite to Men of Learning or of publick Employment,

[and] necessary to the Understanding of our Constitution, Rights, and Liberties.'[11] This connection between classicism, patriotism and the appreciation of English liberties became the standard rationale for nearly all the histories of England from Echard and Tyrrell to Macaulay and Oliver Goldsmith (Hume's history played upon and subverted reader expectations for a work of this type). Thomas Carte, appealing in the *Gentleman's Magazine* for funds to support his project for a scholarly history of England, gave precisely this justification for his enterprise: 'By such an History the People of England will see upon what Foundation their Civil Rights, Privileges and Liberties stand, and be better enabled to support them.'[12] In the event, Carte's *General History of England* (1747) turned out to be a work of unabashed Jacobitism, and not at all the apologia for Revolution-Whig politics which his proposal hinted it would be.

Carte was able to take advantage of public dissatisfaction with the generally low standard of national histories. Politics aside, he delivered a work which was lively and adequately researched and which broke new ground in its depiction of the manners of Anglo-Saxon and medieval times. Carte's work sold poorly, but other works of this period enjoyed enough popular and commercial success to reward substantial publisher investment. John Oldmixon's radical *Critical History of England* (1724), written to refute Clarendon, sold rapidly and in its thousands, or so Oldmixon claimed, although William Guthrie's uneven but sometimes philosophical *General History of England* (three volumes published serially from 1744 to 1751) achieved only mediocre sales.[13] Before Smollett and Hume, all home-grown histories of England faced a formidable competitor in the sophisticated, sceptically Whiggish history of England by the French Huguenot writer Paul Rapin de Thoyras. The fifteen-volume English translation, by Nicholas Tindal, of Rapin's *Histoire D'Angleterre* started to appear in 1725, and was sold in serial form until the last instalment came out in 1731. Thereafter, Rapin's work continued to thrive in new issues, abridgements, epitomes, continuations, and, in extract, as part of the pamphlet wars of the 1730s. Hicks estimates sales of around 18,000 for the work proper during the period 1725–55, a publishing phenomenon to rival Clarendon's history.[14] John Lockman's *A History of England by questions and answers* (1729) disseminated Rapin to an even wider, younger audience, reaching twenty-five editions by 1811. Readers welcomed Rapin's detached, outsider perspective on English national myths and party politics, but at the same time resented the ascendancy of a foreign work. A *Gentleman's Magazine* editorial, commending Carte's historical project to its readers, pointed out that it would be 'an Undertaking that if suitably encouraged, will rescue the nation from the Reproach hinted by Mons. Voltaire, namely that we are beholden to a Frenchman for the best History extant of British Affairs'.[15] There was certainly some money to be made out of anti-Rapin history. Thomas Salmon, an arch-Tory, set out to refute Rapin in his *History of England* (1732–34). The work gained considerable success, but mainly as an appendix to Salmon's enormously popular *Modern History, or the Present State of all Nations* (1724–38), a vast, thirty-one-volume compilation of travel literature and world history. Serially published as volumes 17–27 of this work, Salmon's humane, anti-expansionist, Tory account of English history reached a wide audience (Salmon claimed that over 14,000 volumes were printed).[16]

By the 1750s, and particularly after the Seven Years' War, public demand for a national history – philosophical and detached on the French model, yet patriotic – echoed loudly in the ears of booksellers. Hume's decision to try his hand at such a venture was not uninfluenced by commercial consider-ations, although his *History of England* (1754–62) was initially neither a financial nor a critical success. Unwisely, he offered the first volume, *The History of Great Britain containing the reigns of James I and Charles I* (1754), to the Edinburgh-based firm of Balfour, Hamilton and Neil, who might have sold the whole print run of 2000 if they had not found themselves shut out of London distribution networks. However, the second volume, *The History of Great Britain containing the Commonwealth and the reigns of Charles II and James II* (1756, dated 1757), fared hardly any better with Andrew Millar in London (Millar paid Hume £750 for an edition of 1750 copies). The two subsequent two-volume sets for the Tudor (1759) and medieval (1761, dated 1762) periods achieved sales at around the 3000 mark. Sales of Hume's history took off in the 1770s, and then soared throughout the late eighteenth and nineteenth centuries.[17]

The reason most often cited for the slow start of the *History of England* (and the reason given by Hume himself) was public perception of its Tory bias and political contentiousness. A milder political climate, as well as Hume's extensive revisions to the work, may have taken care of this by the 1770s; by then, Hume's history had simply won out, in terms of its literary reputation, against the other works from which it initially faced stiff competition. For a brief period in the late 1760s, the first four volumes of Catharine Macaulay's *History of England* gave Hume a severe run for his money in the subject area for which he was most celebrated, the history of seventeenth-century England. Macaulay produced an independent, robustly written and politically radical alternative to Hume's patiently historicist reappraisal of the same period. Sales of Macaulay's early volumes were reportedly impressive, and were enhanced when her printer and bookseller Cadell introduced a weekly serialization in 1768. Macaulay then felt confident enough to change publisher, selling the right to Dilly to make an octavo edition of the existing volumes for £900, and the copyright of all future volumes for £1000 each.[18] Unfortunately, these terms may have been over-generous from the publisher's point of view since the remaining four volumes of the history did not perform nearly as well.

A still more formidable challenge to Hume's history came from Smollett's *Complete History of England* (1757–58), a work which, though little regarded today, captured the market at the very time when Millar was trying to get Hume's work off the ground. Hume adopted the obligatory philosophical pose when writing to Millar on the subject: 'I am afraid this extraordinary Run upon Dr. Smollett has a little hurt your Sales: But these Things are only temporary.'[19] Yet he was slightly piqued at the success of a less talented fellow Scottish historian: 'Here I [sit],' he wrote to Robertson, 'near the historical summit of Parnassus, immediately under Dr Smollett.'[20] Smollett's work was published by James Rivington, and its success was sufficiently great and immediate to cause jealousy even among the other members of the Rivington clan.[21] The first edition was a relatively expensive production of three quarto volumes, priced at three guineas when bound, with an initial print run of 1000 copies.[22] Even this may have seemed cost-effective to history buyers: unlike Hume's more detailed work, Smollett offered the whole of English history up to 1688 in fairly succinct form, with a fourth volume (in 1758) taking the story, beyond Hume's 1688 end-point, to 1748. Rivington and Baldwin then embarked upon a serial republication of the whole work, incorporating Smollett's revisions and numerous engravings and maps, which came out in 110 sixpenny numbers. As many as 20,000 copies may have been sold through the numbered parts edition, and Smollett is said to have been paid the almost unprecedented sum of £2000. The four-volume *Continuation* of the history soon followed in fifty weekly numbers between 1760 and 1761, followed by a separate fifth volume in 1765, taking the story to the present day.[23]

Consideration of the enormous success of Smollett's work in relation to the comparative failure of Hume's enables us to see more clearly the relative unimportance of political bias to sales. Hume's perceived Toryism and anti-clericalism are usually given as the reasons for the sluggish early performance of his work, yet Smollett's Toryism, at least, was often more prevalent and overt. Smollett, admittedly, dedicated his history to Pitt, and the work takes some of its patriotic, expansionist tone from the political atmosphere of the Seven Years' War, but he also included forthright defences of the royal prerogative, and a blistering denunciation of the conduct of the Hanoverian troops during the 1745 Rebellion. Smollett's equally politically controversial work prevailed, partly because of its method of presenting historical material, and partly because of the marketing techniques which he and Rivington deployed. *The Complete History* was widely advertised in newspapers such as the *Public Advertiser* (for example, the number for 2 February 1758), and Smollett was able to take advantage of his editorship of the *Critical Review* to puff his own work (although Smollett did review Hume's first volume generously in the *Critical*, 2, 1756). One review in the *Critical*, almost certainly by Smollett himself, let the periodical's readers know just how accessible, affordable and compact they could expect *The Complete History* to be:

> His [Smollett's] aim is to retrench the superfluities of his predecessors, and to present the public with a succinct, candid, and complete history of our own country, which will be more easy in the purchase, more agreeable in the perusal, and less burdensome to the memory, than any work of the same nature.[24]

No unnecessary digressions, appendices or other encumbrances, he promised, would interfere with the enjoyment of the middle-brow reader. Unlike the first editions of Hume's history, moreover, Smollett notes his sources in the margins of his text, a point which he proudly made in the introduction to his work. Smollett was happy to present his work as user-friendly and demand-led (the *Continuation* has an opening address 'To the Public' which claims that the work appears by popular request), even though his approach to history was, in fact, far from bland, and many of his political views were not palatable to the average English Whig reader.

History and the high Enlightenment

The success of Smollett and the mid-eighteenth-century boom in historical sales stimulated a public debate about the nature and role of history which prepared the way for the more advanced works of Robertson, Gibbon and other Enlightenment writers. It must be conceded at the outset that the notion, implicit in the structure of this chapter, that Hume's history and Bolingbroke's writing ushered in a phase of 'high Enlightenment' historical writing relies upon a contentious and not always sustainable distinction between élite and popular historical productions. Jeremy Black has argued persuasively that the distinction, in this period, between enlightened and hack history was far from clear, and this was certainly the case in terms of sales and envisaged audiences.[25] Yet such distinctions are not simply the creation of critical hindsight; they emanate from the eighteenth-century language of marketing, promotion and reviewing. Many of the literary hierarchies which we now adopt were engendered by the original process of fitting books and prices to particular sections of the available readership. Reviewing Smollett's *History of England*, the *Monthly Review* took a side-swipe at the low intellectual level of *Critical Review* readers and the kinds of histories aimed at them: 'With such Readers, every step an Historian takes towards determining the weight of evidence, of the degree of credibility, is an excursion into the regions of dulness.'[26] Self-serving though these remarks may have been, they heralded the beginning of a new phase of intellectual ambition in historical writing and reading, and a new bookselling orientation towards prestigious, single-author productions. As we shall see, the rise of 'philosophical' or 'Enlightenment' history was a commercial as well as an intellectual phenomenon, and one which partly explains why, in the end, Hume's history triumphed over Smollett's.

One mid-eighteenth-century publishing event marked both the high water-mark and end of the compilation histories of the first half of the century, shortly before the transition to the 'philosophical', single-author productions of later years: *The Universal History*. *The Universal History* was the largest historical publishing venture of the eighteenth century, and one which, at the levels of production and content, marked a turning point in contemporary historical culture. The story of the creation, publication and sales of this massive work has been set out in a fascinating article by Guido Abbattista, and need only be briefly summarized here.[27] A subscription was opened for the work in a newspaper in 1729, whereafter a consortium of eight publishers issued seven volumes in cheap monthly instalments, dealing with the ancient world from the time of the Creation. The Ancient Part was completed by 1744, and in 1747 to 1748 there followed a high-quality folio edition costing fourteen guineas. The Modern Part, edited by Smollett and other professional writers, followed this more up-market pattern, appearing volume by volume from 1759 until the forty-fourth and final volume in 1765.

The Modern Part is a work of the Enlightenment in terms of its global conception of history; it covered most of the known non-European world in its first eighteen volumes, and then proceeded to Europe and colonial America, but, in most other respects, it is also a hack production reflecting the values and shortcomings of the commercial history market, with no coherent historical programme and no overall introduction or statement of intent. Smollett was involved, not only as a general editor, but also as contributor to the volumes on Denmark, the German Empire and Sweden, and probably also on Poland and Lithuania.[28] In his sections, as in most others, works such as Voltaire's *Histoire de Charles XII* and *Histoire de l'empire de Russie* are reproduced, translated and run together without acknowledgement. Abbattista finds in the work a general outlook which is patriotic, politically uncontroversial and orthodoxly Protestant, but there is, in fact, little evidence for a consistent editorial line. The work was a sufficient commercial success to support a third edition in 1779 to 1784, but it was critically and commercially overmatched by works with a more decisive, 'philosophical' viewpoint, such as Voltaire's shorter, more cohesive global history the *Essai sur les moeurs*, which first appeared in English translation in 1754, and Guillaume Thomas Raynal's global *Histoire philosophique des deux Indes* (1770, revised 1774 and 1780 with contributions from Diderot).

As a project, *The Universal History* was situated midway between Christian universal history, of the kind represented by Bossuet's *Discours sur l'histoire universelle* (1681), and the Enlightenment cosmopolitanism exemplified by Voltaire and Raynal. The philosophical inferences which might arise from such a global survey – the similarities and differences of people's customs and manners, the effects of climate on political organizations and laws, the varying rates of social evolution and so on – were rarely pointed out by *The Universal History*'s editors, but would certainly have suggested themselves to many readers as they compared and reflected on the diverse national histories. By the 1750s and 1760s, readers had become acquainted with the kinds of philosophical history developed in France by Montesquieu, Voltaire and others, and were eager for more comparative and reflective, less narrowly political kinds of history. Bolingbroke's *Letters on the Study and Use of History* had mapped out a new, distinctly French Enlightenment terrain for English history, promoting – despite the fact that he had contributed patriotic and party-political historical sketches to the opposition paper the *Craftsman* in the 1730s – a cosmopolitan, comparatist approach to European and extra-European history. Bolingbroke's work, originally addressed in the 1730s to Clarendon's descendant Lord Cornbury, was intended for a select audience, but his idea of history as 'philosophy teaching by examples' gained wide currency.

Around the same time as Bolingbroke's posthumous writings, Voltaire's mature historical works began appearing in translation, and English readers became more familiar with the idea of the historian as philosopher rather than as man of state, writing stylish, often idiosyncratic and abrasive history from a distinctive critical perspective. Voltaire's historical works, including the *Essai sur les moeurs* (1756, variously translated as *The General History and*

State of Europe or *An Essay on Universal History*) and the *Siècle de Louis XIV*
(1751), had a huge impact in England. The process of reception is discussed
in detail by A. M. Rousseau in his 'L'Angleterre et Voltaire', in which he
also provides a bibliography of the large numbers of English translations of
Voltaire's works.[29] Voltaire's histories were very widely and favourably
reviewed in the periodicals, and the *Gentleman's Magazine* in particular
devoted extensive space to extracts from his works.[30] Their reputation was
barely dented by the public realization, which dawned with the publication
of *Candide* in 1759, that Voltaire's religious views were far from orthodox,
even for a Roman Catholic.[31] In the same year as *Candide*, one reviewer
commented that 'the writings of Mr. Voltaire are as much in fashion among
the English as Chinese furniture'.[32] The vogue for Voltaire's histories is
explicable, partly in terms of modish francophilia, but also due to their broad
conception of history. For Voltaire's works were social and cultural as well
as political histories. Unlike Thomas Salmon or the editors of *The Universal
History*, Voltaire was able to make sense of the diverse histories of the peoples
of the world through a unified set of philosophical preoccupations, and to
link these to a programme for humanitarian progress: 'the subject he [dis-
cusses],' remarked one reviewer, 'viz. the progress of human understanding
in this age, interests and delights the benevolent writer (as it certainly must
every humane reader).'[33]

Before the reputation of Hume's history became established, Voltaire's
histories embodied the most advanced state of historical thinking available to
English readers. The histories became even more accessible to English readers
after the publication, in 1761 to 1765, of a twenty-five-volume translation of
his complete works, with full annotations.[34] The histories inevitably made up
the greater part of this edition. Smollett was the moving spirit behind this
project, once again putting his faith in the remunerativeness of the popular
history market. He translated all the histories, and provided extensive annotations designed to mediate between the lofty *philosophe* perspectives of the text
and the common-sense notions of the English audience. Some of the notes
simply gloss names and events taken for granted by Voltaire, or supply extra
information about personalities or sensational occurrences. Others, however,
impetuously cut down Voltaire's fashionably French ironic tendencies to
British size, particularly at moments where Voltaire debunks the notion that
European society and religion are superior to the rest of the world. For
example, on one occasion in the *Essai sur les moeurs*, Voltaire points out the
irony of considering Europe's colonial territories as economic dependencies,
since it is, in fact, Europe which depends upon them, whereas they have no

need of Europe. In his note, Smollett replies as a Briton for whom the words 'dependence' and 'independence' touch irrational, patriotic chords:

> Nature has given them [the non-European peoples of the world] no such advantage: for we are naturally as independent as they; and we lived much more independent and comfortably than they do at present, even before we knew them or their country.[35]

Similarly, where matters of religion are concerned, Smollett did not feel that Voltaire's somewhat potent brand of philosophical history could be served undiluted. He replies as a staunch Protestant, illogically intolerant not only of Voltaire's religious unorthodoxy, but also of what he suspects to be his latent Catholic prejudices. Thus Smollett's annotations at once mediated between English readers and the French intellectual world, and reminded them of their distance from it.

Diluted philosophical history remained in vogue throughout the 1750s and 1760s, and no work of history, however hackneyed or plagiarized, was complete without a prefatory declaration of Voltairean ambitions. One of the most successful exponents of watered-down philosophical history was Oliver Goldsmith, whose historical works enjoyed extraordinary popularity until well into the nineteenth century. Goldsmith was a devoted admirer of Voltaire the historian, as well as of Montesquieu, and his essays and poem *The Traveller* (1764) are imbued with the spirit of French historical theory. As a historian, Goldsmith always declared himself an exponent of French-style philosophical history in prefaces and chapter openings, even though the reality was more often plagiarized hack-work which was only philosophical insofar as it reproduced chunks of Voltaire and Hume. Goldsmith's *History of England* (four volumes, 1771) presents itself as a work concerned with the progress of civilization, but turns out to be a mainly political narrative and a readable synthesis of previous histories, including those of Carte, Rapin, Smollett and Hume. Reissued, corrected, updated, abridged and continued up to the present day, the work lived on, reaching its 41st edition by 1865.[36] Goldsmith's bid, in *The History of England*, for philosophical status looked increasingly at odds with the cheap, popular and pedagogical formats in which later editions of the work appeared. Goldsmith was probably also the author of the preface to an edition of the twelve-volume *General History of the World* (originally 1744–51, preface for the 1764–67 edition) which sets out a Voltairean programme for the discussion of the progress of civilization, manners and arts, even though the series of national histories which William Guthrie and others compiled for the work contained nothing of the kind.[37]

Smollett, Goldsmith and their booksellers thus fostered reader expectations for a more sophisticated, stylistically unified kind of history without being able to satisfy it themselves. After Hume and Smollett, discussion, in the periodicals, of the need for a national school of history was replaced by anxieties about its quality. There now existed a discerning, polite audience for high-quality philosophical histories, not only of England but of any aspect of British or world history, but there were few histories to satisfy this requirement. Evidence of this demand is the way in which English readers apparently welcomed Scottish productions – so long as they measured up to philosophical standards – even at the height of English hostility to all things Scottish in the early 1760s. It was William Robertson, even more than Hume, who answered this expectation for polite, philosophical history, encountering little anti-Caledonian feeling on the way to his enormous critical and considerable commercial success. Robertson's *History of Scotland*, published in 1759, was very well received in England. Certainly, it was a work calculated to appeal to English as well as Scottish readers, with its emphasis upon reconciliation, and religious and political moderation as the best means of cementing the Union. Robertson was initially anxious about the possibility of English hostility to a Scottish author, although his fears proved to be needless; leaving nothing to chance, he made the journey down to arrange publication with the London-based publisher Andrew Millar, and devoted a good deal of time to lubricating reviewers and other opinion-formers south of the border. Millar and Thomas Cadell paid him £600 for the copyright, a large sum, although it was reported that they made ten times that amount on the book.[38] Published in two volumes folio, *The History of Scotland* went through five authorized editions and one Dublin reprint during its first four years.

The History of Scotland performed exceptionally well for a single-author, high-brow history, but it was Robertson's second work, *The History of the Reign of the Emperor Charles V* (1769), which marked the first real commercial triumph for British philosophical history. This was a demanding work to read: not merely a biography or the history of a reign, but a massive account of the development of European civilization and Christianity during the late fifteenth and sixteenth centuries. Richard B. Sher, in his authoritative article on the work's publication history, claims that *The History of Charles V* constituted a 'monumental event in Enlightenment print culture'.[39] Robertson negotiated with William Strahan for the almost unprecedented sum of £4000 for the copyright (a figure which quickly became legendary), and Strahan then co-published the work with Thomas Cadell in London, and John Balfour in Edinburgh.[40] The first edition, in three volumes folio, was luxurious and expensive at £2 12s 6d in boards, and it did not, as expected, recoup the copyright costs in the first few months.[41] The second, octavo edition of 1772 did well, however, selling around 8500 copies over the next thirteen years or so, and there were five Dublin pirate editions, presumably all profitable enough. The work met with wide critical acclaim, and it was credited with an originality which, given its indebtedness to other works of the Scottish Enlightenment, it did not entirely possess. The title of its long, introductory essay, 'A view of the progress of society in Europe', set the seal on British philosophical history; readers would, in future, expect a social, indeed socio-logical dimension to political narrative, along with digressions and reflections on the state and progress of mankind, rather than simply linear accounts of successive events.

The success of *The History of Charles V* may have indirectly assisted the fortunes of Hume's history, as well as creating a large audience for Robertson's final major work, *The History of America* (1777). Robertson's success also established the critical terms for the reception of the work of the Scottish Enlightenment's most notable English disciple, Edward Gibbon. Gibbon's *History of the Decline and Fall of the Roman Empire* (1776–88) was more often evaluated by the periodical reviewers in relation to French and Scottish philosophical history than compared to the classical historians of the ancient world, or, indeed, to more recent historians of Rome. The *Decline and Fall* far exceeded all other histories of this period in historical erudition and narrative mastery, and it garnered even greater critical praise. The subject of the decline and fall of the Western Roman Empire, familiar, in outline at least, to all Englishmen, was bound to appeal, but it was a measure of the success of his work that Gibbon was able to extend his readers' interest for three volumes beyond that point, to the long, unfamiliar history of the Byzantine Empire and its Arab, Persian, Central Asian and Latin neighbours.

As well as providing a work of unsurpassed quality, Gibbon's work filled a gap in which there were few English histories highly rated by discerning readers. Before the *Decline and Fall*, most of the Roman histories available were either for the young or the uneducated, or were chronologically limited to the republican and early imperial periods. Of the few sophisticated historical treatments of Roman history, most were concerned with the decline and fall of the Roman Republic, and often raised indirect political questions relevant to contemporary England, such as the strengths and weaknesses of mixed government, and methods of popular representation and land distribution.[42] Nathaniel Hooke's four-volume *Roman History from the Building of Rome* (1738–71) attempted a crypto-Jacobite reading of Rome's Republican era, whereas Conyers Middleton's far more successful *History of the Life of Marcus Tullius Cicero* (1741) examined the demise of the Republic from a court Whig perspective. Later in the century, Adam Ferguson's *History of the Progress and Termination of the Roman Republic* (1783, revised 1799) replied to Hooke's work with a searching, sceptically Whiggish account of the unstable balance of liberty and popular power in this period of Roman history. More popular general works included Echard's *Roman History* (1697), which was later supplanted by Charles Rollin's *Roman History* (originally two volumes in 1739, but reaching sixteen octavo volumes in the 1754 version with a continuation by Crevier), a French work, translated into English and reprinted almost every five years until the 1780s. A relatively affordable, illustrated textbook, Rollin's work was eventually replaced by Goldsmith's two-volume *Roman History from the Foundation to the Fall of the Western Empire*, a work published in 1769 and continuously in print until late in the nineteenth century.[43]

By the time of the publication of the first volume of the *Decline and Fall* in 1776, it had been many years since a scholarly, non-textbook history of the later Roman Empire had been available to English readers. William Wotton's *History of Rome from the Death of Antoninus Pius* (1701), an erudite, concise work which started at the same point in history as Gibbon, had not been reprinted for many years, and there was no English translation of Montesquieu's *Considérations sur les causes de la grandeur des Romains et de leur décadence* (1734). The first instalment of the *Decline and Fall* was expensive – a single quarto volume priced at one guinea unbound – and intellectually demanding, yet it sold out its run of 1000 copies within a few months: 'A thousand Copies are sold . . . which in so short a time is, for a book of that price a very uncommon event', Gibbon wrote, no doubt relieved that, after some reluctance on his part, he had agreed a sizeable print run with the publishing firm of Strahan and Cadell.[44] Robertson's prediction that the apparently irreligious content of chapters 15 and 16 would 'hurt the sale of the book' had proved inaccurate.[45] On the contrary, the controversy which erupted over this portion of the work inflamed readers' curiosity, and Gibbon found himself not only critically esteemed but fashionable: 'My book was on every table, and almost on every toilette', Gibbon later recalled.[46] A second edition of 1500 copies, incorporating Gibbon's revisions, became necessary the same year, and two more came out before the second instalment.

Volumes 2 and 3, taking the story from the relocation of the Empire to Constantinople to the Saxon conquest of Britain, were published in 1781. Cadell printed 4000 copies of the set which he divided into two 'editions' to ensure that sales looked even better than they were.[47] Reviewers were ecstatic and sales brisk, as they were, to a slightly lesser extent, for the final, three-volume instalment of 1788, which carried the narrative all the way to the fall of Constantinople. Strahan and Cadell paid Gibbon a handsome £4000 for these three volumes.[48] They got a reasonable return on this final stage of their investment; Gibbon wrote to Cadell: 'I am happy to find that you express yourself, with some reserve, satisfied with the sale.'[49] In Gibbon, Strahan had found yet another prestigious project to which he could bring not only his considerable publishing acuity but a sense of intellectual commitment: 'though I will not take upon me absolutely to pronounce in what manner it will be received at first by a capricious and giddy public,' he wrote to Gibbon in 1775, 'I will venture to say, it will ere long make a distinguished figure among the many valuable works that do honour to the present age.'[50] Strahan's faith was well rewarded, and the whole of the *Decline and Fall* was a critical and publishing success.

The new history

Gibbon was one of the last eighteenth-century exponents of philosophical history on the grand narrative scale. Other historians of his and the subsequent generation, though they endeavoured to adopt the sociological and economic historical perspectives of Gibbon, Hume and Robertson, were less ambitious in terms of length and chronological scope. Many, particularly Scottish historians, favoured the historical disquisition or the extended essay rather than the grand narrative, often as a means of adding more abstract theoretical reflections or more in-depth historical investigations to the existing state of historical knowledge. Adam Ferguson's condensed, speculative *Essay on the History of Civil Society* (1767) led the way in developing this genre of extended, speculative historical essay, followed by works such as John Millar's *Origin of the Distinction of Ranks in Society* (1771, revised 1779), Lord Kames' *Sketches of the History of Man* (1774), James Dunbar's *Essays on the History of Mankind in Rude and Cultivated Ages* (1780), and Robertson's own one-volume *Historical Disquisition Concerning the Knowledge which the Ancients had of India* (1791). Such works mapped out new territories and categories for historical writing, but they derived their preoccupations and flavour from the academic and scholarly Scottish milieu inhabited by their authors, and thus had limited appeal for the general, polite reader.

As well as creating a special kind of historical discourse for a more

professional readership, such works anticipated and influenced the disaggregation of history into smaller units of narrative or analysis towards the end of
the century. Rather than attempting to replace existing works, historians
increasingly preferred to supplement the huge narrative overviews of British
or world history with detailed accounts of particular eras, institutions or reigns.
The work of Robertson's friend, the Scottish divine Thomas Somerville,
exemplifies this trend; he carried out extensive research for his *History of the
Political Transactions and of Parties, from the Restoration of King Charles II, to the
Death of King William* (1792) in order to revise and deepen the account of
party history given by Hume for this period, and then, in his *History of Great
Britain during the Reign of Queen Anne* (1798), he took his analysis of the
phenomenon of political parties forward into a slightly later period. Even
historians attempting chronologically long-ranging works reflected this new
trend towards the disaggregation of the past. In *The History of Great Britain on
a New Plan* (1771–93, covering the period from the Roman invasion to the
mid-sixteenth century), the Scottish historian Robert Henry partitioned his
subject into ten periods, systematically allocating one book and seven chapters
to each, with separate headings for political developments, economic changes,
'manners' and 'arts'. Henry's innovative format initially attracted few readers,
despite Hume's attempts to puff the work; but the history gradually gained
acceptance, and Henry was eventually paid £3300 for the copyright.[51]

Signs of a retreat from the overarching narrative histories of the high
Enlightenment can be seen in Henry's subdivision of British history into
a series of detailed essays, as well as in the enormous numbers of late
eighteenth-century histories of particular institutions, laws, artistic traditions
and reigns. The consumer demand for comprehensive coverage, which had
prompted such ventures as *The Complete History of England* or *The Universal
History*, weakened or fragmented, as new, more specialist or generically
experimental histories competed for attention. The extent to which this
fragmentation of the history market represented a transformation in English
historical culture is not easy to determine, although some commentators have
argued for something of a historical revolution in the latter part of the
century. Thomas Preston Peardon, author of the only comprehensive survey
of late eighteenth-century English history, makes this case, and finds in this
period a current of 'vigorous dissent' from the 'historical outlook' of Hume,
Robertson and Gibbon which would lead, in the end, to the nineteenth-
century rejection of what he calls 'rationalist' history.[52] However, J. W.
Burrow, in his more authoritative study of nineteenth-century historical
writing, finds deep continuities between the analytical modes and narrative

ambitions of eighteenth-century philosophical history and the Victorian histories of the English past.[53]

To a modern historian searching for general trends, the historical publications of the late eighteenth century certainly present a complicated picture. Many shorter historical works positioned themselves merely as supplements to the larger frame of historical reference offered by the general, complete and universal histories of the previous generation. A number, however, claimed to offer entirely new ways of looking at history, especially those histories dealing with the Anglo-Saxon and English medieval past, and individual studies of literature, manners and religious beliefs. Other works were unintentionally original. They set out to elaborate upon the achievements of previous historians, retaining the analytical categories and procedures of Scottish philosophical history; yet, by subdividing or diversifying the subject matter, and by extending generic boundaries, they effected enormous, unenvisaged changes in the nature and practice of history. Children's history, for example, which grew significantly as a section of the history market in the later eighteenth century, was particularly innovative at the formal level, and pointed the way forward to new kinds of approaches and formats later adopted in adult history. By the later part of the century, the chronologies and epitomes of Rapin and other authors which had circulated for years were superseded by more adventurous, inviting works aimed specifically at children, such as Goldsmith's *History of England, in a Series of Letters from a Nobleman to his Son* (1764), Thomas Lewis' *History of France . . . Designed for the Use of Young Ladies and Gentlemen* (1786), and William Russell's perennially popular *History of Modern Europe, from the Fall of the Roman Empire to 1763* (1779–84), also cast in the form of letters from a nobleman to his son. These were experimental, yet readable, morally didactic works which presented history as a kind of conversation between the older generation and the younger.

Another force for generic innovation, and distinct category of reader, was women, who were often directly addressed and targeted by later eighteenth-century historians, and, in general, their presence as a significant proportion of the readership exerted a transformative pressure on the tone, subject matter and forms of historical narrative. Mary Astell's complaint at the beginning of this period, that history had little relevance to the lives of women, became less valid as historians endeavoured to reflect female concerns and interests. The bluestocking writer Hester Chapone devoted a chapter of her *Letters on the Improvement of the Mind* (1773), an influential educational manual for young women, to 'The manner of reading history'. History, she argued, could compensate women for the lack of a classical education, offer them insights into the male public world and engage the imagination in ways more beneficial than the novel. Historians such as Hume, Gibbon, Robertson and Goldsmith were well aware of the female portion of their readership, and deployed literary techniques and strategies, often borrowed from fictional writing, to sustain their interest. Among other things, this involved the inclusion of more character-based, sentimental modes of historical writing, in which Hume and Robertson in particular excelled.[54]

History's growing generic approximation to the novel in the later eighteenth century attracted more and more female readers; inexorable, linear narratives were diversified or replaced by shorter formats, epistolary forms and biographical vignettes. More importantly, the general expansion of the subject matter of history, beyond political narratives and towards social and cultural life, simultaneously reflected and encouraged reading by women.[55] Later eighteenth-century historians all deferred to the notion that they must include, or even focus upon, the history of 'manners' – a thematic field which encompassed the development of different forms of family and social life, the growth of the arts, sciences and technology, and the evolution of different kinds of ethical and religious beliefs in different regions and historical periods. An important sub-section of the history of manners was the subject of relations between the sexes, and the status, sexual behaviour and social role of women. This subject occupied a large proportion of works such as John Millar's *Origin of the Distinction of Ranks* (1771) and Gilbert Stuart's *A View of Society in Europe* (1778), and interest in this topic grew with the new scholarship into the manners and gender relations of the Dark and Middle Ages. There were also works, notably William Alexander's *History of Women, from the Earliest Antiquity to the Present Time* (1779), devoted exclusively to the analysis of the history of women.

Women played a far more limited role as writers or scholars of history. Catharine Macaulay, although she felt no need to conceal her sex from her readers, was exceptional for her day, as were the Anglo-Saxon scholar Elizabeth Elstob, and Mary Wollstonecraft, the author of a philosophical *Historical and Moral View of the Origin and Progress of the French Revolution* (1794). However, as D. R. Woolf has shown, women made an active contribution to what might be called the 'social circulation' of historical knowledge; they edited historical miscellanies (such as Lady Mary Wray's successful *Historical Miscellany*, 1771), excerpted passages from history in educational anthologies (Wollstonecraft herself included passages from Hume and Robertson in her *Female Reader* of 1789), and put together female-orientated compilations, such as Charlotte Cowley's *The Ladies History of*

England: From the Descent of Julius Caesar to the Summer of 1780 (1780).[56] Women also acted as translators of important historical works (for example, Susannah Dobson's 1784 translation of La Curne de Sainte-Palaye's *Memoirs of Ancient Chivalry* (1759)), and popularized episodes or characters from history in poems, novels or plays (for example, Hannah More's highly successful play *Percy* (1777)). In this way, they played a role in the generic extension of traditional narrative history. The biographical turn of history in the 1790s, in works such as Mark Noble's *Lives of the English Regicides* (1798), was a development encouraged by women writers. Mary Hays recommended biography as a way of writing history in her *Letters and Essays, Moral and Miscellaneous* (1793), before producing her own six-volume *Female Biography* in 1803. Women were pioneers in this kind of history (for example, Elizabeth Hamilton's *Memoirs of Agrippina* (1803)), and it was an area to which, along with art history, they were to contribute extensively during the nineteenth century.

In addition to the growth of a young and female audience for history, there is also evidence of an increasing provincial readership for locally published and targeted history. Rosemary Sweet has made a study of urban histories in the eighteenth century, most of which were produced for local readers in order to appeal to and foster a sense of pride and attachment to their city.[57] These ranged from slender guides to more substantial, wide-ranging works, such as William Hutton's *History of Birmingham* (1781) and his *History of Derby* (1791), or John Whitaker's *History of Manchester* (1771–75). Urban histories became ever more prevalent and popular as the century progressed (Sweet's figures show a steady rise from only two such works in the first decade of the eighteenth century to forty-one in the final decade), with short, cheaply produced volumes making their greatest showing in the later decades.[58] The development of this kind of antiquarianism clearly reflected the growth of urban audiences outside London, and provincial publishing, as well as of internal tourism in England.

County histories and works of ecclesiastical antiquities persisted at a more steady pace, though with no later eighteenth-century projects to rival the massive publications of the late seventeenth century (for example, Edmund Gibson's monumental new edition of Camden's *Britannia* in 1695). The most important development, however, was the readjustment, in the late eighteenth century, of the relationship between antiquarianism and narrative history. Combined with detailed scholarship into the antiquities and archaeological remains of, in particular, the Dark and Middle Ages, the Enlightenment history of 'manners' was transformed into a new kind of cultural antiquarianism. It grew out of the appendices and digressions on the progress of the arts and sciences which had formed a part of so many mid-eighteenth-century works, even those which were otherwise narrowly political histories (such as John Mortimer's *New History of England* (1764–66) which had appendices after each period summarizing the state of civilization, and technological, social and artistic developments). Cultural antiquarianism became a mode of history in its own right, inhabiting and engendering a variety of historical sub-genres. Readers' sense of what belonged to the category of the 'historical' was enlarged: artefacts, pictures, literature and buildings could all be factored into continuous narratives of national history. For booksellers this transformation of English historical culture represented an opportunity to create markets for literary history, sports history, architectural history and so on, as well as for previously neglected areas of Anglo-Saxon and medieval history.

Public interest in the pre-medieval history of the British Isles was initially stimulated by literary scholarship (beginning with James Macpherson's Ossian poems from 1761, and Thomas Percy's *Reliques* in 1765), but an appetite quickly developed for antiquarian narratives of all aspects of this period. The writing of many of these works was motivated by the fierce controversy, on all sides of the English, Scottish and Welsh borders, as to the precise lineage and relative merits of Britain's ancient Celtic or Germanic peoples, and historians competed to construct a plausible narrative account from fragmen-tary evidence. The imperative to piece together a serviceable narrative of the post-Roman conquests and migrations in the British Isles was heeded increas-ingly as the public became more curious about the ethnic or racial basis of their national identity. Percy's popular *Northern Antiquities* of 1770 (an amended translation of the Swiss explorer Paul Mallet's *Introduction à l'histoire de Dannemarc*, 1755) made the Germanic case, while Macpherson's own *Introduction to the History of Great Britain and Ireland* (1771) celebrated the origins and ethnic character of the Celtic-Caledonians. John Smith's *Galic Antiquities* (1780) went still further, idealizing the ancient Celts as a civilized people above the level of the ancient Greeks, whereas John Pinkerton, in his *Dissertation on the . . . Goths* (1787) and John Whitaker, in his *Genuine History of the Britons Asserted* (1772), were implacable defenders in the pro-Germanic camp. Later, Sharon Turner's *History of the Anglo-Saxons* (1799–1805) inaug-urated a renewal of Anglo-Saxon scholarship for the nineteenth century. In all these controversial works of history, the evidence most often adduced was that relating to forms of social and religious life, artistic achievements, and material and moral culture.

Closely related to the national preoccupation with the Germanic (or, in eighteenth-century terminology, 'Gothic') roots of English culture was the revival of medieval history. Antiquarian scholarship on the subject of the political institutions of feudal England was nothing new, and had been practised continuously since the early seventeenth century, often to provide historical ammunition for contemporary party debate.[59] Yet works, particularly of narrative history, relating to the social and cultural life of the medieval period were rare prior to the enormous growth of interest in the third quarter of the century. George, Lord Lyttelton's four-volume *History of the Life of King Henry the Second* (1767–71) was an innovative work in this area which, despite its shortcomings, displayed a far more vivid sense of medieval life than the histories of Robertson or Hume. The work included detailed discussion of English and Welsh manners during the reign of Henry II, as well as political, ecclesiastical and technological developments, and gave an unusually warm account of chivalry as a social institution. Sainte-Palaye's work also precipitated the rediscovery of chivalry, or rather of chivalric manners as not only a military code but a whole way of life which distinguished Gothic Europe from the ancient world. Medieval history blossomed into many genres and subject areas, especially literary history, distinguished by works such as Richard Hurd's *Letters on Chivalry and Romance* (1762), Thomas Warton's *History of English Poetry* (1774–81) and Clara Reeve's *The Progress of Romance* (1785). Other works set out to supply a coherent account of the medieval period as a distinctive and not necessarily inferior epoch in the social and cultural history of English civilization, among them Gilbert Stuart's *View of Society in Europe* and *The History of the Reign of Henry the Second, and of Richard and John* (1790) by the Catholic priest Joseph Berington.[60]

One of the most prolific and successful medievalists of the period was Joseph Strutt who, beginning with *The Regal and Ecclesiastical Antiquities of England from Edward the Confessor to Henry the Eighth* (1773), evinced a real feeling and (sometimes naive) enthusiasm for medieval life. Strutt's main interest, and that of his readers, was in the cultural rather than institutional aspects of medieval history, and he followed his first major work with a three-volume *Complete View of the Manners, Customs, Arms, Habits etc. of the Inhabitants of England* (1775–76) from Anglo-Saxon times. More culturally specific and more enduring was his subsequent *Complete View of the Dress and Habits of the People of England* (1796–99), fully and expensively illustrated with examples from the Saxons to the present day. In the same vein of cultural history, Strutt was also the author of *Sports and Pastimes of the People of England* (1801), a work reprinted throughout the nineteenth century.[61] The kind of partly narrativized, cultural antiquarianism which Strutt practised certainly facilitated the alignment of history and fiction in the novels of Walter Scott and his predecessors, and Strutt himself was the author of an unfinished historical novel, *Queenhoo Hall*, which Scott himself completed.[62] In some respects, Strutt is an emblematic figure for the transformation of late eighteenth-century history. The historical terrain had been widened, and an expanded and diversified readership welcomed increasing varieties and generic subspecies of history. Yet in the ensuing decades, traditional, educative, political history would also continue to flourish, and history would retain much of its prestige, though less of its masculine mystique. The authority of the individual historian, and, with this, his or her earning capacity, had grown considerably during the second half of the century. History in England had not yet acquired the institutional status and more specialist readership accorded to the discipline in Scotland. Instead, nineteenth-century historians such as Henry Hallam and T.B. Macaulay could look forward to a broad, general audience possessed of the patience and enthusiasm to work their way through demanding, multi-volume works.

Notes

1. In Bridget Hill (ed.), *The First English Feminist* (Aldershot, Hants: Gower Publishing, 1986), p. 201.

2. This statistic is given in Philip Hicks' informative study *Neoclassical History and English Culture: From Clarendon to Hume* (Basingstoke: Macmillan, 1996), p. 41.

3. See E. C. Mossner and H. Ransom, 'Hume and the "conspiracy of the booksellers": the publication and early fortunes of the *History of England*', *University of Texas Studies in English*, 29 (1950): 162–82.

4. Quoted in J. A. Cochrane, *Dr Johnson's Printer: The Life of William Strahan* (London: Routledge & Kegan Paul, 1964), p. 83.

5. Advertisement for Smollett's *Continuation of the Complete History of England*, 3 vols (1785).

6. W. S. Lewis (ed.), *Horace Walpole's Correspondence* (New Haven, CT: Yale University Press, 1937–83), Vol. 18, p. 480. See also Laird Okie, *Augustan Historical Writing: Histories of England in the English Enlightenment* (Lanham, MD: University Press of America, 1991), pp. 135–54.

7. For example, J. E. Norton (ed.), *The Letters of Edward Gibbon*, 3 vols (London: Cassell, 1956), letter no. 509.

8. See Bridget Hill, *The Republican Virago: The Life and Times of Catharine Macaulay, Historian* (Oxford: Clarendon Press, 1992). On her research, see Bridget and Christopher Hill, 'Catharine Macaulay's *History* and her catalogue of tracts', *The Seventeenth Century*, 8 (1993): 269–85.

9. See Joseph M. Levine, *The Battle of the Books: History and Literature in the Augustan Age* (Ithaca, NY: Cornell University Press, 1991), pp. 292–302.

10. *Neoclassical History and English Culture*, pp. 62–73. Statistical information on the printing of Clarendon's work is drawn from this study.

11. *A Complete History of England with the Lives of all the Kings and Queens Thereof from the Earliest Account of Time to the Death of . . . William III* (London, 1706), Vol. 1, p. i.

12. *Gentleman's Magazine*, 8 (May, 1738): 227.

13. See Okie, *Augustan Historical Writing*, p. 76.

14. *Neoclassical History and English Culture*, p. 147. On the content of Rapin's work, see Duncan Forbes, *Hume's Philosophical Politics* (Cambridge: Cambridge University Press, 1975), pp. 233–40.

15. *Gentleman's Magazine*, 8 (May, 1738): 227.

16. Okie, *Augustan Historical Writing*, p. 101.

17. Mossner and Ransom, 'Hume and the "conspiracy of the booksellers"'; and Hicks, *Neoclassical History*, p. 196.

18. Bridget Hill, *The Republican Virago*, pp. 49–50.

19. Hume to Millar, 6 April 1758, in J. Y. T. Greig (ed.), *The Letters of David Hume*, Vol. 2 (Oxford: Clarendon Press, 1932), p. 274.

20. Hume to Robertson, 12 March 1759, in *ibid.*, p. 302.

21. In July 1758, William Strahan wrote, 'The great success he [James Rivington] has met in Smollet's History has made him slacken his Career a little, lest his Brothers should make Reprisals upon him while it is publishing in Numbers and interrupt the Sale.' Quoted in Cochrane, *Dr Johnson's Printer*, p. 83.

22. James Raven, *Judging New Wealth: Popular Publishing and Responses to Commerce in England, 1750–1800* (Oxford: Clarendon Press, 1992), p. 36.

23. Lewis Knapp, 'The publication of Smollett's *Complete History* and *Continuation*', *The Library*, 16 (1935): 295–308. On the fifth *Continuation* volume and the reasons for its rapid suppression, see Peter Miles, 'Bibliography and insanity: Smollett and the mad-business', *The Library*, 3 (1976): 214–15.

24. *Critical Review*, 3 (1757): 449. On Smollett's authorship of this review, see the appendix to James G. Basker, *Tobias Smollett: Critic and Journalist* (Newark: Delaware University Press, 1988).

25. Jeremy Black, 'Ideology, history, xenophobia and the world of print in eighteenth-century England', in Jeremy Black and Jeremy Gregory (eds), *Culture, Politics and Society in Britain, 1660–1800* (Manchester: Manchester University Press, 1991), p. 207.

26. *Monthly Review*, 16 (1757): 531.

27. Guido Abbattista, 'The business of Paternoster Row: towards a publishing history of *The Universal History*, (1736–65)', *Publishing History*, 17 (1985): 5–50.

28. See Louis Martz, 'Tobias Smollett and *The Universal History*', *Modern Language Notes*, 56 (1941): 1–14.

29. 'L'Angleterre et Voltaire', *Studies on Voltaire and the Eighteenth Century*, 145–7 (1976), which includes a full bibliography of English translations.

30. See J. Séguin, *Voltaire and the Gentleman's Magazine* (New York: Ross Paxton, 1962).

31. See e.g. 'A critical examination of the respective merits of Voltaire, Rousseau, Richardson, Smollett and Fielding', *The Royal Magazine*, 15 (1766): 145–60.

32. *Critical Review*, 7 (June 1759): 550.

33. *Gentleman's Magazine*, 41 (April 1771): 164.

34. *The Works of M. de Voltaire. Translated from the French. With Notes Historical and Critical.*

By Dr. Smollett and Others, 25 vols (1761–65). See also Eugène Joliat, 'Smollett, editor of Voltaire', *Modern Language Notes*, 54 (1939): 429–36.

35. *Works of M. de Voltaire*, Vol. 4, p. 179.

36. See e.g. Rousseau's discussion of 'L'école historique anglaise de Voltaire' in 'L'Angleterre et Voltaire', *Studies on Voltaire*, 147 (1976): 754–851.

37. See R. S. Crane, 'Goldsmith and Voltaire's *Essai sur les moeurs*', *Modern Language Notes*, 38 (1923): 65–76.

38. See G. B. Hill (ed.), *Boswell's Life of Johnson*, rev. L. F. Powell, Vol. 3 (Oxford: Clarendon Press, 1934), p. 334.

39. Richard B. Sher, 'Charles V and the book trade: an episode in Enlightenment print culture', in Stewart J. Brown (ed.), *William Robertson and the Expansion of Empire* (Cambridge: Cambridge University Press, 1997), p. 164.

40. On relative copyright sales figures, see Raven, *Judging New Wealth*, p. 59.

41. Sher, 'Charles V and the book trade', p. 175.

42. In general, see Frank M. Turner, 'British politics and the demise of the Roman Republic, 1700–1939', in *Contesting Cultural Authority: Essays in Victorian Intellectual Life* (Cambridge: Cambridge University Press, 1993).

43. See Norman Vance, *The Victorians and Ancient Rome* (Oxford: Blackwell, 1997), ch. 3.

44. *The Letters of Edward Gibbon*, Vol. 2, pp. 100, 105.

45. Quoted in Patricia B. Craddock, *Edward Gibbon, Luminous Historian* (Baltimore, MD: Johns Hopkins University Press, 1989), p. 69.

46. G. A. Bonnard (ed.), *Memoirs of My Life* (London: Thomas Nelson, 1966), p. 157.

47. J. E. Norton, *A Bibliography of the Works of Edward Gibbon* (London: Oxford University Press, 1940), pp. 49–50.

48. Craddock, *Edward Gibbon*, p. 262.

49. *Letters*, Vol. 3, p. 143.

50. John, Lord Sheffield (ed.), *The Miscellaneous Works of Edward Gibbon* (London, 1814), Vol. 2, pp. 138–9.

51. See A. S. Collins, *Authorship in the Days of Johnson* (London: Holden, 1927), p. 34.

52. Thomas Preston Peardon, *The Transition in English Historical Writing, 1760–1830* (New York: Columbia University Press, 1933), p. 10.

53. J. W. Burrow, *A Liberal Descent: Victorian Historians and the English Past* (Cambridge: Cambridge University Press, 1981).

54. See Mark Phillips, '"If Mrs Mure be not sorry for poor King Charles": history, the novel, and the sentimental reader', *History Workshop Journal*, 43 (1997): 111–131; Karen O'Brien, *Narratives of Enlightenment: Cosmopolitan History from Voltaire to Gibbon* (Cambridge: Cambridge University Press, 1997), pp. 114–20.

55. See Mark Phillips, 'Adam Smith and the history of private life: social and sentimental narratives in eighteenth-century historiography', in Donald R. Kelley and David Harris Sacks (eds), *The Historical Imagination in Early Modern Britain* (Cambridge: Cambridge University Press, 1997), pp. 318–42.

56. D. R. Woolf, 'A feminine past? Gender, genre and historical knowledge in England, 1500–1800', *American Historical Review*, 102 (1997): 645–79.

57. Rosemary Sweet, *The Writing of Urban Histories in Eighteenth-Century England* (Oxford: Clarendon Press, 1997).

58. *Ibid.*, p. 9.

59. See R. J. Smith, *The Gothic Bequest: Medieval Institutions in British Thought, 1688–1863* (Cambridge: Cambridge University Press, 1987).

60. Aspects of the medieval revival are discussed by Preston Peardon, *The Transition in English Historical Writing*, ch. 5.

61. *Ibid.*, pp. 158–9.

62. See also Mark Phillips, 'Macaulay, Scott and the literary challenge to historiography', *Journal of the History of Ideas*, 50 (1989): 117–33.

CHAPTER 5

BIOGRAPHICAL DICTIONARIES AND THEIR USES FROM BAYLE TO CHALMERS

ISABEL RIVERS

Introduction

In Gilbert West's Spenserian poem *Education* (1751), a knight conveys his son (previously instructed by 'a *Palmer* sage' – John Locke) to Paedia's house. Paedia proudly shows them her magically increasing '*monumental Pile*', adorned with the statues of heroes old and new, and the canto ends with her explaining 'their great Lives' to the youth. Here West adds an important note of clarification and exhortation: the monument is an emblem of the currently appearing *Biographia Britannica*, and he urges his patriotic readers to help its authors 'render as perfect as possible, a Design so apparently calculated to serve the Publick, by setting in the truest and fullest light the Characters of Persons already generally, tho' perhaps too indistinctly known; and reviving from Obscurity and Oblivion, Examples of private and retired Merit'.[1] At the time of writing this note West had read only the first two volumes of *Biographia Britannica* (1747, 1748). After his death the editors made prominent use of his generous piece of advertising: the note appears facing the title-pages of two later volumes (5, 1760; 6, part 1, 1763). On the second occasion they included, in Dryden's translation, Virgil's lines on the worthies seen by Aeneas in the Elysian fields, which West had quoted in Latin at the end of his note to epitomize 'this repository of *British* Glory':

> *Here* Patriots *live, who for their* Country's good,
> *In* fighting fields, *were prodigal of blood;*
> Priests *of* unblemish'd lives *here make abode,*

And Poets *worthy their aspiring God*:
And searching Wits *of more* mechanic parts,
Who grac'd their age with new invented arts;
Those who to worth *their* bounty *did extend*,
And those who knew that bounty *to* commend.[2]

   In his poem West was illustrating the main motive stated in the preface to
the first volume of *Biographia Britannica*, the creation of 'a BRITISH TEMPLE OF
HONOUR, sacred to the piety, learning, valour, publick-spirit, loyalty, and
every other glorious virtue of our ancestors, and ready also for the reception
of the WORTHIES of our OWN TIME, and the HEROES OF POSTERITY'.[3] Yet
this ambition for a continuing national monument of agreed worthies was at
odds with the other main motive for the publication of biographical dictionaries in the eighteenth century, drawn from the model of the *Dictionaire
Historique et Critique* (1697, second edn 1702) of the Huguenot scholar Pierre
Bayle: the aim to provide an easily accessible library in which readers could
locate and compare the quoted arguments of a wide range of writers of
differing persuasions and principles. Eventually the perceived inconsistency of
these motives and the difficulty of meeting the requirements of the second of
them led to the abandonment of the British biographical dictionary on the
grand Baylean scale and a return to an earlier model.
   This chapter is principally concerned with the three great folio dictionaries
on the Baylean model, *A General Dictionary, Historical and Critical* (1734–41),
edited chiefly by Thomas Birch, together with John Peter Bernard and John
Lockman; *Biographia Britannica* (1747–66), edited by William Oldys, together
with Thomas Broughton, John Campbell, Sir Philip Nichols and others; and
the uncompleted second edition of *Biographia Britannica* (1778–95), edited by
Andrew Kippis, together with Joseph Towers and others. In addition to Bayle
it explores the example of the other main continental model, the *Grand
Dictionaire Historique* of the French Catholic priest Louis Moréri (first published
1674), translated and enlarged by Jeremy Collier as *The Great Historical,
Geographical, Genealogical and Poetical Dictionary* (1701); the influential English
antecedents in the biographical collections of Anthony Wood, Edmund
Calamy and John Walker; and the production of a series of popular octavo
dictionaries, beginning with *A New and General Biographical Dictionary*
(1761–62) and concluding with Alexander Chalmers' *The General Biographical
Dictionary* (1812–17). Throughout the period, accounts of lives were widely
published in a variety of forms, either separately or more often as parts of
other works: in funeral sermons, as prefaces to posthumous collected editions,

as characters in memoirs or histories, or as collections of individuals grouped by particular religious denomination, institutional or professional affiliation, interests or talents. The motives and methods of the authors of these accounts were often very different from those of the editors of the dictionaries; in the case of writers such as the dissenter Calamy and the high churchman Walker, for example, their aims were avowedly partisan and polemical. The dictionary writers drew widely on all such accounts, and at the same time were often careful to weigh their respective merits and interpretations. The same procedure was followed by writers of later dictionaries who drew on earlier ones, or by writers of later editions of dictionaries who took account of other dictionaries published in the meantime which commented on the earlier version. There would seem to be no end to the task of the modern historian hoping to disentangle the chain of borrowing, allusion and criticism.

The biographical dictionary was an important, influential and increasingly popular genre in eighteenth-century England, but it is currently under-explored. Modern readers sometimes turn to individual dictionaries for information about specific individuals that is of value to them now, but they rarely ask what their editors hoped to achieve or what their original readers might have found in them at the time.[4] In an attempt to remedy this neglect, the analysis that follows provides a short history of the development of the biographical dictionary and the relationship between the different editions, a broad picture of the philosophies and prejudices of the individual dictionary writers, and an illustration of how the dictionaries can be used to chart the changing fortunes of their subjects.

Historical dictionaries and the Baylean tradition

In the preface to the first French edition of his dictionary (published in Rotterdam, 1697), as translated for one of the two London editions of 1734, Bayle observed that 'the first writers of Dictionaries have committed many faults, but they have done great services, and deserve a glory, of which they ought not to be deprived by their successors'.[5] Writers of new dictionaries regularly prefaced their work with a sketch of the methods, successes and failures of their predecessors, clarifying their relationship to them and their debts where appropriate, setting out their own designs, and claiming the originality and importance of their undertakings. Bayle's original intention, as he explained, was to publish a dictionary of the errors he found in earlier dictionaries, especially Moréri's, but after consultation he changed his mind and devised the method for which he is famous and which was to be so influential for his English imitators.[6] Each article on each individual subject is divided into two parts: one historical, at the top of the page, consisting of a narrative of matters of fact (sometimes of very slight interest); the other critical, in the lower part of the page and in double columns in a smaller typeface (but often taking up most of the page), consisting of a series of remarks keyed to the main article by capital letters. In the left- and right-hand margins of both layers of text are source references, keyed numerically, for both information and quotations provided. This is the model and layout adopted by the English folio biographical dictionaries, though with differences of emphasis that will be discussed below (pp. 149ff). In his preface Bayle carefully explained the function of his remarks and the lengthy quotations they contained. The dictionary was to stand in place of a library both for lovers of learning who could not afford books, and for owners of books who did not have the time to consult them:

> And therefore out of a regard to the readers who have no books, and to the occupations, or laziness of those that have libraries, I have taken care to shew them at once historical facts, and the proofs of them, with many discussions and circumstances, that their curiosity might be fully satisfied.

Citations and abridgements in other works were frequently inaccurate, hence judicious readers had ceased to trust them. The solution was to quote writers' own words as fully as possible.[7]

In the body of his dictionary Bayle elaborated his principles and justified his method from time to time. For example, in the article 'Catius', note D, he celebrated the republic of letters as a free state in which the only authority is that of reason and truth and in which no one is exempt from criticism:

> Every one is there both sovereign and accountable to every one. The laws of civil society have not put the least restraint upon the independency of the state of nature, with regard to error and ignorance. Every private man has in that respect the right of the sword, and may use it, without asking leave of those who govern.[8]

In the article 'Epicurus', note E, he defended at length his painstaking method of collecting and comparing authorities; in 'Marcionites', note E, he recommended that the arguments on both sides in controversies should be drawn up in opposition to one another – as he had done in this particular case – in order to make writers behave more fairly to each other; in 'Rorarius' he noted that 'many persons who delight in the history of opinions' approved of his lengthy remarks under 'Pereira' (on whether beasts have souls), though he recognized that many other readers regarded them as 'mere excrescences'.[9]

Pierre Des Maizeaux, the Huguenot émigré and friend of Bayle, Locke and Shaftesbury, wrote a *Life of Bayle* for the Amsterdam edition of the *Dictionaire* of 1730 which was translated for *The Dictionary, Historical and Critical of Mr Peter Bayle.* Here he very usefully characterized Bayle's method:

> Mr Bayle's work has hardly any thing in common with that of Moreri. It is a Dictionary of a new and singular kind. An infinite variety runs through the whole of it. In the Text or body of the articles, he in a very exact and concise manner gives the history of the persons he treats of, but he makes amends for this Brevity in the Remarks which are subjoined to the text, and which are a sort of commentary on it. He draws the characters of those persons, he clears up the circumstances of their lives, and the motives of their conduct, he examines the judgment which has been, or may be made concerning them. He treats of the most important points of Religion, Morality, and Philosophy. Nay sometimes the text seems to have been made for the sake of the Remarks. He takes occasion from the actions or sentiments of an obscure and almost unknown person, to instruct or agreeably to amuse his reader. So that some Articles which seem to promise nothing at all, are frequently accompanied with the most curious matters. He acts throughout the part of an exact, faithful, and disinterested Historian, and of a moderate, penetrating, and judicious Critic.

Des Maizeaux went on cautiously to explain Bayle's view of the destructive implications of human reason with regard to religion and philosophy, and the positive importance of his sceptical method for historical study:

> He showed that several facts which no body has ever called in question are very uncertain, or even evidently false: from whence it is natural to conclude, that we ought not lightly to give credit to Historians, but rather to suspend our judgment 'till by a rigorous examination we are assured of the truth.[10]

It is worth stressing that although Bayle's English imitators always noted, often with disapproval, his scepticism about the capacity of reason to solve religious and philosophical questions, notably the problem of evil, this aspect of his work (which most interests modern readers)[11] was much less significant for the organization of the English biographical dictionaries than his insistence on citing evidence for facts, providing lengthy quotations from his sources and setting rival authorities against each other.

Bayle's decision to include some subjects and exclude others was partly determined by what was in Moréri; this meant that his dictionary could not

be and was not designed to be free-standing. Moréri's dictionary, especially
after it had gone through many revisions and enlargements both in French
and English, was unique in combining the features of an encyclopedia,
containing information on an enormous range of subjects from antiquity to
the present, with that of a biographical dictionary.[12] As Bayle pointed out in
his entry on Moréri, his predecessor ruined his health working on his
dictionary and did not live to see the second enlarged edition of 1681.[13]
Collier in his entry presented him as a hero: 'it may be said, That he sacrificed
his Fortune and Life for the Publick.'[14] Moréri's most important French editor
was Bayle's rival in the exiled Huguenot community in Holland, the theologian Jean Le Clerc, who produced two editions published in Amsterdam in
1691 and 1702. The first English translation of 1694 (described as 'very
indifferent' in the preface to *Biographia Britannica*)[15] was soon replaced by that
of Jeremy Collier, the non-juring cleric best known now for *A Short View of
the Immorality and Profaneness of the English Stage* (1698). Collier brought out
two volumes of *The Great Historical, Geographical, Genealogical and Poetical
Dictionary* (1701), based on the eighth edition of Moréri corrected and
enlarged by Le Clerc, followed by a *Supplement* (1705, second edn 1727) and
an *Appendix* (1721). The copious title-page of Volume 1 of *The Great
Dictionary* (1701) gives some indication of the extraordinary range of materials
that Moréri and his editors and continuers tried to cram into the format of a
dictionary:

Being a Curious Miscellany of Sacred and Prophane History. Containing, in
short, The Lives and most Remarkable Actions Of the Patriarchs, Judges, and
Kings of the Jews; Of the Apostles, Fathers, and Doctors of the Church; Of
Popes, Cardinals, Bishops, &c. Of Heresiarchs and Schismaticks, with an
Account of their Principal Doctrines; Of Emperors, Kings, Illustrious Princes,
and Great Generals; Of Ancient and Modern Authors; Of Philosophers, Inven-
tors of Arts, and all those who have recommended themselves to the World, by
their Valour, Virtue, Learning, or some Notable Circumstances of their Lives.
Together with the Establishment and Progress both of Religious and Military
Orders, and the Lives of their Founders. As also, The Fabulous History of the
Heathen Gods and Heroes. The Description Of Empires, Kingdoms, Common-
Wealths, Provinces, Cities, Towns, Islands, Mountains, Rivers, and other con-
siderable Places, both of Ancient and Modern Geography; wherein is observed
the Situation, Extent and Quality of the Country; the Religion, Government,
Morals and Customs of the Inhabitants; the Sects of Christians, Jews, Heathens
and Mahometans. The principal Terms of Arts and Sciences; the Publick and
Solemn Actions, as Festivals, Plays, &c. The Statutes and Laws; and withal, the

History of General and Particular Councils, under the Names of the Place where they have been Celebrated. The Whole being full of Remarks and Curious Enquiries, for the Illustration of several Difficulties in Theology, History, Chronology and Geography.

All this is increased for English readers by the inclusion of

The Lives, most Remarkable Actions, and Writings of several Illustrious Families of our English, Scotch and Irish Nobility, and Gentry, and most Famous Men of all Professions, Arts and Sciences: As also, an Exact Description of these Kingdoms; with the most Considerable Occurrences that have happened to this present Time.

In the prefaces to *The Great Dictionary* and the *Supplement*, Collier explained in sprightly fashion the editorial problems he faced and the decisions he had made: he had corrected the style of and errors in the previous English translation, and made considerable additions and alterations to particular topics, especially in the field of English lives and history. He had deliberately not extended his account beyond 1688 (presumably because of his Jacobite sympathies); anything later was either a remainder of the old edition or a continuation by another hand as commissioned by the bookseller (he was thus distancing himself from the claim to contemporaneity of the title-page).[16] In his address 'To the reader' prefacing the *Supplement*, Collier answered readers' objections to errors and omissions and accepted the problem of the conflict between himself and the anonymous continuator.[17] The *Supplement* therefore included a separate section entitled 'A continuation of Mr. Collier's supplement to the great historical dictionary, &c. from 1688, to the Year 1705'. Despite all these difficulties, Collier asserted confidently in the preface to *The Great Dictionary*: '*As for the usefulness of this* Work, *'tis a* Collection *of almost* Universal Knowledge, *and may be call'd rather a* Library *than a* Book.'[18]

Partly because it performs so many disparate functions and provides so much information in so many fields, *The Great Dictionary* is unsatisfactory as a biographical dictionary. Most of the English lives are very short, and contain little in the way of quotations or notes or source material; those that are long, such as the entries under individual monarchs, are not accounts of lives but of events (the entry under Charles I, for example, gives a detailed summary of the stages of the Civil War). They are interesting for the straightforward judgements they contain, and for omissions as much as for inclusions. The methods of Collier/Moréri bear no resemblance to those of Bayle. However, the relationship between them is evident at several points: whereas Bayle frequently draws attention to Moréri's errors and frames some of his articles as rebuttals, the corrected editions of Moréri sometimes list Bayle as a source.

The later biographical dictionaries on the Baylean model take a mixed view of *The Great Dictionary*: they complain about its reliability but attest to its popular success. The preface to the first volume of *A General Dictionary* claims that Le Clerc was reluctant to put his name to the revised edition, and dismisses Collier's version as containing the same or greater defects than the French. However, the article on Collier, 'communicated by a very ingenious and learned Gentleman', contradicts this view:

> tho' it is possible that in so great a variety of matter several errors may still be discovered . . . yet with regard to the choice of proper subjects, and the manner of handling them, to the usefulness of the work and the uniformity of the style, it will justify the good opinion the publick have had of it, and be always the model or the reproach of those that write Dictionaries after him.[19]

The preface to the first volume of the *Biographia Britannica* attributes the scheme of the historical dictionary in its fullest extent to Moréri, and suggests that if Bayle's method and expression could be joined to Moréri's design then the perfect historical and critical dictionary could be made, provided the materials were authentic.[20] The writer of the article on Collier, John Campbell, praises Collier's revisions – 'so well were his endeavours in this kind received by the publick, notwithstanding some exceptions that were taken to them, that few books have met with a better fate, or longer maintained their credit' – and insists on the value of *The Great Dictionary* not only to young scholars 'but even to persons of the greatest abilities, and most comprehensive science, who have but small libraries, and live at a distance from London, and the two Universities'.[21] However, forty years later in the second edition of the *Biographia Britannica* Andrew Kippis added a note berating Campbell for his favourable treatment of Collier. Kippis' objections are as much on religious and political as on scholarly grounds – Collier 'was engaged in defending the most flagrant absurdities, and in exercising the most determined hostilities against the civil and religious interests of these kingdoms' – and he asserts that *The Great Dictionary* is not much used or esteemed at present and has not been of service to him as editor of the *Biographia Britannica*.[22]

The first English translation of Bayle, largely the work of Michel De la Roche, was begun after the publication of the second edition of the *Dictionaire* in 1702 and published in 1710, but like the first translation of Moréri it was unsatisfactory and commercially unsuccessful. Bayle (who died in 1706) was keen to help with an English edition and corresponded with Des Maizeaux on the subject.[23] With the aim of demonstrating the advantages of Bayle's critical method and stimulating interest in a new historical and critical English dictionary, Des Maizeaux published two biographies, *An Historical and Critical Account of the Life and Writings of the Ever-Memorable Mr. John Hales, Fellow of Eton College, and Canon of Windsor. Being a Specimen of an Historical and Critical English Dictionary* (1719) and *An Historical and Critical Account of the Life and Writings of Wm. Chillingworth, Chancellor of the Church of Sarum* (1725). Des Maizeaux's astute choice of mid-seventeenth-century divines of a latitudinarian persuasion whose lives and works continued to provoke considerable controversy provided an excellent illustration of the uses of Bayle's method and a foretaste of the concerns of the English dictionaries that were to employ it. In the dedication of his *Life and Writings of Hales* he explained the relationship between the text and the remarks, and carefully spelled out the limits to his imitation of Bayle: he had sought to imitate Bayle's 'Exactness and Impartiality' while avoiding the things for which Bayle was blamed, his offences to modesty and his apparent objections to religious doctrine. Recognizing the enormous task of undertaking a new dictionary, he hoped that others might join with him or take over the whole execution of such a project; he would willingly resign it to them, 'contenting my self with having been able to excite them by my example'. Des Maizeaux was optimistic about the prospects of such a work: 'whenever the Usefulness, or if I may speak the whole truth, whenever the Necessity of this Work comes to be known; there is ground to believe that all requisite encouragement will be given to those, who shall apply themselves to it.'[24] The harassed Des Maizeaux seems to have been hoping for royal patronage here, but it was rival booksellers who were responsible for the competing versions of a critical and historical dictionary, both indebted to him, which began to appear fifteen years later: one merely a translation of Bayle, *The Dictionary, Historical and Critical of Mr Peter Bayle*, prefixed by Des Maizeaux's life (five volumes, 1734–38); the other, *A General Dictionary, Historical and Critical* (ten volumes, 1734–41), a far more ambitious combination of a new translation of Bayle with a new kind of English biographical dictionary.[25]

The English biographical tradition – Wood, Calamy and Walker

Bayle was not the only significant influence on the folio dictionaries. A set of late seventeenth- and early eighteenth-century English collections played a crucial part in their content, and in one case helped to shape the format not of the folios but of later generations of dictionaries. The most important of these is Anthony Wood's *Athenae Oxonienses: An Exact History of all the Writers and Bishops who have had their Education in the Most Ancient and Famous University of Oxford, from the fifteenth Year of King Henry the Seventh, Dom. 1500, to the End of the Year 1690. Representing The Birth, Fortune, Preferment, and Death of all those Authors and Prelates, the great Accidents of their Lives, and the Fate and Character of their Writings* (two volumes, 1691–92). The second edition (two volumes, 1721) had as its closing date Wood's death in 1695, and included 500 new lives that Wood had left in manuscript to the care of Thomas Tanner.[26] There were 164 subscribers to this edition, of whom thirty-five were booksellers (including Michael Johnson of Lichfield, Samuel Johnson's father). Further manuscript collections intended as supplements to Wood were made at different stages by White Kennett, Humfrey Wanley and Richard Rawlinson.[27] Wood proved an invaluable source of information, but many of his successors, while drawing heavily on his work and paying tribute to its importance, felt obliged to dissociate themselves from his high-church sympathies and sometimes ferocious judgements. Wood, who worked as a freelance antiquarian in Oxford, tells the reader at the beginning of the first volume of *Athenae Oxonienses* how he wrote to three categories of men in his search for information: members of the Church of England, some of whom were very communicative; nonconformists, most of whom were very reluctant to help him, '*not knowing what use might be made of such Communications, to their Disadvantage*'; and Roman Catholics, who were always ready to give him information about their own. He claims that his encomiums of writers from the three groups do not represent his own judgement, but '*domestick Testimonies of the Reputation which each Man had or hath among his own*', a claim hard to credit. Wood portrays himself as an ascetic, with no college position, '*Dead to the World, and utterly unknown to the generality of Scholars in* Oxon', but his biographical dictionary made him famous in the learned world and became a resource that no scholar, whatever his persuasion, could afford to neglect.[28]

Wood arranged his dictionary chronologically, according to his subjects' dates of death; in this respect it differs from the alphabetical arrangement adopted by Moréri, Bayle and the eighteenth-century folio dictionaries. Wood's choice of writers and bishops educated at Oxford is less limiting than it might appear; as is pointed out by the author of the introduction (identified in the 1721 edition as James Harington of Christ Church), '*The Work, in its several commendable Digressions, seems almost to contain an exact and full History of Learning, and of the Learned Men in England'.*[29] Wood's standard pattern is a lively account of a life, in which carefully accumulated details are interspersed with anecdotes and judgements on the subject's conduct as man and writer, followed by a full list of his works. Footnotes are few and are used for bibliographical references only. His method is thus quite unlike Bayle's, but it can be seen to have exerted a significant influence both on Alexander Chalmers' *General Biographical Dictionary* (1812–17) and Leslie Stephen and Sidney Lee's *Dictionary of National Biography* (1885–1900). In his account of writers since 1641 (the subject of his second volume) Wood's sympathies are openly expressed: they are with the executed Archbishop Laud, with the sequestered Anglicans of the Interregnum, such as Peter Gunning and John Fell, and with nonjurors such as George Hickes, while his treatment of latitudinarians such as John Wilkins, Joseph Glanvill and Edward Fowler, and Puritans and nonconformists such as William Prynne, Samuel Annesley, Joseph and Richard Allein and John Flavel, is deliberately insulting.

The later dictionaries acknowledge their debt to Wood under individual lives, but express varying degrees of distaste. The anonymous continuer of the *Supplement to the Great Dictionary*, who does not share Collier's sympathies, observes that Wood ignored the nonconformist Philip Henry, 'perhaps . . . because he could find nothing for his spiteful Teeth to fasten on', but in his account of Wood himself is not unfair: 'There seems to be an Air of Plainness, and of a down-right Honesty, without Affectation or Ceremony, throughout his Histories; for he relates the good and bad of all Persons, and Parties.' His love of the royal cause made him treat the Presbyterians harshly. 'He has told many bold Truths, which created him some Trouble, and many Enemies.'[30] The preface to *A General Dictionary* objects that *Athenae Oxonienses* is 'executed in a very loose and inaccurate manner, with a manifest partiality through the whole, and without any tolerable method, or the least elegance of style and composition'. Birch's article on Wood disappointingly contains no general assessment of his work.[31] Nevertheless, *A General Dictionary* uses Wood where appropriate. The preface to *Biographia Britannica* complains that 'the spleen of the author discovers itself frequently, the composition is by no means elegant, and there is an unusual bluntness and asperity in the language. Yet, with all these defects, it is out of comparison more useful and instructive than any thing that had appeared before' (i.e. among English works).[32] Whereas Birch in *A General Dictionary* accepts Wood's sneer at Glanvill – 'After the Restoration he *turned about*, says Mr. Wood, and *became a Latitudinarian*' – Campbell in *Biographia Britannica* corrects this interpretation:

Mr Glanvill shewed great readiness in conforming, as other eminent and learned persons, who had been educated in those unhappy times, also did, without deserving in the least to be reproached for turning about, because in all probability they followed the light of reason and their own consciences.[33]

Criticism of Wood is voiced even more sharply by John Berkenhout in the preface to *Biographia Literaria* (1777): 'his manner is cynical, his language antiquated, and his civil and religious opinions illiberal.'[34] Chalmers, who draws attention to the corrections and additions in Bliss's new edition of Wood (five volumes, 1813–15), gives a fairer summing up: 'we know not any man to whom English biography is so much indebted, although we may allow, at the same time, that he is deficient in judgment and style.'[35]

Wood had a galvanizing effect on Edmund Calamy, the early eighteenth-century historian of nonconformity. Calamy had tried to help Matthew Sylvester edit the autobiographical and other papers of the nonconformist leader and devotional writer Richard Baxter, published in 1696 in an ill-organized folio as *Reliquiae Baxterianae*. In 1702 Calamy brought out in octavo *An Abridgment of Mr. Baxter's History of his Life and Times. With an Account of many others of those Worthy Ministers who were Ejected after the Restoration of King Charles the Second*. In the preface he devotes several pages to castigating Wood for 'his Rancour and Bitterness in ill Natur'd particular Reflections' and his 'foul Aspersions' on the nonconformists. It was essential to controvert them: 'What must those who come after us think of our supine Neglect, should such malignant Insinuations as his ... be suffer'd to pass uncontradicted.' Calamy thought Wood had ruined an excellent conception in the execution. 'The Truth of it is the *Athenae Oxonienses*, Historically relating the Writers of that Famous University with their Works, was a very Noble Design: But the Canker'd Spirit of the Authour, has spoil'd that which otherwise had been one of the best Books, that a Biographer could easily have met with.'

Chapter 9 of the *Abridgment*, which is over 300 pages long and quite out of proportion to the rest of the book, consists of '*A Particular Account of the Ministers, Lecturers, Fellows of Colledges*, &c. *who were Silenced and Ejected by the* Act for Uniformity: *With the Characters and Works of many of them*', to some extent modelled on Baxter's much shorter account.[36] Calamy went to a great deal of trouble to obtain accurate information, drawing on manuscript catalogues, printed lives, funeral sermons and friends' memoirs. He was well aware of the importance of what he was doing, and regarded this chapter simply as a foretaste: 'Whatever Acceptance this part of my Performance meets with, this I can say, it hath cost me much Time and Pains, in Reading and Abridging so many Printed Accounts and Manuscript Narratives. And yet 'tis but a Specimen of what I intend.' In addition to the motives of setting the nonconformist record straight and strengthening contemporary dissent against high-church intolerance, Calamy saw a more general educational and moral value in his biographical accounts:

> If any think it unseasonable to revive the Memory of these Good Men, I would desire them to consider, that there's a great deal of Curiosity in the Age we live in, which inclines Men of sense and tho't, to be inquisitive into the Notions, the Conduct and Fate, of those, of a different Stamp from themselves, as well as of those who stand upon the Square with them, that they may have the better Understanding of Humane Nature, as well as of their own Country, under its several different Faces.[37]

Calamy twice enlarged his 'specimen': in the second edition of *An Abridgement of Mr. Baxter's History of his Life and Times* (1713), *An Account of the Ministers, Lecturers, Masters and Fellows of Colleges and Schoolmasters* constituted the second volume, and *A Continuation of the Account of the Ministers etc* (1727) took up two volumes. The latter was described by Campbell in *Biographia Britannica* as 'A work of prodigious industry and labour, and which is alone sufficient to transmit his memory with honour to posterity, as it has supplied the learned world with a noble collection of memoirs, which otherwise in all probability had been dissipated and lost.'[38] In the preface to the second volume of the 1713 *Abridgement* Calamy noted that the first edition had soon been bought up and read with approval by persons of quality and divines of the Church of England as well as dissenters, though '*many were incens'd to that Degree, that they knew not how to keep their indignation within any tolerable Bounds*'. Yet in the interests of toleration on both sides, Calamy was pleased to learn that an account of the sufferings of the episcopal party in the period 1640 to 1660 was being compiled, and he wished that he could have taken advantage of its publication before his second edition.[39]

The work to which he referred, published the following year, was John Walker's *An Attempt towards Recovering an Account of the Numbers and Sufferings of the Clergy of the Church of England, Heads of Colleges, Fellows, Scholars, &c. who were Sequester'd, Harrass'd, &c. in the late Times of the Grand Rebellion: Occasion'd by the Ninth Chapter (now the Second Volume) of Dr. Calamy's Abridgment of the Life of Mr. Baxter.* Just as Calamy's work was intended to strengthen the position of dissent, so Walker, who dedicated his book to the archbishops, bishops and clergy then assembled in Convocation, wrote in

defence of the established church. His lengthy preface is particularly interesting
for his account of the difficulties he encountered in finding materials for his
lives – 'because the Path was in a manner wholly untrodden, I found my self
oblig'd, first, to Encounter the Difficulty of Beating out my Road, as well as
that of Travelling it afterwards' – and of the places he searched, such as
libraries and public offices, the individuals who helped him, the printed
sources he used (*Athenae Oxonienses* was particularly important), and the
manuscripts he consulted. He had originally intended to produce only lists of
the cathedrals, the two universities, and the clergy of London and Devon, but
he decided this would be 'only a Dry and Sapless Alphabet', so instead he
followed the method of Calamy's *Abridgment* and gave a short account of each
sufferer as well as of his sufferings.[40] The book is divided into two parts, the
first a narrative of events, the second an account of individuals, arranged by
place (the cathedrals, the colleges of Oxford and Cambridge, and individual
parishes by diocese), with references to sources in marginal notes. Wood is
much used, and so, for the relevant lives, is Izaac Walton, whose account of
Robert Sanderson, first published in 1678, was one of the earliest attempts to
provide a portrait of the sequestered Interregnum Anglicans.[41]

The works of Wood, Calamy and Walker are not biographical dictionaries
as conventionally understood. They are not arranged alphabetically (though
their indexes make alphabetical searches easy), and they have very specific
objectives, Wood to record Oxford's extraordinary importance as a nurse of
learning, to celebrate her loyal sons and castigate her disloyal ones, Calamy to
honour the memory of the nonconformist ministers who lost their livings
after 1660, Walker to honour the memory of the Church of England clergy
who lost their livings in the 1640s and 1650s. Their readers could not avoid
their partisan interpretations of the lives and actions of their subjects, but their
works were of enormous value for the writers of biographical dictionaries
who came after them. Their individual lives form the basis of many of the
accounts in the dictionaries, even where the writers feel obliged to dissociate
themselves from the particular political or religious leanings of their sources.
Equally important is the very high standard of research that they set. They
hunted down printed books and manuscripts, public and private records, they
made detailed written enquiries to any who might be in possession of papers
or information which might help them in their accounts, and they provided
prefatory statements detailing their methods. It was the fusion of these
methods with those of Bayle that gave the folio dictionaries their distinctive
character.

The folio biographical dictionaries on the Baylean model

The success of the folio dictionaries depended on the energy, intelligence, competence, and indeed the good health of their editors and contributors. The title-pages of *A General Dictionary* list John Peter Bernard, Thomas Birch and John Lockman in that order as authors, with George Sale as contributor of the articles relating to Oriental history, but Birch, who was only 26 years old when he joined the editorial team in 1732, emerged as by far the most productive and important member.[42] A Quaker by upbringing, Birch took orders in the Church of England, but spent most of his extraordinarily industrious working life as a biographer, editor and historian and as an active member of learned societies. Working on *A General Dictionary* must have been a gruelling process. It was published from 1734 to 1741 by a consortium of booksellers in monthly parts of twenty sheets, for which the editors shared £24 per month; the price to the public for each part was 3s 6d, 'which it is presumed will not be thought unreasonable, considering the Labour such a Work requires, and the Number of Books in most Languages that have been purchased to complete it'. The original intention was that the work should be published in six folio volumes with twelve monthly numbers per volume; this plan was soon modified to eight volumes with nine monthly numbers, presumably to give the editors more time, but ten volumes were eventually needed.[43] All the additional articles (i.e. additional to the translation of Bayle) were indicated by a hand ☞ in the margin; new remarks added to Bayle's articles were enclosed within crotchets (i.e. square brackets). The authors of the great majority of the additional articles were identified by initial as H, T, P and I. At the end of the chronological table of lives provided at the beginning of Volume 10, the meaning of the initials was revealed: P stood for Bernard, T and H for Birch, and I for Lockman. James Osborn calculated that Birch wrote 618 of the 889 new biographies, 'an achievement that makes much twentieth-century scholarship seem mere Lilliputian botanizing'.[44]

The decision (presumably made by the booksellers) to combine a new translation of Bayle's historical and critical dictionary with a new English biographical dictionary created some conflicts and anomalies but also had very important intellectual consequences. Anger was voiced by the owners of *A General Dictionary* at the decision by a rival consortium to publish a different five-volume translation of Bayle simultaneously, *The Dictionary, Historical and Critical of Mr Peter Bayle* (1734–38). The advertisement for the latter, 'A character and recommendation of Monsieur Bayle's dictionary', printed at the front of Volume 1 (1734), forcefully emphasizes the populist aspect of this undertaking: it will be sold in parts,

> by which every Reader, who can afford a *shilling once a Fortnight*, will in three or four Years time be Master of a Library, *a great Library* in a *few Volumes*; from whence our common Artificers and Farmers, and even their Wives and Children, may gather much Learning as well as much Entertainment, and acquire more Instruction, and better Principles, at their own Fireside, than others bring with Expence from Places of great Name, where real Ignorance and wretched Notions have usurped the Seat of Erudition, but still cover themselves with it's Cloak.

The corresponding advertisement prefacing the first volume of *A General Dictionary* objected (from a sight of the first number) that the rival version was as full of errors as the previous translation of 1710. However, the editors of *A General Dictionary* did not need to fear the competition of the much cheaper *Dictionary, Historical and Critical*; their much more ambitious version, twice the length because of the additional material, set new standards for biography and was to exercise an enormous influence on subsequent dictionaries, whereas the rival translation seems to have disappeared from literary history.

Building a dictionary round Bayle created obvious problems. Some of Bayle's entries, particularly on English subjects, were deemed inadequate; partly because of the awkward relationship between his dictionary and Moréri's, there were deliberate omissions; and Bayle's philosophical scepticism and erotic interests were potentially embarrassing. The first case was dealt with by printing Bayle's articles but supplementing them with additional ones based on better scholarship. Some interesting theological examples from Volume 2 are Arminius, where Birch's very long addition draws on Gaspar Brandt's *History of the Reformation in the Low Countries* (1724) and Peter Heylyn's *Historia Quinqu-Articularis* (1660); Thomas Barlow, where Birch uses Wood 'to supply the defects of Mr. Bayle's Article of this great and learned Writer'; and Peter Baro, where Bernard announces, 'Mr. Bayle's account of this great Man being very imperfect, and even erroneous, we shall here supply his defects, and correct his errors', and further berates Des Maizeaux for misinforming Bayle about the status of Calvinism in the Church of England.[45]

The anticipated objections of readers to Bayle's embarrassing aspects – 'the vein of unbounded Scepticism, and the sallies of a loose imagination, which he has indulged in several articles' – are confronted in the preface to the first volume: nothing is retrenched, and 'we can only condemn whatever is obnoxious in it'. The preface goes on carefully to differentiate the new part of the dictionary from Bayle's in these respects:

However we are confident, that no reasonable complaint can be formed against any part of our own performance, as carried beyond the just freedom of reveal'd Religion, or inconsistent with the most severe modesty. And we doubt not but that a just account of the Lives and Writings of great and valuable Men will prove of more real and extensive advantage to the interests of Religion and Virtue, than all the efforts of Scepticism can to the contrary.

Bayle's lengthy self-defence under four headings – 'I. To the Encomiums bestowed on Persons, who denied either the Providence or Existence of the Deity. II. To the Objections of the Manichees. III. To the Objections of the Sceptics. IV To obscene Touches.' – was included in Volume 10. Occasional attempts were made to render him less dangerous. Thus Bernard's article on Bayle quoted a statement made by Bayle to De la Roche three or four years before he died, 'that it was impossible for the most subtle Atheists to confute the arguments grounded upon the contrivance and wisdom conspicuous in the several parts of the Universe', and concluded 'that Mr. Bayle was more orthodox than many persons imagine'.[46] For readers who compared Bayle's articles with Birch's, *A General Dictionary* would on one level have appeared to be a kind of dialogue between Bayle's scepticism and the natural religion that underpinned eighteenth-century Anglicanism.[47]

A particularly interesting aspect of the new articles in *A General Dictionary* is the adaptation of Bayle's system of critical remarks. The preface to Volume 1 announces that the editors have used materials in dedications, prefaces, funeral sermons and pamphlets in addition to works such as Wood's, but what is striking is the regular appearance of manuscript material in the remarks. The reader is often presented with the raw material of research, rather than with analysis. For example, Birch's article on John Milton (itself a supplement to Bayle's) quotes at length from the Trinity College manuscript; the very brief main text of Birch's article on Henry Oldenburg is accompanied by long extracts from his letters to Robert Boyle.[48] The article on Lord Russell avowedly exists as an excuse for the publication of manuscript material: 'RUSSEL, the name of an ancient and illustrious family, from which was descended William Lord Russel, of whom we shall give an article, in order to insert some original letters and papers never before published.'[49] The remarks contain letters by Gilbert Burnet and Lady Russell on the subject of Russell's trial and execution. Birch's article on John Trenchard prints from the manuscript Samuel Clarke's objections to Trenchard's articles on religion published in the *British Journal*; his article on Lady Winchilsea includes previously unpublished poems.[50] Each article contains quantities of information about individuals who are not the ostensible subject of that article, and Volume 10 includes an invaluable index designed precisely to help users gain access to this information: 'The particulars inserted in this Index, are only such as are not to be found in the Dictionary, in the Articles to which they properly belong.'

Birch seems to have had a particular interest in bibliographical details, rather than in the arguments or beliefs of the divines, philosophers, scientists or poets he wrote about. His method was often to catalogue an author's works in a long note and to give details of the contents of one of them. In his articles on controversial writers, such as Anthony Collins (Volume 4), Bernard Mande-ville (Volume 7) and Thomas Woolston (Volume 10), this took the form of providing very full lists of replies by their opponents. Birch's obsession with detail is noted with different emphases by his successors. The verbose Kippis in his article on Birch in the second edition of Biographia Britannica excuses Birch's failure to select: 'If . . . [Birch] carried the fault of minuteness to an excess, it least of all becomes us Biographers to blame it.'[51] The brisk Chalmers, whose article on Birch in The General Biographical Dictionary is extracted from Kippis, adds a telling remark by Ralph Heathcote, a friend of Birch and one of Chalmers' predecessors on A New and General Biographical Dictionary: 'He had a favourite position, that we could not be possessed of too many facts.'[52]

Biographia Britannica, published in seven volumes from 1747 to 1766, was, as its title made clear, digested in the Manner of Mr Bayle's Historical and Critical Dictionary, with an obvious debt to A General Dictionary. According to Andrew Kippis, the volumes appeared in weekly numbers beginning in 1745.[53] The contributors were identified by initials derived from their places of residence, but no key was given; however, in the prefaces to the first and second volumes of the second edition, Kippis identified them as follows: T stood for the Revd Thomas Broughton, Reader to the Temple, C for the Revd Philip Morant of Colchester, G for William Oldys of Gray's Inn, P for Sir Philip Nichols, E and X for John Campbell, then living in Exeter Court, R for the Revd Mr Hinton of Red Lion Square, H for Henry Brougham, and D for Mr Harris of Dublin. I and Z were not identified.[54] The antiquarian Oldys, who had himself written at least one article for A General Dictionary, contrib-uted twenty-two articles to the first five volumes (he died in 1761) and was probably responsible for the preface to the first volume.[55] The preface emphasizes the advantage of Bayle's method –'and this advantage in the hands of a man of extensive learning, lively imagination, and happy expression, appeared with all it's lustre' – but it goes on to argue that it was a mistake for booksellers to attempt to complete the dictionaries of Bayle and Moréri by augmenting them with additional articles and supplements. (Though *A General Dictionary* is not mentioned in the preface, it is implicitly criticized here.) Instead, it would be more practicable and useful to compile in Bayle's method in the several countries of Europe 'complete Bodies of the *Personal Histories* of the great and eminent persons that have flourished in them'. 'And will not some honour arise, some proportion of glory be due to the country, where this design, so useful to learning in general, as well as so beneficial to that country itself, shall be first set on foot?' The *Biographia Britannica*, subtitled *The Lives of the Most Eminent Persons who have flourished in Great Britain and Ireland, from the earliest Ages, down to the present Times*, thus advertises itself as the first of a new kind of dictionary, 'a kind of general MONUMENT erected to the most deserving of all ages, an expression of gratitude due to their services, and the most probable means of exciting, in succeeding times, a spirit of emulation, which might prompt men to an imitation of their virtues.' A survey of existing collections of biographies from John Boston in the reign of Henry IV through to Wood, and of examples of individual lives and memoirs shows that 'there has nothing appeared of the same nature with our design'. The *Biographia* will include not only divines and scholars, but statesmen, captains, seamen, patriots, 'all who have rendered themselves remarkable in publick posts, or deserve to be remembered for their private virtues'. One of the uses of the dictionary is that it will be continually added to, so that

> every man of genius, every person endowed with a generous and liberal spirit, will become more steady and more assiduous, as well as more eager in pursuit of knowledge and virtue, when he is sensible that his labours will not be buried in oblivion, but that whatever he gloriously atchieves will be faithfully recorded.

At the same time the editors have chosen Bayle's method, not because of his reputation among the learned, 'but because it appeared to us the most natural, easy, and comprehensive, the best adapted to our purpose, and the most likely to give our readers satisfaction'. The importance of the notes from the point of view of historical scholarship is stressed: they 'make a perpetual commentary, in the manner of BAYLE, in which all doubtful points are examined, disagreeing relations compared, and the truth, from thence, set in a clear light.' Passages scattered in works on other subjects are thus secured from being overlooked. The articles function as 'both a Supplement and a Key, not only to our General Histories, but to particular Memoirs'.[56]

There would seem to be an inherent tension between the traditional humanist motive of writing lives for the purposes of glory and emulation and the application of the Baylean critical method to the scrutiny of historical sources. Some readers evidently deplored the hagiographic aspect: Berkenhout in the preface to *Biographia Literaria* thought the adulatory portraits should be attributed to philanthropy, and also answered an implicit criticism of the style as old-fashioned by defending the contributors' credentials as professional historians: 'If it be true that their language is that of the last century, it may be answered, that politer men would probably have been deficient in more essential knowledge and abilities.'[57] Kippis in his article on Campbell suggested that public interest flagged after the first two volumes, but revived as a result of Gilbert West's encomium at the end of his poem *Education*,[58] 'from which time the undertaking was carried on with increasing reputation and success'. Kippis attributed much of this reputation and success to Campbell's articles:

> He was not satisfied with giving a cold narration of the personal circumstances relative to the eminent men whose lives he drew up, but was ambitious of entering into such a copious and critical discussion of their actions or writings, as should render the Biographia Britannica a most valuable Repository of historical and literary Knowledge.[59]

Campbell, who was admired by Johnson for his 'very extensive reading',[60] covered a vast range of historical and political subjects during his forty-year career as a professional writer, culminating in his *Political Survey of Britain* (four volumes, 1774); presumably because of his other commitments he contributed only to the first four volumes of the *Biographia*. His articles include Charles Blount, Sir Thomas Browne, Edmund Calamy, Jeremy Collier, Oliver Cromwell, Richard Cumberland, Joseph Glanvill and Thomas Hobbes, the last surprisingly sympathetic. Some of them, notably that on Cromwell, are very long, partly because of the general but misguided tendency in the *Biographia* to interpret the Baylean method of commentary as an opportunity for very extensive quotation from historical sources, far more than appears in *A General Dictionary*.

The relationship between the two dictionaries is more complex than might at first appear. The later dictionary, with its national remit, includes figures missing from the earlier, but sometimes the opposite is true. Where there is an overlap, the later is often the fuller and superior version, but this is not invariably the case. Campbell's accounts of Browne and Calamy are certainly superior to Birch's. Campbell justifies his 'copious account' of Browne for patriotic reasons: 'it seems to be a reflection on his countrymen, that while his fame is so great abroad, there should be nothing of this sort worthy of his memory, performed at home.'[61] Articles in the *Biographia* tend to be more complimentary than their equivalents in *A General Dictionary*: thus Archbishop Laud is portrayed much more favourably by Morant than by Birch.[62] Sometimes an article in the *Biographia* is better informed than its *General Dictionary* counterpart because more source material or a new assessment has been published in the interim: thus Sir Philip Nichols' account of Benjamin Whichcote makes use of Samuel Salter's important preface to his edition of Whichcote's *Moral and Religious Aphorisms* (1753), unavailable to Birch.[63] Birch's article on Sir Walter Ralegh is indebted to Oldys' important life, published with Ralegh's *The History of the World* (1736), and Birch added his own life to Ralegh's *Works* (1751). Nichols took the opportunity of his derivative article to castigate David Hume for maligning a national hero in the first volume of his *History of Great Britain* (1754): Hume 'has taken much unworthy pains to fix Sir Walter as an odious character in the English annals.'[64] The *Biographia* is indebted to other works by Birch published long after *A General Dictionary*: the Supplement to the *Biographia* includes articles on the dramatist and philosopher Catharine Cockburn (author unidentified) and the evangelical James Hervey (by Nichols), which are derived from the invaluable lives by Birch prefacing Cockburn's *Works* (1751) and Hervey's *Letters* (1760).[65]

Despite its stated aims, the *Biographia* is not confined to the celebration of worthies. For example, throughout the dictionary there is considerable interest in the period of the Civil War and in the motives of its participants. Nichols gives the following explanation for his account of the leveller John Lilburne (who is treated cursorily by Birch in *A General Dictionary*):

> one main design in enlarging upon this article, was to produce a large variety of instances, which may serve as a commentary to the History of the Rebellion [by Clarendon], the plan of which would not admit of being so particular. Another principal end herein, has been to give a series of proofs not commonly known, of the infinite guile and subtlety of Cromwell.[66]

Morant used his article on the Quaker James Nayler as an opportunity for an essay on the dangers of enthusiasm:

> This blind and ungovernable guide has, at different times, led an incredible number of persons of weak judgment and a strong imagination, through a maze of such strange and unaccountable follies, as, one would imagine, could never have entered into the thoughts of a creature endowed with Reason.[67]

Elsewhere in the *Biographia* a passion for sharing the fruits of research and stimulating further work is paramount. Nichols' article on the antiquarian

Ralph Thoresby is largely devoted to the text of Thoresby's unfinished manuscript history of the north of England from the time of the Britons and Romans to the end of the sixth century, 'in hopes that it may excite some able hand to carry it on and compleat the noble design of its Author in it'.[68] The article on Edmund Spenser includes a detailed account of Spenser's manner of allegorizing from Spence's *Polymetis* (1747), 'which, as the book is not in very many hands, we shall lay before the Reader'.[69] The article on the Marian martyr Nicholas Ridley, based on the life by Glocester Ridley (1763), provides a moving example of the kind of detail the dictionary writers loved. Nichols observes that 'there is one particular related by the writer of his life, which has escaped, if I mistake not, the diligence of others, and therefore, being somewhat curious, shall be preserved here.' What follows is an account of the supper Ridley gave for his friends the evening before his martyrdom, with an itemized bill, consisting of bread and ale, shoulder of mutton, pig, plover, cheese and pears, and wine, totalling 2s 6½d.[70]

The developing characteristics of the English Baylean dictionary – the love of detail, the urge to fill columns of notes with quotations, the struggle to keep up with recent publications in order to remain true to Bayle's original concept of the dictionary as a library – eventually brought about its extinction. The second edition of the *Biographia Britannica* was undertaken by Andrew Kippis, Presbyterian minister and tutor at the dissenting academies of Hoxton and Hackney, after Johnson had declined the booksellers' invitation.[71] The Bodleian Library copy contains, bound in at the front of the first volume, the contract, dated 22 February 1776, between Kippis and the booksellers Rivington, Davis, Longman, Cadell and Robinson. Kippis undertook to make corrections and improvements to the original and to add important lives of those who had either been omitted by the previous editors or who had died since publication. The work was to consist of eight folio volumes of about 200 sheets each, for which Kippis was to be paid 100 guineas a volume.[72] Publication began in 1778, but at the time of Kippis' death in 1795, halfway through the sixth volume, he had only reached the letter F.[73] His rate of progress makes it only too clear that his interpretation of the Baylean method was unworkable, even though he had a great deal of help. New articles and additional notes and observations, increasingly numerous as the volumes progressed, were distinguished by brackets. Kippis was responsible for the articles marked K, and Joseph Towers, also a Presbyterian minister and compiler of the first seven volumes of the octavo *British Biography* (1766–72), for those marked T. In addition, several scholars are thanked for information in the prefaces to each volume, including Thomas Astle, Thomas Percy,

Francis Blackburne, Richard Gough, Sir David Dalrymple (Lord Hailes), Sir John Hawkins and John Nichols, and others are identified as contributing whole articles.[74]

Kippis' prefaces provide a full account of his aims and methods, together with increasingly self-conscious apologies for his delays. He wished to conduct the work with 'real impartiality' and 'a philosophical liberality of mind', while at the same time insisting on his editorial viewpoint: 'We scruple not to declare our attachment to the great interests of mankind, and our enmity to bigotry, superstition, and tyranny, whether found in Papist or Protestant, Whig or Tory, Churchman or Dissenter.' He saw the second edition of the *Biographia* as an important contribution to the eighteenth-century science of man:

> [Biography] may be regarded as presenting us with a variety of events, that, like experiments in Natural Philosophy, may become the materials from which general truths and principles are to be drawn. When Biographical knowledge is employed in enlarging our acquaintance with Human Nature, in exciting an honourable emulation, in correcting our prejudices, in refining our sentiments, and in regulating our conduct, it then attains its true excellence. Besides its being a pleasing amusement, and a just tribute of respect to illustrious characters, it rises to the dignity of SCIENCE; and of such science as must ever be esteemed of peculiar importance, because it hath MAN for its object.[75]

Kippis was convinced of the rightness of Bayle's method for this purpose (with the standard rejection of Bayle's 'scepticism and licentiousness'), though it is clear from his prefaces that many correspondents were dissatisfied. He repeatedly spelled out what he was doing. In cases where he disagreed with his predecessors, he added notes declaring his difference of opinion and the reasons for it. (Thus just as Bayle took issue with Moréri, Birch with Bayle and Campbell with Birch, so did Kippis with Campbell and others.) He always cited his authorities, and never referred to a book which he had not seen. If his information came from secondary sources, he cited those sources.[76] He thought it an essential aspect of the *Biographia* to provide details of the writings of learned men and the controversies to which they gave occasion:

> In the vast variety of publications, accumulating from age to age, it is scarcely possible that the knowledge of many of them should be preserved in any other way than by a work of this nature. Every man of letters, however extensive his reading may be, must feel the full force of this observation.

Kippis acknowledged that some readers disliked the use of reflections and remarks, 'though recommended by the example of such Biographers as a

Tacitus and a Plutarch, a Bayle and a Johnson'.[77] Some objected to too much
fresh matter. 'But considering the present solicitude for Biographical knowledge, it seems better to err on the side of excess than of defect.' Some thought
the choice of subjects for new articles should be limited to very distinguished
statesmen and warriors. 'But as a History of British Literature, the Biographia
ought to contain as much information, and include as great a variety of
objects, as the nature of the design can admit.' Kippis' answer to the complaint
that Bayle's method sometimes made the text too scanty in relation to the
notes was to make the text as full as possible, but he nevertheless insisted that
'the form of Bayle will be found, on the whole, best suited to a Work, in
which accounts of books, extracts from authors, original letters, and critical
discussions are frequently necessary'.[78] It was important to give copious
accounts of books because they were continually being displaced,[79] but Kippis
did the same for books he believed were likely to last. In his article on Elijah
Fenton, he quoted Johnson's objection in his *Lives of the Poets* (1779–81) that
Fenton included too many long quotations from Clarendon in his edition of
Edmund Waller: 'Illustrations drawn from a book so easily consulted, should
be made by reference rather than transcription.' Kippis replied to this
objection, fundamentally at odds with the Baylean method of the *Biographia*,
that it was better for readers 'not to be obliged too frequently to have recourse
to authors who, though well known, may not always be readily at hand'.[80]
Indeed, in his additional note to Campbell's article on Sir Thomas Browne,
Kippis claimed that for quoting at length from Johnson's life of Browne
prefixed to *Christian Morals* (1756), 'we shall receive the thanks of our
readers'.[81]

Kippis' desire for a dictionary that would be among other things a record
of literary history and a conveniently accessible library is perfectly consistent
with Bayle's original plan, but in the face of the publishing explosion of the
late eighteenth century it was manifestly impossible. Kippis had seriously
misjudged the time and space needed to bring the *Biographia* up to date on
this model, and he had too many other commitments as a dissenting
spokesman to be able to carry on the work any faster. His critics thought he
over-emphasized the importance of dissent in the life of the nation, though in
the preface to the first volume he carefully heaped praise on Oxford and
Cambridge and made no reference to the dissenting academies or the Scottish
universities.[82] In his funeral sermon his colleague Abraham Rees, himself a
dissenting minister, educationalist and author of an encyclopedia, praised
perhaps too warmly Kippis' industry, knowledge and judgement as editor of
the *Biographia* and the quality of his remarks and reflections, but observed

fairly that those who considered the time and labour necessary and the range of his other engagements would 'admire his unwearied diligence and perseverance rather than find fault with the slow progress of such a publication'.[83]

With the death of Kippis, the English Baylean folio dictionary died too. This does not mean that its reputation collapsed. Richard Watson, in the unpaginated 'Catalogue of books in Divinity' appended to the sixth volume of his *Collection of Theological Tracts* for clerics and students (1785, reprinted 1791), recommended both *A General Dictionary* (noting that for those who were unable to buy it, Bayle, Moréri or Collier would serve instead) and the second edition of *Biographia Britannica*, which Watson thought would become 'one of the most complete works of the kind that ever appeared in any Language'. However, quite apart from the failure to complete it, the *Biographia* faced competition from the increasing popularity both of collections of lives of specific groups, such as admirals, doctors, dramatists, preachers and women, and of much cheaper octavo biographical dictionaries which provided summary narratives and a brief list of references but none of the detailed footnote remarks and reflections of the Baylean kind. Kippis' collaborator Towers had previously pointed out in the preface to *British Biography* that the *Biographia* (i.e. the first edition) and *A General Dictionary* were too voluminous and too highly priced to come into ordinary hands or be generally read.[84] The most successful of the octavo dictionaries, *A New and General Biographical Dictionary* (eleven volumes, 1761–62), was international in its coverage, though with a bias towards the British and Irish, and went through a number of revisions and expansions (twelve volumes, 1784; fifteen volumes, 1798–1810), of which the most important was that by Alexander Chalmers, *The General Biographical Dictionary* (thirty-two volumes, 1812–17). The preface to the first volume of the first edition surveys existing biographical dictionaries (Bayle, *A General Dictionary*, *Biographia Britannica*, *Athenae Oxonienses* and Collier), and finds fault with all of them. Bayle's is dismissed as 'nothing more than a vehicle for his criticism', 'the transcript of a voluminous common-place book', and 'rather a miscellany of critical and metaphysical speculations, than a system of Biography'. Dictionaries that use Bayle's method are liable to the same objections. *A New and General Biographical Dictionary*, on the other hand, deliberately avoids 'mere criticism, minute enquiries and discussions'.[85] Chalmers, in the important advertisement prefacing Volume 1 of his revision, explains his additions and improvements. He defends his rewriting of most of the lives in whole or in part and his inclusion of many new ones. Biography is a form that progresses: 'every new work, if performed with equal industry and accuracy, must excel the past in utility and copiousness.' Other improvements to which he draws attention are the number of references to authorities and the copious lists of each author's writings, but this does not mean that Chalmers has any time for the Baylean method. He is contemptuous of the 'ostentatious minuteness' of the *Biographia* and *A General Dictionary*.[86] The article on Bayle is utterly dismissive. After the usual complaints about Bayle's impertinent treatment of religion and his obscenity, it continues: 'Considered in a critical light, this Dictionary may be allowed to form a vast mass of information, but the plan is radically bad. . . . It is much to be regretted that his reputation was such as to render this mode of writing Biography a fashion.'[87] By the early nineteenth century this fashion had passed.

Changing fortunes of writers in the biographical dictionaries

The modern reader is more likely to be interested in the scholarly than the patriotic elements of the English Baylean dictionary, and in particular in the idea of scholarship as interdependent, progressive and evolving. A valuable but neglected aspect of the dictionaries which deserves much broader exploration than is possible here is their function as a record of the changing reputations of writers through the century. What follows is a brief outline of how three important religious, philosophical and literary writers of the later seventeenth and early eighteenth centuries were treated in the dictionaries. The writers chosen for illustration here are Bunyan, Shaftesbury and Dryden, but Hales, Chillingworth, Tillotson, Hobbes, Locke, Milton, Marvell and Behn would have been equally revealing.

John Bunyan is a very interesting example of a major English author who was relatively neglected by the biographical dictionaries until the late eighteenth century. He is not mentioned by Calamy,[88] nor in Collier's *Great Dictionary* or *Supplement*, nor in *A General Dictionary*. There is a surprisingly favourable reference in the second edition of *Athenae Oxonienses* under Edward Fowler, with whom Bunyan clashed; he is described as 'Author of several useful and practical Books; among which one is entit. *The Pilgrim's Progress*'.[89] There is a very brief entry by Broughton in *Biographia Britannica*; regrettably note F, which should have been about *Pilgrim's Progress*, is missing, presumably because of a printer's error. In the entry under Fowler Morant dismisses him as 'the Antinomian'.[90] However, in the years between the two editions of the *Biographia* Bunyan's reputation changed dramatically, and the process can be observed in the second edition. Kippis adds a remark in which he draws on the favourable but unsubtle entry in *A New and General Biographical Dictionary*, and quotes the very high praise (though he thinks it is carried too far) in James Granger's *A Biographical History of England*: 'Bunyan, who has been mentioned among the least and lowest of our writers, . . . deserves a much higher rank than is commonly imagined', alongside Spenser and Homer.[91] Chalmers in turn, in *The General Biographical Dictionary*, criticizes Kippis for disagreeing with Granger, and quotes Johnson's high praise of *Pilgrim's Progress* as recorded by Boswell. Chalmers' entry charts the change in Bunyan's literary reputation. For many years his allegory was

> confined to the serious part of the world for whom it was intended, and was seldom noticed by others but as the production of an illiterate man, calculated to please illiterate people. . . . But Bunyan's want of education is the highest praise that can be given. Such a defect exhibits the originality of his genius in the strongest light: and since more attention has been paid by men of critical taste to his "Pilgrim's Progress," he has been admitted into a higher rank among English writers, and it seems universally acknowledged that nothing was wanting to advance him yet higher but the advantages of education, or of an intimacy with the best writers in his own language.[92]

The reputation of the third Earl of Shaftesbury, the author of *Characteristicks*, moved in the opposite direction. Birch's valuable article in *A General Dictionary* draws on information from the fourth Earl and an excellent assessment of Shaftesbury's importance as a philosopher provided by his nephew James Harris. Harris' material in note R is taken over almost verbatim in *A New and General Biographical Dictionary*.[93] Further, in *A General Dictionary* there are references to and quotations from Shaftesbury (particularly from his letters) in the articles on Antoninus Philosophus (i.e. Marcus Aurelius), Gilbert Burnet, Ralph Cudworth, Locke, Henry More and Whichcote (all by Birch), the last containing lengthy extracts from Shaftesbury's preface to Whichcote's *Select Sermons*.[94] *Biographia Britannica*, however, treats Shaftesbury less seriously. There is no separate article in the main dictionary, only a complimentary but lazy reference to him under his grandfather the first Earl as 'a nobleman of extraordinary parts and learning, as from his celebrated writings appears'. This omission is remedied in the supplement in the article by Nichols, who is, however, cautious in his praise: 'The elegance and politeness of the *Characteristics* always has been, and is still, the universal admiration of all parties: this is the charm which captivates and binds.' There are further references to Shaftesbury in the supplement, in Nichols' articles on Hutcheson and Which-cote.[95] In the second edition Kippis is more critical. In a note added to

Broughton's article on Samuel Clarke, Kippis observes that Shaftesbury's ethical system, which made inroads into Clarke's, is now declining because of the popularity of David Hartley's principle of association. In his important article on Shaftesbury he makes use, unusually, of Birch's in *A General Dictionary* rather than reprinting Nichols' in the supplement to the *Biographia*, but he adds considerably more detail about critical responses to Shaftesbury, and notes the alterations in his standing:

> For a considerable time he stood in high reputation as a polite writer, and was regarded by many as a standard of elegant composition. His imitators, as well as admirers, were numerous, and he was esteeemed the Head of the School of the sentimental Philosophy. Of late years, he has been as much depreciated as he was heretofore applauded; and in both cases the matter has been carried to an extreme. At length, it is to be hoped, that he will find his due place in the ranks of literature; and that, without being extravagantly extolled, he will continue to be read, and in some degree to be admired.[96]

Chalmers in *The General Biographical Dictionary* draws on both Birch and Kippis, and does not add significantly to the interpretation of Shaftesbury or his reputation; he does, however, provide more information about Shaftesbury's edition of Whichcote.[97]

The standing of poets in the dictionaries can partly be gauged by the frequency of quotation. In the case of John Dryden this is especially marked, particularly in contexts in which modern readers might not expect to find him. Wood quotes with approval Dryden's portraits of Achitophel and Zimri from *Absalom and Achitophel* in his accounts of the first Earl of Shaftesbury and the second Duke of Buckingham in *Athenae Oxonienses*.[98] The anonymous author of the account in the 'Continuation' of Collier's *Supplement* is obtuse in his observation that Dryden's fancy was in decline in his translation of Virgil,[99] a view that is contradicted by the extraordinary use made of Dryden's translations in *A General Dictionary*. Birch's article on Dryden unsurprisingly quotes at length and with great approval – the 'Ode on St Cecilia's Day' is judged to be 'perhaps one of the most perfect pieces in any language' – but Dryden's voice is heard throughout the dictionary.[100] For example, there are lengthy quotations from *An Essay of Dramatic Poesy* under Ben Jonson, and 'To the memory of Mr Oldham' appears in its proper place.[101] Dryden is even more prominent as a translator in the parts of the dictionary for which Birch was not responsible. Bayle explained in the preface to his second edition of 1702 that one of the reasons he quoted long Latin passages was that many of his readers were little acquainted with French but skilled in Latin.[102] The

English editors made no such assumption about their readers' skill. Bayle's original articles on classical figures (probably translated by Bernard and Lockman)[103] are illustrated in the remarks in existing translations by English writers following the Latin, so that Dryden is a considerable presence in the articles on Ovid and Virgil, the goddess Juno, and Augustus' sister Octavia.[104] In the last of these Bayle introduces with 'transports of admiration' Anchises' lament in Book 6 of the *Aeneid* for the death of Octavia's son Marcellus (drawn on by Dryden for his poem on Oldham), the Latin followed by Dryden's version. The passage that *Biographia Britannica* was to adopt as a motto appears in the article on Virgil in Latin and in Dryden's version.[105] Despite the lengthy articles on Dryden in both editions of the *Biographia Britannica* (Kippis expands Broughton's account by incorporating much of Johnson's from *Lives of the Poets*),[106] the careful reader of *A General Dictionary* would be able to gain a much better sense of his role as the principal transmitter of Latin literature in English. Dryden is thus a very important beneficiary not only of the Baylean method of lengthy quotation, but also of the decision to combine a translation of Bayle with an English biographical dictionary.

In 1882 the initial plan of George Smith, publisher of *The Dictionary of National Biography*, was for a cyclopedia of universal biography, but on the advice of its first editor, Leslie Stephen, he decided to limit his plan to the national biography of the British Isles and Colonies. Its second editor, Sidney Lee, in his account of the completed *Dictionary* in 1900, claimed that 'Only one venture in national biography of an exhaustive and authoritative kind had been previously carried to completion in this country', namely the *Biographia Britannica* and its unfinished second edition. He harshly dismissed Chalmers' *General Biographical Dictionary* as an inadequate experiment. Surprisingly, he made no reference at all to *A General Dictionary* nor to the *Biographia*'s indebtedness to Bayle.[107] The Baylean method of critical remarks on which the great eighteenth-century folio dictionaries were built was simply ignored. This chapter has tried to show some of the lasting virtues of that method, despite the fact that it was superseded. Des Maizeaux had observed (to the objection of the octavo dictionary writers) that Bayle's text seemed to have been made for the sake of the remarks; the thousands of double columns in the Baylean dictionaries undoubtedly provided a particular kind of arena in which scholars could engage in the eighteenth-century culture of controversy – religious, philosophical, political and literary – an arena in which, as Bayle had said, every man had the right of the sword. The Baylean editors and their forebears are as much heroes as the '*sculptur'd Chiefs*' who adorn Paedia's '*monumental Pile*'.[108]

Notes

1. Gilbert West, *Education, a Poem. Canto the First* (London, 1751), stanzas iv–viii, xc–xcii, pp. 6–9, 51–2. Only one canto was published.

2. *Biographia Britannica: Or, The Lives of the Most Eminent Persons who have flourished in Great Britain and Ireland, from the earliest Ages, down to the present Times: Collected from the best Authorities, both Printed and Manuscript, and digested in the Manner of Mr Bayle's Historical and Critical Dictionary*, Vol. 6, Part 1 (London, 1763); West, *Education*, p. 52. The translation is of *Aeneid*, Book 6, ll. 660–4.

3. *Biographia Britannica*, Vol. 1 (1747), p. viii.

4. There are general accounts (not always satisfactory) in Donald A. Stauffer, *The Art of Biography in Eighteenth-Century England* (Princeton, NJ: Princeton University Press, 1941), ch. 4, and Lawrence Lipking, *The Ordering of the Arts in Eighteenth-Century England* (Princeton, NJ: Princeton University Press, 1970), ch. 3.

5. *The Dictionary, Historical and Critical of Mr Peter Bayle. The Second Edition*, Vol. 1 (London, 1734), p. 10. The preface is dated 23 October 1696. For the differences between the two London editions see pp. 143, 149–50 below.

6. For the influence of his method on the continent see Anthony Grafton, *The Footnote* (London: Faber and Faber, 1997), ch. 7.

7. *The Dictionary, Historical and Critical of Mr Peter Bayle*, Vol. 1, p. 6.

8. *A General Dictionary, Historical and Critical: In which a New and Accurate Translation of that of the Celebrated Mr. Bayle . . . is Included*, Vol. 4 (London, 1736), p. 207 (hereafter *A General Dictionary*).

9. *Ibid.*, Vol. 5 (1737), pp. 48–9; Vol. 7 (1738), p. 417; Vol. 8 (1739), pp. 768–9.

10. 'The Life of Mr Bayle', *The Dictionary, Historical and Critical of Mr Peter Bayle*, Vol. 1 (1734), p. lxxvi. The 'Life' is prefixed by a letter from Des Maizeaux (also translated from the 1730 Amsterdam edition) in which he explains that he first wrote a life at Shaftesbury's request after Bayle's death in 1706; this was published in 'a very imperfect English translation' in 1708 as *The Life of Mr. Bayle. In a Letter to a Peer of Great Britain*. The 1730 version is much more substantial. The same passage from the 1730 'Life' (in a different translation) is quoted in the preface to *A General Dictionary*, Vol. 1 (1734), n.p., but the 'Life' itself is not included.

11. See e.g. Pierre Bayle, *Historical and Critical Dictionary: Selections*, trans. with introduction and notes by Richard H. Popkin (Indianapolis: The Library of Liberal Arts, 1965).

12. There is an account of the many editions of Moréri from 1674 to 1740 in the preface to *Biographia Britannica*, Vol. 1 (1747), p. vi. Johnson told Boswell, 'we [the English] have no such book as Moréri's Dictionary', in *Journal of a Tour to the Hebrides, Boswell's Life of Johnson*, ed. G. B. Hill, rev. L. F. Powell (Oxford: Clarendon Press, 1964), Vol. 5, p. 311.

13. *A General Dictionary*, Vol. 7 (1738), p. 654.

14. *The Great Historical, Geographical, Genealogical and Poetical Dictionary*, Vol. 2 (1701), under 'Moreri', n.p. (hereafter *The Great Dictionary*).

15. *Biographia Britannica*, Vol. 1 (1747), p. vi.

16. *The Great Dictionary*, Vol. 1 (1701) (A2ᵛ).

17. Jeremy Collier, *A Supplement to the Great Historical, Geographical, Genealogical and Poetical Dictionary . . . Together with A Continuation from the Year 1688, to 1705, by another Hand*, 2nd edn (London, 1727), n.p.

18. *The Great Dictionary*, Vol. 1 (1701) (A2ᵛ).

19. *A General Dictionary*, Vol. 4 (1736), pp. 392n, 394.

20. *Biographia Britannica*, Vol. 1 (1747), pp. vi–vii.

21. *Ibid.*, Vol. 4 (1748), pp. 1410–11, n.G. For the attribution of articles in the *Biographia Britannica* see p. 152 below.

22. Andrew Kippis (ed.), *Biographia Britannica: Or, the Lives of the Most Eminent Persons who have Flourished in Great Britain and Ireland, from the Earliest Ages, to the Present Times: Collected from the Best Authorities, Printed and Manuscript, and digested in the Manner of Mr. Bayle's Historical and Critical Dictionary*, 2nd edn, Vol. 4 (London, 1789), pp. 18, 20; cf. the critical account of Collier in the preface to *A New and General Biographical Dictionary; containing An Historical and Critical Account of the Lives and Writings of the Most Eminent Persons in every Nation; Particularly the British and Irish; From the Earliest Accounts of Time to the present Period*, Vol. 1 (London, 1761), pp. v–vi.

23. Pierre Bayle, *An Historical and Critical Dictionary . . . with many Additions and Corrections, made by the Author himself, that are not in the French Editions*, 4 vols (London, 1710). See Léo Pierre Courtines, *Bayle's Relations with England and the English* (New York: Columbia University Press, 1938), pp. 48–9, 55–9.

24. *Life and Writings of Hales*, pp. iv–vi, ix–x; cf. preface to *Life and Writings of Chillingworth*, pp. a–aᵛ.

25. Des Maizeaux is thanked for his assistance in the preface to *A General Dictionary*, Vol. 1 (1734), n.p.

26. *Athenae Oxonienses*, 2nd edn (1721), Vol. 1, 'The Booksellers to the Reader', n.p.; *A General Dictionary*, Vol. 10 (1741), pp. 190–2, under Wood; *Biographia Britannica*, Vol. 6, Part 1 (1763), p. 3903, under Tanner; Philip Bliss (ed.), *Athenae Oxonienses*, Vol. 1 (1813), pp. 10–14; David C. Douglas, *English Scholars 1660–1730*, 2nd rev. edn (London: Eyre & Spottiswoode, 1951), pp. 159–60; M. J. Sommerlad, 'The Continuation of Wood's *Athenae Oxonienses*', *The Bodleian Library Record*, 7 (1966): 264–71. The extent of Tanner's alterations to Wood's papers is a matter of dispute. The second edition of *Athenae Oxonienses* (1721), Vol. 2, pp. 934ff., included writers who were still alive at the date of Wood's death, e.g. John Evelyn, George Hickes, John Howe, Edward Fowler, Robert South, John Locke and Thomas Sprat.

27. Samuel Johnson hoped that John Nichols would take over the task: see *Boswell's Life of Johnson*, Vol. 4, p. 161; Bruce Redford (ed.), *The Letters of Samuel Johnson*, Vol. 4 (Oxford: Clarendon Press, 1994), pp. 78–9. Wanley's ms. additions were communicated to Kippis by Thomas Astle, *Biographia Britannica*, 2nd edn, Vol. 1 (1778), preface, p. xx.

28. *Athenae Oxonienses*, Vol. 1 (1691), 'To the Reader', n.p.

29. *Ibid.*, Vol. 2 (1692), introduction, n.p.

30. *A Supplement to the Great Dictionary*, 2nd edn (1727), 'A Continuation of Mr. Collier's Supplement', under Henry and Wood, n.p.

31. *A General Dictionary*, Vol. 1 (1734), n.p.; Vol. 10 (1741), pp. 190–2.

32. *Biographia Britannica*, Vol. 1 (1747), p. xi.

33. *A General Dictionary*, Vol. 5 (1737), p. 430, referring to *Athenae Oxonienses*, Vol. 2 (1692), p. 495; *Biographia Britannica*, Vol. 4 (1757), p. 2203.

34. *Biographia Literaria; Or a Biographical History of Literature: Containing the Lives of English, Scotish, and Irish Authors, from the Dawn of Letters in these Kingdoms to the Present Time, chronologically and classically arranged*, Vol. 1 (London, 1777), p. ix.

35. Alexander Chalmers (ed.), *The General Biographical Dictionary: Containing an Historical and*

Critical Account of the Lives and Writings of the Most Eminent Persons in Every Nation; Particularly the British and Irish; from the Earliest Accounts to the Present Time, Vol. 32 (1817), p. 266.

36. *Reliquiae Baxterianae* (1696), Part 3, §§ 202–8.

37. *Abridgment of Mr. Baxter's History of his Life and Times* (1702), preface, n.p. See David L. Wykes, 'To Revive the Memory of Some Excellent Men:' Edmund Calamy and the Early Historians of *Nonconformity* (London: Dr. Williams's Trust, 1997).

38. *Biographia Britannica*, Vol. 2 (1748), p. 1111. A revision of Calamy was made by Samuel Palmer, *The Nonconformist's Memorial*, 2 vols (London, 1778), 3 vols (London, 1802). Kippis added to the second edition of *Biographia Britannica*, Vol. 3 (1784), pp. 142–5, a long note including details of and extracts from the ms. of Calamy's *Historical Account of My Own Life*, first published in two volumes in 1829, and a long list of his publications, with a reference to Palmer.

39. *Abridgment*, 2nd edn (1713), Vol. 2, pp. xvi, xxvii–xxviii.

40. *Sufferings of the Clergy* (1714), pp. xxiii–xxv, xxviii. Calamy replied critically in *The Church and the Dissenters Compar'd, as to Persecution* (London, 1719); he incorporated this into *A Continuation* (1727).

41. Walker's account of the sequestered clergy of Christ Church, Oxford is heavily indebted to Wood. For Sanderson and George Morley, for whom Walker used both Wood and Walton, see *Sufferings of the Clergy*, pp. 104–5. Birch used Walton's lives of John Donne and George Herbert in *A General Dictionary*, Vol. 4 (1736), pp. 631–7, and Vol. 5 (1737), p. 124. The preface to *Biographia Britannica*, Vol. 1 (1747), p. xii, cites Walton's Sir Henry Wotton as an example of an admirably well-written life. Johnson approved of George Horne's intention in 1774 to publish an edition of Walton (not carried out): 'Walton's time is at last come'; Bruce Redford (ed.), *The Letters of Samuel Johnson*, Vol. 2 (1992), p. 139. The best modern edition is Geoffrey Keynes (ed.), *The Compleat Angler. The Lives of Donne Wotton Hooker Herbert & Sanderson with Love and Truth & Miscellaneous Writings* (London: The Nonesuch Press, 1929).

42. See A. E. Gunther, *An Introduction to the Life of the Rev. Thomas Birch D.D., F.R.S. 1705–1766* (Halesworth, Suffolk: The Halesworth Press, 1984), and James M. Osborn, 'Thomas Birch and the *General Dictionary* (1734–41)', *Modern Philology*, 36 (1938–39): 25–46.

43. *A General Dictionary*, Vol. 1 (1734), preface [advertisement], n.p.; [second] preface, n.p. On the original contract see Osborn, 'Birch and the *General Dictionary*', pp. 31–2; Gunther, *Birch*, p. 13. The actual publication rate was as follows: Vol. 1 (1734), Vols 2 and 3 (1735), Vol. 4 (1736), Vol. 5 (1737), Vols 6 and 7 (1738), Vols 8 and 9 (1739), Vol. 10 (1741). Vol. 10 includes an appendix of omitted articles.

44. Osborn, 'Birch and the *General Dictionary*', p. 32. For Johnson's opinion of and debt to Birch see *Boswell's Life of Johnson*, Vol. 1, pp. 159–60.

45. *A General Dictionary*, Vol. 2 (1735), pp. 284, 671, 688, 694. See Sommerlad, 'The continuation of Wood's *Athenae Oxonienses*', pp. 270–1, for a very interesting passage on Barlow in Wood's ms. that was cut by Tanner.

46. *A General Dictionary*, Vol. 3 (1735), p. 89.

47. See e.g. the adjacent articles in Vol. 5, Epictetus (by Birch) and Epicurus (by Bayle); Birch's article on William King, which quotes Edmund Law's criticism of Bayle's method of using authorities (Vol. 6, p. 536); the additional reflections by the unidentified translator to Bayle's article on Pyrrho (Vol. 8).

48. *A General Dictionary*, Vol. 7 (1738), n.AA, pp. 582–7; Vol. 8 (1739), n.A, pp. 20–3.

49. *Ibid.*, Vol. 8, p. 816.

50. *Ibid.*, Vol. 9 (1739), n.B, pp. 628–32; Vol. 10 (1741), n.B, p. 179.

51. *Biographia Britannica*, 2nd edn, Vol. 2 (1780), p. 323. Kippis supplemented his article on Birch in Vol. 3 (1784) under 'Corrigenda & Addenda'.

52. Chalmers (ed.), *The General Biographical Dictionary*, Vol. 5 (1812), p. 287.

53. *Biographia Britannica*, 2nd edn, Vol. 3 (1784), p. 211, under Campbell. The publication rate (much slower than that of *A General Dictionary*) was as follows: Vol. 1 (1747), Vol. 2 (1748), Vol. 3 (1750), Vol. 4 (1757), Vol. 5 (1760), Vol. 6, Part 1 (1763), Vol. 6, Part 2 (1766). The last volume includes a supplement, an appendix to the supplement and an index.

54. *Biographia Britannica*, 2nd edn, Vol. 1 (1778), p. xx, Vol. 2 (1780), p. viii. The information in Vol. 2 is slightly revised. The full details are in a manuscript note bound into the Bodleian Library copy of Vol. 1, shelfmark I 1. 7 Art. Kippis wrote articles on Broughton, Vol. 2, pp. ix–x, and Campbell, Vol. 3, pp. 209–15; he was intending to write on Harris, Morant and Oldys (see Vol. 2, p. viii).

55. See Chalmers (ed.), *The General Biographical Dictionary*, under Oldys, Vol. 23 (1815), pp. 337–8; Osborn, 'Birch and the *General Dictionary*', p. 46; Pat Rogers, 'William Oldys', in George Watson (ed.), *The New Cambridge Bibliography of English Literature*, Vol. 2. *1660–1800* (Cambridge: Cambridge University Press: 1971), col. 1747; Lipking, *The Ordering of the Arts*, pp. 78–9. Lipking states erroneously that Joseph Towers was Oldys's co-editor.

56. *Biographia Britannica*, Vol. 1 (1747), pp. vii–xiii.

57. *Biographia Literaria*, Vol. 1 (1777), pp. x–xi.

58. See n.1 above.

59. *Biographia Britannica*, 2nd edn, Vol. 3 (1784), p. 211.

60. Boswell, *Journal of a Tour to the Hebrides*, p. 324. See also *Boswell's Life of Johnson*, Vol. 1, p. 417; Vol. 2, p. 447.

61. *Biographia Britannica*, Vol. 2 (1748), p. 993, n.A; cf. Birch's account of Browne, *A General Dictionary*, Vol. 3 (1735), pp. 609–12. For Calamy, cf. *ibid.*, Vol. 4 (1736), pp. 28–30, and *Biographia Britannica*, Vol. 2, pp. 1110–12.

62. *Ibid.*, Vol. 5 (1760), pp. 2886–904; *A General Dictionary*, Vol. 6 (1738), pp. 641–8. Laud is highly praised in *Athenae Oxonienses*, Vol. 2 (1692), pp. 30–2, 2nd edn (1721), Vol. 2, pp. 55–70.

63. *Biographia Britannica*, Vol. 6, Part 2 (1766), supplement, pp. 193–5; *A General Dictionary*, Vol. 9 (1739), pp. 136–8.

64. *A General Dictionary*, Vol. 8 (1739), pp. 678–91; *Biographia Britannica*, Vol. 5 (1760), p. 3483.

65. *Ibid.*, Vol. 6, Part 2 (1766), supplement, pp. 31–2, 92–4. Birch is identified as the author of the life of Hervey in *Biographia Britannica*, 2nd edn, Vol. 3 (1784), in 'Corrigenda & Addenda' under Birch.

66. *Biographia Britannica*, Vol. 5 (1760), p. 2961; cf. *A General Dictionary*, Vol. 7 (1738), pp. 77–9.

67. *Biographia Britannica*, Vol. 5 (1760), pp. 3202–3.

68. *Ibid.*, Vol. 6, Part 1 (1763), p. 3934.

69. *Ibid.*, pp. 3807–8.

70. *Ibid.*, Vol. 6, Part 2 (1766), supplement, p. 152.

71. *Boswell's Life of Johnson*, Vol. 3, p. 174.

72. Shelfmark I 1. 7 Art. Also bound in is a receipt for 9 guineas paid by Kippis for a thirty-second share of the *Biographia*.

73. The publication rate was as follows: Vol. 1 (1778), Vol. 2 (1780), Vol. 3 (1784), Vol. 4 (1789), Vol. 5 (1793), Vol. 6, Part 1 (undated, presumably 1795, after Kippis' death). Vol. 6 ends with Sir Michael Foster, written by M. Dodson. This volume (not noted in *ESTC*) is extremely rare; the Bodleian copy contains the statement at the top of the first page: 'Of this part I know but one copy existing. A.C.' (?Alexander Chalmers).

74. *Biographia Britannica*, 2nd edn, Vol. 1 (1778), pp. xx–xxi; Vol. 2 (1780), p. viii; Vol. 3 (1784), p. viii; Vol. 4 (1789), p. viii; Vol. 5 (1793), n.p.

75. *Ibid.*, Vol. 1 (1778), p. xxi.

76. *Ibid.*, Vol. 1, pp. xx–xxi.

77. *Ibid.*, Vol. 2 (1780), pp. vii–ix.

78. *Ibid.*, Vol. 3 (1784), pp. vii–viii.

79. *Ibid.*, Vol. 4 (1789), pp. vii–viii.

80. *Ibid.*, Vol. 6, Part 1 (?1795), p. 37; Johnson, *Lives of the English Poets*, ed. G. B. Hill (Oxford: Clarendon Press, 1905), Vol. 2, pp. 261–2.

81. *Biographia Britannica*, 2nd edn, Vol. 2 (1780), pp. 634–7.

82. *Ibid.*, Vol. 1 (1778), p. xxi. Boswell retracted his criticism that the second edition was 'too much crowded with obscure dissenting teachers', in *Boswell's Life of Johnson*, Vol. 3, p. 174. Richard Hurd thought it 'full of the nonsense and impertinence of those people', in Francis Kilvert, *Memoirs of the Life and Writings of the Right Rev. Richard Hurd, D.D.* (London: Richard Bentley, 1860), p. 152.

83. Abraham Rees, *A Sermon preached . . . upon Occasion of the Much Lamented Death of the Rev. Andrew Kippis* (London, 1795), pp. 46–7.

84. *British Biography*, Vol. 1 (1773 edn), p. v.

85. *A New and General Biographical Dictionary*, Vol. 1 (1761), pp. iv–vii.

86. Chalmers (ed.), *The General Biographical Dictionary*, Vol. 1 (1812), pp. v–viii.

87. *Ibid.*, Vol. 4 (1812), pp. 221–2.

88. Technically Bunyan would not qualify for entry in Calamy, as he was not an ejected minister, but Calamy found room for several other nonconformists who did not meet his own criteria.

89. *Athenae Oxonienses*, 2nd edn (1721), Vol. 2, p. 1030.

90. *Biographia Britannica*, Vol. 2 (1748), pp. 1208–9; Vol. 3 (1750), p. 2013.

91. *Biographia Britannica*, 2nd edn, Vol. 3 (1784), pp. 12–13; *A New and General Biographical Dictionary*, Vol. 2 (1761), pp. 426–8; James Granger, *A Biographical History of England, from Egbert the Great to the Revolution: Consisting of Characters disposed in different Classes, and adapted to a Methodical Catalogue of Engraved British Heads*, 3rd edn, *With Large Additions and Improvements* (London, 1779), Vol. 3, pp. 346–8. The first edition of *A Biographical History of England* (1769), Vol. 2, pp. 247–8, gives a much more muted account. For bibliographical details of Granger see *Boswell's Life of Johnson*, Vol. 3, appendix F, pp. 484–5.

92. *The General Biographical Dictionary*, Vol. 7 (1813), pp. 288–93; *Boswell's Life of Johnson*, Vol. 2, p. 238. See N. H. Keeble, ' "Of him thousands daily Sing and talk": Bunyan and his Reputation', in Keeble (ed.), *John Bunyan: Conventicle and Parnassus* (Oxford: Clarendon Press, 1988).

93. *A General Dictionary*, Vol. 9 (1739), pp. 179–86; *A New and General Biographical Dictionary*, Vol. 3 (1761), p. 448. For Harris' contribution see Clive T. Probyn, *The Sociable Humanist: The Life and Works of James Harris 1709–1780* (Oxford: Clarendon Press, 1991), pp. 61–4, 80.

94. *A General Dictionary*, Vol. 2 (1735), p. 45, n. U; Vol. 3 (1735), p. 708, n. AA; Vol. 4 (1736), p. 488; Vol. 7 (1738), pp. 147–8, n. N, 148; Vol. 7, p. 653; Vol. 10 (1741), pp. 137–9, n. E.

95. *Biographia Britannica*, Vol. 3 (1750), p. 1469; Vol. 6, Part 2 (1766), pp. 34–9, 104, 193–5.

96. *Biographia Britannica*, 2nd edn, Vol. 3 (1784), p. 608; Vol. 4 (1789), pp. 266★–98★.

97. *The General Biographical Dictionary*, Vol. 10 (1813), pp. 220–7.

98. *Athenae Oxonienses*, Vol. 2 (1692), p. 546; 2nd edn (1721), Vol. 2, p. 804.

99. *Supplement to The Great Dictionary*, 2nd edn (London, 1727), n.p.

100. *A General Dictionary*, Vol. 4 (1736), pp. 676–87; cf. the account in Birch, *The Heads of Illustrious Persons of Great Britain, Engraven by Mr. Houbraken, and Mr. Vertue. With their Lives and Characters*, Vol. 2 (London, 1751), pp. 39–40.

101. *A General Dictionary*, Vol. 6 (1738), pp. 399–407; Vol. 8 (1739), pp. 23–6.

102. *The Dictionary, Historical and Critical of Mr Peter Bayle*, Vol. 1 (1734), 'Advertisement concerning the Second French Edition', p. 17.

103. See Osborn, 'Birch and the *General Dictionary*', p. 32.

104. *A General Dictionary*, Vol. 8 (1739), pp. 86–112; Vol. 10 (1741), pp. 11–20; Vol. 6 (1737), pp. 478–95; Vol. 8, pp. 10–12.

105. *Ibid.*, Vol. 8, p. 10, n. C; *Aeneid*, Book 6, ll. 860–87; Vol. 10, p. 15, n. E; *Aeneid*, Book 6, ll. 660–4. See n. 2 above.

106. *Biographia Britannica*, Vol. 3 (1750), pp. 1749–61; 2nd edn, Vol. 5 (1793), pp. 373–98.

107. Sidney Lee, 'A statistical account of the *D.N.B.*', appendix 2 to *The Compact Edition of the Dictionary of National Biography* (Oxford: Oxford University Press, 1975), Vol. 2, p. 2995, first published as preface to *The Dictionary of National Biography*, Vol. 63 (1900), pp. lxi–lxii.

108. See n.1 above.

CHAPTER 6

REVIEW JOURNALS AND THE READING PUBLIC

ANTONIA FORSTER

Byron's joke about Keats being killed by the *Quarterly Review* has deep roots. When Ralph Griffiths, after a few controversial years as a general bookseller, decided in 1749 that there was a niche in the expanding book trade for a publication offering general readers 'some idea of a book before they lay out their money or time on it',[1] he could hardly have imagined that his *Monthly Review* would last for nearly a century and begin a phenomenon that has been part of the literary world ever since. Within a few years the familiar process was well underway: booksellers were using quotations in advertisements, authors were attacking reviewing as corrupt and unfair, and the success of the *Monthly Review* was spawning imitators.

The myth that real book reviewing or reviewing in anything like the modern sense began only with the *Edinburgh Review* has clung to life, despite many demonstrations of its falsity. In her 1992 revision of *Mary Wollstonecraft*, Claire Tomalin, while taking back the 1802 starting date by fourteen years, was still maintaining that the *Analytical Review* (1788) 'was the first British literary and scientific monthly aimed at the general public and made up almost entirely of book reviews';[2] numerous twentieth-century publications (and indeed the *Analytical*'s own prefatory material) make it clear that this is not true. Benjamin Christie Nangle's 1934 and 1955 volumes of *The Monthly Review . . . Index of Contributors and Articles* provided a great deal of information about the theory and practice of eighteenth-century reviewing,[3] as did the work of Smollett scholars interested in the *Critical Review*, from Claude Jones' series of articles in the 1940s and 1950s[4] to Robert D. Spector's articles and book in the 1950s and 1960s[5] and James G. Basker's *Tobias Smollett: Critic and Journalist* (1988); Lewis M. Knapp's work from the 1930s to the 1950s examined aspects of the practice of both the *Monthly* and *Critical*,[6] and Derek

Roper's *Reviewing Before the Edinburgh, 1788–1802* (1978) looked back very
effectively to the beginnings as well as examining the later period in great
detail. There are many more, including Frank Donoghue's interesting *The
Fame Machine: Book Reviewing and Eighteenth-Century Literary Careers* (1996).

The beginnings

Griffiths changed the literary marketplace for ever by introducing a new
element into the relationship between authors, booksellers and the reading
public. Book reviewing soon became an inextricable part of the book business,
as it remains today. The fifteenth-century German printing revolution had
been less a new discovery than a putting together of several existing technol-
ogies in the realization of how these could be used in the production of
books. Griffiths' revolutionary journal did nothing new in essence, but, with
brilliant timing, combined existing ideas into something quite new, and so
began the modern age of bookselling.

Of course there had been some kinds of book reviewing before, principally
by the abstract-and-extract method, going back in some sense 2000 years but
more realistically dating from the French learned journals of the seventeenth
century such as Denis De Sallo's *Journal des Sçavans,*[7] published in Paris and
Amsterdam. This journal, which lasted from 1665 to 1753, started a trend
copied by a number of English periodicals such as the *Memoirs of Literature*
(1710–14 and 1717), edited by Michel de la Roche, and the *History of the
Works of the Learned* (1737–43). These periodicals had extremely limited
coverage, however, addressing themselves, as the latter title suggests, to erudite
works with small potential audiences. Comprehensive, or would-be comprehensive, coverage of publications in general was offered by the lists of recent
publications in the *Gentleman's* and *London* magazines, but these, with only
occasional exceptions, were simply book lists.

Griffiths could see that the expanding book market was simultaneously
creating a market for a tool to enable readers to grasp it. He spelled this out in
an advertisement added to the first (May 1749) number of the *Monthly Review*:

> When the abuse of title-pages is obviously come to such a pass, that few readers
> care to take in a book, any more than a servant, without a recommendation; to
> acquaint the public that a summary review of the productions of the press, as
> they occur to notice, was perhaps never more necessary than now, would be
> superfluous and vain.

The cure then for this general complaint is evidently, and only, to be found in a periodical work, whose sole object should be to give a compendious account of those productions of the press, as they come out, that are worth notice; an account, in short, which should, in virtue of its candour, and justness of distinction, obtain authority enough for its representations to be serviceable to such as would choose to have some idea of a book before they lay out their money or time on it. This is the view and aim of the present undertaking; and as it must necessarily stand or fall by the merit of the execution, on that we rest the issue, without offering to prepossess the Public in its favour.[8]

That was all that was on offer in the first number – 'a compendious account of those productions of the press, as they come out, that are worth notice' or, as an early newspaper advertisement described it, 'Giving an Account, with proper Abstracts, of the new Books, Pamphlets, &c. as they come out'[9] – and it did not sound particularly revolutionary. Griffiths, who had worked for Jacob Robinson when Robinson was publishing *The History of the Works of the Learned*, was well acquainted with the long-established form of learned journal and appeared at first to be changing very little.

The first number, however, though it began with Henry Grove's *System of Moral Philosophy* and a translation of a French treatise on the senses, included in its six items reviews of a current poem, Aaron Hill's *Gideon*, and a current play, Smollett's *The Regicide*. This step towards wider coverage was soon followed, in the July number, by a giant leap, the promise to 'register all the new Things in general, without exception to any, on account of their lowness of rank, or price' (*MR* 1, 1749: 238).[10] Of necessity this brought about a change in format which remained part of this and all the review journals which followed: a distinction between the handful of long articles character-istic of the learned journals, and the new mixture of long and short articles required by the new approach. While the *Monthly*'s first and second eighty-page numbers had contained just six long articles each, the third contained in addition some information about nineteen further works of lesser importance. Now, as a footnote to a newspaper advertisement for the *Monthly*'s seventh number explained:

This Work exhibits a View of every new Thing whatever that comes out; a Circumstance that must render it of more extensive Use than any Undertaking of the Kind ever set on Foot before, which were all restricted to only the capital Books; whereas this is calculated to prevent our Readers from being imposed on by artful Title Pages and Advertisements; and to shew them by a fair Represen-tation, what they may really expect from any new Piece, before they lay out their Time and Money on it. [11]

It was not simply a matter of article length; giving brief coverage to 'all the new Things' required rethinking the long-sanctified abstract-and-extract method which was the literal meaning of reviewing and was based on the principle of giving readers enough information to enable them to judge for themselves. In the first number's review (by Griffiths himself) of Hill's *Gideon* the original method was spelled out:

> herein we shall not, in the language of critics, pretend to describe, in terms of the art, the beauties or imperfections (as doubtless imperfections there are, even in the greatest authors) of the production before us. No, but we shall take, what we believe our readers will think a much more agreeable and useful method; we shall extract from the work itself a few of such passages as we shall judge proper to give a tolerably adequate idea of the whole.
>
> (*MR* 1, 1749: 66–7)

Variations of this method continued to be used throughout the century, but it coexisted with the giving of critical judgements and doing precisely what is scorned in the original definition: describing 'beauties or imperfections'. This was at first considered inferior and apologies were frequently offered when, for reasons ranging from lack of space to obscenity or tedium, the review gave 'only a characteristical sketch of some articles' (*MR* 6, 1752: 449).

The response from authors and booksellers to this new phenomenon had some similarities to the response from the Catholic Church to the invention of printing: a combination of fear of the consequences and determination to make use of its capacities. We have now for so long taken general book reviewing for granted that it may be difficult to imagine the startling effect it had in those early days when Griffiths, whose previous claims to fame were his publication of two seditious works of his own after the 1745 rebellion (*Ascanius* and *Copies of the papers delivered by the 9 Rebels*) and his part in the publication of *Memoirs of a Woman of Pleasure* [*Fanny Hill*], began this enterprise. Griffiths had been a bookseller for under a decade when he began the *Monthly Review*, perhaps for only four years (the first imprint with his name is dated 1740, but this appears to be an error), but had been in serious trouble on these three occasions; on the last he is said to have threatened 'with a large Hammer' the man who came to execute the Duke of Newcastle's warrant,[12] but he managed to wriggle out of all three. His varied experiences and connections as a general bookseller appear to have given him a good eye for the market, and his correspondence throughout his long life shows that he was widely regarded as a fount of knowledge about all aspects of publishing.

Authors and booksellers

Within a few years of the beginning of the *Monthly Review*, soon followed by a number of imitators and by the introduction of review sections into existing and new magazines, both authors and booksellers were wondering what had hit them. Charles Churchill's 1761 poem *The Apology* expressed the astonishment:

> How could these self-elected monarchs raise
> So large an empire on so small a base?
> In what retreat, inglorious and unknown,
> Did Genius sleep when Dulness seized the throne?[13]

A correspondent to the *London Chronicle* in 1759 further spells out what had happened:

> if we reflect how much we are influenced by the opinions of our companions, by the judgment of the public, and even by the verdict of those, who, on the first day of every month, have assumed a right of pronouncing sentence upon the productions of their contemporaries, we shall find that we seldom sit down to read with that freedom from prejudice, which a Judge ought to possess. The decisions of all these tribunals we have often experienced to be rash and fallible; but we are lazy enough to acquiesce in them without farther examination.[14]

In the same year William Kenrick's pamphlet *A Scrutiny; or the Criticks criticis'd* had admitted: 'While the publick continues to be supplied with such a swarm of writings as issue monthly from the press, it is not to be doubted that our literary reviews will find readers',[15] and the preface to *A compleat Catalogue of all Books and Pamphlets Published for Ten Years past; With their Prices, and References to their Characters in the Monthly Review*, published in 1760, claimed that 'By the Help of such candid Assistance, Purchasers are relieved from the Risk of incurring a fruitless Expence, or of wasting their Time in unprofitable Attention'.[16] The evidence that readers did in fact allow the judgements of reviewers to influence their book-buying is meagre, but authors and booksellers thought they did. Before the end of 1750 review material was being used in book advertisements. The first example I have found is, it must be said, an advertisement in a Griffiths newspaper for a Griffiths publication,[17] but it was soon followed by others – and the place of the reviewers was fixed, only to become stronger.

The business of reviewing

In 1760 a pamphlet entitled *The Battle of the Reviews* declared ringingly that 'Criticism is a Matter of too great Importance to be made a Trade of, or to serve Views purely lucrative, in either Author or Bookseller',[18] but there was by then, eleven years after the beginning of the *Monthly Review* and four years after the *Critical*, a well-established 'Business of criticism' filling an apparently accurately diagnosed need in the reading public. Smollett's preliminary advertisement for the *Critical Review*, published in 1755 to prepare the ground for his new review journal, had complained about seeing in his predecessor 'the noble Art of Criticism reduced to a contemptible Manufacture subservient to the most sordid Views of Avarice and Interest, and carried on by wretched Hirelings, without Talent, Candour, Spirit, or Circumspection',[19] but the *Critical*'s approach to the business in fact differed very little from that laid down by the *Monthly Review*.

The great similarities between the two journals, sometimes forgotten in modern times in a canonical snobbery which assumes that the *Critical* must be more 'literary' because it began as Smollett's, were and are obvious, no matter how much readers are told that they should not confound 'a work undertaken from public spirit with one supported for the sordid purposes of a bookseller' (*CR* 7, 1759: 372). The fact that Griffiths was a general bookseller until 1762 was a complication, and, despite jokes on the subject in the *Monthly Review* – 'since honest *Griffiths* is concerned, we are to recommend this production as the book of books, or the only book in the world, for wit, and humour, and elegance, and all that, as mr. *Bays* has it' (*MR* 10, 1754: 392) – some prejudice was inevitable. However, the network of connections between booksellers in the period was so byzantine that it is extremely difficult to pin down all the varied influences and pressures on critical judgements; the shareholders of the *St. James's Chronicle*, for example, begun by Henry Baldwin, who included Griffiths (a founding shareholder and an active proprietor for more than forty years) and several other booksellers and reviewers, among them Henry's brother Robert Baldwin, one-time publisher of the *Critical*, would make an interesting case study on their own. Sordid purposes and personal rancour were quite well distributed between the review journals.

Connections or not, however, the editors of the review journals had their burdens considerably increased by the difficulties of obtaining books for review, sending books to reviewers and, more important, retrieving the books again. We know most about the technicalities of this procedure as far as the

Monthly Review is concerned, as details appear in many letters in Griffiths' surviving correspondence, chiefly in the Bodleian Library and in the Osborn collection in the Beinecke Library at Yale, but available details from other journals suggest that the problems were much the same. Booksellers did not usually send free books for review, although the *Monthly*, for example, must be assumed to have had no difficulty with Griffiths' publications and the *English Review* with those of its publisher, John Murray, but the several examples of booksellers who were also publishers of Reviews account for only a small percentage of publications in any journal. When Francis and Charles Rivington set up the *British Critic*, their agreement of 1793 with Robert Nares and William Beloe, the editor and deputy editor, specified that the Rivingtons

> shall and will provide Copies of all such Books or Publications for the perusal of the said Robert Nares as he shall think proper to criticise or review in the said British Critic which copies the said Robert Nares is to return immediately after they are respectively reviewed.[20]

Reviewers for the *Monthly* were allowed to keep the books if they paid for them, and Griffiths would subtract the cost from what was owing in payment for reviews (they were paid by the octavo sheet, with the *Monthly*'s well-paid reviewers earning between £2 and 4 guineas,[21] the same for quotations as for original material, another encouragement to substantial extracts), but the others were firmly retrieved. Some booksellers lent them – there is a later reference in a letter of 1818 by George Edward Griffiths to Murray's having sent a parcel of books 'for the use of the M.R., on return'[22] – but this did not alter the need for retrieval. All this was going on behind the scenes, with the only public window some occasional comments in the Reviews about the difficulty of obtaining certain books mentioned by readers but not obtainable in London,[23] and a few hints, as in the *London Review* (*LR* 1, 1775: 164), that it would be a good idea for authors to send copies of their books.

The expanding market

The most remarkable aspect of the establishment of the early general review journals is the rapidity with which readers appear to have been brought to accept the argument that such a publication is something 'which no one, conversant in the Literary World, ought, in justice to themselves, to be without',[24] and that 'it certainly is of the highest Utility to the Public to have a just and judicious Criticism upon the modern Productions, whereby Works of Merit may not only be rescued from Oblivion, but much Expence, and what is of infinite more Concern to Mankind, their Time may be saved'.[25] William Strahan's ledgers show that the *Monthly Review*'s initial May 1749 print run of 1000 declined to 750 and then 500 but returned to 1000 in 1750–51 and rose to 1250 in 1752, 2250 in 1756, 2500 in 1758, 3000 in 1768 and 3500 in 1776;[26] as Derek Roper points out, the 1803 sales of the *Edinburgh Review*, 'then reckoned a dazzling success', were 2000.[27] No such records survive for Archibald Hamilton's printing of the *Critical Review*, but such evidence as there is suggests that it did not catch up with its rival; C. H. Timperley's figures for 1797[28] are 5000 for the *Monthly*, 3500 for the *Critical* and for the recently established *British Critic* (which had begun publication in 1793), and 1500 for the fading *Analytical Review*, launched in 1788 and soon to fail in 1799. As 'Philo-Musarum' had written to the *London Evening-Post* in 1774, offering some criticisms of his own and echoing Griffiths' point made twenty-five years earlier,

> it is natural for every body to be inquisitive concerning the merit of recent publications, and as few have leisure or desire to read all, many may be glad to have such pieces pointed out to them as are most worthy their attention.[29]

For Griffiths the challenge had been to create a market, or rather, to transform and expand the small, specialized existing market for reviewing learned works, whereas for all the rivals who followed his journal (which outlived its next longest-lasting competitor, the *Critical*, by twenty-seven years, finally perishing in 1844), the difficulty was to move into the existing market and to differentiate the newcomer from established journals. Despite the aggression of Smollett's attacks on the seven-year-old *Monthly* as 'patched up by obscure Hackney Writers, accidentally enlisted in the service of an undistinguishing Bookseller'[30] and its claims, quoted in part above, of a higher purpose, the *Critical*'s changes to the established reviewing format were minimal, as was true for most of the subsequent review journals. They all made changes, but continuity is more noticeable than change, no matter how grand the claims. Just as the *Critical* directed particular venom at the *Monthly*'s 'sordid Views of Avarice' and 'obscure Hackney writers' while conveniently ignoring its own similar financial dealings and equally anonymous reviewers (some of whom were the same people, including Smollett himself), William Kenrick's *London Review* in 1775 justified the new journal by attacking the anonymity of reviewers in other journals (a group which had included Kenrick himself) and claimed to 'disdain the subterfuge of concealment' while not in fact identifying the individual authors of any of its own reviews.[31]

On its entry in 1783 the *English Review* managed to take the high road and avoid attacks on its long-established rivals; instead, the new journal promised some non-review elements of a type to be found in magazines, keeping one of these promises (to provide monthly political coverage) and failing to keep most of the rest (such as provision of biographical materials and extensive coverage of the arts). The three other major eighteenth-century entries into the field, the *Analytical Review* (1788), the *British Critic* (1793), and the *Anti-Jacobin Review* (1798), revert to attack mode, the first principally on critical-theoretical grounds (arguing that the review journals should not be giving opinions but instead, by providing 'analytical' accounts, allowing readers to judge for themselves) and the other two on political grounds. The *British Critic*, founded by conservative Church of England churchmen explicitly alarmed by what they saw as the dangerously liberal attitudes of the existing review journals (Joseph Johnson's notoriously radical *Analytical Review* especially), argued that good literary criticism is not enough and that the 'principal Reviews have long been animated by a spirit very hostile . . . to the whole establishment in Church and State' (*BC* 1, 1793: 1), and the more extreme and wittier *Anti-Jacobin*, whose title proclaimed its social and political attitudes, expressed disgust that 'Reviewers, sinking the critic in the partisan, have insidiously contributed to favour the designs of those writers who labour to undermine our civil and religious establishments, and, by a shameful dereliction of duty, to cast an odium on their opponents' (*AJR* 1, 1798: 2). With the advent of these two explicitly conservative journals inspired by the political ferments of the 1790s, the paper wars in review journals were heating up. This did not go unopposed: political and religious prejudice in the existing reviews forms a major plank too in the platform of the *New London Review*; its prospectus complains dramatically of both the 'undue ascendancy' of party politics 'with all the feuds and asperities incident to the passions of venality and ambition' and the warping of the 'benign genius of Religion' which 'has become the tool of interest to one faction, the ladder of preferment to another, and the but [*sic*] of ridicule to a third'.[32] All, whatever they said, were trying to establish a commercial foothold in the literary world, to find an economically viable position in the relationship between authors, publishers and readers.

The political differences between the *Monthly* and *Critical* Reviews have been exaggerated and over-simplified, as in Samuel Johnson's famous comment: 'The Monthly Reviewers . . . are not Deists; but they are for pulling down all establishments. The Critical Reviewers are for supporting the constitution, both in church and state.'[33] Many dissenters wrote for the

Monthly, but many of its reviewers were Church of England clergymen too. Later, especially in the turbulent 1790s, as I indicated above, political differences were important distinguishing features of some of the new journals. As Emily Lorraine de Montluzin has commented, 'To a greater degree than any other literary journal of its day, with the possible exception of the *Anti-Jacobin Review*, the *British Critic* was a periodical with a mission.'[34]

Reviewing methods: opinions and quotations

The *Analytical Review*'s complaint in 1788 that 'the writers of literary journals, flattered by the attention paid to their decisions, and gratified by the influence they have obtained over authors, have filled their publications with little else than their own opinions and judgments' (*AR* 1, 1788: i) has a confusing air; the question of giving critical judgements had ceased to be a question thirty-five years earlier. The *Analytical*, however, was arguing for a return to what it saw as the true, pure aim of a literary journal: 'to give such an account of new publications, as may enable the reader to judge of them for himself' (*ibid.*); that is, to present readers with abstracts and extracts instead of opinions, as the journals for the learned had done. In the very early days reviewers had pointed out to their inexperienced audience that 'a few passages from the work will give the reader the best idea of it' (*MR* 1, 1749: 461) or 'we leave the reader to form his own judgment of it on others' (*MR* 2, 1749–50: 331); as time went on they were most likely to be given as 'a specimen of the author's manner' (*MR* 45, 1771: 147) or 'in confirmation of our praise' (*CR* 30, 1770: 382) or because in order 'that we may not be thought to pronounce dogmatically, the reader shall judge from specimens' (*CR* 11, 1761: 135). The supposed return to first principles in the *Analytical Review* was selective and did not amount to much, and the journal was giving opinions in its first volume – for example, having informed the public in one review that 'analysis of novels will seldom be expected' (*AR* 1, 1788: 208), the *Analytical* goes on in the next review to complain about 'foolish titles' and the 'tedious insipidity' of *Agitation: Or the Memoirs of George Woodford* and in the next to describe *Henrietta of Gerstenfeld* as being 'much superior to the generality of those mis-shapen monsters, daily brought forth to poison the minds of our young females, by fostering vanity, and teaching affectation' (pp. 208–9).

One of the complaints made in the early days highlights a conflict between the Reviews and the reading public on one side and, on the other, booksellers and authors: the point that the giving of extracts may harm the sale of books.

David Mallet's sarcastic pseudonymous pleading as 'Butler Swift' in the 'Epistle Dedicatory' to his *Tyburn to the Marine Society* expresses a more general concern when he asks 'the Most ingenious and very learned the Writers and Compilers, male and female, of our present MAGAZINES, REVIEWS, CHRONICLES, and other daily, weekly or monthly Storehouses of Wit, Taste, Science, and Erudition' not to pick any of his 'choicest and most beautiful flowers' in extracts.[35] Reviewers often remind readers that the extracts are intended to induce them 'to purchase and peruse the whole excellent performance' (*CR* 1, 1756: 491) or to 'excite an earnest desire, in many, to read the work itself' (*MR* 35, 1766: 21). On other occasions, however, they show some awareness of the concerns of authors and booksellers when they declare that they will not 'transgress farther upon this publication, lest [they] forestall the reader's curiosity' (*CR* 28, 1769: 267), or say cheerfully that they forbear further quoting 'lest our good Cousin should think himself rather injured than served by the measure of our commendation' (*MR* 38, 1765: 185). Readers want or need extracts, as the reviewers comment on many occasions, and their wishes must inevitably come first, but Griffiths jokes more than once about the other side of this point, as he does in a review of John Armstrong's anonymous poem *A Day* published by Andrew Millar:

> We cannot resist the temptation to enrich our page with the following extracts, wherein [are] some very just invectives, and admonitory hints, which we would recommend to the particular notice of our Readers in general, but especially our *London* Readers. By your leave, then, Dr. A. or Mr. Editor, or Mr. Andrew Millar; – we must make bold to borrow a few of your lines: – ye shall be heartily welcome, in turn, to as many from us, if possibly any thing of ours should ever be deemed worth the stealing.
>
> (*MR* 24, 1761: 77)

The role of the critic

From the early days many reviewers had expressed some version of the claim made by James Kirkpatrick in the *Monthly Review* in 1759 of 'designing to act with constant equity between the Writers we review, and the Readers we intend to inform or entertain' (*MR* 21, 1759: 467): Oliver Goldsmith had defined 'the true Critic's province' in a review in 1757 as 'To direct our taste, and conduct the Poet up to perfection' (*MR* 16, 1757: 427); ten years later another reviewer commented on the reviewers' aiming to 'do *justice* to the Public, and at the same time answer the *expectations* of Authors' (*MR* 36,

1767: 176); and in 1788 a reply to a correspondent says that the reviewers' 'utmost wish is, to do justice to the Public, as well as the Authors (*good* and *bad*) whose works they are, by their plan, obliged to notice' (*MR* 80, 1789: 286). There are many similar examples. However, in commercial literary enterprises the interests of readers naturally take precedence. It is readers who are paying to be told, despite the best deflecting efforts of authors' prefaces and booksellers' advertisements, whether a book or pamphlet is worth reading; they may also be paying to be entertained by the rudeness with which some authors or their works are disposed of or to be flattered by assumptions of common ground between authors and reviewers, with the generally used grand editorial 'we' of the review journals contributing to a sense of institutional authority in which the reading public is assumed to be on the same side.

With many of the early attacks on reviewers focusing, like Churchill's lines quoted above, on presenting the periodical critics as 'presumptuous and self-erected tribunals',[36] 'these self-erected Censors of the Republick of Letters'[37] and 'these self-constituted Critics, these Russian autocrators in literature',[38] considerable effort is made in the Reviews' pages to establish common ground with readers and, as the *British Critic* puts it, place the reviewers as 'confidential friends of the great host, the public, who, having assisted in the decoration and arrangement of the table, are admitted to a respectable place among the company' (*BC* 3, 1794: iv). With one side of the picture maintaining, as do two newspaper correspondents in 1765, that the reviewers are 'a Set of Men without any Pretensions to Taste, Wit or Judgment, deciding in a most dictatorial Manner upon every literary Composition which may appear'[39] who '*bestride the World of Literature* with rather too magisterial an Air',[40] it is all the more important that the reviewers keep reminding readers of shared standards. 'We shall ever be glad to learn the sentiments of our candid Readers' (*MR* 30, 1764: 496), writes the *Monthly Review*, and it is true that the *Monthly* gives a great deal of space throughout the century to replying to correspondents in a section at the end of most monthly numbers. The *Critical* does much less of this, despite claiming to be 'open to conviction and reproof' (*CR* 1, 1756: 96) and ready to 'thankfully receive every correction administered by the lenient spirit of candour' (*CR* 10, 1760: 162), but it does give some space to such replies to correspondents, as do most of the later journals. The tone taken was generally reasonable, if occasionally with gritted teeth, and with some spleen in the *Critical*'s early days, but the *London Review* provided some breakdowns in the expected gentlemanly politeness, as when a reader who has been unable to understand the argument of one review is roundly insulted:

in offering our strictures to the public, on the various productions of literature that come before us, we do not engage, either to furnish our readers with *understanding*, or to teach them the several arts and sciences necessary for them to know, in order to comprehend such strictures.

(*LR* 9, 1779: 98)

Even the *Monthly*'s patience wore out sometimes, particularly with correspondents who failed to pay the postage, as we see, for example, in 1788:

We have, of late, been too much annoyed with impertinent and expensive letters.–People who have nothing to do, should have some consideration for those who have useful employment for every moment.

(*MR* 79, 1788: 704)

This section was a popular part of the *Monthly Review*'s pages at least, as letters of complaint illustrate on the two occasions in 1752 and 1783 when the *Monthly* decided to print the correspondence section on the blue paper covers in which the monthly numbers were sold and which were normally discarded by the binders of each volume. In 1752 a letter to Griffiths from the poet Mary Jones asked that he 'wd. allow [the] Letters a white Leaf; because we grudge yr. Book binder's Claim to 'em in blue'.[41] Griffiths listened on this occasion, but then in 1783 the *Monthly Review* decided to try the idea again: 'For the future, our CORRESPONDENCE, and NOTES to Correspondents, will be printed on the last leaf of the Blue Cover of the Review; to which our Readers are referred for the Correspondence, &c. of the present month' (*MR* 69, 1783: 448). A 'considerable number' of the *Monthly Review*'s readers reacted as Jones had done years before and the bright idea was given up after only a month:

It has been observed to us, that our Articles of Correspondence are often as entertaining, and may sometimes prove as useful, as other parts of the publication; that it is not always of a temporary nature; and that when the Reviews are bound in volumes, it must be totally lost.–In conformity, therefore, with the desire of our friends, we return to the accustomed mode of arranging our materials.

(*MR* 69, 1783: 526)

In the early days the reviewers use a number of interesting metaphors to define or clarify their roles, some pointing to the public and some to authors. When the *Monthly* uses the phrase 'tasters to the public' in 1755 and goes on to explain that this requires that the reviewers 'apprize the connoisseur of what is, or is not, fit for his table' (*MR* 13, 1755: 399), readers are the only concern; the same is true of the term 'monitors to the public' used in 1772 (MR 46, 1772: 97). The Critical's 'officers of the literary police' who 'bring the offenders to justice' (CR 21, 1766: 60–1), on the other hand, are principally concerned with keeping authors in order, as, with varying degrees of hostility, are the Monthly's 'beadles of Parnassus' (MR 38, 1768: 248) and 'liege knights of the Muses' (MR 49, 1773: 202) and the Critical's comment that the reviewers have 'inclosed what was once a common field' (CR 30, 1770: 467). When the Critical writes of literary thief-catchers in 1764, the image is aimed at authors, who are the thieves, but the role here is defined in relation to the public:

> Is literary, the only, justice that is to be denied the privilege of thief-catchers, for detecting those practices in shop-lifting? . . . We shall, therefore, once for all, declare, that we apprehend our province is not only critical but useful, in as strict a sense as the office in Bow-street, because it may prevent many from being gulled out of their money.
>
> (CR 17, 1764: 439)

This aspect of the reviewers' role, saving the gullible reading public from the cheats of authors and booksellers, is much stressed in the early years of reviewing. Time and again the reviewers reflect with disfavour on 'those arts of Publication which have often been practised, to the prejudice of Literature, the abuse of the Public, and the disgrace of Individuals' (MR 26, 1762: 360) and 'the many specious title-pages to which the ingenuity of authors and booksellers has daily recourse, for the allurement of the public' (CR 33, 1772: 73). 'It is vain', writes a reviewer in the Critical Review in 1760, 'for those sons of industry to rack their invention to pass off old, threadbare, and tattered subjects for new, while the public countenances persons whose business it is to detect the imposture' (CR 10, 1760: 302).

The reviewers' selfless critical labours to save the stupid or naive reader from deception or simply to provide useful information are stressed repeatedly from the beginning, often in terms of duty and obligation. Expressions such as 'our duty to the public obliges us . . .' (CR 18, 1764: 58), 'the discharging our duty to the public, with fidelity and justice' (MR 46, 1772: 272), and 'the obligation we are under, of pointing out the merits and demerits of new publications' (MR 40, 1769: 24) abound. There are also innumerable reminders, particularly in the early years, of the sufferings brought about by what the London Review calls the 'toils of critical investigation' (LR 10, 1779: 63). The Monthly complains, for example, as do all the review journals at one time or another, about the 'vile drudgery' (MR 11, 1754: 470) of reviewing fiction, the *London* refers to 'the horrid fatigue, of poring over the numerous pages of sterility and dullness, which our profession, as Reviewers, obliges us to peruse' (*LR* 6, 1777: 321), the *New London Review* laments being 'compelled to plod through volumes of ribaldry and nonsense, in search of something to commend' (*NLR* 1, 1799: 508), and the *British Critic*, which had earlier referred to the fable of Sisyphus as a tempting image of 'ungrateful labour perpetually recommencing' (*BC* 3, 1794: iii), asks readers to 'weigh but for a moment the arduous task of conducting a publication, which professes to give an account of every printed book' (*BC* 16, 1800: 226).

In the earliest days the reviewers in the *Monthly* and *Critical* Reviews liked at least to pretend that the public was being properly guided and would form appropriate judgements, although there are many indications that they believed nothing of the sort. A reviewer may declare that the favourable reception accorded by the public to a work approved by the reviewers 'is a proof of the justice of its discernment, with regard to literary productions' and that he has 'rarely known an instance of its failing to distinguish between such masterly performances as the present pamphlet, and the ordinary produce of the press' (*MR* 28, 1763: 396), but many other comments make it clear that no such confidence exists. William Rose, for example, writes of the third edition of *A Comparative View of the State and Faculties of Man with those of the Animal World*, 'It gives us no small pleasure to find that the opinion we formed of this very ingenious and entertaining work is so amply confirmed by the public approbation' (*MR* 35, 1766: 221), and the *Critical* writes of the second edition of *Letters that Passed between Theodosius and Constantia*, 'We are pleased to find that the warm encomiums we bestowed on the first edition of these entertaining and instructive letters, have received the sanction of public approbation' (*CR* 17, 1764: 80). If it were indeed true, as the *Critical* observes, that 'the public voice has generally seconded [their] criticisms' (*CR* 18, 1764: 165 [265]), it would seem unnecessary to comment on the pleasure felt on certain occasions when their voice and the public's are in agreement. This sort of comment continued, and we see, for example, William Enfield opening his review of Hugh Blair's *Sermons* with 'It is an inexpressible gratification and encouragement to us in our literary labours, when we find our literary judgment concerning the merit of important publications confirmed by the general suffrage of the world' (*MR* n.s. 15, 1794: 51). On one occasion the *Critical* says dogmatically: 'We have the pleasure to know, that the public voice has always seconded our censures: for on what shelves are now those books to be found which we have condemned? – The answer is ready, On those of grocers, fruit-shops, and trunkmakers' (*CR* 22, 1766: 470). On other

occasions, however, the *Critical* says that it would 'chuse to examine productions of genius by another standard than the public approbation, which is
sometimes capricious and arbitrary' (*CR* 14, 1762: 131); similarly, the *Monthly*,
while calling it 'an invidious office to oppose the public judgment', reserves
the right to 'venture to appeal from the people to themselves' (*MR* 24, 1761:
181). The confident assertions go on: 'We are happy', says the *Critical* in a
1791 advertisement, 'that the confidence of the Public in our judgment has
been so great and uniform.'[42]

The calm assumption of authority might even extend to announcing that
the reviewers 'look upon themselves to be in some measure responsible for
the morals as well as the taste of their readers' (*CR* 18, 1764: 314). Certainly
they regard themselves as having both the power and the duty to form public
taste, the 'delicate task of directing the public taste with respect to literature
and science' (*CR* 8, 1759: 271). This may involve cruel treatment of authors
'to expose the fastidious pretenders to wit, literature and the polite arts' (*CR*
18, 1764: 57), as duty to the public requires the reviewers 'to exert [their]
utmost endeavours to diminish the number of useless volumes with which it
is deluged' (*CR* 12, 1761: 363). Almost all the review journals, early and late,
express reluctance that duty forces them to treat authors harshly – although
'Politeness . . . must give way, in some measure, with us Reviewers, to truth;
and our duty to the public must take place of our complaisance to individuals'
(*MR* 20, 1759: 276) – but cheerfully insult and savage author after author,
sometimes justifying this as their duty and occasionally admitting to bad
temper brought about by reading too many bad books. The *Gentleman's
Magazine*'s reviewers offer a commonly made case when they argue that
'concern for the interests of Literature urges them to the severity of free and
unreserved censure' (*GM* 58, 1788: 441), and the *Critical Review* speaks for
many when it argues that 'Every author who writes without talents, is a
grievance, if not an impostor, who defrauds the public; and every critic has a
right to detect the imposition' (*CR* 1, 1756: 287). Reviewers may say briskly,
as does the *European Magazine*, 'Bad poetry is an unpardonable crime, no man
being under the necessity of writing verse' (*EM* 10, 1786: 420★) or that 'the
Quixotes of the pen view their objects of atchievement through a delusive
medium' (*CR* 31, 1771: 300–1), but on many occasions reviewers try to
present themselves as reluctantly doing their duty to steer deluded would-be
writers in another direction. They may hint to an author to 'betake himself to
some employment which his talents may be better adapted to, than they are
for procuring a subsistence by the trade of book-making' (*MR* 19, 1758:
581–2) or, in cases of 'confirmed, incorrigible dulness', kindly explain, 'If we

disperse the luminous vapour which misled the steps of the literary wanderer, we erect the steady beacon to be his future and his safer guide' (*CR* 34, 1772: sig. a1r).

Established institution

By 1772 the *Critical* can say with some accuracy that the Reviews 'are purchased by almost all the literary societies at present established; one of which, at least, subsists in every town of note' (*CR* 34, 1772: 479). It is difficult to establish just how much notice the book-buying and book-borrowing public took of the reviewers' judgements, as I have said, but there is plenty of evidence of a general belief that the public did listen to reviewers. I have written elsewhere about the extensive use by booksellers in advertisements, particularly in the last quarter of the century, of review quotations and references to reviews,[43] and the columns of most newspapers taking book advertisements produce plenty of evidence of this. As advertisements became more expensive with increased stamp duties late in the century, the practice continued, supporting the view that the reviewers' verdicts had authority. Unwilling acknowledgement of the point by many authors also supports this. As Thomas Underwood writes in a poem of 1768, ' 'tis plain the Town/Are much inclin'd to favour or condemn,/As these *confed'rate Wits* will suffer them';[44] twenty years later William Renwick refers to the *Monthly* and *Critical* Reviews as 'the publications by which the public voice is so generally determined'.[45] Country readers, according to 'P.D.', a correspondent to the *Public Advertiser*, 'are apt to be guided in the Choice of Books and Pamphlets by the Decisions of our Periodical Critics, scarce ever venturing to purchase without the Sanction of their Opinion',[46] and another correspondent to the same paper points out the 'ridiculous and lamentable' fact that 'the public Taste is directed by these incompetent Judges, whose peremptory Decisions seldom fail to be wrong, and very often are so to the utmost degree of Absurdity'.[47] Wrong or not, the reviewers are defied, attacked and pleaded with in hundreds of prefaces, dedications, postscripts, poems, pamphlets and letters in newspapers and magazines, all testifying to the strength of the writers' belief, whether acknowledged or denied, that the public was listening to reviewers and that the way to literary success was via their favourable judgements.

In 1790 a writer in *Walker's Hibernian Magazine* had reminded readers of the reviewers' function as 'indexes or way-posts' in the confusion of ever-increasing numbers of publications, although there is a lighthearted caution:

> It is the province of these gentlemen to inform the public what books are really good, bad, or indifferent; but such is the imperfection of human nature, that the booksellers, albeit very desirous to obtain them, have never yet been able to procure a set of infallible reviewers. There is always some little flaw, speck, or imperfection in what they do, and they often differ so very materially from one another, that although we can pretty nearly guess some one may be right, yet it is beyond all power of conjecture to find out who that one is.[48]

In March 1800, more than half a century after the *Monthly Review*'s beginnings, the author of a complaining letter to the *Gentleman's Magazine* wrote reminding one of the *Monthly*'s reviewers of the journal's 'original design and professions' and intention that the work 'should, in virtue of its candour, and justness of distinction, obtain authority enough for its representations to be serviceable to such as would choose to have some idea of a book before they lay out their money or time on it'.[49] This is a timely reminder of the function and purpose of reviewing; review journals flourished and multiplied in the eighteenth century and afterwards because enough readers did want 'some idea of a book' before buying or even borrowing it and because, whatever the reservations and complaints, they did give some degree of authority to the reviewers. There might be voices crying, as did the 1802 prospectus for a new series of *Monthly Epitome, Or, Readers Their Own Reviewers*, that the abuse of literary journals and their use as 'vehicles of party, and even of private resentment' have 'in great measure rendered them useless, so far as respects the opinion of Reviewers',[50] but reviewers were there to stay.

Notes

1. This 'Advertisement' is bound following the table of contents at the beginning of Vol. 1 of the *Monthly Review* in the Bodleian Library's copy (Griffiths' own annotated set) but is bound at the end of the first number, i.e. between pp. 80 and 81, in the British Library's copy.

2. Claire Tomalin, *The Life and Death of Mary Wollstonecraft* [1974], revised edn (London: Penguin, 1992), p. 94n.

3. Benjamin Christie Nangle, *The Monthly Review First Series 1749–1789: Indexes of Contributors and Articles* (Oxford: Clarendon Press, 1934) and *The Monthly Review Second Series 1790–1815: Indexes of Contributors and Articles* (Oxford: Clarendon Press, 1955).

4. Claude E. Jones, 'Contributors to the *Critical Review* 1756–1785', *Modern Language Notes*, 61 (1946): 433–41; 'The *Critical Review* and some major poets', *Notes and Queries*, n.s. 3 (1956): 114–15; 'The *Critical Review*'s first thirty years', *Notes and Queries*, n.s. 3 (1956): 78–90;

'Dramatic criticism in the *Critical Review*, 1756–1785', *Modern Language Quarterly*, 20 (1959): 18–26, 133–44; 'The English novel: A *Critical* view', *Modern Language Quarterly*, 19 (1958): 147–59, 213–24; 'Poetry and the *Critical Review*, 1756–1785', *Modern Language Quarterly*, 9 (1948): 17–36.

5. Robert D. Spector, 'Additional attacks on the *Critical Review*', *Notes and Queries*, n.s. 3 (1956): 425; 'An attack on the *Critical Review* in *Political Controversy*', *Notes and Queries*, n.s. 22 (1975): 14; 'Attacks on the *Critical Review*', *Periodical Post Boy* (June 1955): 6–7; 'Attacks on the *Critical Review* in the *Court Magazine*', *Notes and Queries*, n.s. 5 (1958): 308; 'Attacks on the *Critical Review* in the *Literary Magazine*', *Notes and Queries*, n.s. 7 (1960): 300–1; *English Literary Periodicals and the Climate of Opinion During the Seven Years' War* (The Hague: Mouton, 1966); 'Further attacks on the *Critical Review*', *Notes and Queries*, n.s. 2 (1955): 535; 'The *Monthly* and its rival', *Bulletin of the New York Public Library*, 64 (1960): 159–61.

6. Lewis M. Knapp, 'Griffiths's "Monthly Review" as printed by Strahan', *Notes and Queries*, n.s. 5 (1958): 216–17; 'Ralph Griffiths, author and publisher 1746–50', *The Library*, 4th ser., 20 (1939): 197–213; *Tobias Smollett: Doctor of Men and Manners* (Princeton, NJ: Princeton University Press, 1949).

7. For more information about the early developments, including the contention that there was book reviewing of a sort in *c.* 140 BC, see Edward A. Bloom, ' "Labors of the learned": Neoclassic book reviewing aims and techniques', *Studies in Philology*, 54 (1957): 537–63.

8. See n. 1 above.

9. *London Evening Post*, 17–20 June 1749.

10. References to the principal review journals and reviewing magazines will be abbreviated and incorporated parenthetically in the text. The titles and abbreviations are as follows: *Analytical Review (AR); Anti-Jacobin Review (AJR); British Critic (BC); Critical Review (CR); English Review (ER); European Magazine (EM); Gentleman's Magazine (GM); London Review (LR); Monthly Review (MR)*.

11. *General Advertiser*, Wednesday, 20 December 1749.

12. See Knapp, 'Ralph Griffiths', pp. 210–11.

13. Charles Churchill, *The Apology. Addressed to the Critical Reviewers* (London, 1761), p. 5.

14. Letter dated 2 April, *London Chronicle*, 5 (1759): 361.

15. [William Kenrick], *A Scrutiny; Or the Criticks criticis'd: being an Examination into the Censorial Merits of the Authors of the Critical Review: Occasion'd by Their extraordinary Account of a Poem, entitled Epistles Philosophical and Moral: A work whose moral Tendency is here impartially consider'd, and its Arguments illustrated and defended against the palpable Misrepresentations of those candid Criticks. By the Editor of those Epistles* (London, 1759), p. 1.

16. *A compleat Catalogue of all Books and Pamphlets Published for Ten Years past; With their Prices, and References to their Characters in the Monthly Review. The Whole forming a General Index to all the Articles in the first Twenty Volumes of the said Review, viz. from its Commencement in May 1749, to June 1759, both inclusive* (London: Printed for R. Griffiths in the Strand, and may be had of any Bookseller in Great Britain and Ireland, 1760), pp. iii–iv.

17. *General Advertiser*, 14 December 1750; advertisement for the then-forthcoming *Revolutions of Genoa*, reviewed in the *Monthly* in its original French version.

18. *The Battle of the Reviews* (London, n.d.) [1760], p. vi.

19. *Public Advertiser*, Friday, 9 December 1755.

20. Indenture 19 August 1793, London Metropolitan Archives Library Ms. F/RIV/4.

21. For further details see Antonia Forster, *Index to Book Reviews in England 1749–1774* (Carbondale: Southern Illinois University Press, 1990), p. 16, n. 32.

22. Letter to Isaac Disraeli, Bodleian Mss. Dep. Hughenden 244/3 fol. 126r.

23. See Forster, *Index to Book Reviews in England 1775–1800* (London: The British Library, 1997), pp. xxxviii–xxxix.

24. Advertisement for the October 1749 number of the *Monthly Review*, *General Advertiser*, 2 November 1749.

25. *The London Advertiser and Literary Gazette*, Monday, 3 June 1751.

26. Lewis M. Knapp, 'Griffiths's "Monthly Review" as printed by Strahan', *Notes and Queries*, n.s. 5 (1958): 216–17. Knapp's source is British Library Add. Mss. 48,800.

27. Derek Roper, *Reviewing before the Edinburgh 1788–1802* (Newark: University of Delaware Press, 1979), p. 24.

28. C. H. Timperley, *Encyclopaedia of Literary and Typographical Anecdote*, 2nd edn (London: Bohn, 1842), p. 795.

29. *London Evening-Post*, 26–28 May 1774; letter dated 18 May.

30. *Public Advertiser*, Friday, 9 December 1755.

31. *London Review*, 37 (1775): 107.

32. Prospectus, *The New London Review* [London, 1799; British Library 898.f.1(3)], p. 1.

33. James Boswell, *Boswell's Life of Johnson*, ed. George Birkbeck Hill, rev. L. F. Powell, Vol. 3 (Oxford: Clarendon Press, 1934), p. 32.

34. Emily Lorraine de Montluzin, 'Attributions of authorship in the *British Critic* during the editorial regime of Robert Nares, 1793–1813', *Studies in Bibliography*, 51 (1998): 243.

35. [David Mallet], *Tyburn to the Marine Society. A Poem* (London, 1759), pp. v and x–xii.

36. *Political Register*, 1 (1767): 122.

37. George Canning, *An Appeal to the Publick, from the Malicious Misrepresentations, Impudent Falsifications, and Unjust Decisions, of the Anonymous Fabricators of the Critical Review* (London, 1767), p. 9.

38. John Sayer, *The Temple of Gnidus a Poem From the French Prose of M. Secondat, Baron de Montesquieu* (London, 1765), p. v.

39. Letter, signed 'Candidus' and dated from George's Coffee–house 24 December 1765, *Public Advertiser*, Friday, 24 December 1765.

40. Letter, signed 'T.X. Y.Z.' and dated 10 December, *Public Advertiser*, Friday 20 December 1765.

41. Bodleian Add. Mss. C89 fol. 172r.

42. *London Chronicle*, 69 (29 January to 1 February 1791): 109.

43. *Index . . . 1749–1774*, p. 9; *Index . . . 1775–1800*, pp. xxxvii–xxxviii.

44. T[homas] Underwood, 'Liberty', in *Poems, &c. by T. Underwood, Late of St. Peter's College, Cambridge* (Bath, 1768), p. 220.

45. [William Renwick], *The Solicitudes of Absence. A Genuine Tale* (London, 1788), p. x.

46. Letter signed 'P.D.' and dated from York on 6 April *Public Advertiser*, 14 May 1761.

47. Letter signed 'Anti-Zoilus', *Public Advertiser*, 14 April 1772.

48. 'Essay on book making', *Walker's Hibernian Magazine* (August 1790): 119–20.

49. Letter signed 'X.Y.Z.', *Gentleman's Magazine*, 70 (1800): 228. See n. 2 above for original advertisement.

50. Prospectus [BL 11902. *c.* 26 (110)] for new series, 'enlarged and improved' of *Monthly Epitome, Or, Readers Their Own Reviewers* to be published on 1 February 1802, p. 1.

CHAPTER 7

LITERARY SCHOLARSHIP AND THE LIFE OF EDITING

MARCUS WALSH

Developments and varieties in literary scholarship

It was during the eighteenth century that English literary scholarship established itself, formally, culturally, institutionally and commercially. The scope
and consequence of its developments arguably surpassed those of any other
mode of literary writing in the period, with the possible exception of prose
fiction. Some initial indication of its variety and progress within the wider
world of letters might be given by two very different cases, from opposite
ends of the century.

In 1711 John Urry, a Student of Christ Church, Oxford, was asked by
more senior members of the college, and particularly by the Dean, Francis
Atterbury, to undertake a new edition of Chaucer. Urry was not keen, despite
his 'skill in the Northern language spoken in the lowlands of *Scotland*'. When
he died in 1715 the project was handed on to his transcriber, Thomas
Ainsworth. When Ainsworth died in his turn in 1719 the cup was passed into
the almost equally unwilling hands of Timothy Thomas, another Christ
Church graduate, by 'a Person, whose commands I was in all Duty bound to
obey' (that is, Dr Smalridge, the then Dean).[1] The result of this succession of
unrefusable offers, published by subscription in 1721, was an imposing folio
volume, garnished with cuts before each poem. From the scholarly point of
view, however, 'Urry's' Chaucer was less imposing. The text was treated
(despite claims of collation of the manuscripts, and of the printed editions) in
a particularly cavalier fashion; Chaucer's later and altogether more learned
editor Thomas Tyrwhitt warned that Urry's 'strange licence . . . of lengthen-
ing and shortening Chaucer's words, according to his own fancy, and of even
adding words of his own, without giving his readers the least notice, has made

the text of Chaucer in his Edition by far the worst that was ever published'.[2] A number of spurious works are foisted into the Chaucerian canon. The only evidence of philological scholarship is to be found in the glossary prepared by Timothy Thomas, where there is some use of a variety of lexicographical resources, and even an occasional textual and explanatory comment. No formal textual or explanatory notes accompany the text, though further short glossaries provide brief anglicizations of Chaucer's French and Latin words and tags, and a 'Short Account of some of the Authors Cited by Chaucer' provides elementary identifications: '*Boccace*, a famous *Italian* Poet, born at Florence, contemporary with Chaucer.' Clearly, with the exception of Timothy Thomas' belated efforts, this Chaucer was not the product of practised and appropriately informed specialists working within a consolidated academic tradition. Apparently, too, it assumed no very broad or developed relevant literary reading in its intended audience, nor any very developed demand for textual accuracy.

An almost total contrast is offered by Thomas Tyrwhitt, and his own edition of the *Canterbury Tales*, published in four octavo volumes in 1775, with a further volume, containing a glossary, in 1778. Thomas Tyrwhitt is an instance of a significant late eighteenth-century phenomenon, the gentleman-scholar dedicated to the enthusiastic pursuit of letters, though he spent part of his life in public office. Educated at Eton and Oxford, Tyrwhitt was called to the Bar in 1755 but did not practise. Appointed Deputy Secretary of War in December 1756, he none the less resided for most of the year in Oxford, where he held a fellowship at Merton. He combined his literary interests from 1762 with his clerkship of the House of Commons, publishing his *Observations and Conjectures upon some Passages of Shakespeare* in 1766. After his retirement from office in 1768 he published his edition of Chaucer, as well as involving himself in Shakespearean and classical scholarship, and the Rowley controversy. Tyrwhitt's edition of the *Canterbury Tales* indicates how far not only Chaucerian studies, but also methods and institutions of vernacular literary scholarship, and assumptions about readers, had come since Urry's edition. Tyrwhitt's edition provides a text 'formed . . . throughout from the Mss.', rather than from previous printed editions (with the exception of those by Caxton), substantially avoiding the 'arbitrary innovations' of Urry. It undertakes to contextualize and interpret Chaucer's writing by enquiring into 'the state of our language and versification at the time Chaucer wrote', and by tracing 'his allusions to a variety of forgotten books and obsolete customs'.[3] The first volume provides copious scholarly prolegomena. The preface is followed by 'An Account of Former Editions of the Canterbury Tales'; an impressive list of manuscripts consulted, with the abbreviations by which they are cited (those listed include nine 'in the [British] Museum', six in the Bodleian Library, four at Cambridge, and a number lent by other scholars and collectors); and an 'Abstract of the Historical Passages of the Life of Chaucer', which provides what is known, as Tyrwhitt puts it, of 'the principal facts in Chaucer's life, which are attested by authentic evidence'. The text of the *Canterbury Tales* is followed, in the fourth volume, by further analytical and explanatory apparatus: Tyrwhitt's 'Essay on the Language and Versification of Chaucer', an 'Introductory Discourse to the Canterbury Tales', and the notes. The notes provide explicatory comments; parallels within the *Tales*, with other works by Chaucer, and with other writers of Chaucer's time; historical references, including (as one might expect, given Tyrwhitt's training) legal statutes; lexicographical materials; and invocations of the manuscript readings. Tyrwhitt's learning is worn lightly, but the notes none the less reflect the widest reading in English, Italian, Spanish, French and classical literatures; a list of authors referred to by Tyrwhitt might begin with Dante, Leland, Froissart, Walsingham, Mariana, Du Cange, Sir John Mandevile, Holinshed, Lydgate, Gower, Gratian and Hoccleve. The glossary provided in Volume 5 is explicitly designed to be used by the reader in conjunction with the notes, and avails itself of such lexicographical and encyclopaedic sources as Chambers, Junius, Ray and Cotgrave. This is an edition supported by a life spent among books, and among fellow scholars (Tyrwhitt's friends included George Steevens and Edmond Malone). It displays throughout Tyrwhitt's daunting and committed historical and philological scholarship. The text is based on an extensive examination of the manuscripts, and on resort to a substantial range of public and private scholarly collections. In the annotation a thoroughgoing attempt is made to explain Chaucer's distant and difficult poetry to contemporary readers. Tyrwhitt's editing, unlike Urry's, lasted; his edition was reissued in 1798 and frequently reprinted thereafter, and even the late nineteenth-century Chaucer specialist W. W. Skeat drew on Tyrwhitt's notes, though his later, chaster editorial methodology balked at Tyrwhitt's relative openness to conjectural emendations and additions.

The difference between Urry's and Tyrwhitt's Chaucers is certainly evidence of progress. An apparatus like Tyrwhitt's could scarcely have been published in 1721; neither the substance of its scholarship, nor its editorial methodologies, as far as they related to vernacular literature, were developed at that date. Equally, an edition as textually and exegetically feeble as Urry's would not have found countenance among serious and self-conscious literary readers in the 1770s. The difference between these two works is also a witness, however, to formal and cultural variation within even a single genre of English literary scholarship. In this chapter I shall concentrate on editing, the most prolific form of English vernacular literary scholarship in this period, and I shall pay much less attention to such other genres as literary history, literary criticism, translation and literary biography, within which very substantial processes of development and formation also occurred.[4] Even restricting the focus of investigation for the most part to editions of works of English literature reveals however a variety of institutions, forms and processes of production, and modes and scenes of consumption.

Conceptions and roles of the scholarly editor

English literary scholarship today, however contested it often seems to those involved in it, is a relatively mature and homogeneous discipline, centred for the greater part in the university. Literary scholars are usually university academics; their readers are usually fellow students and fellow academics. Such relatively settled institutions of production, and recognizable and defined markets, did not exist as the discipline of vernacular (as opposed to biblical or classical) literary scholarship, and the genres associated with it, were instituted in the early eighteenth century. By the end of the century, as is demonstrated, for example, by Malone's great 1790 Shakespeare and its predecessors, and such central achievements in literary history and biography as Thomas Warton's *History of English Poetry* and Samuel Johnson's *Lives of the Poets*, institutions, methods and corpora of knowledge had been established, however much they differed from their modern equivalents. There is no simple linear narrative of the coming into being of an eighteenth-century literary scholarship, but it is possible to trace some of its routes, and to describe some of its key features and manifestations.

Who practised literary scholarship, and how in particular did the role, concept and practice of the scholarly editor arise? A significant proportion of Britain's literary heritage was effectively owned by the Tonson publishing house, founded in the latter decades of the Restoration period by Jacob Tonson, continued from 1720 by his nephew Jacob II, and from 1736 by the latter's son, Jacob III, with whom the dynasty died in 1767. Before the end of the seventeenth century Jacob Tonson I had published magnificent editions of English poets, including the folio Miltons of 1688, 1691 and 1695. More significantly from the point of view of the development of literary scholarship and editorial method, at the beginning of the eighteenth century the Tonson house began to publish poetical and dramatic works produced by an individual, often a named individual, editor. These publications present themselves not simply as reprints (however elegant), but, to a greater or lesser extent, as critical editions, embodying more or less evident and more or less authoritative scholarship. In some early cases the Tonsons sought to improve the literary cachet of their editions, and hence their sale and the value of their copyright, by employing poets of established reputation. The six-volume octavo Shakespeare of 1709 was edited by the poet and playwright Nicholas Rowe. A major element of added scholarly value of Rowe's edition was the Life of Shakespeare, which was reprinted, in various forms, throughout the century. Alexander Pope's edition of Shakespeare (1723–25) included a very small number of brief explanatory footnotes, but was more significant for its expressions of poetic taste and judgement, in its preface, and in Pope's starring of the 'most shining passages' and degradation of 'excessively bad' passages in Shakespeare's plays. In other cases, and increasingly, Tonson's commissioned editors were writers by trade, generally less well known, but often possessed of more relevant learning, and more concerned to develop an informed and coherent editorial method. One such was John Hughes, a poet, scholar and dramatist, who edited the ambitious and successful six-volume duodecimo Tonson edition of Spenser in 1715, and the 1719 duodecimo *Paradise Lost*, in each case carrying out a collation of the original texts.[5] Another was Lewis Theobald, who brought himself to the attention of Tonson and the world with the demolition, in his *Shakespeare Restored* (1726), of Pope's Shakespearean textual editing. In 1733 Tonson published Theobald's edition of Shakespeare, a milestone in its application of extensive knowledge of playhouse practice, and of dramatic and other literature of Shakespeare's time, both to the establishment and explanation of the text.[6] Pope's implied audience in his edition of Shakespeare had been a gentleman or gentlewoman humanist reader (rather than a playgoer), who preferred a mostly clean page and could do without elaborate scholia, for (as Pope allowed himself to claim, in his translation of the *Iliad*) 'Men of a right understanding generally see at once all that an Author can reasonably mean'.[7] Theobald's far more extensive, elaborated and illustrated explanatory annotations are evidently based on different assumptions about readerly understanding and editorial responsibility. The work of Theobald on Shakespeare, both in his edition and in *Shakespeare Restored*, was an important moment in the realignment of literary humanism. Now methods of 'intelligent editing' (to use Theobald's phrase) previously confined to the Latin and Greek classics and the Bible were being applied to 'canonical' works of English literature. A new literary scholarship based on historical and philological knowledge was being forged, and made new kinds of demand on its practitioner.

To those demands the university, operating thus far in the century to an older classical and theological curriculum, was not (as Urry's Chaucer shows) necessarily hospitable. The majority of scholars of English literature operated outside the academy, dependent on the product of their writings, or on income from another profession or private resources. In the early absence of substantial public library holdings of vernacular writings, they most often found books in their own libraries, built up even at the expense of personal impoverishment, or in those of their associates or friends.[8] By no means surprisingly, many of those involved in literary scholarship were trained in, and often still pursued, one of the lettered professions. Some were lawyers. Lewis Theobald was the son of an attorney, and briefly practised as an attorney himself before becoming a professional writer. Isaac Reed, editor of the 1785 variorum Shakespeare, like Theobald began his career in legal articles. Unlike Theobald, however, he continued this career as a conveyancer in chambers in Gray's and then in Staple Inn, in tandem with his literary work. Others combined literary scholarship with a clerical career. Zachary Pearce was vicar of St-Martin-in-the-Fields when he wrote his *Review of the Text of Milton's Paradise Lost* (1732–33), the most critically forceful and contextually informed response to Richard Bentley's notorious edition of *Paradise Lost* (1732); he rose in the Church to become Bishop of Rochester in 1756. When William Warburton published his edition of Shakespeare in 1747 he was in the midst of a career which was to take him to the bishopric of Gloucester. Relatively few literary scholars held college positions. Richard Farmer, Master of Emmanuel College, Cambridge, untroubled by the pressures to produce research under which modern academics labour, published only the magisterial and hugely influential *Essay on the Learning of Shakespeare* (1767). The scholarly high point of the altogether more productive career of Thomas Warton, Fellow of Trinity College, Oxford, was his massive *History of English Poetry* (three volumes: 1774, 1778, 1781). A small number of literary scholars were gentlemen rendered independent by inherited wealth or sinecures. Edward Capell's tenure of the office of Deputy Inspector of Plays afforded him sufficient income and leisure to dedicate himself to the study of Shakespeare and Elizabethan literature, resulting in his *Prolusions, or Select Pieces of Ancient Poetry* (1760), and his edition of Shakespeare (1768) with its remarkable apparatus, the *Notes and Various Readings* (1774, 1779–81). Charles Jennens, one of the richest men in the country, could pursue his passion for Shakespearean textual scholarship in the luxury of his great house at Gopsal in Leicestershire.[9]

In the eighteenth century the scholarly community of producers and readers was predominantly but not exclusively male. As in other periods the determinants of access to leisure, means and education were multiple, and included but were by no means confined to gender. A number of women took part in literary scholarship, both classical and (in its nature less circumscribed by class or gender) vernacular. Elizabeth Carter was educated by her father Nicholas, perpetual curate of Deal Chapel and preacher at Canterbury Cathedral, learning Latin and Greek, and subsequently Hebrew, French, Italian, Spanish, German, and, late in life, Portuguese and Arabic. She was introduced to Samuel Johnson by Edward Cave, who had published her *Poems upon Particular Occasions* in 1738. In 1741 she met Catherine Talbot, granddaughter of Dr William Talbot, Bishop of Durham. Carter's most significant work of literary scholarship, a translation of *All the Works of Epictetus* (1758), was initially intended only for family use within Catherine Talbot's reading circle, which included the Bishop of Oxford, Dr Secker, and his wife, but Talbot initiated the project of publishing the work by subscription. Within the learned Talbot/Secker group, most of the men but few of the women could make use of writings in Greek; within the larger community, gentlemen who had less Greek than Latin (and may have forgotten what small Latin they had once possessed) were as much in need of Carter's translation, if they wished to understand this central Stoic text, as women readers. The subscription, which was energetically prosecuted by Dr Secker, was hugely successful: there were just under 1000 subscribers at a guinea apiece, including a large number of titled names, a larger number of clergy including a very high proportion of the bishops, and some two dozen college heads and fellows. A quarter of the subscribers were women. The subscription afforded Carter a modest independence, and allowed her to devote the remainder of her life to literary interests, in converse and correspondence with such luminaries as Sir Joshua Reynolds, Edmund Burke, Horace Walpole, Hannah More and Elizabeth Montagu.

Elizabeth Montagu, sister of Sarah Scott Robinson and relative of Zachary Grey, developed her literary interests as a girl in Cambridge, partly under the influence of the controversialist and divine Conyers Middleton. Marrying the wealthy Edward Montagu in 1742 she was in a position, from the early 1750s, to take a lead in London literary society, hosting assemblies at her husband's town house, where the participants included Lord Lyttelton, Walpole, Johnson, Burke, David Garrick and Reynolds. Montagu's *Essay on the Genius and Writings of Shakespear, Compared with the Greek and French Dramatic Poets* (1769) is a robust defence of Shakespeare, 'our great national classic', against the carping particularly of Voltaire. Montagu positions her book as part of a national project of literary culture and criticism. Her title is a no doubt conscious echo of Joseph Warton's *Essay on the Genius and Writings of Pope* (1756–82). In an implicit Protestant sneer at the Roman Catholic and especially the French sequestration of Scripture sacred and secular, Montagu insists that in England 'Learning . . . is not confined to ecclesiastics, or a few lettered sages and academics; every English gentleman has an education, which gives him an early acquaintance with the writings of the ancients'. There is no doubt a feminine modesty here (Montagu's book does not bear her name on its title-page), but it is not clear that Montagu excludes herself on gender grounds from the ranks of English gentlemen whose bent critical bows face the cavalry of captious France. Nevertheless, Montagu is diffident. In her introduction she acknowledges the superior scholarship of the editors, and allows that she is engaged in a secondary exercise of critical disquisition:

> some of the most learned and ingenious of our critics have made correct editions of his works, and enriched them with notes. The superiority of talents and learning, which I acknowledge in these editors, leaves me no room to entertain the vain presumption of attempting to correct any passages of this celebrated author; but the whole, as corrected and elucidated by them, lies open to thorough enquiry into the genius of our great English classic.

Specifically, Montagu identifies the antiquarian and contextualizing part that the editors have played in clarifying the 'lighter characters' of the Shakespearean text, which 'have been restored by critics whose learning and penetration traced back the vestiges of superannuated opinions and customs'; the learned here are set against 'rash critics' and 'witlings', though the anonymous Montagu does not here claim to be among the vanguard of scholarship. At the end of her essay on *Julius Caesar* she hopes that 'this weak attempt to vindicate our great dramatic poet, will excite some critic able to do him more ample justice'. There is perhaps a female note of self-effacement here, though these are modesty *topoi* of a kind by no means uncommon in the scholarship of non-professional writers at this time.[10]

The scholarly edition: forms, functions, methods

By the 1730s and 1740s editors and publishers (especially the Tonsons) had effected something of a revolution in the form, character and function of the literary edition. The scholarly editorial treatment of the vernacular literary text had become a powerful and recognizable mode, making literary works readable to an eighteenth-century audience, and starting to have a significant effect in the establishment of a broadening vernacular canon. In a number of editions of English poets, including Spenser, Milton and Butler, as well as Shakespeare, are to be found (with a good deal of variation) most of the characteristic methods and formal elements we have already seen in Thomas Tyrwhitt's edition of the *Canterbury Tales*: a concern for textual accuracy which entailed resort to and close collation of manuscript sources and of the earliest printed editions, careful explanation of textual method, biographical and historical accounts of the author and the author's publications, the employment in annotation of literary and historical scholarship in the service of interpretation of the text, and the provision of glossaries and indexes and other aids to the reader's use and understanding.

John Upton's two-volume edition of Spenser's *Faerie Queene*, published by Tonson in 1758, might be taken as a representative instance. Upton's preface provides a biographical account of Spenser, as well as his well-known argument for the coherence and unity of Spenser's poem, on essentially classical grounds.[11] Upton claims to print the text 'as the Author gave it', using for his 'groundwork' the first editions of 1590 and 1596, and endeavouring to follow Spenser's spelling. He provides a glossary, 'Explaining the Difficult Words and Phrases', and making extensive references to other poets, including Homer, Virgil, Horace, Chaucer, Lydgate, Gower, Douglas, Tasso, Ariosto and Shakespeare. Upton's notes to the *Faerie Queene* (printed in the second volume after the clean text of the poem) display a similarly broad range of reference and learning, in Greek, Latin and English literature of all kinds (though the romance as a genre makes few appearances), British history, philology, Christian theology, classical philosophy, and, extensively, the Bible. Frequently interpretation is made on the basis of Spenser's 'manner', and, more specifically, his verbal uses. Sources are identified or surmised and analogues postulated, and the reader is provided with general information; but for the most part these notes are focused on particular explanation of the words of Spenser's text. So Upton's note on Repentance's use of salt water (*Faerie Queene*, 1. 10. 27), after citing and incorporating the variant reading of the 1596 quarto and 1609 folio, includes explanatory references to Euripides and Shakespeare, as well as to the biblical books of Psalms, Isaiah and Peter. His note on Spenser's account of the Castle of Alma (*Faerie Queene*, 2. 9. 22) – always a major crux for exegetes of the poem – provides (as well as Upton's extended Christian meditation on the nature of man) references to Cicero, Macrobius, Sallust, Manilius, Milton and Dryden.[12]

Thomas Warton, in his 1785 edition of Milton's *Poems upon Several Occasions*, both states and demonstrates a mature methodology and format of editing. He claims to have examined and compared 'the authentic copies published under the author's immediate inspection', and he provides, at the end of his volume, a list of 'Original Various Readings', as well as a list of the editions of Milton's shorter poems. In his preface, Warton not only stresses the evaluative and interpretative uses of 'comparing Milton with himself', but also traces the development of this practice in Milton editing, noting that neither Patrick Hume nor Richard Bentley made any significant comparative use of the shorter poems in their scholia on *Paradise Lost* of 1695 and 1732, and pointing out Zachary Pearce's primacy in the provision of such 'collateral evidences' in his *Review of the Text of Paradise Lost*. Warton provides (as did many scholarly editors) an explicit apology for his annotations:

> The chief purpose of the Notes is to explain our author's allusions, to illustrate or to vindicate his beauties, to point out his imitations both of others and of himself, to elucidate his obsolete diction, and by the adduction and juxtaposition of parallels universally gleaned from both his poetry and prose, to ascertain his favourite words, and to shew the peculiarities of his phraseology.

Warton insists that Milton's allusions are not restricted to Shakespeare, Spenser and the classical writers. His style, diction and ideas 'are also to be traced in other English poets, who were either his contemporaries or predecessors, and of whom many are now not commonly known'. Much of Milton's imagery derives from such sources, and hence the failure of previous editors (including Thomas Newton) to explore this Gothic library has resulted in failures both of understanding and appreciation.[13]

Warton's claim to be bringing to the understanding of Milton a new range of illustrative and explanatory knowledge is justified in his practice. In his typically extensive notes, for example, on the concluding speech of the Spirit in *Comus* (lines 976 ff.) he cites (among others) Homer, Pindar, Virgil, Fulgentius, Apuleius, Spenser, Tasso, Ariosto, Marino, Shakespeare, Jonson, Michael Drayton and William Browne (author of 'Britannia's Pastorals'). Apollonius Rhodius is cited as a specific source for the skill in singing of Hesperus' three daughters, Ovid as a specific source for Milton's description of the 'golden tree' (line 983) around which they sing. Among many noted parallels with Milton's other poems, and with *Paradise Lost* in particular, are the Spirit's reference to 'the gardens fair/Of Hesperus' of *Comus* (lines 981–2), and the 'Hesperian gardens' and 'Hesperian fables' of *Paradise Lost* (3. 568, 4. 250). Parallels are used to provide clear interpretative evidence: for example, Milton's use of the word 'chime' in the sense of 'music' – 'Higher than the sphery chime', *Comus* (line 1021) – is explained and illustrated by reference to passages in *Paradise Lost* (11. 559), *Paradise Regained* (2. 363), 'At a Solemn Music' (line 20), and 'On the Morning of Christ's Nativity' (line 128), as well as in Jonson, Dryden and others.[14]

The most significant case of development and establishment of a method and a format however is to be found in the field of Shakespearean editing in the last third of the eighteenth century, with the successive and cooperative work of Samuel Johnson, George Steevens, Edmond Malone and Isaac Reed. Before Johnson, significant collected editions of the dramatic works of Shakespeare had been published almost exclusively by the house of Jacob Tonson (Sir Thomas Hanmer's edition, published by the Oxford University Press in 1744, is the most obvious exception), and by single editors: Rowe, Pope, Theobald, Hanmer and Warburton. Even the idiosyncratic Edward Capell continued this tendency with his *Mr. William Shakespeare his Comedies, Histories, and Tragedies* (ten volumes, 1768), an edition produced almost exclusively by Capell's solitary efforts, but published none the less by the house of Tonson.[15] Samuel Johnson's own edition was published by Tonson, together with a number of other publishers, under his own by then distinguished and saleable name in 1765. In the following year George Steevens published Proposals for a new variorum, and Johnson, impressed by Steevens' *Twenty of the Plays of Shakespeare* (1766), a faithful old-spelling reprint of quarto texts, was happy to accept Steevens' offer to prepare a revised and expanded variorum version of his edition. The new Johnson/Steevens edition of 1773, the first variorum Shakespeare, was published by a consortium of some thirty-three publishers, Jacob Tonson having died in 1767, and the Tonson rights to Shakespeare having been sold in 1772. The 1773 variorum was substantially the work of Steevens, who provided many new notes, and time and again added tellingly apposite contextual illustrations to existing notes; Johnson provided eighty-four new notes, and revised a further seventy.[16] In 1778 a further revision of Johnson/Steevens appeared, the second variorum. The 1778 edition benefited from a huge number of suggestions and corrections provided by Edmond Malone, whose two important supplementary volumes, containing editions of Shakespeare's poems and sonnets, of 'seven plays that have been ascribed to him', and a number of additional notes, were published in 1780. In 1785, Steevens having declared that he had now joined the ranks of 'dowager editors', a further version of the variorum was published, with Isaac Reed's revisions. And in 1790 was published the edition which most commentators consider the high point of eighteenth-century Shakespeare editing, the sophisticated text and massive apparatus of Edmond Malone's edition.

These successive variorum editions constitute an inheritance of editorial form, and of scholarship, as well as of property among publishers.[17] A series of editors produced, for an evolving consortium of booksellers in the London book trade, a series of editions each of which built on its predecessors, using some or all of their elements, developing their forms, adding to previous knowledge and understanding. Malone's great 1790 edition is in substantial and important ways a distinctive and individual achievement, but it is also an organic development of content and conventions in the editions of Johnson, Steevens and Reed. The format is not a pompous folio (like Urry's Chaucer) or a majestic quarto (like Tonson's 1720 Milton), but a workmanlike octavo in ten volumes, ranging with its variorum predecessors. The object of such editions is not display but use, more specifically use by readers who believed that understanding of Shakespeare, as of other past writers, depended on the dialectical exercise and communication of a substantial body of pertinent knowledge. Malone's prolegomena are considerably more extensive than those that went before, occupying all of Part 1, and a substantial portion of Part 2 of his divided first volume. Their greater bulk reflects Malone's huge invest-ment of effort in research among primary sources, including the office-book of Sir Henry Herbert, and papers in the Stamp Office, Chancery, the Lord Chamberlain's office, Dulwich College, the Stratford and Worcester registers, and elsewhere. Some of his work is substantially original. Malone's definitive essay, 'An Attempt to Ascertain the Order in which the Plays of Shakspeare were Written', which had first been published in Steevens' edition of 1778, occupies some 120 pages of Part 1 of his first volume. Also to be found in the first volume is Malone's essay on 'Shakespeare, Ford, and Jonson'. His 'Historical Account of the Rise and Progress of the English Stage', a ground-breaking account of the English theatre from the earliest drama (where Malone draws on Thomas Warton's work) to the eighteenth century, concen-trating on Shakespeare's own period, takes up nearly three hundred pages of Part 2. Some of Malone's prolegomena are based on what others had created before him, but so extensively changed as to be virtually his own. Malone reprints, for example, as previous editors had done, Rowe's 1709 Life of Shakespeare, but accompanied by his own massive annotations, which authen-ticate Shakespeare's biography and challenge the legendary or anecdotal parts of Rowe's narrative. Many elements of Malone's prolegomena repeat those of his predecessors, with more or less extensive corrections, additions and revisions by Malone himself: a 'List of the most Authentick Ancient Editions of Shakspeare's Plays', a 'List of Detached Pieces of Criticism on Shakspeare, his Editors, &c.', a 'List of Plays altered from Shakspeare', 'Extracts of Entries on the Books of the Stationers' Company', 'Translations from Classick Authors'. Malone's edition continues to reprint a number of elements which are now almost obligatory in the make-up of the scholarly Shakespeare edition: the preface of Pope as well as that of Johnson, and Steevens' advertisement (but not the prefaces of Theobald, Hanmer or Warburton); Heminge and Condell's dedication and preface to the 1623 Folio; and Shakespeare's will.

Malone's tenacious, thoroughgoing and individual uses of and additions to an already existing succession of literary scholarship are perpetually visible too in the body of his edition of Shakespeare. The notes variorum of Malone, and of previous explicators, appear at the foot of each text page, an efficient but busy block of smaller type squeezing Shakespeare's words to the top, and often reducing them to a trickle. An important issue of form and use is involved here. Many editions of English classics, including many scholarly editions such as Upton's 1758 Spenser, Capell's 1768 Shakespeare and Tyrwhitt's 1775 Chaucer, had offered a clean reading text, uncluttered on the page by the impedimenta of philological apparatus, with explanatory notes following the text, or in a later volume, or even (as in Capell's case) in a later year. Many others however presented a text accompanied by more or less substantial footnotes: key examples are Richard Bentley's 1732 *Paradise Lost*, Lewis Theobald's 1733 *Shakespeare* and Zachary Grey's 1744 *Hudibras*. The separation of text and note attempts, it may be argued, to combine a reading text that aspires to a humanist elegance with the authenticating materials of philological scholarship. To accompany a text with substantial footnotes is to insist on the editorial act of contextualization and explanation, and to implicate the reader in the complexities of exegesis and understanding. How the notes of an edition are placed goes to the heart of an argument about the relative authority of author and editor, about the function and status of exegetical scholarship, and about reading practices, which had raged almost from the start of the century. A writer in the *Grub Street Journal* in the early 1730s, with distinguished scholarly editions of a Latin and an English classic in his sights, lamented editorial usurpations of authorial privilege:

> to be commented on, is only the Fate of the greatest and brightest Genius's, and to comment the Task of the heaviest Pedants . . . it's no longer BENTLEY at the Tail of HORACE, or THEOBALD at the Tail of SHAKESPEAR; but as if the Authors

Works were become their Properties, they call them BENTLEY's *Horace*, or
THEOBALD's *Shakespear*.[18]

During the 1770s and 1780s the volume and placement of notes became an
especially important part of this argument. A writer in the *English Review*, for
example, congratulates Edward Capell for having 'printed his notes by
themselves, not forcing them upon the student of Shakespeare, but leaving
the perusal to his choice'. By contrast, Johnson in his 1765 edition, and
Steevens in 1773 and 1778, had forced upon the reader's attention not only
their own notes but those of other scholars and editors:

> Johnson . . . adopted a multiplicity of notes from various writers into his edition.
> Mr. Steevens has carefully preserved all this farrago, and, beside it, we are now
> treated with the annotations of himself, Dr. Farmer, Mr. Tyrwhit, Mr. Malone,
> &c. &c. &c. . . . all these inestimable notes are printed at the bottom of the
> page, so that a reader, at all inquisitive, can scarcely keep his eyes from them,
> and is frequently drawn into the whirlpool; in spite of all his efforts.[19]

Similarly, the *British Critic* thought 'it . . . now a very general opinion, that
poor Shakespeare is . . . over whelmed and oppressed with notes till his
delightful pages become absolutely terrific', even preferring the sparsely
annotated (not to say inconsequential) edition of Joseph Rann (Oxford,
1786).[20] Other writers however welcomed the copious and immediately
accessible explanatory materials of the variorum editions. The *Critical Review*
found that the explicatory annotations of the 1778 Johnson/Steevens edition
transform the reader's literary experience and understanding: 'In tracing the
many valuable illustrations in this edition of Shakespeare, we seem as if almost
rendered contemporary with the poet; so clearly are the manners, the customs,
and the language of those times delineated by the investigation of the editor.'[21]

Malone continues the format developed and confirmed by Johnson, Steevens and Reed, and provides in his preface a definitive version of the argument
both for weighty scholarly annotation and for its intimate interaction on the
page with the text. In so doing, he is conscious of the development of
scholarly vernacular editing as a methodology, and of its consequences, and in
his view its advantages, for the practice of reading distant and difficult literary
works. To place notes at the end of each volume, rather than 'subjoined to
the text', as some friends had suggested to him, would have the consequence
that 'many readers would remain uninformed, rather than undergo the trouble
occasioned by perpetual reference from one part of a volume to another'.
Malone tackles head-on the accusation that authors have become submerged
under a flood of scholiastic editorial pedantry. 'An idle notion has been

propagated, that Shakspeare has been *buried under his commentators'*; but such a notion thoughtlessly perpetuates a view appropriate only in the age of (as Malone would think) Bentley, Theobald and Warburton:

> During the era of conjectural criticism and capricious innovation, notes were indeed evils; while one page was covered with ingenious sophistry in support of some idle conjecture, and another was wasted in its overthrow, or in erecting a new fabrick equally unsubstantial as the former.

Now, however, 'conjecture and emendation have given place to rational explanation'. The establishment and interpretation of Shakespeare's text, and the labour of editors, no longer an exercise in quarrelsome egotism, is now based on reason and evidence, and serves the interest of the understanding reader:

> While our object is, to support and establish what the poet wrote, to illustrate his phraseology by comparing it with that of his contemporaries, and to explain his fugitive allusions to customs long since disused and forgotten ... if even every line of his plays were accompanied with a comment, every intelligent reader would be indebted to the industry of him who produced it.

Neither the project nor its supporting rhetoric was entirely new; both Lewis Theobald and Edward Capell certainly thought of themselves as offering 'rational explanation' to an 'intelligent reader' who wished to go beyond superficial or intuitive response to informed understanding. The volume of notes in Malone's edition (or in Steevens') however goes appreciably beyond Theobald, and even beyond Capell. Further, Steevens and Malone do much more than add to the inherited body of scholia. Steevens' additions to Johnson's notes offer time after time the most pertinent contemporary illustration, and the most cogently appropriate evidence for interpretation. Malone, in his preface, accurately describes the selective and dialectic hermeneutic methodology of his own annotations, claiming to have given 'the true explication of a passage, by whomsoever made, without loading the page with the preceding unsuccessful attempts at elucidation'.[22] The meaning of Shakespeare's words is drawn out in the notes of Malone's edition, and to a substantial extent in those of his predecessors, by a project which is both collaborative and critical, each crux explained by a series of attributed comments, guiding the reader to understanding.

Scholarship: circulation and collaboration

The cooperative forms of the late eighteenth-century variorum Shakespeare
were to some extent made possible by the development of social processes of
collaboration among literary scholars and readers. These processes were not
entirely unanticipated. Theobald, for instance, had conducted during the
course of his work on his edition a lengthy Shakespearean correspondence
with William Warburton.[23] From about the mid-eighteenth century, however, there developed a newly complex scholarly economy of conversation
and correspondence, lending and borrowing, annotation, bequeathing, referring and assisting. The overlapping circles of scholarly friendship included
Samuel Johnson, the Warton brothers, Elizabeth Carter, Charlotte Lennox,
Elizabeth Montagu, Horace Walpole, Thomas Gray, Thomas Percy, George
Steevens, John Nichols, Thomas Tyrwhitt, Edmond Malone, Isaac Reed and
Richard Farmer – though significantly they excluded such isolated and
provincial workers as Edward Capell and Charles Jennens (and Steevens'
friendship was not in continuously good repair with anyone except Johnson,
and the equable Isaac Reed). These networks of scholarly communication
centred on Oxford, Cambridge and, especially, London. Scholars met in the
university colleges, in the new library of the British Museum – where Johnson,
Reed, Percy, Steevens and Tyrwhitt were among the first to hold reader's
tickets[24] – and in literary clubs – not only Johnson's famous club, but also the
Eumélean Club (of which Farmer was a member) and the Unincreasable Club
(of which Isaac Reed was president). Sometimes they worked in close personal
contact with each other. Reed, for example, welcomed fellow scholars to
Staple Inn to use his personal library, amounting to nearly 9000 volumes of
poetry, drama and pamphlets, and indeed Steevens corrected all the proof-
sheets of his 1793 variorum through the night in Reed's chambers, 'and
benefited largely from Reed's suggestions'.[25] They contributed remarks and
suggestions and formal notes for each other's writings. Steevens, Thomas
Warton and Percy, for example, were among those who provided notes to
the appendix of Johnson's 1765 Shakespeare. Tyrwhitt contributed notes on
Shakespeare to Steevens, Malone (for his supplement in 1780) and Reed.
Both Reed and Steevens assisted Johnson with information for the *Lives of the
Poets*, and Johnson appealed to his friend Richard Farmer for information
about the poets Ambrose Philips, William Broome and Thomas Gray (though
Farmer, characteristically, did not reply).[26] They shared books of all kinds
between them. Garrick lent Steevens Shakespearean quartos, for example,

for the latter's *Twenty Plays of Shakespeare* (1766). In a strikingly extended but not atypical instance of the circulation of information within the world of literary scholarship, George Steevens made a transcript in 1788 from Richard Farmer's copy of a curious 1595 pamphlet, *Maroccus Extaticus or Bankes Bay Horse in a Trance*, which he gave to Isaac Reed, from whom it passed to Edmond Malone.[27] They also bequeathed books to each other. When Steevens died in 1800, he left Isaac Reed a corrected copy of his edition of Shakespeare, and from this Reed produced his revised twenty-one-volume version in 1803. Malone's books were willed to his elder brother Lord Sunderlin, who allowed James Boswell, jun. to keep them until he had finished his work on his revision of Malone, published in 1821, after which they passed to the Bodleian.[28]

Occasionally this circulation of scholarship amounted in practice to small-scale manuscript publication and distribution. Perhaps the best known and most demonstrably influential instance of this phenomenon is Oldys' Langbaine.[29] William Langbaine's *Account of the English Dramatick Poets*, first published in Oxford in 1691, became the single most important source of information for eighteenth-century literary scholars about the history and biography of the English stage, not in its own right, but because of Oldys' extensive and learned manuscript annotations. William Oldys the antiquary, best known now for his editorial work with Samuel Johnson on the catalogue of the Harleian library, annotated his first copy of Langbaine's *Dramatick Poets* before leaving London for Yorkshire in 1724. On his return he discovered that his landlord had sold his books and papers, including this first Langbaine, which was to pass into the possession of Thomas Coxeter, and thence to Theophilus Cibber, and form the basis of Cibber's additional notes in the *Lives of the Poets of Great Britain and Ireland in the Time of Dean Swift* (five volumes, 1753). Having lost his labour once, Oldys promptly started again, spending part of the remaining years of his life in covering a second copy of Langbaine (purchased in 1727) with voluminous annotations, written in a tiny hand in the margins and between the lines. Oldys' notes here constitute, in effect, a publication, indeed one of the most important publications for eighteenth-century scholarship on the native dramatic tradition. Oldys' second copy was purchased at an auction of Oldys' books and papers by Dr Thomas Birch, Secretary of the Royal Society, who loaned it to Bishop Thomas Percy. Percy in his turn transcribed Oldys' notes, with some of his own, into a copy of Langbaine bound in four interleaved volumes, which then passed to Monck Mason, to Halliwell Phillips, and finally to the library of the British Museum. George Steevens made a further transcript from Oldys' second copy of Langbaine, with additions of his own, into another copy of Langbaine's book; and this in its turn was transcribed by Joseph Haslewood into a copy of Langbaine bound in two interleaved volumes, in which may now be found the autograph or copied manuscript annotations not only of Oldys, Percy and Steevens, but also of Isaac Reed, R. Wright, Haslewood himself, and probably Edward Utterson. This copy incorporates especially clearly an inheritance or tradition of Langbaine. It is perhaps the richest of several more or less parallel individual physical instances of preservation of all that can be gathered of a sequence of manuscript commentators upon Langbaine's *Dramatick Poets*. Nor is this mere preservation. There is good evidence that those involved in the duplication of Oldys' notes assumed that their work would be seen and used by others. In both the Percy and Haslewood copies prefatory manuscript glosses (by Percy, Steevens and Haslewood) explain the nature, provenance and transmission of the notes, and ensure that a reader of these handwritten notes will understand how they work, how they embody and articulate the tradition.[30] These copies of Oldys' scholia on Langbaine (and the scholia of others on Oldys' scholia) were not only read but extensively used by many editors, historians and biographers of the drama. The 'Anecdotes of Shake-speare, from Oldys's Mss. &c.' printed in George Steevens' 1778 variorum edition are only one of the more explicit and formal uses of a resource central to eighteenth-century scholarship in these areas. The history of the copies of Oldys' annotations on Langbaine demonstrate the existence of an economy of knowledge related to, but also different from, that of the printed book.

Occasional manuscript annotation in margins or interleaves was common-place, of course, but such thoroughgoing annotation as Oldys provides is remarkable for its scholarly completeness and assumption of an audience. It is none the less not unique.[31] There are some functional similarities in the case of Edmond Malone's autograph annotations in his copy of Edward Capell's edition of *Mr. William Shakespeare his Comedies, Histories, and Tragedies* (ten volumes, 1768). In a prefatory note on a front flyleaf of Capell's first volume, signed and dated 20 June 1781, Malone explains the grounds and procedures of the marginal corrections he has written throughout this copy. Though Capell was 'a very industrious and careful *collator* of the old copies', he was in Malone's view 'a man of very mean understanding, and *totally* unacquainted with the phraseology of our ancient English Writers', and consequently Capell has in many places disturbed the '*genuine* reading of the ancient copies' and made room for 'the arbitrary interpolations of Warburton, Theobald, or Hanmer', as well as 'fantastick alterations of his own'. Hence, Malone explains, in the present manuscript commentary he has 'restored the ancient readings' and 'marked such emendations as deserve to be admitted into the text with the initial letter of the Commentator by whom each emendation was proposed'. On the recto of the next flyleaf Malone gives, as he would in a printed edition, a list of abbreviations for the names of the Shakespearean commentators to whom he refers, and advises that 'where the emendation is considered to be just, the initial Letter is placed in the *external* margin; where it is faulty, in the *internal*'. This, then, is a formal, careful record whose symbols are intended to be understood by others. Malone's manuscript notes run throughout these ten volumes of Capell's 1768 Shakespeare. The notes are generally written at the foot; where space runs out, he uses the top margin, and he uses the inner and outer margin as he indicates in his manuscript prefatory account of abbreviations and editorial procedures. Malone's written footnotes are keyed by line number on the page to Capell's unnumbered text, like Capell's own printed footnotes. Capell's printed copy in fact is formally developed by Malone's manuscript additions in part according to the conventions already used within it. The notes constitute a very thorough textual apparatus on the variations in Capell's text from the copies. In its completeness, its accuracy, its consistent use of formal editorial conventions and its care to make its own conventions understood, Malone's annotated Capell is in effect an edition, constructed according to at least some of the standards of a printed edition, intended to be usable by readers. The textual alterations and apparatus added by Malone's pen (together with his further occasional comments about Capell's ignorance) make this a kind of small-scale manuscript variorum.[32]

Scholarship's readers

Malone could invest so much time and effort in these manuscript annotations because he could expect his little book to be circulated at least in his own circle of Shakespearean learning. Printed works of literary scholarship, and most scholarly editions, were of course aimed at a very much larger though not a mass market. Prices were relatively high. Urry's Chaucer cost 30s. in sheets (50s. on royal paper), Zachary Grey's two-volume edition of Butler's *Hudibras* (1744) 15s., Thomas Newton's *Paradise Regained* of 1750 10s. in sheets. Theobald's 1733 Shakespeare cost his subscribers 2 guineas apiece. The 'pond'rous volumes' of Thomas Hanmer's edition were less good value at 3 guineas. Both Warburton's and Johnson's Shakespeares were priced at £2 8s. Edward Capell's bare text of Shakespeare, published in 1768, cost

2 guineas, the three volumes of *Notes and Various Readings* published between 1779 and 1781 3 guineas; the total cost of 5 guineas was no doubt not the least of the objections to his edition. Readers of the Johnson and Steevens variorum of 1773 paid £3 for the ten bound volumes. Malone's variorum cost £3 17s. in 1790. These are all expensive books, and notably expensive in comparison with such cheaper popular editions as those published by the Donaldsons, the house of Foulis or John Bell. The five duodecimo volumes of Bell's 1773 edition of Shakespeare, for instance, sold for 15s., and a 1772 edition of *The Works of Andrew Marvel* (a reprint of Edmund Curll's two-volume duodecimo of 1726) could be had for 6s. They compare in price (adjusted for inflation) rather more closely, however, with modern scholarly editions of English poets, or with the complete sets of, for example, the Arden or Oxford Shakespeares. Print runs of eighteenth-century learned works and editions were usually under a thousand, but very considerable sales could be achieved over time. Though the sales of Warburton's Shakespeare could be described by a contemporary as 'slow-pac'd',[33] no fewer than seven London editions of Theobald's Shakespeare, in octavo and duodecimo formats, had been published by 1773, reaching (according to Steevens) a total of 11,360 copies.

The most reliable and particularized indication of readership in the eighteenth century is provided by subscription lists, and this is especially true for literary editions, a high proportion of which were published by this method. Different kinds of editions were aimed at very different markets, and printed lists reflect this (as well as how the efforts of the individuals who solicited the subscriptions were directed). The magnificent two-volume quarto Milton issued by the bookseller Jacob Tonson in 1720 was aimed equally at establishing Milton's prestige and Tonson's. The poet's text is beautifully printed in large type, without any editorial intrusion on the text page or anywhere else (though Addison's famous *Spectator* papers are reprinted at the end of Volume 2, together with a topic index). Its intended destination is evidently the houses of the great and good, and indeed the subscription list has a markedly courtly and aristocratic bias. Something over one-third of its fit audience of some 340 subscribers bore titles (including the Earl of Burlington, Lord Bathurst, the Duke of Chandos, Lord Oxford and Lord Hervey), or held senior office in law or government. Alexander Pope and Matthew Prior are among the other subscribers. Only nine of the subscribers were female, of whom all but two were titled. Lewis Theobald's more functional, less elegant and more scholarly 1733 edition of Shakespeare has an appreciably more varied and rather larger subscription list. The proportion of women is very much higher (about one in eleven), and the proportion of titled names very much lower (about one in eight). Literary names are better represented than in other comparable subscription lists, then or later in the century: Theobald's subscribers included James Thomson, Colley Cibber, Henry Fielding, Samuel Richardson, Richard Steele and Edward Young. The worlds of scholarship (Bentley, Thirlby, Upton, Warburton), the pictorial arts (Thornhill, Hogarth), music (Pepusch) and the theatre (Rich, Cibber, Quin) are also significantly represented. Markedly different again, both from the 1720 Milton and the 1733 Shakespeare, is the subscription list of a 'popular' edition. John Bell's *Shakespeare's Plays, As they are now performed at the Theatres Royal in London* (1773) was aimed at a very different market, and undertook a very different function. Bell's neat duodecimo volumes were intended 'as a companion to the theatre' (Vol. 1, p. 7), for the pocket rather than the library table or desk. The subscription list here is substantially longer, made up for the most part of members of the professional and trading classes. The title of Bell's typical subscriber is 'Mr' (occasionally 'Mrs'). The dukes and earls among his subscribers are overwhelmingly outnumbered by clerics, academics, surgeons, merchants and druggists. In all these lists the great majority of the subscribers are private individuals. Libraries, book-clubs and booksellers usually make up a very small percentage of the whole. A number of books – Ralph Church's 1758–59 edition of the *Faerie Queene* and Elizabeth's Carter's *Epictetus* among them – found subscribers in some half a dozen Oxford and Cambridge college libraries, and Zachary Grey's edition of *Hudibras* found a place in several college, town and cathedral libraries.

Subscription lists evidence in a wide variety of ways the particular social and cultural positioning of works of literary scholarship, in many cases delineating a characteristic audience or even confirming an agenda. Samuel Butler might not have seemed the author most likely to appeal to a mid-eighteenth-century readership, yet Zachary Grey's massively annotated edition of *Hudibras* (1744) had a relatively enormous subscription sale of some 1600 copies. Zachary Grey, vicar of St Giles and St Peter's in Cambridge, was a committed churchman, and had long been embroiled in controversy against dissent and Presbyterianism.[34] This polemic is continued in the editorial materials of his *Hudibras*. Grey explains that Samuel Butler's satiric purpose was 'to expose the Hypocrisy and Wickedness of those, who began and carried on the Rebellion, under a Pretence of promoting Religion and Godliness; at the same time that they acted against all the precepts of Religion'. To understand this purpose, the eighteenth-century reader requires, and Grey provides, detailed contextualization. In his preface he gives an extended 'abstract' of Presbyterian and Independent church governance. His dense line-by-line annotations to the poem itself amount to a politico-religious project of identifying and illustrating the targets of Butler's complex religious satire. By no means surprisingly, therefore, Grey's subscription list leans heavily to a learned and clerical audience. At least half of his subscribers were individual churchmen and college fellows. A substantial number of college and cathedral libraries also subscribed. Equally striking are the number of Cambridge names, both university and local clergy, in the list. Conversely (and by no means unusually) there are very few obviously 'literary' names; Christopher Smart, Richard Hurd and Horace Walpole are the exceptions (and the subscription of all three may be explained by their Cambridge connections). Only 3 per cent of Grey's subscription purchasers were female, an unusually low proportion (7 or 10 per cent was common for scholarly vernacular editions).

Equally scholarly in its way, Elizabeth Elstob's edition and translation of *An English-Saxon Homily on the Birth-Day of St Gregory* (1709) had a very different agenda, and a very different readership. It has recently been argued that for Elstob, 'Saxon studies was a route to self-discovery as a woman living in the eighteenth century', an alternative to a male-dominated classicism, and that Elstob, in her preface, offers an explicit defence of 'women's rights to learning and to Christian authority'. The work is dedicated to Queen Anne. The Anglo-Saxon text is accompanied by a translation not in Latin, but in a language 'accessible to a wider audience', the 'mother tongue' of English. Elstob's own portrait appears within the initial illuminated 'G' of the transla-tion, echoing the portrait of Gregory himself in the initial which opens the original text.[35] The subscription list for Elstob's volume contains as one might expect a number of antiquarians and scholars, including Thomas Hearne the antiquary, Joshua Barnes the Cambridge professor of Greek, and George Hickes the Anglo-Saxonist. There are, too, local connections of a number of kinds. There are several subscribers from Canterbury (where Elstob's uncle Charles was a prebendary), and from Oxford (where Elstob had set up home with her brother William from 1698 to 1702). Almost one in ten of the subscribers are from Newcastle, Elstob's birthplace, and many more from the northern cities of Leeds, Durham, Gateshead and Stockton. Much the most striking feature of the subscription list, however, is that no fewer than 116 of the small total of 271 subscribers are women. Titled women, significantly, outnumber titled men by a ratio of nearly four to one.

Conclusions

Even from the beginning of the eighteenth century, vernacular scholarly editing assumed diverse forms, and addressed markets various in profession, gender and social class. The passing decades witnessed the growth of complex and matured communities of literary scholarship, whose members assisted each other's work, and within which books and other documents circulated widely. Book layouts and editorial methodologies developed, and took on some shared and recognizable, though never monolithic or hypostatized, shapes. The publication especially of the more significant editions evoked regular contributions to a continuing debate about issues of function and authority in editing. A readership for the learned edition, distinguishable but not wholly separate from that for the popular edition, including but by no means confined to the literary scholars themselves, grew throughout the century. By the decades of Steevens and Malone the market for editions of English literary classics had become, like any mature market, stratified. Publishers and editors could find a niche and a substantial sale not only for popular reprints but also for learned editions with their carefully edited texts and extensive apparatus. Scholars were able to assume in their readers some knowledge or at least acceptance of the consequence of historical, cultural, literary and biographical contexts of the texts they edited. They could assume, too, and understand the need to satisfy, an increasing expectation of textual exactness. The market for literary learning depended on shared though fluid conceptions of a canon of English literature which had come into being during the course of the century. The existence and lineaments of that canon itself, in its turn, had substantially depended on the work and interests of the publishers and scholars of an English literary inheritance.

Acknowledgement

Part of my research for this chapter was carried out during the tenure of a fellowship of the British Library Centre for the Book, whose help I am glad to acknowledge.

Notes

1. *The Works of Geoffrey Chaucer* (London: Lintot, 1721), preface.
2. *The Canterbury Tales of Chaucer*, 5 vols (London: Payne, 1775, 1778), Vol. 1, p. xx. William Thomas made extensive ms. corrections to the text in a copy of Urry's Chaucer which he presented to the British Museum in 1764 (now British Library 643.m.4).
3. *The Canterbury Tales of Chaucer*, Vol. 1, pp. i, ii, xx ff.
4. On the development of literary history, a classic work is René Wellek, *The Rise of English Literary History* (New York: University of North Carolina Press, 1941). See also Lawrence Lipking, *The Ordering of the Arts in Eighteenth-Century England* (Princeton, NJ: Princeton University Press, 1970); and David Fairer's important recent account in his introduction to *Thomas Warton's History of English Poetry* (London: Routledge, and London and New York: Thoemmes Press, 1998).
5. On Hughes' editorship of Milton, see R. G. Moyles, *The Text of Paradise Lost: A Study in Editorial Procedure* (Toronto: University of Toronto Press, 1985), pp. 48–51.
6. For extended discussions of Theobald and his methods, see Peter Seary, *Lewis Theobald and the Editing of Shakespeare* (Oxford: Oxford University Press, 1990); and Marcus Walsh, *Shakespeare, Milton and Eighteenth-Century Literary Editing* (Cambridge: Cambridge University Press, 1997), pp. 126–49.
7. *The Twickenham Edition of the Poems of Alexander Pope*, Vol. 7: *The Iliad of Homer*, Books I–IX, ed. Maynard Mack *et al.* (London: Methuen and New Haven, CT: Yale University Press, 1967), p. 82.
8. Lewis Theobald, Edward Capell, Richard Farmer, George Steevens, Isaac Reed and Edmond Malone were among those who devoted appreciable resources to the collection of hundreds of texts of Shakespeare and his near contemporaries. See *The Catalogue of the Library of Lewis Theobald, Deceas'd* (London, 1744); W. W. Greg, *Catalogue of the Books Presented by Edward Capell to the Library of Trinity College in Cambridge* (Cambridge: printed for Trinity College at the University Press, 1903); *Dictionary of National Biography* s.vv. Richard Farmer, George Steevens; *A Catalogue of the Curious & Extensive Library of the Late Isaac Reed, Esq. . . . Which will be sold by Auction, by Messrs. King and Lochee* (London, 1807); *Catalogue of Early English Poetry and other Miscellaneous Works Illustrating the British Drama, Collected by Edmond Malone, Esq. and now Preserved in the Bodleian Library* (Oxford, 1836); *A Catalogue of the Greater Portion of the Library of the Late Edmond Malone, Esq. . . . Which will be sold by Auction, By Mr. Sotheby* (London, 1818); Peter Martin, *Edmond Malone, Shakespearean Scholar: A Literary Biography* (Cambridge: Cambridge University Press, 1995), pp. 277–9.
9. See Gordon Crosse, 'Charles Jennens as editor of Shakespeare', *Library*, ser. 4, 16 (1935): 236–40.
10. *An Essay on the Genius and Writings of Shakespear* (1769), pp. 1, 3, 15, 288.
11. Jonathan Kramnick suggests that Upton's use of philological learning in his annotation is intended as a solution to 'the problem of Spenserian archaism', argues for the primacy of Upton's treatment of Spenser as a classic, and considers Upton's contribution to 'the understanding of high cultural genres' in his *Making the English Canon: Print-Capitalism and the Cultural Past, 1700–1770* (Cambridge: Cambridge University Press, 1998), pp. 164–8.
12. John Upton (ed.), *Spenser's Faerie Queene* (London: Tonson, 1758), Vol. 1, pp. xl–xli; Vol. 2, pp. 408, 480–1.
13. Thomas Warton (ed.), *Poems upon Several Occasions . . . by John Milton* (London: Dodsley, 1785), pp. xxiv, 606–18, 618–20, vii, ix, xix, xx, xxi.

14. *Ibid.*, pp. 256–65.

15. On Capell, see Walsh, *Shakespeare, Milton and Eighteenth-Century Literary Editing*, pp. 175–98.

16. Arthur Sherbo (ed.), *Johnson on Shakespeare* (New Haven, CT: Yale University Press, 1968), Vol. 7, p. xxxix.

17. For an important recent discussion, see Nick Groom's introduction in Vol. 1 of *The Johnson–Steevens Edition of the Plays of William Shakespeare* (London: Routledge/Thoemmes, and Tokyo: Kinokuniya, 1995).

18. *Gentleman's Magazine*, 4 (March 1734): 135, quoting from *Grub Street Journal*, 14 March, No. 220.

19. *English Review*, 3 (1784): 176, 179.

20. *British Critic*, 3 (1794): 645; 6 (1795): 300. Cited by Brian Vickers, *Shakespeare. The Critical Heritage*, Vol. 6 (London: Routledge & Kegan Paul, 1981), p. 78.

21. *Critical Review*, 47 (1779): 172.

22. Malone, *The Plays and Poems of William Shakspeare* (1790), Vol. 1, Part 1, pp. xliv, liv–lvii.

23. See Seary, *Lewis Theobald*, pp. 102–30.

24. P. R. Harris, *A History of the British Museum Library 1753–1973* (London: the British Library, 1998), Appendix 3.

25. *Dictionary of National Biography*, s.v. Isaac Reed.

26. Bruce Redford (ed.), *The Letters of Samuel Johnson. Volume 3: 1777–1781* (Oxford: Clarendon Press, 1992), p. 257.

27. *Catalogue of Early English Poetry . . . Collected by Edmond Malone*, p. 47.

28. *Ibid.*, advertisement.

29. A somewhat different case is represented by the antiquary William Cole (1714–82), who published virtually nothing of his own, but communicated his knowledge widely among friends and correspondents (including Gray, Farmer, Nichols and Alban Butler), and 'rendered substantial assistance to many authors by supplying them either with entire dissertations or with minute communications or corrections' (*Dictionary of National Biography*). He bequeathed nearly a hundred folio manuscript volumes, containing results of his enquiries, to the British Museum.

30. William Oldys' second copy of the 1691 Langbaine is now British Library C.28.g.1.; Percy's transcription is British Library C. 57.L.12.; and the Steevens/Haslewood copy is C.45.d.14, 15.

31. For a significant discussion of a thorough but apparently more private case of manuscript annotation of the 1785, 1790 and 1793 variorums, see Paul Nelsen, 'Chedworth and the territoriality of the reader', in Joanna Gondris (ed.), *Reading Readings: Essays on Shakespeare Editing in the Eighteenth Century* (Cranbury, NJ, and London: Associated University Presses, 1998), pp. 140–63.

32. Malone's annotated Capell is British Library C.60.g.10.

33. In a letter from 'T. P.', *Gentleman's Magazine*, 20 (June 1750): 252.

34. For instance, in *A Vindication of the Church of England* (1720), *Presbyterian Prejudice Display'd* (1722), and numerous other publications through to the 1740s.

35. Kathryn Sutherland, 'Editing for a new century: Elizabeth Elstob's Anglo-Saxon manifesto and Aelfric's St Gregory homily', in D. G. Scragg and Paul E. Szarmach (eds), *The Editing of Old English* (Cambridge: D. S. Brewer, 1994), pp. 213–37. My quotations are from pp. 217, 225 and 228.

CHAPTER 8

THE PRODUCTION AND CONSUMPTION OF THE EIGHTEENTH-CENTURY POETIC MISCELLANY

MICHAEL F. SUAREZ SJ

Introduction

The New Cambridge Bibliography of English Literature records nearly 5000 'poetical miscellanies, song books, and verse collections of multiple authorship' published between 1701 and 1800.[1] In fact, the actual figure is considerably higher. This chapter attempts to advance our understanding of eighteenth-century verse miscellanies, not by surveying vast numbers of such collections, but by scrutinizing a relatively small selection of texts. Eschewing a biblio-metric approach dependent upon sweeping statistical analyses of surviving eighteenth-century miscellanies, my investigation is organized according to seven principal divisions.

Following the introduction, the second part of this chapter considers works published by retail subscription to determine what they can (and cannot) tell us about their likely readerships. The subject of the third section is the composite nature of miscellanies. Tracing a series of intertextual connections among verse collections, I highlight the complexities of their transmission while alerting the reader to the importance of commercial considerations for the ways these texts are compiled, produced and marketed. This theme is amplified in the fourth and fifth parts of the investigation which scrutinize, first, piratical miscellanies, and then unauthorized continuations of poetry collections. Both kinds of opportunistic exploitation reveal how booksellers profited from the success of their competitors, most especially of Robert

Dodsley's bestselling miscellany, *A Collection of Poems. By Several Hands* (3 vols, 1748; 4 vols, 1755; 6 vols, 1758). The unusual history of a poetic miscellany compiled and published by George Pearch – in which the bookseller effectively writes from the grave to condemn the tactics of his rivals, and his greatest adversary becomes his posthumous publisher – is the subject of the sixth section. Finally, the conclusion briefly considers what we can learn from studying miscellanies so closely, and makes a case for the knowledge that these texts can provide not only about eighteenth-century reading habits and literary tastes, but also about the networks of social, historical, aesthetic and economic relations inextricably linked to their production and consumption.

The examples I have chosen are predominantly 'literary' miscellanies, rather than collections which would ordinarily be characterized as political, religious, juvenile, comic, Scots, educational or musical. No consideration is given, however, to 'made-up' miscellanies, which were typically created by binding together a group of smaller publications and adding a title-page to announce the collection's contents.[2] Although the mixing of literary modes is a common feature of many miscellanies, I have generally avoided works in which prose serves more than an editorial function.

In the vast majority of cases, poetical miscellanies were created as money-making endeavours, although most of their prefaces or advertisements claim that their compilation provides a valuable service to literature by preserving verses which otherwise might well have perished. The anonymous editor of *Deliciæ Poeticæ; or Parnassus Display'd* (1706), for example, notes that some of the poems in his collection 'are now unhappily out of Print, others handled [*sic*] about only in Manuscript'. Accordingly, the publication of this miscellany is said to perform an important curatorial function by rescuing meritorious compositions 'from the danger of some of the Copies being lost, by not appearing in Print at all; of others, by not being Reprinted, which has been the undeserved Fate of too many admirable Composures'.[3] In keeping with this assumed role, the editor, who is probably the bookseller John Nutt, signs himself 'PHILOMUSUS'. In fact, as we will observe below, miscellanies were an important means by which booksellers packaged poetry, creating products that both responded to and created markets for verse. Many of the miscellanies we encounter in the following pages were targeted at readers from specific social and economic classes, age groups or geographical regions.

This chapter focuses on miscellanies rather than anthologies. Miscellanies are usually compilations of relatively recent texts designed to suit contemporary tastes; anthologies, in contrast, are generally selections of canonical texts which have a more established history and a greater claim to cultural importance. The miscellany, then, typically celebrates – and indeed constructs – taste, novelty and contemporaneity in assembling a synchronous body of material. It should be distinguished from the anthology, which honours – and perpetuates – the value of historicity and the perdurance of established canons of artistic discrimination in gathering texts recognized for their aesthetic legitimacy. Although the relationship between anthologies and the formation of the poetic canon in the second half of the eighteenth and the first decades of the nineteenth century is a fascinating topic, I believe that the particular circumstances surrounding the often complex 'life-histories' of poetic miscellanies also make these texts a highly rewarding if somewhat unconventional subject of scholarly investigation. Throughout this enquiry, my aim is to employ the allied disciplines of bibliography and book history to enrich our comprehension of texts generally neglected, but of genuine importance for the light they can shed on attitudes to the legitimate use and the illicit appropriation of literary property, the commercial determinants of textual transmission, interactions among publishing booksellers, the changing reputations of poets, and trends in the habits of eighteenth-century readers.

Retail subscription and readership: the markets for verse miscellanies

When studied with due circumspection, the many verse miscellanies sold by retail subscription are useful for giving us a sense of what their readerships may generally have been like. The sagacious American bibliographer Hugh Amory rightly cautions, however, that a subscription list is often taken as a precise indication of a work's readership, when in fact 'Nothing in the list proves that [subscribers] ever paid the second half of their subscription, much less that they ever read their copies if they did.' He also points out that not infrequently 'Subscribers . . . were greatly out-numbered by subsequent purchasers, and their weight in any account of the work's reception and readership must be gauged accordingly.'[4] Amory's admonition is highly salutary for students of bibliography and book history; nevertheless, in the absence of other evidence, we may at least understand such lists as being broadly indicative of the kinds of customers to which the book was marketed. Hence, we may cautiously scrutinize subscription lists for what they generally reveal about the types of readers likely to be associated with particular books. We must consider, however, that in the mid- and late eighteenth century, subscribers typically paid an additional 50 per cent or more for a book than did those customers who bought it from a shop at the retail price. For many, subscribing may have been more an exercise of patronage or vanity than a manifestation of the desire to own and read the book itself. Because of the kinds of people who would ordinarily have been solicited to subscribe, we may expect the names on a subscription list generally to reflect both a higher proportion of social and cultural élites and a more affluent clientele than the readership of the book as a whole. By virtue of their social status, wealth, occupations, political affiliations and sheer numbers, subscribers furnish publishing projects not only with economic capital, but also with cultural capital that may often be essential to a work's reputation and commercial success.[5] Subscribing is at once a form of conspicuous consumption and of public approbation in a way that conventional retail purchasing is not.

Bearing these facts in mind, let us consider a few subscription miscellanies to see what they may reveal. *A Miscellany of Poems by Several Hands* (1731), edited by John Husbands, a Fellow of Pembroke College, Oxford, has earned a minor place in the annals of literary history because it contains Samuel Johnson's first known publication, a Latin translation of Pope's 'Messiah'. Husbands' 491 subscribers, who took 583 copies, reflect the learned audience that the collection was meant to edify and entertain. Twenty different Oxford colleges are represented; fifty-seven subscribers are styled 'M.A.' and 130 are members of the clergy. Fourteen peers grace the subscription list, including one duchess, two countesses, two earls, a viscount and a baron. Surprisingly, only one subscriber hails from a Cambridge college. Among the most conspicuous consumers of the miscellany was Richard Savage, who later became Johnson's London companion in poverty and the subject of his first great biography. Ever wishing to cut a great figure in the polite world, he subscribed for twenty copies. Husbands' *Miscellany of Poems* is very much an Oxford production not only because it was edited and published there, but also because most of its authors and many of its subscribers have discernible connections with the university or its members. The contents of the collection, including Latin poems and imitations of classical poets, were well suited to its learned readership.

An altogether different kind of miscellany is *The Poetical Museum. Containing Songs and Poems on Almost Every Subject. Mostly from Periodical Publications* (1784), published and printed by George Caw in Hawick, in the Scottish Borders, approximately 40 miles from Carlisle and 50 miles from Edinburgh.[6] This local miscellany is particularly noteworthy because its subscription list reveals the occupations of its largely working-class readership. The miscellany, one of Caw's earliest surviving imprints, is generally well printed in 400 octavo pages, though very poor-quality paper was used, probably to keep the cost of the book to a minimum. The number of subscribers is a modest 158. Caw noted, however, 'There are a good many subscribers, whose names do not appear in the above list; but all that were given in are inserted.'[7]

As one would expect, the great majority of those listed are locals: most are from Hawick, others live nearby in Dam-side, Jedburgh, Melrose, Martin and Selkirk. Ten subscribers hail from Edinburgh, including seven printers, suggesting that Caw had professional associations in that city. Another ten, including a man from Hawick who put his name down for twelve copies, belong to the category of 'merchant'; among the ten shoemakers, one from Kincardine subscribed for twenty copies, though he was outdone by a mason (one of four on the list) from Langholm who paid at least half of the subscription for twenty-six copies. In contrast, the only bookseller listed, a man from Jedburgh, took only six copies, although a printer in Kelso subscribed for twelve, and a dyer from Ednam put his name down for thirteen copies. Eight men are listed as 'surgeon', six as 'wright', four as 'weaver' and three as 'stockingmaker'. There are three men from Edinburgh, and three from elsewhere, whose profession is 'writer'. ('Writer' should not be construed as 'author', but as the Scots equivalent of a solicitor.) Only two clergymen, both from Hawick, appear on the list, a number that seems surprisingly low. Other categories of employment with two subscribers each are watchmaker, saddler, miller, and baker. One subscriber represents each of the following occupations: smith, candle-maker, skinner, breeches-maker, leather-dresser, tobacconist, vintner, farmer, manufacturer, schoolmaster and bookbinder (in Hawick). While one man is styled as 'Dr', four are listed as 'Esq.'. The names of forty-seven men do not include any occupation, though it is impossible to determine whether in most cases this was because they were considered 'gentlemen', or – as I think more likely in the great majority of instances – because no information was given. Only nine subscribers are women, none of whom are distinguished by their employment.

Caw's passing reference in his preface to 'those subscribers who chose to take their copies in numbers' reveals that *The Poetical Museum* was issued in parts, and helps to explain how the volume was made affordable to its largely artisan readership (a2ʳ). Purchasing one sheet at a time, subscribers were able to make twenty-five small payments (viii + 392 pp. = 25 octavo sheets) and so buy on a kind of instalment plan a book they perhaps could not purchase outright. Part-issue, in turn, enabled Caw both to reach a broader market and charge more per sheet than he would have when selling an ordinary book. In addition, this method of publication allowed the entrepreneurial printer to receive income while incurring production costs, thus lowering his capital risk. It also made it possible for Caw to adjust the size of each print run as his list of subscribers making weekly payments inevitably diminished.[8]

Identifying the sources of his miscellany, Caw writes, 'The greatest part of the modern [songs and poems] are selected from periodical publications; the more ancient from the best collections of Scottish and English poetry. Several originals are inserted' (a2[r]). Most of the texts will be unfamiliar to modern readers, though there are poems by Rowley/Chatterton and Alan Ramsay, 'The Highland March' by Sir Harry Erskine, and some songs from Vauxhall. The Scots glossary appended to the text suggests that Caw hoped to sell the miscellany to his English neighbours – Newcastle was some 60 miles distant. Many miscellanies sold by retail subscription were local enterprises. Though commonly forgotten by literary historians, these collections were often important sources of poetry for groups of provincial readers.

Caw is unpretentious about the origins of his miscellany and its readership. Other booksellers, however, were more deceitful. In order to attract both contributors and customers, they masqueraded their miscellanies as the productions of a literary élite to which a select group of deserving others might have the privilege of being admitted. At the end of the century, for example, the Glasgow bookseller John Murdoch published *The Polyhymnia: Being a Collection of Poetry, Original and Selected* ([1799]). Ostensibly 'By A Society of Gentlemen', the 'Society' principally comprised the bookseller himself. The pretentiously titled *Polyhymnia* was sold in twenty weekly parts, each an octavo half-sheet with its own title-page and pagination; when the book was completed, an engraved title-page was given free to subscribers who had purchased the whole. Several of the parts have little notes 'To Correspondents', informing them that their poems are under consideration, or promising that a verse or riddle will be answered. The poetry is very minor indeed, though the conclusion of the final number is wonderfully absurd for its inflated rhetoric. The gentlemen editors testify to 'their regret, at being obliged, for the present, to relinquish an intercourse, which it was their pride to cultivate, and their ambition to deserve'. They are grateful

for the distinguished favour which their Miscellany has experienced, from the learned, the good, and the fair. . . . The inhabitant of the palace did not disdain to unite his efforts with those of the tenant of the cottage. The philosopher descending from the pinnacle of science, became the associate of the unlearned mechanic. . . . Such an association was delightful . . . it was a confederacy worthy of the golden age – mankind were once more brethren.

Alas, the 'higher duties which we owe to society, compel us to bid, perhaps a short farewell, to our readers.'[9] Although Murdoch was obviously attempting to develop a reputation that would ensure the success of subsequent volumes, the *Polyhymnia* was to be no more.

The publishers of verse miscellanies commonly targeted a particular audience. *The Lover's Manual. Being a Choice Collection of Poems from the most approv'd Modern Authors. With Several Original Pieces* (1753), published by Samuel Silver, a bookseller and retailer of household goods in Sandwich, is a good case in point. The *Manual* attracted 443 subscribers from Sandwich, Dover, Deal, Ash, Ramsgate, Canterbury, Margate, Folkstone and the surrounding area. Tellingly, the London bookseller Charles Hitch, whose name appears on the imprint as a vendor of the miscellany, took only six copies. In his preface Silver explains that 'the Hopes, that the following Collection . . . might become the means of exalting and refining the Notions and Conceptions of the younger Part of the World concerning the Nature of Love, was my sole Inducement to make it publick'.[10] Appropriately, one-third of the subscribers are clearly unmarried, 117 being 'Miss' and 37 'Master'. Women account for almost 30 per cent of the subscribers, though one might reasonably speculate that the female readership of such a romantic collection was greater still.

Despite the high-mindedness of Silver's professed motive in publishing *The Lover's Manual*, a work dedicated 'To the Youth of Great-Britain', paratextual matter at the conclusion of the volume provides a salutary reminder of the bookseller's commercial enterprise. Three-and-a-half pages of advertising alert the reader to the many goods which Silver sells, including 'Books of all Sorts, New and Second Hand', 'Almanacks', 'Ballads' and 'Penny Histories', 'Account Books', 'Writing Books' and 'Pocket Books', as well as fiddle strings, thread, needles, children's shoes, case knives, nutmeg graters, sugar, spice, starch, flour, mustard, and various pills and elixirs. If Silver's miscellany could lead the young and marriageable to discover 'the Nature of Love', then he could also supply both ardent newlyweds and jaded couples with all they needed to keep house. For Silver, as for others whose business was tied to books, a collection of poems was a commodity to be marketed and sold so that his investment might realize the maximum return. Miscellanies were an attractive, because potentially very profitable, product for booksellers at every level in the market; from the publisher's perspective, one of the principal advantages of verse collections was that there was usually no need to pay fees to any of the authors whose work was being used.

So far we have examined miscellanies published in Oxford, Hawick, Glasgow and Sandwich, though of course London, as the centre of the English book trade, was the origin of many such volumes. *The Grove; Or, A Collection of Original Poems, Translations, &c.* (1721), anonymously compiled by Lewis Theobald and published in the capital, featured verses by Donne, Dryden, Butler, Suckling and others. Among the small but generally distinguished list of 190 subscribers – who took 103 copies on royal paper and 175 copies on standard 'small' paper – are seventeen peers, including the Earl of Anglesey, the Earl of Rockingham, the Earl of Orrery and Lord Montague. Most intriguing is the fact that 'Mr. Pope' took four royal-paper copies of Theobald's miscellany. The high proportion of large paper copies and the fact that few of those taking multiple copies were booksellers further indicate the subscribers' wealth and status. Yet, despite its refined subscribing clientele, which one might imagine would have contributed to strong sales in book-shops, the miscellany did not sell as well as the publisher had evidently expected. In 1732 the sheets were reissued with a new title-page, now proclaiming that *The Grove* was 'Collected and Published by Mr. Theobald', who had won some measure of literary fame in the intervening years. Subscription lists can be deceiving.

In the ordinary course of events, miscellanies (and other books) offered via subscription were subsequently sold at a lower price to retail customers from bookshops. As we have seen, if the work failed to attract sufficient custom, then it may have been reissued, often with a new title-page announcing a 'second edition'. Occasionally, however, this pattern was reversed. *Poems by the most Eminent Ladies of Great Britain and Ireland. Re-Published from the Collection of G. Colman and B. Thornton . . . with Considerable Alterations, Additions, and Improvements*, published by subscription *c.* 1785, is a version of *Poems by Eminent Ladies*, a work first issued in 1755. A Dublin edition followed in 1757. A 'new' London 'edition' appeared in 1773 as *Poems by the most Eminent Ladies of Great-Britain and Ireland*, though it was in fact merely a reissue of the remaining 1755 sheets.[11] Ironically, in the 'Advertisement' to the subscription edition, the new editor explains that one must be bold to 'attempt an improvement, or even the smallest alteration, in a work of such deserved celebrity'.[12] In fact, the 1755 miscellany was not well reviewed; its reissue eighteen years later suggests no great reputation, despite the helpful biographical notes of the original editors George Colman and Bonnell Thornton.[13]

The poor reception of the miscellany helps to explain why the anonymous editor made the 'Considerable Alterations, Additions, and Improvements' advertised on the revised collection's title-page. In addition to providing works by the eighteen women poets featured in the 1755 miscellany – Barber, Behn, Carter, Lady Chudleigh, Cockburn, Grierson, Jones, Killigrew, Leapor, Madan, Masters, Lady M. W. Montagu, Monk, the Duchess of Newcastle, Philips, Pilkington, Rowe and Lady Winchelsea – the subscription miscellany added poems by another sixteen: Barbauld, Brooke, Sally Carter, Chapone, Collier, Darwall, Greville, Heys, Lennox, Pennington, Pye, Roberts, Savage, Scott, Thrale, Tomlins, and Miss Whateley (who is, in fact, the same person as the already named Mrs Darwall).[14] These additions undoubtedly increased the appeal of the volumes for contemporary readers, though many works by the original group were omitted to make room for the new poets. The subscription list for the 1780s miscellany includes such cultural luminaries as Joshua Reynolds and Horace Walpole. Of the 396 subscribers, twenty-seven are Peers, eleven are listed as 'Dr' or 'Revd Dr', and nine are military men – including two generals and a vice-admiral. Surprisingly, only ninety-eight subscribers, a quarter of the list, are women, though many copies for wives and daughters must have been subscribed for under their husbands' and fathers' names. Taken at face value, this miscellany's preliminary matter – title-page, advertisement and subscription list – suggests that the editor has built on the success of a respected work by bringing an old favourite up to date. In fact, he has breathed new life into a work that had been a critical and commercial failure.

Begged, borrowed or stolen: miscellanies as composite texts

Although the c.1785 edition of *Poems by the most Eminent Ladies of Great Britain and Ireland* is unusual in having been sold by subscription after its exemplar came to the public through bookshops, it is nevertheless typical of many eighteenth-century verse miscellanies in being closely related to one or more earlier publications. While it is hardly surprising that collections of poetry are often extracted from a variety of single-author publications, the degree to which 'new' miscellanies are related to antecedent collections has not been generally recognized. Many miscellanies appropriated select pieces from earlier poetry collections, thus forming what were essentially anthologies of miscellanies. Moreover, successful miscellanies routinely attracted unacknowledged abridgments, self-professed 'supplements', 'improved' versions and close (wholly unauthorized) imitations from opportunistic booksellers. These inter-textual features of many miscellanies, though seldom acknowledged, are essential for understanding their production and consumption.

Poems by the most Eminent Ladies of Great Britain and Ireland is a good case in point. Chantel Lavoie has revealed that the anonymous editors of the 1785 text 'borrowed heavily from a four-volume collection compiled by James Harrison and titled *The Lady's Poetical Magazine, or Beauties of British Poetry*', which was published in 1781–82. Moreover, 'Harrison had, in turn, borrowed older material from the first edition of *Poems by Eminent Ladies* to include in *The Lady's Poetical Magazine*.'[15] Thus, the 1781–82 collection utilized the 1755 anthology, the 1785 version of which used material from the 1781–82 volumes. It is plausible that the 1785 compilers may have elected to remain anonymous because they owned neither the Colman and Thornton text, nor the works they had arrogated from Harrison.

Not all such borrowings were illicit, however. Careful scrutiny of the first edition of Robert Dodsley's three-volume *A Collection of Poems. By Several Hands* (1748) indicates more than a hundred works by authors who had already published verses through Dodsley or his close associate Mary Cooper, a successful trade publisher.[16] Moreover, at least forty-four additional poems came from periodicals and miscellanies that Dodsley and/or Cooper had previously sold.[17] In all, then, over 85 per cent of the poems in the first edition of the *Collection* may be said to come from 'in-house' sources. As James Tierney has noted, Dodsley began publishing his *Collection* less than four months after he discontinued *The Museum: or, Literary and Historical Register*, a fortnightly journal consisting of essays, historical and literary memoirs, and poetry. The miscellany thus may have been conceived in part as a quick way to sell the substantial backlog of poems left over from his abandoned periodical.[18] Dodsley was understandably reluctant to invest a great deal in his miscellany until he saw how it would perform in the market; his thirteen years as a bookseller had taught him that, in a rapidly changing and highly competitive environment, few miscellanies could sustain multiple editions.[19]

In the preface to the fourth edition of J. Noble's two-volume miscellany, *The Muse in Good Humour: Or, A Collection of Comic Tales* (1745; 1st edn 1744), the compiler wonders at 'the uncommon Success' of the collection, a 'few months having produc'd no less than four Editions of the former Part, and two of the latter'.[20] Of the poems included in his miscellany, the compiler admits that 'the greater Part . . . are only detach'd Pieces from the Works of various Authors that were before Printed', but he notes that gathering them together saves the reader with a predilection for such verse both time and money. Among the poets represented are Dryden, Oldham, Rochester, Sedley, La Fontaine, Congreve, Gay, Swift, Prior, Samuel Cobb, Hildebrand Jacob and Richard Savage.

Sensing that there was money to be made, a rival bookseller produced a copy-cat miscellany with a very similar title, *The Muse in Good Humour: Or, A Collection of the Best Poems, Comic Tales . . . &c.* (1745). Unwilling to undertake such a blatantly unprofessional tactic under his own name, the bookseller (or possibly a self-publishing compiler) issued the work through Mary Cooper. This new miscellany, though obviously modelled upon Noble's selection, is far less artful and entertaining. It enjoyed only moderate success: although the first volume sold sufficiently well to justify the publication of a second (published in two parts), neither volume reached a second edition. In contrast, Noble's miscellany went through a fifth edition in 1746, a sixth in 1751, a seventh in 1766 and an eighth in 1785, making it one of the most popular poetry miscellanies of the century. The success of this collection, and indeed of other diverting miscellanies it undoubtedly influenced – such as *The Foundling Hospital for Wit* (1743–49) and its successors *The New Foundling Hospital for Wit* (1768–72) and *An Asylum for Fugitives* (1776–79) – should remind us that poetry was an important form of light entertainment in the eighteenth century. Although collections of comic poetry have been critically neglected because they are commonly regarded as insufficiently 'literary', miscellanies of light verse and of songs occupied a significant niche in the literary marketplace. Clearly, further research is needed in this area.

We have briefly considered three examples of the ways in which miscellanies are profoundly intertextual: the arrogation of another bookseller's verses (in this case a reciprocal theft), the appropriation of the publisher's own poetry backlist (and of works in the possession of close associates), and the close imitation (almost to the point of imposture) of a competitor's successful collection. The composite nature of poetry miscellanies will continue to be a dominant theme throughout the remainder of this chapter.

Piracies of Dodsley's *Collection* and other miscellanies

Commercially successful miscellanies did not go unnoticed by others competing in the market. Understandably, a number of booksellers sought to capitalize on the reputation of Dodsley's well-respected and highly profitable *Collection of Poems* by producing unauthorized 'supplements' to the *Collection*; others were still less scrupulous in their use of Dodsley's miscellany. In 1751, for example, a Dublin conger, or group of booksellers in financial partnership, began a two-year programme of publishing a series of successful titles taken from the London market. Among the first of these 'moral piracies' was the 1751 Dublin edition of Dodsley's *Collection of Poems by Several Hands*. Because the so-called Statute of Anne (1710) establishing copyright did not extend to Dublin, the conger could legally view Dodsley's popular miscellany as a commodity that might be exploited to make a profit. The strategy of the Dublin booksellers was to make their miscellany look like Dodsley's *Collection*, even reproducing the title-page vignette of Apollo and the Nine Muses, and copying the separate title-page preceding Lyttelton's 'Progress of Love' (which began Volume 2 of Dodsley's miscellany). The half-title of each volume, the first page the reader would see, proclaims the work '*DODSLEY*'s COLLEC-TION', and the accompanying edition statement, 'The THIRD EDITION', was clearly meant to lend legitimacy and authority to the text which follows. Yet, the imprint is in no way false and there is no question of forgery or of producing an inexpensive piracy for sale in England. This was a book intended for sale in Ireland; the 'Advertisement' promoted the work not as a reprint of the popular London miscellany but as an improved version of what Dodsley had done:

> The Design of the following Volumes (to use Mr. *Dodsley*'s own Words) is to preserve to the Public those poetical Performances which seem to merit a longer Remembrance, than would probably be secured to them, by the Manner wherein they were originally published. But as the *English* Editor, who collected these Poems, enjoyed the conversation and acquaintance of their Authors, it is probable his good Nature sometimes over-ruled his Judgement, and that he printed some Pieces rather to gratify the Desires of others than his own Taste. The Editors of this Edition, being under no Restraint, have selected those which have been mostly admired, not with a View to lessen the Merit of the few that are omitted, but to furnish out the most agreeable Entertainment for their Readers; and to give place to some Pieces not printed in the *English* Edition, the general Approbation of which gives them a Claim to the Protection of the Public: Among these are, the Battle of the Sexes, *Hammond*'s Love-Elegies, *Akenside*'s Odes, and the *Nymph* of *Bristol* Spring, by Mr. *Whitehead*.[21]

Thus the conger makes a virtue out of necessity – suggesting that distance from the London literary scene enables Dublin editors to make a more judicious selection. It is revealing that, though they invoke Dodsley, nowhere do they identify who Dodsley is; as a publisher of Pope, a successful dramatist, the editor of the *Select Collection of Old Plays* (1744 [1745–46]) and the *Collection of Poems*, and a leading London bookseller whose name was associated with most of the best poets of the day, Dodsley needed no introduction. The Dublin booksellers capitalize upon his authority even as they subvert it – 'it is probable his good Nature sometimes over-ruled his Judgement' – in order to insinuate that their product is superior to his.

Among the conspicuous omissions from the three-volume *Collection* were poems by Thomas Tickell, Lady Mary Wortley Montagu, William Collins, William Shenstone, Stephen Duck, William Whitehead, Matthew Green, Gilbert West, John Dyer, Thomas Edwards, James Thomson and Thomas Gray. Seven new poems 'By Mr. R—— H——N', who has not been identified, were added to the first volume of the Dublin *Collection*. It seems probable that these poems, which appear to have been previously unpublished, were composed by an Irish author whose work was known to the Dublin conger. In Volume 2 the editors also added two poems by Henry Brooke, a Dublin native. The inclusion of Brooke's poems was a shrewd marketing idea; the introduction of recent work by a local poet and playwright of such considerable renown would undoubtedly have boosted sales of the Dublin miscellany and helped to convey the impression that the *Collection of Poems in Two Volumes* was more than a distillation of a London bookseller's miscellany.

In addition, the Dublin editors included poems by James Hammond, Samuel Wesley, Mark Akenside, Thomas Gray, William Whitehead and Christopher Smart in order to distinguish their miscellany further from Dodsley's and, in some cases, to emphasize its more contemporary character. These works were added *en bloc* at the end of Volume 2. The publication of Gray's *Elegy Written in a Country Church-Yard* (first published by Dodsley with the assistance of Walpole in February 1751) in the Dublin *Collection* may have been that miscellany's most attractive feature. Smart's 'Solemn Dirge, Sacred to the Memory of His Royal Highness Frederic Prince of Wales' was the most recently published work of all those in the miscellany. Frederick had died on 20 March 1751; Smart's poem, composed shortly thereafter, was set to music by John Worgan, organist at Vauxhall Gardens, and noticed favourably in the *Gentleman's Magazine* for April.[22] The inclusion of these and other new poems was a clever marketing strategy, showing that the newly improved Dublin *Collection* was up-to-date in a way that Dodsley's miscellany was not. Although one inevitably wishes that some of the omitted pieces had been retained, the 1751 Dublin 'Third Edition' is in some respects a better miscellany than Dodsley's own three-volume edition. It therefore seems curious that, despite its currency and seemingly well-managed exploitation of Dodsley's *Collection*, the Dublin 'edition' was never reprinted.[23]

Perhaps there were no more Dublin piracies of the *Collection of Poems* in part because of Dodsley's close relationship with George Faulkner, the publisher of Swift and one of the leading figures in the Dublin book trade.[24] Though it is difficult to know why, Scots booksellers did not produce any piratical editions of the *Collection* until after Dodsley's death. Not surprisingly, it was Alexander Donaldson who published the first Scots piracy, *A Select Collection of Poems, From the most approved Authors* (Edinburgh, 1768) in two octavo volumes.[25] Although 95 per cent of the pages in Donaldson's miscellany are taken from Dodsley's work, the Scot's prefatory 'Advertisement' nowhere divulges his debt, but wryly notes instead that the poems 'have been carefully selected by Gentlemen well known in the Poetical World'. Donaldson boasts that these poems constitute 'undoubtedly the best Collection (of their size), in the English language yet offered to the Publick', and he thanks 'the Gentlemen who favoured him by selecting the materials for this Collection'.[26] This disingenuous acknowledgement was probably intended to deceive unwitting English customers, for the *Select Collection*'s imprint states that it was 'sold at [Donaldson's] Shops in London and Edinburgh'. Because Dodsley's *Collection* had been recently published in editions of 1763, 1765 and 1766, Donaldson undoubtedly needed to obscure the derivative nature of his miscellany if he was to have much chance of selling it in England. (Perhaps Donaldson also hoped that his duplicitous advertisement, along with the generic title of his miscellany, might help it escape the notice of James Dodsley, Robert's younger brother and business partner, who took sole charge of the firm when Robert retired in 1761.)

Donaldson did add eight poems not found in Dodsley's miscellany; only one of these, 'The Hermit, A Ballad, Supposed to be written by Dr. Goldsmith', is of any literary consequence, though it is not by Goldsmith. These minor additions comprise just 5 per cent of the total number of pages in Donaldson's two volumes, which are predominately a selection of the best and most popular works found in Dodsley's *Collection*. With poems by Tickell, Johnson, Dyer, Shenstone, Collins, Chesterfield, Lyttelton, Thomson, Goldsmith, Gray *et al.*, *A Select Collection of Poems* sold well: in addition to the 1768 octavo, there were duodecimo editions in 1768 and 1772.

In 1763 Donaldson published an impressive miscellany which is not indebted to Dodsley, *A Select Collection of Modern Poems, by the Most Eminent Hands*. Its title-page boasts works by Milton, Prior, Hughes, Addison, Dryden, Congreve, Green, Gay, Pope, Arbuthnot, Parnell, Tickell, Lord Lansdowne and Blacklock. Some of the poems have helpful introductions and explanatory notes, a sign of editorial competence and care. The selection and sequence of texts similarly evince the compiler's intention to configure his miscellany so that readers will take pleasure in the resonances among the poems he has chosen. At the end of the miscellany, for example, Pope's *Eloisa to Abelard* is immediately followed by James Cawthorn's *Abelard to Eloisa*, first published in 1747. Although the contents are not grouped thematically but organized by author, the compiler has arranged his selection so that four works on the same subject – Addison's *Song for St. Cecilia's Day*, Dryden's *Alexander's Feast; or, The Power of Music*, Congreve's *A Hymn to Harmony, in Honour of St. Cecilia's Day*, and Pope's *Ode for Music, On St. Cecilia's Day* – appear in the space of seven poems. Donaldson and his associates had created a fine miscellany. Or had they?

In 1744 the Glasgow bookseller John Gilmour published *A Select Collection of Modern Poems, by the Most Eminent Hands*, featuring works by Milton, Prior, Hughes, Addison, Dryden, Congreve, Gay, Pope, Parnell and Lord Lans-downe, among others. The four St Cecilia's Day compositions appear in identical order with the same intervening poems. Donaldson's indebtedness to Gilmour's work becomes still more evident when we observe that, with the exception of *Comus*, all the poems appearing in Gilmour's 1744 miscellany are found in Donaldson's 1763 volume, though the bookseller has evidently added value to the later work by including supplementary poems. It would seem, then, that Donaldson used the 1744 miscellany as the basis of his *Select Collection*. Further investigation reveals, however, that Gilmour published a second edition of his miscellany in 1750, adding poems by Milton, Tickell, Addison, Pope, Arbuthnot, Matthew Green, Elizabeth Carter and others.[27] Arbuthnot and Tickell joined the roster of 'Eminent Hands' on the title-page, now a dozen names long. It was this second edition that Donaldson appropri-ated, deleting the masque, but otherwise following Gilmour's sequence exactly. To this augmented second edition Donaldson added nine poems: two unidentified hymns, three works by Blacklock, and one poem each by William Hamilton, David Mallet, Pope and James Cawthorn. The names of Blacklock and Green now raised the count of poets adorning the title-page to fourteen.[28]

The first and second editions of the miscellany were printed by Robert Urie for John Gilmour, both of whom remained active in Glasgow into the early 1770s. Urie was a printer of unusual skill who, like many entrepreneurial printers, sometimes sold and published books; Gilmour, less prominent in the Glasgow publishing world, was a bookbinder and occasional bookseller. Because imprints do not necessarily reveal the financial relationships underly-ing the publication of books, it is impossible to know who actually under-wrote the cost of publishing the miscellany; it is certainly possible that the more prosperous Urie may have owned a share in the work.[29] Nor do we know whether the owner actually sold *A Select Collection of Modern Poems* to Donaldson, or whether this bookseller – notorious for disregarding the professional understanding of a perduring 'courtesy copyright' among members of the English book trade – also saw fit to appropriate the miscellany from his Scots colleague because most of its poems were no longer within the terms of copyright. Whatever the case, *A Select Collection of Modern Poems* provides us with a paradigmatic example of how the contents of poetry miscellanies change and develop over time. Of course, booksellers produce such collections partially in response to the public's taste, but the miscellanies themselves are also instruments in directing that same public's relish for particular authors and kinds of poetry.

Like Donaldson in Edinburgh, the Foulis brothers in Glasgow understood that Dodsley's *Collection* could be exploited to produce a highly marketable miscellany at minimal cost. *Select Poems from a Larger Collection* (Glasgow: R. & A. Foulis, 1775) is a modest assemblage of forty poems filling 151 duodecimo pages.[30] All are taken from Dodsley. Only nine poems come from volumes 1–3, while thirty-one were originally published in volumes 4–6, including fifteen from Volume 4. The compiler has shown little care about the ordering of the poems in his abridgment: the selected verses follow the same sequence found in Dodsley's volumes. The one exception to this unimaginatively imitative succession is that Johnson's *London*, originally printed in Volume 1, has been taken out of the sequence to become the final poem in the Foulis miscellany. No mention is made of Dodsley, nor of the *Collection of Poems*. The only editorial comment appears in a brief 'Advertisement' on the verso of the title-page: 'The Editor has here omitted those poems, which he has formerly published in the compleat works of their respective authors.' Obviously Robert and Andrew Foulis did not want to compromise the success of their backlist by making many of their best works available in a single, inexpensive volume.

The idea of abridging Dodsley's *Collection* was quickly copied by another Glasgow business, which issued a similar miscellany in 1776. Boldly naming their volume *Select Poems, From Dodsley's Collection*, the booksellers called attention to the miscellany's pedigree, which would undoubtedly have attracted customers, but also carried the risk that James Dodsley would take legal action in an attempt to protect what he regarded as his literary property. No such challenge was mounted, however, perhaps because the Lords' decision against the idea of perpetual copyright in *Donaldson v. Becket* (1773) meant that many of the works in Dodsley's *Collection* were in the public domain and could be reprinted with impunity. In any case, the *Select Poems* could have had little, if any, effect on the English market, which must have been nearly saturated by the six editions of the six-volume *Collection* published between 1758 and 1775. In the following year, the Glasgow booksellers developed a product designed to appeal both to those who had purchased the 1776 *Select Poems* and to owners of Dodsley's *Collection*. *Select Poems and Ballads, From Miscellanies Printed Since the Publication of Dodsley's Collection* (1777) proclaimed in its 'Advertisement' that 'all the poems in this volume are taken from late collections'.[31] Although the duodecimo volume was a mere twenty sheets long, it professed to be a miscellany of miscellanies that attempted to present the most worthy verses that had appeared in such collections during the past twenty years. Regrettably, the selection is far less genuinely representative than its title might suggest – the editor himself identified twenty of its thirty-six works as having been taken from Thomas Percy's *Reliques of Ancient English Poetry* (which James Dodsley had published in 1765). Also included in the Glasgow miscellany are three poems by Thomas Warton, a work wrongly attributed to Swift, verses by Christopher Anstey, and Malcom M'Gregor's immortal 'Ode to Mr. Pinchbeck, Upon His Newly Invented Patent Candle Snuffers'. Despite its obvious shortcomings, *Select Poems and Ballads* is of interest not only because it marks a contemporary Scots understanding of Dodsley's miscellany as a liminal event in the publishing history of British verse miscellanies, but also because it epitomizes the fact that, in the opportunistic world of eighteenth-century publishing, miscellanies tend to beget miscellanies. Of course, piracy is generally neither a subtle nor a particularly nuanced form of such textual begetting. Far more engaging are the miscellanies produced to exploit the reputation of a competitor's product, so that an established poetry collection's market success might actually enhance customer recognition and sales of a new book. It is to such works that we will now direct our attention.

Imitations and unauthorized continuations: profiting from Dodsley's success

The title-pages of the first two volumes of *The Poetical Calendar* (1763), a twelve-volume miscellany edited by Francis Fawkes and William Woty, proclaim that it is 'intended as a Supplement to Mr. Dodsley's Collection', though the 'Advertisement' (v–vi) mentions neither Dodsley nor the *Collection*.[32] Issued in slim monthly volumes, *The Poetical Calendar* resembles

Dodsley's miscellany neither in heft nor in layout, nor in ornaments and illustrations. Moreover, the *Calendar* diverges from its supposed model by including a higher proportion of previously unpublished contemporary poems. It seems, then, that Fawkes and Woty – or perhaps the bookseller John Coote – were endeavouring to make use of the market-leading miscellany's success by associating their production with the *Collection of Poems*. We do not know whether public reaction or the threat of reprisals from James Dodsley led to the omission of any reference to the *Collection* on the title-pages of volumes 3–12, although as a marketing ploy the mere mention of the highly popular miscellany could scarcely have been effective. Other booksellers, as we will see below, were far more assiduous in their attempts to exploit the *Collection*'s success for their own advantage.

Considered in its own right, *The Poetical Calendar* deserves more critical attention than it has received. It includes works ascribed to Milton, Cowley, Congreve, Pope, Spence, Bishop Atterbury, Locke, Gray, Collins, Lyttelton, Tickell, Dyer, Akenside, Smart, Thomas Warton, Horace Walpole, Ambrose Philips, Robert Dodsley, John Hawkesworth, John Gilbert Cooper, Samuel Johnson and Paul Whitehead, although many of the poems are by unknown authors. Fawkes and Woty themselves inserted more than thirty of their own compositions. Johnson furnished a character of Collins, which he later incorporated into his *Lives*.[33] Because each volume opens with a series of verses on the month and the activities of the season, the *Calendar* has the feel of a substantial monthly magazine. It is useful to think of *The Poetical Calendar* either in this regard, or as a miscellany issued in monthly parts – its nearly 1500 pages in small octavo would have made four ample volumes. A number of the surviving copies are bound in six volumes, each amounting to almost 250 pages. A second edition was printed in 1763–64.[34]

In 1767, the booksellers Richardson and Urquhart made a more concerted effort to profit from the renown of Dodsley's miscellany. Their *Collection of the Most esteemed Pieces of Poetry, that have appeared for several Years. With [a] Variety of originals, by the late Moses Mendez, Esq; and other Contributors to Dodsley's Collection, to which this is intended as a Supplement* generally imitates the layout and *mise-en-page* of its forebear. The work closely follows Dodsley's in its use of fleurons and tailpieces and in the initial engraving illustrating the opening poem. The 'Advertisement' explains that 'The Editor's chief intention in making the following Collection was to bring into one point of view the best pieces that have appeared since the conclusion of Dodsley's Collection'. He affirms that his miscellany is as entertaining as Dodsley's because 'some of the volumes in that are made up of the publications of a few years;

whereas this contains whatever has been applauded in the course of twenty'.[35] In other words, he suggests that *A Collection of the Most esteemed Pieces of Poetry* is more akin to an anthology than to a miscellany.

Many of the poets in the 230-page octavo volume had been represented in the *Collection of Poems*, among them William Collins, William Mason, Edward Moore, Mark Akenside, James Grainger, Richard Berenger, Thomas Tickell, David Garrick, Horace Walpole, John Ellis, John Gilbert Cooper, Samuel Johnson and William Whitehead. Richard Glover, though not in the *Collection*, had seen his principal works published from Dodsley's shop at Tully's Head. The celebrity of other notable authors in Richardson and Urquhart's miscellany – Oliver Goldsmith, Tobias Smollett, David Mallet – helps to account for their presence.

Another indication of how seriously the 'editor' (presumably the booksellers themselves) designed and marketed the miscellany as a continuation is the brief note added to the end of the Contents (viii) apologizing to the reader for inadvertently including a single song, 'Winifreda', which had already appeared in Dodsley's *Collection*. The editors of *A Collection of the Most esteemed Pieces of Poetry* took further care to associate their work with Dodsley and his miscellany by the inclusion of Richard Berenger's 'Verses to Mr. Dodsley', a poem first published in the *London Chronicle* of 22–25 April 1758. When the bookseller omitted his own *Melpomene: or The Regions of Terror and Pity* (1757) from volumes 5 and 6 of the *Collection* (1758), Berenger's poem lauded both the ode itself and his friend's manifest humility. Robert Dodsley's 'Answer' is also included in the miscellany, further suggesting that Richardson and Urquhart went to no small pains to authorize their miscellany by forging a strong connection with its most successful predecessor.

It is strange that the booksellers should have featured the '*Variety of originals, by the late Moses Mendez*' on the title-page of their miscellany. Mendez (or 'Mendes' as he is sometimes called) was not an especially respected poet, though James Thomson and Paul Whitehead had been among his literary friends, and several of his musical entertainments were performed with considerable success at Drury Lane. His best-known work is *The Seasons* (1751) which, like most of his verse, was written in close imitation of Spenser. Richardson and Urquhart had no discernible association with Mendez, who died almost a decade before their miscellany appeared. It is ironic, then, that *A Collection of the Most esteemed Pieces of Poetry* was commonly known to contemporary readers as 'Mendez', especially given that only three of his poems are included in the miscellany.[36] One can only speculate that, in addition to exploiting a connection with a successful collection, the booksellers were attempting to draw in a readership who would have associated Mendez's name with popular works of musical theatre such as *The Chaplet*, *Robin Hood*, *The Double Disappointment* and *The Shepherd's Lottery*. Then as now, fame sold books.

The case of a 1771 miscellany, *The Choice Spirit's Chaplet: Or a Posey from Parnassus*, further illustrates the extent to which booksellers might go to have their miscellanies identified with a stage celebrity. This collection describes itself as a '*Select Collection of Songs, from the Most Approved Authors; many of them Written and the Whole Compiled by George Alexander Stevens, Esq*'. Stevens was famous for his 'Lecture on Heads', a hugely successful one-man show satirizing contemporary foibles; it was said to have earned its originator £10,000.[37] When he was performing in Whitehaven in 1767, Stevens was asked by John Dunn, a local bookseller, if he would kindly peruse a manuscript collection of popular songs, indicating which compositions were best and offering attributions when he was able. Stevens, who had enjoyed some repute as a song writer for the stage, appears to have been flattered, and duly obliged. Dunn subsequently published his miscellany as '*Compiled by George Alexander Stevens*', though in the intervening four years he had no contact with the actor. Dunn's title, *The Choice Spirit's Chaplet*, was obviously intended to evoke Stevens' *The Choice Spirit's Feast: A Comic Ode* (1754), thereby strengthening the miscellany's association with him and establishing Stevens' credentials as a compiler by calling to mind his long versifying career. Despite Dunn's efforts, *The Choice Spirit's Chaplet*, a volume of 360 pages in duodecimo, did not sell sufficiently well to require a second edition.[38] The alleged compiler fared better than the opportunistic bookseller, however. Inspired by Dunn's miscellany, Stevens quickly published at his own expense a collection of his lyrics: *Songs, Comic, and Satyrical* (Oxford, 1772), which later saw two additional English editions (1782, 1788) and one each in Dublin (1778) and in Philadelphia (1778), where his 'Lecture on Heads' had been particularly well received.[39] For Stevens, theatrical celebrity proved a profitable asset in the publishing world.

The strange case of George Pearch's *Collection of Poems*

Soon after he was freed from his apprenticeship in May 1767, George Pearch set up as a bookseller in Cheapside. That same year, his name appeared on the imprints of just three titles, none of which he seems wholly to have owned. In the following year the journeyman published or co-published eleven works, including *A Collection of Poems in Two Volumes. By Several Hands*, a miscellany that closely imitated Dodsley's *A Collection of Poems in Six Volumes. By Several Hands* in far more than its title. Pearch's miscellany studiously followed Dodsley's in its format, length, *mise-en-page*, engravings, use of ornaments and price per volume (3s.). Its title-pages boldly sport a copy of the engraved vignette of Apollo and the Nine Muses that had become distinctly associated with the miscellany from Tully's Head. Similarly, the first poem in each volume is accompanied by an engraving in the same style as those we find in Dodsley's *Collection*. Of course, such sedulous imitation was no mere flattery but an audacious commercial gambit, a stratagem most blatantly expressed on the half-titles of the new miscellany: 'A Collection of Poems. Being Two Additional Volumes to Mr. Dodsley's Collection.' As we have seen, Richardson and Urquhart advertised that their 1767 *Collection of the Most esteemed Pieces of Poetry* was '*intended as a Supplement*' to Dodsley's miscellany, but the upstart Pearch now had the temerity to announce that his new volumes were actually enlargements of the famous compendium. Pearch had gone to considerable trouble and expense to make sure that the appearance of his miscellany gave credence to that claim.

The bookseller's 'Advertisement' in the opening pages of the collection does not attempt to deceive the reader into believing that the work had been authorized by Dodsley, but claims that it is as good as Dodsley's, containing poems that had appeared in the ten years since Dodsley's volumes were concluded, 'with the addition of many other pieces, which with all his diligence were overlooked by him'.[40] Accordingly, Pearch 'hopes [his volumes] will not be considered as an improper Supplement to the work of which they are designed as a Continuation' (p. 2), and he justifies his undertaking with a candid evaluation of the market:

> the favourable reception which Mr. Dodsley's elegant Collection of Poems obtained from the public, is sufficient to encourage any person who has the means in his power to continue that deservedly esteemed Miscellany. Several attempts of this sort have been made, but none have acquired so much reputation as to render the present undertaking useless or unnecessary. (p. 1)

Although he has furnished his miscellany with some of the most highly regarded 'poetical pieces of the last thirty years', he concludes his prefatory matter with an observation, taken from the final lines of Dodsley's 'Advertisement', about the impossibility of forming a selection in which every piece satisfies the taste of every reader (p. 2).

There is no known surviving correspondence between them, but James

Dodsley, one of the wealthiest and most powerful booksellers in London, must have threatened to take action against Pearch for advertising his miscellany as 'Being Two Additional Volumes to Mr. Dodsley's Collection'.[41] Soon after the initial publication of his miscellany, Pearch began selling a second issue in which the half-titles had been altered to read only 'A Collection of Poems', followed by the volume number.[42] Although they no longer made so brazen a claim, they too were designed to imitate Dodsley's miscellany. Pearch suppressed the boldest reference to his exemplar, but all the other imitative features remained. How was the text received? The *Monthly Review*, devoting just two sentences to its notice, was savage in its assessment: 'A continuation of Mr. Dodsley's plan, but without his judgment. Many trifling and injudicious performances are recorded here, which ought to have rested in the oblivion which had overtaken them.'[43] The *Critical Review* was more fair in its appraisal, which read in part, 'It is sufficient . . . to say, that [the poems selected by Pearch] are not at all inferior in beauty, sentiment, genius, versification, or any other excellence, to those pieces contained in the collection which they are intended to continue.'[44]

However mixed the reviewers' reactions, the sale of Pearch's continuation was sufficiently encouraging for him to double the size of his miscellany only two years later. Published to coincide with the appearance of Dodsley's 1770 edition of the *Collection*, Pearch's *A Collection of Poems in Four Volumes. By Several Hands* (1770) retained the same 'Advertisement' and continued to emulate the *Collection* in appearance. Once again, the *Monthly Review* was brutally dismissive: 'In our Catalogue for September 1768, we inserted the two preceding volumes of this collection. What was said of them may be said of these, and with the strictest regard to truth.'[45] Despite its earlier plaudits for volumes 1 and 2, the *Critical Review* was now also dismissive:

> This collection of poems is inferior to Mr. Dodsley's: – it contains, however, a number of such performances as have appeared for twenty or thirty years past, together with a few original compositions. – When we have said this, we apprehend we have said enough.[46]

Although the critics showed disdain for Pearch's *Collection*, the public seemed not to care – the four-volume miscellany continued to sell well. When James Dodsley published another edition of his brother's celebrated miscellany in 1775, George Pearch once again quickly printed a new edition of his complementary volumes, now altering the half-titles to read, 'A Collection of Poems; Consisting of Valuable Pieces, Not Inserted in Dodsley's Collection, or Published Since. With Several Originals, By Eminent Writers.'

Pearch died shortly afterwards, but not before he had written to the editors of the *Gentleman's Magazine* to allege that the poor critical reception of his miscellany could be accounted for by the undue influence of two booksellers who believed that Pearch's *Collection* threatened their respective interests. When printing the accusation, the editor explained, 'Had Mr. Pearch been living, this would not have appeared; but the requests of the dead are sacred.' Pearch had written:

> On the first publication of this work in 1768, it was most severely censured by the Reviewers; and upon republishing a new edition in 1770, with an additional 3rd and 4th vol. they repeated their condemnation with aggravated inveteracy. Yet from an index, which I have interleaved, with extracts and references to the Monthly Reviews, it appears that the compilers of that work have very highly commended no less than one hundred and seventeen poems here inserted. . . . If I had not a very good opinion of the general conduct of the M[onthly] Reviewers, I should not so much concern myself respecting their censure; and if they would divest themselves of the shackles some of the leading booksellers have placed on them, it would give me a much higher idea of their merit. That these booksellers had this influence in my case, I have the greatest reason to suppose from the high degree of acrimony Mr. Dodsley expressed at my styling the volumes 'supplementary to his brother's collection.' Mr. Becket likewise used every effort in his power to condemn them in his Review, because, truly, he pretended to claim a property in Collins's Eclogues and Odes, having lately reprinted them from the *Poetical Calendar*.[47]

The bookseller's missive occupies most of what is ostensibly a review of the 1775 third edition. Pearch's charge not only helps to account for the excoriating quality of the reviews quoted above, but also enables the editor of the *Gentleman's Magazine* to redress some of the wrong that has been done; he describes Pearch's *Collection* as 'this truly meritorious selection'.

Although we cannot be certain, it seems plausible that James Dodsley, angered by the presumptuousness of the young bookseller and, perhaps, worried that the new miscellany could diminish the 'polite' reputation of his brother's production, might well have asked Ralph Griffiths, editor of the *Monthly Review*, to assail the collection in his periodical. As one of the most important booksellers in the kingdom, Dodsley must have been able to influence the reviews when necessary.[48] Pearch's charge against the bookseller Thomas Becket, who also owned a share of the *Monthly Review*, is supported by the fact that Becket and P. A. de Hondt published several editions of *The Poetical Works of Mr. Collins* (1765, 1765, 1771) which included fourteen poems appearing in both *The Poetical Calendar* and all the editions of Pearch's

Collection. Another motive for Becket's condemnation might have been Becket's business associations with James Dodsley. Although this link may have been unknown to Pearch, evidence from imprints indicates that between 1760 and 1770 the two booksellers co-published at least four titles and appeared together as selling another twenty-four works, most of which had been printed for their respective authors.[49] This business relationship, which continued into the 1770s, suggests that Becket may have had more than one reason for condemning Pearch's miscellany.

James Dodsley's attitude to Pearch's encroachment should not lead the reader to believe that Dodsley was himself particularly strict or high-minded regarding literary property or the rough-and-tumble of the book trade. Although he was a member of the Stationers' Company which had an official role in policing the trade, Dodsley seems, on at least one occasion, not to have been squeamish about invading the copyrights of others.[50] In 1779 he published *A Collection of Poems. Containing The Minstrel . . . Owen of Charon. Essay on Man. Deserted Village. Traveller. The Grave. The Hermit of Warkworth. Sir Eldred of the Bower and the Bleeding Rock. The Diaboliad . . .* , a miscellany featuring the work of '*Beattie, Langhorne, Pope, Goldsmith, Blair, Percy, Moore [sic., Hannah More] and Kenrick*'. With the exception of Percy, whose *Reliques* he had published, and of Pope, whose work was no longer in copyright, James Dodsley appears to have had a legitimate claim to publish none of the poems by the other authors in this duodecimo volume of more than 320 pages. Though it may seem curious that the imprint reads, 'London: Printed for R. Dodsley, in Pall-Mall, 1779', I do not believe that the imprint is intentionally misleading, despite the fact that Robert Dodsley died in 1764. The name 'R. Dodsley' continues to appear in imprints throughout the 1770s and into the 1780s, while the formula 'J. Dodsley, in Pall-Mall' was certainly used by James Dodsley at the time this book was printed (there are surviving imprints of 1777 and 1779 in this form, for example).[51]

What are we to make of Dodsley's renegade miscellany? One possible explanation is that it signals his response to what was happening in the publishing world. We know that there was an ever-growing number of verse miscellanies – a dozen such collections, not counting John Bell's *The Poets of Great Britain* or *The Works of the English Poets*, appeared in 1779 alone. We may also observe that, although copyright was commonly respected for single-author productions, it was often and increasingly ignored in multi-author collections. As one editor observed in the preface to his 1775 miscellany, 'In compiling this volume, I had one difficulty to encounter respecting the right of literary property, which few collectors have ever thought of, or at least have not regarded'.[52] It seems, therefore, that James Dodsley elected, in this case at least, to follow the practices of his competitors.

If Dodsley really did use the monthly reviews to denounce Pearch's *Collection*, then the subsequent history of this miscellany is especially ironic. In 1783 Dodsley published the deceased bookseller's volumes 'by Assignment from the Executors of G. Pearch'. As if correcting Pearch's original act of *hubris*, the half-titles now read, 'A Collection of Poems, Intended as a Supplement to Mr. Dodsley's Collection'. Like the 1782 edition of Dodsley's *Collection*, the four-volume 'Supplement' was also enriched with biographical and explanatory notes by Isaac Reed, so that 'Dodsley' and 'Pearch' could be sold together as a ten-volume set. Remarkably, Dodsley's 'Advertisement to the Present Edition' of the Pearch volumes refers to 'the present Collection, which long ago has been thought not unworthy of accompanying the elegant Miscellany to which it was designed as a Supplement'.[53] What brought about this volte-face?

If James Dodsley's decision to authorize the 'Supplement' and associate his brother's 'classic' volumes with a relatively recent imitation produced by a fairly minor, rival bookseller seems curious – especially in light of his attempts to defame Pearch's miscellany – then information from fixed-price book-sale catalogues can help to explain why he chose to do so. In the catalogues, we find that many members of the book trade who sold their stock by means of retail catalogues regularly listed Dodsley's 1775 edition with Pearch's four volumes as 'Dodsley's *Collection of Poems* 10 vols.' Indeed, more than half of all the copies of the 1775 *Collection* offered for sale in the catalogues were 'bundled' in this way.[54] Therefore, it seems that Dodsley chose to buy into Pearch's miscellany because it was already perceived and sold by other booksellers as a legitimate part of his miscellany.[55] The imitative design of the 1768 and 1770 editions and the editor's careful selection of poems had obviously made their mark. Of course, since Pearch owned the complementary miscellany until his death, Dodsley's own newspaper advertisements for the 1775 edition give no indication of this trend. At the same time, Pearch's advertisements proffering his work as a supplement to the long-established *Collection* seem more the announcement of an ardent wish than the reflection of what was actually transpiring in the market. Pearch's miscellany became incorporated into Dodsley's not merely because James Dodsley saw a profitable marketing opportunity, but chiefly because booksellers and consumers had already accepted Pearch's bold conception of his books as 'Additional Volumes to Mr. Dodsley's Collection'.

Ever the shrewd businessman, and doubtless wishing that his brother's collection would continue to have pride of place over the *arriviste* miscellany, James Dodsley cleverly instructed Isaac Reed to add the biographical notes to the 1783 'Pearch' not only 'in conformity to the original plan' of the 1782 six-volume *Collection*, but also 'in subordination' to it, so that information provided in the notes to the original miscellany was not repeated in its supplement (x–xi).[56] Because twenty-nine of the eighty-five authors identified in the 1783 'Pearch' were also in the 1782 'Dodsley', consumers who wanted to own a fully annotated 'Pearch' could not purchase the four volumes alone, but had to buy the six-volume 'Dodsley' as well. This strategy was particularly important because the imprint of the supplement suggests that James Dodsley did not wholly own Pearch's miscellany, but only had a share in a work he published 'by Assignment from the Executors of G. Pearch'. Dodsley's partial stake in the literary property also helps explain why he chose to bring out the annotated *Collection*, which belonged exclusively to him, a year before he saw fit to publish the supplement. As we have observed, the annotated 'Pearch' was designed to invigorate sales of the 1782 'Dodsley', yet the experienced bookseller must also have anticipated that the success of the six-volume set would stimulate the market for the four volumes of his erstwhile rival. Selling the miscellany and its supplement in two stages also made good business sense in terms of pricing. The 1782 *Collection* in trade bindings cost £1 4s., a not inconsiderable sum. Buying six volumes in one year, and four volumes in the next, must surely have made the combined 'set' affordable to some consumers who would have found the outlay for ten volumes all at once too much to afford.

Clearly, Dodsley's timing in releasing the two new editions was clever, but what led him to commission Isaac Reed to produce an annotated *Collection of Poems* in the first place? Perhaps not surprisingly, the answer to this question leads us to another miscellany. Between 1780 and 1782 John Nichols published *A Select Collection of Poems; With Notes, Biographical and Historical* in eight volumes. Although some of the notes were written by Nichols himself, many others were supplied by Isaac Reed, who also annotated Dodsley's *Select Collection of Old Plays* (1780), and was known as one of the most learned and reliable editors of his day.[57] An annotated *Collection of Poems* would further establish its classic status and might well invigorate an already saturated market for the miscellany. In addition, by publishing editions of 'Dodsley' and 'Pearch' that conformed to the eight volumes of 'Nichols', the bookseller was making available a multi-volume selection of the century's poetry that might compete with the large collections – such as *The Works of the English Poets* (for which Johnson was writing his *Prefaces*

Biographical and Critical), and Bell's *The Poets of Great Britain* – that were beginning to populate the market. To understand how this is so, we ought to turn briefly to Nichols' miscellany.[58]

A Select Collection of Poems professedly owes a great deal to earlier verse miscellanies. Rather than mask the work's derivative nature, Nichols' 'Advertisement' promotes it as an epitome of miscellanies. 'On Dryden's foundation the present superstructure is begun', he explains, but the *Select Collection* goes beyond Dryden's because subsequent miscellanies have also contributed to the work: 'almost every undertaking of a similar nature has been consulted, and material parts incorporated.'[59] The *Select Collection* has been 'formed principally from that of Dryden', though in addition 'Collections formed by Fenton and Steele have been epitomized; whilst Pope's, Pemberton's, Lintot's, and C. Tooke's have occasionally contributed to [its] embellishment' (vii–viii). 'Dryden's foundation' is the work commonly known as 'Tonson's *Miscellany*', or 'Tonson's *Miscellanies*', a collection of poems in six volumes published between 1684 and 1709. Dryden greatly assisted the bookseller Jacob Tonson in editing the four volumes published in the poet's own lifetime, which are sometimes known as 'Dryden's *Miscellanies*'. Tonson's *Miscellanies* achieved no small measure of fame, not only because of Dryden's editorial acumen, but also because many of his best poems appear in these volumes.[60] 'Fenton' is *Oxford and Cambridge Miscellany Poems* (B. Lintot, [1708]), a substantial production of 400 pages in large octavo edited by Elijah Fenton. 'Steele' is obviously *Poetical Miscellanies, Consisting of Original Poems and Translations* (J. Tonson, 1714). Declared to be 'By the Best Hands' and 'Publish'd by Mr. Steele', this volume includes works by Pope, Parnell, Tickell, Philips, Gay, Thomas Warton (the elder), Young, and Steele himself.

'Pope's' is neither *Pope's Miscellany*, which was pseudonymously published by Edmund Curll (masquerading as 'R. Burleigh') in two parts in 1717, nor the Swift–Pope *Miscellanies* (two vols, 1728; Vol. 3, 1733; Vol. 4, 1735). Rather, it is *Miscellaneous Poems and Translations, By Several Hands* (B. Lintot, 1712; 2 vols, 1720), a work that sold very well and was almost certainly edited by Pope.[61] Pope probably also edited 'Lintot's', which is *Poems on Several Occasions. By His Grace the Duke of Buckingham, . . . Sir Samuel Garth, . . . Bevil Higgons . . . And other eminent Hands* (B. Lintot, 1717).[62] 'Pemberton's' is *Poems and Translations. By Several Hands* (J. Pemberton, 1714), which was edited by John Oldmixon.[63] 'Tooke's' seems to be *A Collection of Poems: viz. The Temple of Death: By the Marquis of Normanby. An Epistle to the Earl of Dorset: By Charles Montagu, Lord Halifax . . . With Several Original Poems, Never Before Printed, by the E. of Roscommon. The E. of Rochester. The E. of Orrery . . .*

(D. Brown; and B. Tooke, 1701), which has a fascinating bibliographical history dating back to 1672.[64]

Calling attention to his use of these miscellanies, all published in the first two decades of the century, Nichols authorizes his own collection by suggesting that his volumes bear the imprimatur of literary history, the sanction of the author-editors Dryden, Pope, Oldmixon, Fenton and Steele, and of several once-prominent literary booksellers as well. (It is no accident that the editor dedicates his work to Thomas Percy, celebrated for his *Reliques*, for Nichols too is interested in literary recovery.) In addition, Nichols is signalling the market niche for the *Select Collection* – the gems in this miscellany belong to an earlier golden era of miscellanies from 'Dryden' and its immediate successors, rather than from 'Dodsley' and those which followed. Although the eight volumes do include their share of recent poems, the authors represented in the frontispiece engravings – Dryden, Sir William Temple, William King, Sir Richard Steele, Bishop Francis Atterbury, William Duncombe, John Cleveland and Joseph Spence – indicate the degree to which Nichols' collection looks back to an earlier era.

Noting in his 'Advertisement' that the selections in his *Collection* do not include any of the same poems found in Dodsley, Pearch, or in the sixty volumes of the 'English Poets', Nichols modestly informs the reader, 'To all or either of these, therefore, this Selection will be a suitable appendage' (p. viii). By linking his brother's *Collection of Poems* with those of Nichols and Pearch, then, James Dodsley made available an annotated set of eighteen volumes, published between 1780 and 1783, covering the first three-quarters of the century. In this, as in much else, he was perspicacious. With the advent of Bell's *Poets* and Johnson's *Poets*, of Charles Cooke's *Pocket Editions of Select British Poets* (thirty-six vols, 1794–1801), and of collections such as Robert Anderson's *Works of the British Poets* (thirteen vols, 1792–95) and Alexander Chalmers' *Works of the English Poets* (twenty-one vols, 1810), the position of the verse miscellany in the literary marketplace was shifting.[65] Although there was no decline in their popularity, miscellaneous collections of verse now had to compete against works that claimed to be more genuinely representative of the best productions by the best British poets. In light of such broad canonical publishing projects, the professed curatorial function of many miscellanies may have seemed trivial. Yet the reading public's enjoyment of the poetic miscellany – with its attendant pleasures of fashion and novelty, of discovery and variety – appears to have continued undiminished.

Conclusion: what we might learn

The bewildering number and variety of poetry miscellanies, each with its own often complex intertextual relationships, has made scholars, perhaps understandably, reluctant to study the miscellany as a vital means for the publication and consumption of poetry in the eighteenth century. In his 1984 introduction to *The New Oxford Book of Eighteenth-Century Verse*, Roger Lonsdale suggested that 'we still know very little' about 'the landscape of eighteenth-century poetry', in part because of our inattention to 'the innumerable miscellanies by several hands'.[66] Many of these composite texts are highly uneven; almost all are commercially driven, opportunistic productions. Very few individual collections have exercised much influence on the formation of the poetic canon as we know it today – although their collective effects have yet to be adequately registered by literary historians. Yet if we wish genuinely to understand the marketing and reading of poetic texts in this period, we can no longer ignore the miscellanies which played such an important role in literary dissemination and consumption. Considered with bibliographical acumen, each miscellany may usefully be regarded as a *textus*, a fabric woven from many strands, and hence contribute to our understanding of the networks of relations – social, literary, cultural and commercial – involved in the transmission of its component parts. Typically compiled by booksellers or by authors intent on directing and pleasing the market, these collections have much to teach us about the poetry-reading public and its appetites. Even a schematic survey of these miscellanies' contents suggests that our perception of eighteenth-century reading habits and literary predilections is not sufficiently capacious. Clearly, there is a great deal we have yet to learn about the miscellanies in which so many poetic texts were published and read. Lacking adequate maps, few scholars have been willing to venture into so vast an uncharted territory. Yet the fascinating interplay between texts and readers that routinely occurred as verse miscellanies were produced, marketed and construed indicates that this immense *terra incognita* will amply reward our further explorations.

Acknowledgements

The author wishes to thank Dr Lesley Higgins for her generous assistance in the preparation of this chapter. A version of this chapter was delivered before members of the Bibliographical Society of America in January 2001. I am grateful for their questions and suggestions. Dr Chantel Lavoie also deserves thanks for generously answering my queries.

Notes

1. George Watson (ed.), *The New Cambridge Bibliography of English Literature*, Vol. 2 (Cambridge: Cambridge University Press, 1971), cols 341–429.

2. Usually, each poem (or group of poems by a single author) in a made-up miscellany has a separate title-page, register and pagination because each was printed as an individual unit of sale. Thus the miscellaneous collection allowed the bookseller to sell poems individually and in a compilation. *A Collection of Modern Poems* (London: J. James, 1762), for example, consists of eight poems ranging in size between eight and more than eighty pages long.

3. *Deliciæ Poeticæ; or Parnassus Display'd* (London: J. Nutt, 1706), pp. A2^v, A3^r.

4. Hugh Amory, 'Virtual readers: the subscribers to Fielding's *Miscellanies* (1743)', *Studies in Bibliography*, 48 (1995): 102, 104.

5. It was not uncommon for booksellers to print many more copies than the number subscribed for; these were sold by the bookseller at the usual retail price. In addition, because a large percentage of subscribers never took their copies, the sale of these unclaimed copies in the ordinary retail market was an important source of revenue. See, for instance, Keith Maslen, 'Printing for the author: from the Bowyer printing ledgers, 1710–1775', who adduces an example in which 1000 copies of a book were printed for 732 copies subscribed, just 148 of which were actually taken: *An Early London Printing House at Work: Studies in the Bowyer Ledgers* (New York: The Bibliographical Society of America, 1993), p. 103. (Maslen's essay originally appeared in *The Library*, 5th ser., 27 (1972): 302–9.) See also Amory, 'Virtual readers', who notes that for Fielding's *Miscellanies* (1743) 149 royal-paper and 258 ordinary-paper copies were delivered to subscribers, though the total print runs for each were 250 and 1000 copies (p. 104).

6. George Caw was a printer and occasional vendor of books whose name survives in forty-two pre-nineteenth-century imprints from 1783 to 1800. Imprint evidence suggests that he was active in Hawick from 1783 to 1787, before moving to Edinburgh in 1788 to work his trade in the metropolis. It is possible that George Caw was a relation of Alexander Caw, a bookbinder active in Edinburgh *c.* 1776–84, and of John Caw, a bookbinder and bookseller in the same city who, George H. Bushnell speculates, may have been Alexander's brother and business partner; see H. R. Plomer, G. H. Bushnell and E. R. McC. Dix, *A Dictionary of the Printers and Booksellers Who Were at Work in England, Scotland, and Ireland from 1726 to 1775* (London: The Bibliographical Society, 1968), pp. 290–1.

7. *The Poetical Museum. Containing Songs and Poems on Almost Every Subject. Mostly from Periodical Publications* (Hawick: G. Caw, 1784), p. 392.

8. Subscribers for part-issue books, who paid for each instalment at regular intervals and received a printed sheet upon tendering their money, often did not have their names printed in a list that was appended to a text. The subscription list commonly found in a work's 'prelims' was predominantly used for those who paid half the asking price of a book before it was published and, perhaps, half again once it had been printed. Both forms of 'subscription' helped the publisher to finance the production costs of the book, and both kinds of subscribers paid more for the volume than the same number of sheets would have cost if purchased at the standard retail price from a bookshop.

9. *The Polyhymnia: Being a Collection of Poetry, Original and Selected. By A Society of Gentlemen* (Glasgow: John Murdoch, [1799]), Part 20, pp. 6–8.

10. *The Lover's Manual. Being a Choice Collection of Poems from the most approv'd Modern Authors. With Several Original Pieces* (Sandwich: S. Silver; sold by C. Hitch and L. Hawes [in London], 1753), p. A3ᵛ.

11. On the miscellany, see Margaret J. M. Ezell, *Writing Women's Literary History* (Baltimore, MD: Johns Hopkins University Press, 1993), pp. 69, 73, 90–1, 112–13 and 118; Barbara Benedict, *Making the Modern Reader: Cultural Mediation in Early Modern Literary Anthologies* (Princeton, NJ: Princeton University Press, 1996), pp. 160–5; and Chantel Lavoie, '*Poems by Eminent Ladies*: the encyclopedic anthology of 1755', *1650–1850: Ideas, Aesthetics, and Inquiries in the Early Modern Era*, 8 forthcoming (2002).

12. *Poems by the most Eminent Ladies of Great Britain and Ireland. Re-Published from the Collection of G. Colman and B. Thornton . . . with considerable Alterations, Additions, and Improvements*, 2 vols (London: W. Stafford [1784 or 1785?]), p. [viii]. The imprint reads, 'Printed and Sold by W. Stafford', but in many copies the phrase 'and Sold' has been struck out by hand. Unusually, there is no date in the imprint. W. Stafford is known to have been active in the trade only in 1784–85; hence, *ESTC* assigns a date of '1785?'. Benedict (*Making the Modern Reader*, p. 160) follows Ezell (*Writing Women's Literary History*, p. 112) in asserting a publication date of 1780, but neither offers any evidence to justify her claim. Ezell hardly inspires bibliographical confidence by affirming of the 1773 volumes, 'This popular text was enlarged' (the text was a reissue of the 1755 edition); by calling the 1780s miscellany 'the fourth edition' (it was the third); by referring to 'the changes that this anthology underwent in its five editions' (only three are known); or by stating that in the expanded miscellany 'the number of authors had been increased to thirty-three' (there were thirty-four) (p. 112). There is no *ESTC* record of a work published in 1780 that could correspond to the *Poems by the most Eminent Ladies of Great Britain and Ireland*. Ezell lists only the 1755 first edition in her bibliography, so it is impossible to ascertain what other editions or issues she consulted. Benedict's study is distressingly unreliable; see my review in *Modern Philology*, 97 (1999): 283–6.

13. See *Monthly Review*, 12 (1755): 512.

14. See Chantel Lavoie, '*Poems by Eminent Ladies*: a study of an eighteenth-century anthology', unpublished PhD Thesis, University of Toronto, 1999, Appendix D, pp. 310–21, esp. pp. 313 and 321.

15. Chantel Lavoie, '*Poems by Eminent Ladies*: a study of an eighteenth-century anthology', p. 279. Lavoie's argument is convincing; in addition to comparing the contents of the collections, she demonstrates that the error of not knowing that Miss Whateley and Mrs Darwall are the same person is common to both the 1781–82 and the 1785 anthologies.

16. On Cooper as a trade publisher, see Michael Treadwell, 'London trade publishers 1675–1750', *The Library*, 6th ser., 4 (1982): 99–134. On Dodsley's *Collection*, the bestselling poetry miscellany of the eighteenth century, see Michael Suarez, 'The formation, transmission, and reception of Robert Dodsley's *Collection of Poems by Several Hands*' and 'Who's who in Robert Dodsley's *Collection of Poems by Several Hands*', which constitute the introduction to the facsimile edition of Robert Dodsley and Isaac Reed (eds), *A Collection of Poems by Several Hands (1782)*, Vol. 1 (London: Routledge/Thoemmes Press, 1997), pp. 1–230. See also my 'Trafficking in the muse: Dodsley's *Collection of Poems* and the question of canon', in Alvaro Ribeiro and James G. Basker (eds), *Tradition in Transition: Women Writers, Marginal Texts, and the Eighteenth-Century Canon* (Oxford: Oxford University Press, 1996), pp. 297–313; and 'Dodsley's *Collection of Poems* and the ghost of Pope: the politics of literary reputation', *Papers of the Bibliographical Society of America*, 88 (1994): 189–206.

17. Among these are twenty-seven from *The Museum* (1746–47), nine from *Philomel. Being*

a Small Collection of only the Best British Songs (1744), and eight from *The Public Register: or the Weekly Magazine* (1741). Dodsley subsequently appropriated still more poems for his expanding miscellany from Cooper-associated productions. On the close business relationship between Dodsley and Mary Cooper, see the entry for Thomas and Mary Cooper in the *New Dictionary of National Biography* (forthcoming 2004).

18. James E. Tierney, '*The Museum*, the "Super-Excellent Magazine"', *Studies in English Literature*, 13 (1973): 509–11.

19. See Arthur E. Case, *A Bibliography of English Poetical Miscellanies, 1521–1750* (Oxford: Oxford Bibliographical Society, 1935). Throughout the late 1730s and 1740s, Dodsley and/or Cooper were involved in a significant number of miscellanies; among the works they published or sold were *The Theatre of Wit*; *Pastorella; or, The Sylvan Muse*; *The Muse's Banquet*; *Cupid*; and *The Muse in Good Humour*. Shortly before undertaking the *Collection of Poems by Several Hands*, Dodsley was the principal seller for R. Cross' *A Collection of Poems on Several Occasions* (1747), a miscellany of Restoration verse.

20. *The Muse in Good Humour: Or, A Collection of Comic Tales, &c. From Chaucer, Prior, Swift, La Fontaine, Dr. King, and other eminent Poets. Together with some Originals*, Part I, 4th edn (London: J. Noble, 1745), p. [A2ʳ]. The 2nd edn of Part II appeared in 1745 and was paired with the 4th edn to make a set: see Case, *A Bibliography of English Poetical Miscellanies 1521–1750*, pp. 327–8 (nos 450.1–2).

21. *A Collection of Poems in Two Volumes By Several Hands*, Vol. 1 (Dublin: P. Wilson, J. Exshaw, J. Esdall, R. James, S. Price and M. Williamson, 1751), pp. aʳ⁻ᵛ.

22. *Gentleman's Magazine*, 21 (1751): 190, cited in Christopher Smart, *The Poetical Works of Christopher Smart*, ed. Karina Williamson and Marcus Walsh, Vol. 4 (Oxford: Clarendon Press, 1987), pp. 435–6.

23. For a more detailed discussion of the 1751 Dublin 'edition', see the introduction to my facsimile edition of *A Collection of Poems*, Vol. 1, pp. 25–32.

24. James E. Tierney, 'Literary piracy and the eighteenth-century book trade: the cases of George Faulkner and Alexander Donaldson', *Factotum*, 17 (1983): 25–35; and Tierney, 'More on George Faulkner and the London book trade', *Factotum*, 19 (1984): 8–11. Although Dodsley promised to send Faulkner the later volumes of his miscellany in sheets prior to their publication in London, there is no evidence that Faulkner or any of his close associates ever published an edition of Dodsley's *Collection*: see Robert Dodsley, *The Correspondence of Robert Dodsley, 1733–1764*, ed. James E. Tierney (Cambridge: Cambridge University Press, 1988), p. 300 (Dodsley to Faulkner, 28 October 1757).

25. Donaldson became famous for his successful challenge of perpetual copyright in *Donaldson v. Becket*; see Mark Rose, *Authors and Owners: The Invention of Copyright* (Cambridge, MA: Harvard University Press, 1993), pp. 92–112.

26. *A Select Collection of Poems, From the most approved Authors*, Vol. 1 (Edinburgh: Printed by A. Donaldson, and sold at his Shops in London and Edinburgh, 1768), p. [a2ʳ].

27. Case (*A Bibliography of English Poetical Miscellanies*, p. 325) notes that a 'third edition was published in 1757', though *ESTC* records no such edition.

28. Despite his celebrity, Mallet is not identified as the author of *Edwin and Emma* in the miscellany, nor is his name listed on Donaldson's title-page, perhaps because this poem had been published anonymously, perhaps because it was the property of Donaldson's competitor Andrew Millar.

29. Gilmour and Urie appear together on twelve surviving imprints between 1744 and 1769, four of which belong to the years 1750–51.

30. See Philip Gaskell, *A Bibliography of the Foulis Press*, 2nd edn (Winchester: St Paul's Bibliographies, 1986), p. 333, no. 587.

31. *Select Poems and Ballads, From Miscellanies Printed Since the Publication of Dodsley's Collection* (Glasgow: Printed by R. Chapman and A. Duncan, 1777), p. a2^r.

32. *The Poetical Calendar. Containing a Collection of Scarce and Valuable Pieces of Poetry: With a Variety of Originals and Translations, by the Most Eminent Hands. Intended as A Supplement to Mr. Dodsley's Collection*, 12 vols (London: J. Coote, 1763).

33. Cf. James Boswell, *Boswell's Life of Johnson*, ed. G. B. Hill and L. F. Powell, Vol. 1 (Oxford: Clarendon Press, 1934), p. 382.

34. See Harold Forster, *Supplements to Dodsley's Collection of Poems*, Oxford Bibliographical Society Occasional Publication No. 15 (Oxford: Oxford Bibliographical Society, 1980), p. 2.

35. *A Collection of the Most esteemed Pieces of Poetry, that have appeared for several Years. With [a] Variety of originals, by the late Moses Mendez, Esq; and other Contributors to Dodsley's Collection, to which this is intended as a Supplement* (London: Richardson and Urquhart, 1767), p. [a2^r].

36. In the 2nd edn (1770), Mendez's *The Seasons* was among the eleven poems Richardson and Urquhart added; nineteen poems, including Berenger's verses to Dodsley and their accompanying reply, were omitted.

37. See Gerald Kahan, *George Alexander Stevens and the Lecture on Heads* (Athens, GA: University of Georgia Press, 1984). Additional information on Stevens and the publications associated with him is taken from the *DNB* and the *ESTC*.

38. Although *The Choice Spirit's Chaplet* was published with two different imprints in 1771, my collation indicates that they are not separate editions.

39. See Gerald Kahan, 'The American career of George Alexander Stevens' lecture on heads', *Theatre Survey: The American Journal of Theatre History*, 18, 2 (1977): 60–71.

40. *A Collection of Poems in Two Volumes. By Several Hands*, Vol. 1 (London: G. Pearch, 1768), p. 2. Page references for subsequent citations are given parenthetically in the body of the text.

41. For a catalogue of James Dodsley's correspondence – including both extant letters and untraced letters cited in auction house and autograph dealer catalogues – see James Tierney, *The Correspondence of Robert Dodsley*, Appendix E, pp. 555–9.

42. See Harold Forster, *Supplements to Dodsley's Collection of Poems*, p. 6. For the contents of Pearch's *Collection*, including a catalogue of poems added and omitted in the subsequent editions of the miscellany (1768b, 1770, 1775, and 1783), see Forster, pp. 27–40. Pearch's contents may also be found at *http://miavx1.muohio.edu/~update/pearch.htm*, a site produced by Laura Mandell, Department of English, Miami University of Ohio. On the elimination of poems by Horace Walpole, George Keate and Mark Akenside in the second issue, see Herman W. Liebert, 'Walpole and Pearch', in Warren Hunting Smith (ed.), *Horace Walpole: Writer, Politician, and Connoisseur* (New Haven: Yale University Press, 1967), pp. 293–7.

43. *Monthly Review*, 39 (1768): 242. This unsigned notice is identified in Ralph Griffiths' copy as having been written by John Langhorne ('L'). On Griffiths' identifications, see Benjamin Christie Nangle, *The Monthly Review First Series 1749–1789: Indexes of Contributors and Articles* (Oxford: Clarendon Press, 1934).

44. *Critical Review*, 26 (1768): 229.

45. *Monthly Review*, 43 (1770): 154.

46. *Critical Review*, 30 (1770): 236.

47. *Gentleman's Magazine*, 45 (1775): 593–4.

48. On the routine accusations in this period that booksellers had inappropriate dealings with

the editors and their reviewers, see Antonia Forster, *Index to Book Reviews in England 1775–1800* (London: The British Library, 1997), pp. xxiv, xxxviii and xl.

49. On the common phenomenon of author-funded publishing in the eighteenth century, see Maslen, 'Printing for the author: from the Bowyer Printing Ledgers, 1710–1775', pp. 302–9.

50. On the company's activities in the eighteenth century, see Cyprian Blagden, *The Stationers' Company: A History, 1403–1959* (London: George Allen & Unwin, 1960), pp. 229–52; and Blagden, 'The Stationers' Company in the Eighteenth Century', *Guildhall Miscellany*, 10 (1959): 36–53.

51. In 1777 'R. Dodsley' appears on three imprints, in 1778 on one, and in 1779 on five (not including an additional one in which his name is paired with his brother's). Intriguingly, the first edition of John Duncombe's *An Elegy, Written in Canterbury Cathedral* bears the imprint 'Canterbury: Printed by Simmons and Kirkby, for R. Dodsley, London, 1778', but the bookseller's initial has been overstamped with a 'J', presumably by Simmons and Kirkby themselves.

52. William Giles (ed.), *A Collection of Poems on Divine and Moral Subjects, Selected from Various Authors* (London: Sold by Buckland; Keith; Vallance and Simmons; and Matthews, 1775), pp. ix–x. Although Giles' preface boldly contrasts his selection with 'the rubbish found in almost every collection of this kind' (p. ix), his miscellany attracted just 222 subscribers, including the four London bookselling firms listed in the imprint, who each took twenty-five copies. Giles' subscription list, which names twelve clergymen and thirty-six women, suggests small circles of acquaintances as it records, for example, fourteen subscribers from Margate and eleven from St Peter's (Broadstairs) nearby.

53. *A Collection of Poems in Four Volumes* (London: Printed by Assignment from the Executors of G. Pearch, For J. Dodsley, 1783), p. ix.

54. See my 'English book sale catalogues as bibliographical evidence: methodological considerations illustrated by a case study in the provenance and distribution of Dodsley's *Collection of Poems*, 1750–1795', *The Library*, 6th ser., 21 (1999): 350–3.

55. Of course, the booksellers had a financial motive: there is more money to be made from ten volumes than from six.

56. On Reed's editing of the 1782 *Collection*, see Arthur Sherbo, *Isaac Reed, Editorial Factotum*, University of Victoria English Literary Studies Monograph No. 45 (Victoria, BC: University of Victoria Press, 1989), pp. 35–41; and my introduction to the facsimile edition of *A Collection of Poems by Several Hands*, pp. 74–8.

57. Others too – including John Kynaston, Thomas Percy, Robert Lowth and Joseph Warton – supplied biographical information and suggested authors or particular works for inclusion in the miscellany; see George Baldwin Elick, 'Kind hints to John Nichols, by Joseph Warton and others', *Notes and Queries*, 3 (1956): 76–8.

58. For a highly informative account of Bell's publication (109 vols, 1777–82), see Thomas F. Bonnell, 'John Bell's *Poets of Great Britain*: the "Little Trifling Edition" revisited', *Modern Philology*, 85 (1987): 128–52.

59. John Nichols, *A Select Collection of Poems; With Notes, Biographical and Historical*, Vol. 1 (London: J. Nichols, 1780–82), p. vii.

60. Each volume was published by Tonson with a separate title: *Miscellany Poems* (1684); *Sylvæ: Or the Second Part of Poetical Miscellanies* (1685); *Examen Poeticum: Being the Third Part . . .* (1693); *The Annual Miscellany: For the Year 1694. Being the Fourth Part . . .* (1694); *Poetical Miscellanies: The Fifth Part* (1704); and *Poetical Miscellanies: The Sixth Part* (1709). Case, *A Bibliography of English Poetical Miscellanies 1521–1750*, pp. 115–23 (no. 172), is helpful, though incomplete. When the six volumes were published together in 1716 and 1727, their title-pages claimed that they were 'Publish'd by Mr. *Dryden*', a practice reflecting the wording of some

earlier editions of individual volumes. On the combined editorial efforts of Dryden and Tonson in producing the first four volumes, see Kathleen M. Lynch, *Jacob Tonson, Kit-Cat Publisher* (Knoxville: University of Tennessee Press, 1971), pp. 21–3 and 29.

61. *Miscellaneous Poems and Translations*, which contains several of Pope's poems (including the first publication of *The Rape of the Locke*), appeared in a second edition in 1714. In 1717 Lintot published *Poems on Several Occasions: By . . . Buckingham, . . . Wycherley, Lady Winchilsea, . . . Garth, N. Rowe, . . . Mrs. Singer . . . And other eminent Hands*. An altered version of this miscellany became Vol. 2 of the 3rd edn of *Miscellaneous Poems and Translations* (1720). It was to this or a subsequent edition in two volumes (1722, 1726–27, 1732) that Nichols almost certainly refers. The most convincing argument for Pope's having edited the miscellany from 1712 to 1726 is found in Norman Ault, *New Light on Pope* (London: Methuen, 1949), pp. 27–38.

62. Among the poems Nichols appropriated from 'Lintot' for his miscellany are 'On Buckingham House' by Mr. Buckeridge (5.160) and 'To Mr. Pope' by Bevil Higgons (3.114).

63. In the same year a 2nd edn was published as *Original Poems and Translations. By Several Hands* (J. Pemberton, 1714).

64. *ESTC* reveals no possible match for a poetry miscellany associated with 'C. Tooke', either as editor or publisher. The bookseller 'B. Tooke' seems much more likely, especially considering that the 'B' and the 'C' were adjacent in the divided-lay, English-pattern type cases used by English compositors in this period. Personal names are, of course, notoriously difficult to correct. Tooke's *A Collection of Poems* (1701) (which, despite its joint imprint, concludes with three pages of 'Books lately Printed for B. Tooke') is a revised and enlarged edition of *A Collection of Poems by Several Hands. Most of them Written by Persons of Eminent Quality* (London: F. Saunders, 1693), a miscellany reissued with a cancel title-page in 1695 as *The Temple of Death . . . The Second Edition Corrected*. The 1693 miscellany was, in turn, edited and enlarged from *A Collection of Poems, Written upon Several Occasions, by Several Persons. With many Additions, Never before in Print* (London: T. Collins and J. Ford; W. Cademan, 1673), which itself is a version of *A Collection of Poems, Written upon Several Occasions, by Several Persons. Never Before in Print* (London: H. Kemp, 1672) with thirty-one additional songs and poems. Thus the catena of appropriation runs 1672, 1673, 1693, [1695], 1701, a span of thirty years. A 2nd edn of Tooke's large octavo *Collection* (1701) appeared in the same format in 1702; a duodecimo 3rd edn was published in 1716. All the poems in the 1672 and 1673 volumes are anonymous; in the 1693 miscellany only three are wholly unattributed, while four poems are said to be 'By a Person of Honour' [Charles Sackville, Lord Dorset]. Twelve pieces by Sir George Etherege and the twenty by Sir Charles Sedley, the two most represented contributors in the 1693 collection, also appeared in the 1672 and 1673 miscellanies. A number of other works are common to all three miscellanies, though Francis Saunders (who signs the introductory matter) considerably improved and expanded the work of his predecessors. No doubt the publication of works such as *Poems by Several Hands, And on Several Occasions Collected by N[ahum]. Tate* (1685), Charles Gildon's *Miscellany Poems on Several Occasions* (1692) and, especially, the first two volumes of Tonson's *Miscellanies* (1684, 1685) had raised the standard. The 1701 *Collection* includes most of the poems appearing in that of 1693, with substantial additional matter.

65. On the growing number of multi-volume collections and the marketing of the British poetic canon as a commodity, see Thomas Bonnell's forthcoming book, *The Most Disreputable Trade: Publishing the Classics of British Poetry, 1765–1810*.

66. Roger Lonsdale (ed.), *The New Oxford Book of Eighteenth-Century Verse* (Oxford: Oxford University Press, 1984), p. xxxv.

SELECT BIBLIOGRAPHY

1 The Book Trades

Primary works

Belanger, Terry. 'A directory of the London book trade, 1766', *Publishing History*, 1 (1977): 7–48.

Boswell, James. *Boswell's Life of Johnson*, ed. George Birkbeck Hill and L. F. Powell, 2nd edn, 6 vols. Oxford: Clarendon Press, 1964.

Collier, J. *The Parents and Guardians Directory*. London, 1761.

Dibdin, Thomas Frognall. *Bibliomania; Or Book Madness: A Bibliographical Romance*. London, 1811.

Grosley, Pierre Jean. *A Tour to London: or, New Observations on England and its Inhabitants*, trans. Thomas Nugent, 2 vols. London, 1772.

The House of Longman, 1794–1914, microfilm edn. Cambridge: Chadwyck Healey, 1978.

Nettel, Reginald (ed.). *Journeys of a German* [Carl Philip Moritz] *in England in 1782*. London: Jonathan Cape, 1965.

Nichols, John. *Literary Anecdotes of the Eighteenth Century*, 9 vols. London, 1812–15, repr. edn New York, 1966.

Tierney, James E. (ed.). *The Correspondence of Robert Dodsley 1733–1764*. Cambridge: Cambridge University Press, 1988.

West, William. *Fifty Years' Recollections of an Old Bookseller*. London, 1837.

Williams, Clare (ed.). *Sophie in London, 1786 Being the Diary of Sophie von la Roche*. London: Batsford, 1933.

Secondary works

Alston, Robin. *Library History Database*. http:www.r-alston.co.uk/contents.html, 1998–.

Alston, Robin. *Order and Connexion: Studies in Bibliography and Book History*. Woodbridge: Boydell and Brewer, 1997.

Altick, Richard D. *The English Common Reader: A Social History of the Mass Reading Public 1800–1900*. Chicago, IL: University of Chicago Press, 1957.

Aspinall, A. 'Statistical accounts of the London newspapers in the eighteenth century', *English Historical Review*, 63 (1948): 201–32.

Baines Reed, Talbot. *A History of the Development of Old English Letter Foundries*, rev. edn by A. F. Johnson. London: Faber and Faber, 1952.

Ball, Johnson. *William Caslon, 1693–1766: The Ancestry, Life and Connections of England's Foremost Letter-Engraver and Type-Founder*. Kineton: Roundwood Press, 1973.

Belanger, Terry. 'Booksellers' sales of copyright: aspects of the London book trades, 1718–1768'. Unpublished PhD dissertation, Columbia University, 1970.

Belanger, Terry. 'Booksellers' trade sales 1718–1768', *The Library*, 5th ser., 30 (1975): 281–302.

Belanger, Terry. 'Publishers and writers in eighteenth-century England', in Isabel Rivers (ed.), *Books and their Readers in Eighteenth-Century England*. Leicester: Leicester University Press, 1982.

Besterman, Theodore (ed.). *The Publishing Firm of Cadell and Davies: Select Correspondence and Accounts, 1783–1836*. London: Oxford University Press, 1938.

Blagden, Cyprian. 'Booksellers' trade sales 1718–1768', *The Library*, 5th ser., 5 (1951): 243–57.

Blakey, Dorothy. *The Minerva Press 1790–1820*. London, 1939.

Blayney, Peter W. M. *The Bookshops in Paul's Cross Churchyard*. Occasional Papers of the Bibliographical Society, no. 5, London, 1990.

Borsay, Peter. 'The English urban renaissance: the development of a provincial urban culture c. 1680–c. 1760', *Social History*, 2 (1977): 581–603.

Borsay, Peter and McInnes, Angus. 'Debate: leisure town or urban renaissance?', *Past and Present*, 126 (February 1990): 189–202.

Boyce, George, Curran, James, and Wingate, Pauline (eds). *Newspaper History from the Seventeenth Century to the Present Day*. London, and Beverly Hills, CA: Constable and Sage, 1978.

Brack, O. M. Jun. (ed.). *Writers, Books, and Trade: An Eighteenth-Century English Miscellany for William B. Todd*. New York: AMS Press, 1994.

Bruntjen, Sven H. A. *John Boydell, 1719–1804: A Study of Art Patronage and Publishing in Georgian London*. New York: Garland Press, 1985.

Clayton, Timothy. *The English Print 1688–1802*. New Haven, CT: Yale University Press, 1997.

Coleman, D. C. *The British Paper Industry, 1495–1860*. Oxford: Clarendon Press, 1958.

Collins, A. S. *Authorship in the Days of Johnson: Being a Study of the Relation Between Author, Patron, Publisher, and Public, 1726–1780*. London: R. Holden and Co, 1927.

Collins, A. S. *The Profession of Letters: A Study of the Relation of Author to Patron, Publisher, and Public, 1780–1832*. New York: Dutton, 1929.

Corfield, P. J. *The Impact of English Towns, 1700–1800*. Oxford: Oxford University Press, 1982.

Cranfield, G. A. *The Development of the Provincial Newspaper, 1700–1760*. Oxford: Oxford University Press, 1962.

Crump, Michael and Harris, Michael (eds). *Searching the Eighteenth Century*. London: British Library, 1983.

Dowell, Stephen. *A History of Taxation and Taxes in England*, 3rd edn, 3 vols. London: Frank Cass, 1965.

The English Short Title Catalogue. London: British Library, in progress.

Ferdinand, C. Y. *Benjamin Collins and the Provincial Newspaper Trade in the Eighteenth Century*. Oxford: Clarendon Press, 1997.

Fergus, Jan and Thaddeus, Janice Farrar. 'Women, publishers, and money, 1790–1820', *Studies in Eighteenth-Century Culture*, 17 (1988): 191–207.

Fontaine, Laurence and Postel-Vinay, Gilles (eds). *Des Personnes aux institutions: Réseaux et culture du crédit du XVIe au XXe siècle en Europe*. Louvain-la-Neuve: Bruylant-Academia, 1997.

Foxon, David and McLaverty, James. *Pope and the Early Eighteenth-Century Book Trade*. Oxford: Clarendon Press, 1991.

Harris, Michael. *London Newspapers in the Age of Walpole: A Study of the Origins of the Modern English Press*. London: Associated University Press, 1987.

Hunt, Arnold, Mandelbrote, Giles and Shell, Alison (eds). *The Book Trade and its Customers 1450–1900*. Winchester, and New Castle, DE: St Paul's Bibliographies and Oak Knoll Press, 1997.

Hutt, Allen. *Fournier: The Compleat Typographer*. London: Muller, 1972.

Innes, Joanna. 'Jonathan Clark, social history and England's "ancien régime"', *Past and Present*, 115 (May 1987): 165–200.

Isaac, Peter and McKay, Barry. *Images and Texts: Their Production and Distribution in the 18th and 19th Centuries*. Winchester, and New Castle, DE: St Paul's Bibliographies and Oak Knoll Press, 1997.

Lippincott, Louise. *Selling Art in Georgian London: The Rise of Arthur Pond*. New Haven, CT: Yale University Press, 1983.

Love, Harold. *Scribal Publication in Seventeenth-Century England*. Oxford: Clarendon Press, 1993.

McDowell, Paula. *The Women of Grub Street: Press, Politics and Gender in the London Literary Marketplace 1678–1730*. Oxford: Oxford University Press, 1998.

McInnes, Angus, 'The emergence of a leisure town: Shrewsbury, 1660–1760', *Past and Present*, 120 (August 1988): 53–87.

McKitterick, David. *Set in Print: The Fortunes of an Idea, 1450–1800: The Lyell Lectures, 2000*. Oxford, forthcoming, 2001.

Mann, Phyllis G. 'Death of a London bookseller', *Keats-Shelley Memorial Bulletin*, 15 (1964): 11.

Marston, E. *Sketches of Booksellers of Other Days*. London (n.p.), 1901.

Maslen, K. I. D. and Lancaster, John. *The Bowyer Ledgers: The Printing Accounts of William Bowyer, Father and Son*. London and New York: Bibliographical Society and Bibliographical Society of America, 1991.

Maxted, Ian. *The London Book Trades 1775–1800*. Folkestone: Dawson, 1977.

Mumby, Frank Arthur. *Publishing and Bookselling*. London: Jonathan Cape, 1934.

Myers, Robin. *The Stationers' Company Archive, 1551–1984*. Winchester: St Paul's Bibliographies, 1990.

Myers, Robin and Harris, Michael (eds). *Author–Publisher Relations in the Eighteenth and Nineteenth Centuries*. Oxford: Oxford Polytechnic Press, 1983.

Myers, Robin and Harris, Michael (eds). *Economics of the British Booktrade, 1605–1939*. Cambridge: Chadwyck Healey, 1986.

Myers, Robin and Harris, Michael (eds). *Sale and Distribution of Books from 1700*. Oxford: Oxford Polytechnic Press, 1982.

Myers, Robin and Harris, Michael (eds). *Serials and their Readers, 1620–1914*. Winchester, and New Castle, DE: St Paul's Bibliographies and Oak Knoll Press, 1993.

Myers, Robin and Harris, Michael (eds). *Spreading the Word: The Distribution Networks of Print, 1550–1850*. Winchester, and New Castle, DE: St Paul's Bibliographies and Oak Knoll Press, 1990.

Myers, Robin and Harris, Michael (eds). *The Stationers' Company and the Book Trade 1550–1990*. Winchester, and New Castle, DE: St Paul's Bibliographies and Oak Knoll Press, 1997.

Pardoe, F. E. *John Baskerville of Birmingham: Letter-Founder and Printer*. London: F. Muller, 1975.

Pollard, H. G. and Ehrman, A. *The Distribution of Books by Catalogue*. Cambridge: Roxburghe Club, 1965.

Pollard, M. *Dublin's Trade in Books 1550–1800*. Oxford: Clarendon Press, 1989.

Raven, James. *Judging New Wealth: Popular Publishing and Responses to Commerce in England, 1750–1800*. Oxford: Clarendon Press, 1992.

Raven, James. 'New reading histories, print culture, and the identification of change: the case of eighteenth-century England', *Social History*, 23 (1998): 268–87.

Raven, James. 'The Noble brothers and popular publishing', *Library*, 6th ser., 12 (1990): 293–345.

Raven, James and Forster, Antonia. *The English Novel 1770–1799: A Bibliographical Survey of Prose Fiction Published in the British Isles*, Vol. 1. Oxford: Oxford University Press, 2000.

Raven, James, Small, Helen and Tadmor, Naomi (eds). *The Practice and Representation of Reading in England*. Cambridge: Cambridge University Press, 1996.

Raven, James, Hall, Nigel *et al*. *Mapping the Print Culture of Eighteenth-Century London*. http://members.tripod.co.uk/bookhistory/, 1999–.

Rees, Thomas and Britton, John. *Reminiscences of Literary London from 1779 to 1853*. London, 1896.

Rose, Mark. *Authors and Owners: The Invention of Copyright*. Cambridge, MA: Harvard University Press, 1993.

Shorter, Alfred H. *Water Paper Mills in England*. London: Society for the Protection of Ancient Buildings, 1966.

Solomon, Harry M. *The Rise of Robert Dodsley: Creating the New Age of Print*. Carbondale: Southern Illinois University Press, 1996.

Sutherland, James. *The Restoration Newspaper and its Development*. Cambridge: Cambridge University Press, 1986.

Sweet, Rosemary. *The English Town 1680–1840: Government, Society and Culture*. London: Longman, 1999.

Thomson, Alistair G. *The Paper Industry in Scotland, 1590–1861*. Edinburgh: Scottish Academic Press, 1974.

Timperley, C. H. *Encyclopaedia of Literary and Typographical Anecdote*. London, 1842.

Treadwell, Michael. 'London trade publishers 1675–1750', *The Library*, 6th ser., 4 (1982): 99–134.

Updike, Daniel Berkeley. *Printing Types: Their History, Forms and Use: A Study in Survivals*, 2 vols. Cambridge, MA: Belknap Press, 1962.

Walker, R. B. 'Advertising in London newspapers, 1650–1750', *Business History*, 15 (1973): 112–30.

Wallis, Philip. *At the Sign of the Ship: Notes on the House of Longman, 1724–1974*. London, private edn, 1974.

Walters, Gwyn. 'The booksellers in 1759 and 1774: the battle for literary property', *Library*, 5th ser., 29 (1974): 287–311.

Wiles, R. M. *Serial Publication in England before 1750*. Cambridge: Cambridge University Press, 1957.

Zachs, William. *The First John Murray and the Late Eighteenth-Century Book Trade*. London: British Academy and Oxford University Press, 1998.

2 The Bible and its Readers

Primary works

Bate, Julius. *A New and Literal Translation from the Original Hebrew, of the Pentateuch of Moses, and of the Historical Books of the Old Testament, to the End of the Second Book of Kings*. London, 1773.

Blackwell, Anthony. *The Sacred Classics Defended and Illustrated*, 3rd edn, 2 vols. London, 1737.

Blake, William. *Annotations to Richard Watson*, ed. G. Ingli James. Cardiff: University College Cardiff Press, 1984.

Blayney, Benjamin. *Jeremiah and Lamentations. A New Translation*. Oxford, 1784.

Blayney, Benjamin. *Zechariah. A New Translation*. Oxford, 1797.

Bowyer, William (ed.). *Critical Conjectures and Observations on the New Testament*, 3rd edn, ed. J. Nichols. London, 1782.

Durell, David. *Critical Remarks on the Books of Job, Proverbs, Psalms, Ecclesiastes, and Canticles*. Oxford, 1772.

'An Essay upon the English Translation of the Bible', *Bibliotheca Literaria*, 4 (1723): 1–23.

Fortescu, Alexander. *The Holy Family Bible*. Winchester, 1774.

Geddes, Alexander. *Dr Geddes's Answer to the Queries, Counsils and Criticisms that have been communicated to him since the Publication of his Proposals for Printing a New Translation of the Bible*. London, 1790.

Geddes, Alexander. *The Holy Bible, or the Books accounted sacred by Jews and Christians, otherwise called the Books of the Old and New Covenants*, 2 vols. London, 1792–97.

Harwood, Edward. *A Liberal Translation of the New Testament*, 2 vols. London, 1768.

Holloway, Benjamin. *The Primaevity and Preeminence of the Sacred Hebrew, above all other Languages, Vindicated*. Oxford, 1754.

Holmes, Robert. *The First Annual Account of the Collation of the Mss. of the Septuagint-Version*. Oxford, 1789.

Houbigant, Charles. *Prolegomena in Scripturam Sacram*. Paris, 1753.

Hunt, Thomas. *De usu dialectorum Orientalium ac praecipue Arabicae, in Hebraico codice interpretando, oratio*. Oxford, 1748.

Johnson, Anthony. *An Historical Account of the several English Translations of the Bible and the Opposition they met with from the Church of Rome*. London, 1730.

Kennicott, Benjamin. *The State of the Printed Hebrew Text of the Old Testament Considered*, 2 parts. Oxford, 1753–59.

[Le Cène, Charles]. *An Essay for a New Translation of the Bible*, trans. H[ugh] R[oss], 2 parts. London, 1701–2.

Lewis, John. *A Complete History of the Several Translations of the Holy Bible, and New Testament, into English*, 2nd edn. London, 1739.

Lowth, Robert. *De sacra poesi Hebraeorum*. Oxford, 1753.

Lowth, Robert. *Lectures on the Sacred Poetry of the Hebrews*, trans. G. Gregory with notes by J. D. Michaelis, 2 vols. London, 1787.

[Lowth, Robert]. *A Letter to the Right Reverend Author of* The Divine Legation of Moses Demonstrated. Oxford, 1765.

Lowth, Robert. *Isaiah. A New Translation*. London, 1778.

Macauley, John S. and Greaves, R. W. (eds). *The Autobiography of Thomas Secker Archbishop of Canterbury*. Lawrence: University of Kansas Libraries, 1988.

[Mace, Daniel]. *The New Testament in Greek and English*, 2 vols. London, 1729.

Newbery, John. *The Holy Bible Abridged*. London, 1757.

Newcome, William. *An Attempt Towards an Improved Version, a Metrical Arrangement, and an Explanation of the Twelve Minor Prophets*. Dublin, 1785.

Newcome, William. *An Attempt Towards an Improved Version, a Metrical Arrangement, and an Explanation of the Prophet Ezekiel*. Dublin, 1788.

Newcome, William. *An Historical View of the English Biblical Translations*. Dublin, 1792.

Ostervald, J. F. *The Necessity and Usefulness of Reading the Holy Scriptures*, trans. John Moore, new edn. London, 1770.

Palmer, Samuel (ed.). *A New Translation of the New Testament of our Lord and Saviour*

Jesus Christ. Extracted from the Paraphrase of the late Philip Doddridge, 2 vols. London, 1765.

Purver, Anthony. *A New and Literal Translation of All the Books of the Old and New Testament*, 2 vols. London, 1764.

Report from Select Committee on King's Printers' Patents. London, 1832.

Scarlett, Nathaniel. *A Translation of the New Testament from the Original Greek*. London, 1798.

Secker, Thomas. *Eight Charges delivered to the Clergy of the Dioceses of Oxford and Canterbury*, ed. Beilby Porteus and George Stinton. London, 1769.

Sharpe, Gregory. *Two Dissertations: I. Upon the Origin, Construction, Division, and Relation of Languages. II. Upon the Original Power of Letters*. London, 1751.

Travis, George. *Letters to Edward Gibbon*, 3rd edn. London, 1794.

Trimmer, Sarah. *An Abridgment of the New Testament, consisting of Lessons Composed from the Writings of the Four Evangelists*. [London, 1793].

Wesley, John. *Explanatory Notes upon the New Testament*. London, 1755.

Secondary works

Belaval, Yvon and Bourel, Dominique (eds). *Le Siècle des Lumières et la Bible*. Paris: Beauchesne, 1986.

Bentley, G. E. jun. 'The holy pirates: legal enforcement in England of the patent in the Authorized Version of the Bible ca. 1800', *Studies in Bibliography*, 50 (1997): 372–89.

Berg, J. van den. 'The Leiden professors of the Schultens family and their contacts with British scholars', *Durham University Journal*, 75 (1982–83): 1–14.

Bottigheimer, Ruth B. *The Bible for Children from the Age of Gutenberg to the Present*. New Haven, CT: Yale University Press, 1996.

Bultmann, Christoph. *Die biblische Urgeschichte in der Aufklärung*. Tübingen: Mohr Siebeck, 1999.

Burton, Edwin H. *The Life and Times of Bishop Challoner (1691–1781)*, 2 vols. London: Longmans, 1909.

Carson, D. A. and Woodbridge, John D. (eds). *Hermeneutics, Authority, and Canon*, new edn. Grand Rapids, MI: Baker Books, 1995.

Carson, D. A. and Woodbridge, John D. (eds). *Scripture and Truth*, new edn. Grand Rapids, MI: Baker Books, 1992.

Carter, Harry. *A History of Oxford University Press, Volume I: To the Year 1780*. Oxford: Clarendon Press, 1975.

Darlow, T. H. and Moule, H. F. *Historical Catalogue of Printed Editions of the English Bible 1525–1961*, revised and expanded by A. S. Herbert. London: British and Foreign Bible Society, 1968.

David, Alun Morris. 'Christopher Smart and the Hebrew Bible: Poetry and Biblical criticism in England (1682–1771)', unpublished Cambridge University PhD thesis, 1994.

Deconinck-Brossard, Françoise. 'England and France in the eighteenth century', in Stephen Prickett (ed.), *Reading the Text. Biblical Criticism and Literary Theory*. Oxford: Blackwell, 1991.

Drury, John (ed.). *Critics of the Bible 1724–1873*. Cambridge: Cambridge University Press, 1989.

English, John C. 'John Hutchinson's critique of Newtonian heterodoxy', *Church History*, 68 (1999): 581–97.

Fox, Adam. *John Mill and Richard Bentley*. Oxford: Blackwell, 1954.

Frei, Hans W. *The Eclipse of Biblical Narrative*. New Haven, CT: Yale University Press, 1974.

Fuller, Reginald C. *Alexander Geddes*. Sheffield: Almond Press, 1984.

Green, Ian. 'Développement et déclin de la production des Bibles en Angleterre entre 1530 et 1730', in Bertram Eugene Schwarzbach (ed.), *La Bible imprimée dans l'Europe moderne*. Paris: Bibliothèque nationale de France, 1999.

Hilton, Mary, Styles, Morag and Watson, Victor (eds). *Opening the Nursery Door*. London: Routledge, 1997.

Hitchin, Neil W. 'The politics of English Bible translation in Georgian Britain', *Transactions of the Royal Historical Society*, 6th ser., 9 (1999): 67–92.

Howsam, Leslie. *Cheap Bibles. Nineteenth-Century Publishing and the British and Foreign Bible Society*. Cambridge: Cambridge University Press, 1991.

Katz, David S. 'The Chinese Jews and the problem of biblical authority in eighteenth- and nineteenth-century England', *English Historical Review*, 105 (1990): 893–919.

Kugel, James L. *The Idea of Biblical Poetry*. Baltimore, MD: Johns Hopkins University Press, 1981.

Lamb, Jonathan. *The Rhetoric of Suffering. Reading the Book of Job in the Eighteenth Century*. Oxford: Clarendon Press, 1995.

Levine, Joseph M. *The Autonomy of History*. Chicago, IL: University of Chicago Press, 1999.

McKane, William. 'Benjamin Kennicott: an eighteenth-century researcher', *Journal of Theological Studies*, NS 28 (1977): 445–63.

McKane, William. *Selected Christian Hebraists*. Cambridge: Cambridge University Press, 1989.

McKitterick, David. *Cambridge University Library. A History. The Eighteenth and Nineteenth Centuries*. Cambridge: Cambridge University Press, 1986.

McKitterick, David. *A History of Cambridge University Press*, 2 vols to date. Cambridge: Cambridge University Press, 1992–98.

McLachlan, H. 'An almost forgotten pioneer in New Testament criticism', *Hibbert Journal*, 37 (1938–9): 617–25.

Mitchell, Jim. 'Bible publishing in eighteenth-century Britain', *Factotum*, 20 (1985): 11–19.

Muller, Richard A. *Post-Reformation Reformed Dogmatics*, 2 vols. Grand Rapids, MI: Baker Books, 1987–93.

Norton, David. *A History of the Bible as Literature*, 2 vols. Cambridge: Cambridge University Press, 1993.

Reventlow, Henning Graf. *The Authority of the Bible and the Rise of the Modern World*, trans. John Bowden. London: SCM Press, 1984.

Walsh, Marcus. 'Profession and authority: the interpretation of the Bible in the seventeenth and eighteenth centuries', *Literature and Theology*, 9 (1995): 383–98.

3 Theological Books

Primary works

Blackburne, Francis. *The Confessional*. London, 1767; 3rd enlarged edn, 1770.

Blackburne, Francis. *Memoirs of Thomas Hollis*. 2 vols. London, 1780.

Blackburne, Francis. *Remarks on Johnson's Life of Milton*. London, 1780.

Blackburne, Francis. *The Works, Theological and Miscellaneous*, 7 vols. Cambridge, 1804–5.

Bury, Arthur. *The Naked Gospel*. London, 1690.

Butler, Joseph. *The Analogy of Religion, Natural and Revealed*. London, 1736.

Clerc, Jean le. *An Historical Vindication of the Naked Gospel*. London, 1690.

Doddridge, Philip. *Calendar of the Correspondence of Philip Doddridge (1702–1751)*, ed. Geoffrey F. Nuttall. London: Historical Manuscripts Commission, 1979.

Doddridge, Philip. *The Family Expositor*, 6 vols. London, 1739–56.

Fielding, Henry. *Joseph Andrews*, ed. Martin C. Battestin. Oxford: Clarendon Press, 1967.

Froude, James Anthony. *Nemesis of Faith*. London: John Chapman, 1849.

Gibbon, Edward. *The Autobiographies*, ed. John Murray. London: John Murray, 1896.

Gibbon, Edward. *The Decline and Fall of the Roman Empire*, ed. David Womersley, 3 vols. Harmondsworth: Penguin, 1994.

Graves, Richard. *The Spiritual Quixote*, ed. Clarence Tracy. London: Oxford University Press, 1967.

Gray, Thomas. *Correspondence of Thomas Gray*, ed. Pagey Toynbee and Leonard Whibley, 3 vols. Oxford: The Clarendon Press, 1935.

Hume, David. *Essays, Moral, Political and Literary*, ed. Eugene F. Miller. Indianapolis: Liberty Fund Press, 1987.

Hurd, Richard. *Discourse, By Way of a General Preface to the Quarto Edition of Bishop Warburton's Works*. London, 1794.

Hurd, Richard. *The Early Letters of Bishop Richard Hurd 1739–1762*, ed. Sarah Brewer. Woodbridge: Boydell Press, 1995.

Hurd, Richard. *Letters on Chivalry and Romance*. London, 1762.

Jervis, Thomas. *Reflections on the State of Religion and Knowledge.* London, 1801.

Lardner, Nathaniel. *Credibility of the Gospel History.* London, 1730.

Law, William. *A Practical Treatise on Christian Perfection.* London, 1726.

Law, William. *A Serious Call to a Devout and Holy Life.* London, 1729.

Middleton, Conyers. *The History of the Life of Marcus Tullius Cicero,* 2 vols. London, 1741.

Middleton, Conyers. *A Letter from Rome,* 5th edn. London, 1742.

Middleton, Conyers. *A Letter to Dr Waterland.* London, 1731.

Middleton, Conyers. *The Miscellaneous Works,* 4 vols. London, 1752.

Nichols, John. *Literary Anecdotes of the Eighteenth Century,* 9 vols. London, 1812–15.

[Nichols, Sir Philip]. 'Milton', in *Biographia Britannica,* 7 vols. London: 1747–66, Vol. 5, pp. 3106–119.

Parkinson, James. *The Fire's Continued at Oxford.* London, 1690.

Pope, Alexander. *The Dunciad,* ed. Valerie Rumbold. Harlow: Longman, 1999.

Sterne, Laurence. *Sermons of Parson Yorick.* 2 vols. London, 1760.

Sterne, Laurence. *The Life and Opinions of Tristram Shandy, Gentleman,* ed. Melvyn and Joan New, 2 vols. Gainesville: University of Florida Press, 1978.

Tindal, Matthew. *Christianity as Old as the Creation.* London, 1730.

Warburton, William. *The Alliance of Church and State.* London, 1736.

Warburton, William. *The Divine Legation of Moses Demonstrated,* 2 vols. London, 1738–41.

Warburton, William. *The Doctrine of Grace.* London, 1763.

Warburton, William. *Julian.* London, 1750.

Warburton, William. *Letters From a Late Eminent Prelate to One of His Friends.* London, 1809.

Warburton, William. *Pope's Literary Legacy: The Book-Trade Correspondence of William Warburton and John Knapton With Other Letters and Documents 1744–1780,* ed. Donald W. Nichol. Oxford: Oxford Bibliographical Society, 1991.

Warburton, William. *A Selection from Unpublished Papers,* ed. Francis Kilvert. London: 1841.

Warburton, William (ed.). *The Works of Shakespeare,* 8 vols. London, 1747.

Waterland, Daniel. *Advice to a Young Student.* Cambridge, 1730; 2nd edn, Oxford, 1755.

Waterland, Daniel. *Scripture Vindicated.* London, 1731.

Waterland, Daniel. *Sermons on Several Important Subjects of Religion and Morality,* 2 vols. London, 1742.

Watson, Richard. *Anecdotes of the Life of Richard Watson.* London, 1817.

Watson, Richard. *An Apology for the Bible.* London, 1796.

Watson, Richard. *An Apology for Christianity.* London, 1776.

Watson, Richard. *A Collection of Theological Tracts,* 6 vols. London, 1785.

Watts, Isaac. *Scripture History.* London, 1736.

Wollaston, William. *The Religion of Nature Delineated.* London, 1722.

Young, Edward. *Night Thoughts*, ed. Stephen Cornford. Cambridge: Cambridge University Press, 1989.

Secondary works

Bourdieu, Pierre. *The Field of Cultural Production*. Cambridge: Polity Press, 1993.

Brewer, John. 'Reconstructing the reader: prescriptions, texts and strategies in Anna Larpent's reading', in James Raven, Helen Small and Naomi Tadmor (eds), *The Practice and Representation of Reading in England*. Cambridge: Cambridge University Press, 1996.

Cash, Arthur H. *Laurence Sterne: The Later Years*. London: Methuen, 1986.

Doherty, F. M. 'Sterne and Warburton: another look', *British Journal for Eighteenth-Century Studies*, 1 (1978): 20–30.

Donoghue, Frank M. *The Fame-Machine*. Cambridge: Cambridge University Press, 1996.

Evans, A. W. *Warburton and the Warburtonians*. London: Oxford University Press, 1932.

Goldgar, Anne. *Impolite Learning*. New Haven, CT: Yale University Press, 1995.

Haydon, Colin. *Anti-Catholicism in Eighteenth-Century England, c. 1714–80*. Manchester: Manchester University Press, 1993.

Hudson, Nicholas. *Writing and European Thought 1600–1830*. Cambridge: Cambridge University Press, 1994.

Jarvis, Simon. *Scholars and Gentlemen*. Oxford: Clarendon Press, 1995.

Kramnick, Jonathan Brody. *Making the English Canon: Print Capitalism and the Cultural Past, 1700–1770*. Cambridge: Cambridge University Press, 1998.

Lyons, Nicholas. 'Satiric technique in *The Spiritual Quixote*', *Durham University Journal*, 66 (1973–74): 266–77.

Nangle, Benjamin Christie. *The Monthly Review First Series 1749–1789*. Oxford: Clarendon Press, 1934.

New, Melvyn. 'Sterne, Warburton, and the burden of exuberant wit', *Eighteenth-Century Studies*, 15 (1981–82): 245–74.

Patterson, Annabel. *Early Modern Liberalism*. Cambridge: Cambridge University Press, 1997.

Redwood, John. *Reason, Ridicule and Religion*. London: Thames and Hudson, 1976.

Rivers, Isabel. *Reason, Grace, and Sentiment*, Vol. 1: *Whichcote to Wesley*. Cambridge: Cambridge University Press, 1991; Vol. 2: *Shaftesbury to Hume*. Cambridge: Cambridge University Press, 2000.

Robbins, Caroline. *The Eighteenth-Century Commonwealthman*. Cambridge, MA: Harvard University Press, 1959.

Rose, Mark. *Authors and Owners: The Invention of Copyright*. Cambridge, MA: Harvard University Press, 1993.

Seary, Peter. *Lewis Theobald and the Editing of Shakespeare*. Oxford: Clarendon Press, 1990.

Sitter, John. *Literary Loneliness in Mid-Eighteenth-Century England*. Ithaca, NY: Cornell University Press, 1982.

Tyacke, Nicholas. 'Religious controversy', in Tyacke, ed., *Seventeenth-Century Oxford*, *The History of the University of Oxford*, Vol. 4. Oxford: Clarendon Press, 1997.

Walsh, Marcus. *Shakespeare, Milton, and Eighteenth-Century Literary Editing*. Cambridge: Cambridge University Press, 1997.

Young, B. W. *Religion and Enlightenment in Eighteenth-Century England*. Oxford: Clarendon Press, 1998.

Young, B. W. '"Scepticism in excess": Gibbon and eighteenth-century Christianity', *Historical Journal*, 42 (1998): 79–99.

Young, B. W. '"See *Mystery* to *Mathematics* fly!": Pope's *Dunciad* and the critique of religious rationalism', *Eighteenth-Century Studies*, 26 (1993): 435–48.

Zwicker, Steven. 'Reading the margins: politics and the habits of appropriation', in Kevin Sharpe and Steven N. Zwicker (eds), *Refiguring Revolutions*. Berkeley: University of California Press, 1998.

4 The History Market

Primary works

Alexander, William. *A History of Women, from the Earliest Antiquity to the Present Time*, 2 vols. London, 1779.

Berington, Joseph. *The History of the Reign of Henry the Second, and of Richard and John*. Birmingham, 1790.

Bolingbroke, Henry St John, Viscount. *Letters on the Study and Use of History*. London, 1752.

Burnet, Gilbert. *The History of the Reformation of the Church of England*, 3 vols. London, 1679–1715.

Carte, Thomas. *A General History of England*, 4 vols. London, 1747–55.

Chapone, Hester. *Letters on the Improvement of the Mind*, 2 vols. London, 1773.

Clarendon, Edward Hyde, Earl of. *History of the Rebellion and Civil Wars in England*, 3 vols. Oxford, 1702–4.

Clarendon, Edward Hyde, Earl of. *The Life of Edward Earl of Clarendon . . . Published from his original manuscripts*. Oxford, 1759.

A Complete History of England with the Lives of all the Kings and Queens thereof from the earliest Account of Time to the Death of . . . William III, 3 vols. London, 1706.

Cowley, Charlotte. *The Ladies History of England: From the Descent of Julius Caesar to the Summer of 1780*. London, 1780.

Dunbar, James. *Essays on the History of Mankind in Rude and Cultivated Ages*. London, 1780.

Echard, Laurence. *The History of England*, 4 vols. London, 1707–18.

Echard, Laurence. *The Roman History*. London, 1697.

Ferguson, Adam. *An Essay on the History of Civil Society*. Edinburgh, 1767.

Ferguson, Adam. *The History of the Progress and Termination of the Roman Republic*. London, 1783, revised 1799.

A General History of the World, 12 vols. London, 1764–67.

Gibbon, Edward. *The History of the Decline and Fall of the Roman Empire*, 6 vols. London, 1776–88.

Goldsmith, Oliver. *The History of England*, 4 vols. London, 1771.

Goldsmith, Oliver. *A History of England, in a Series of Letters from a Nobleman to his Son*. London, 1764.

Goldsmith, Oliver. *The Roman History from the Foundation to the Fall of the Western Empire*, 2 vols. London, 1769.

Guthrie, William. *A General History of England*, 3 vols. London, 1744–51.

Hamilton, Elizabeth. *Memoirs of the Life of Agrippina*, 3 vols. Bath, 1804.

Henry, Robert. *The History of Great Britain*, 6 vols. London, 1771–93.

Hooke, Nathaniel. *The Roman History from the Building of Rome*, 4 vols. London, 1738–71.

Hume, David. *The History of Great Britain*, Vol. I: *The Reigns of James I and Charles I*. Edinburgh, 1754; Vol. II: *The Commonwealth, and The Reigns of Charles II and James II*. London, 1757 [1756].

Hume, David. *The History of England, under the House of Tudor*, 2 vols. London, 1759.

Hume, David. *The History of England, from the Invasion of Julius Caesar to the Accession of Henry VII*, 2 vols. London, 1762.

Hume, David. *The History of England, from the Invasion of Julius Caesar to the Revolution in 1688*, 8 vols. London, 1778.

Hurd, Richard. *Letters on Chivalry and Romance*. London, 1762.

Hutton, William. *An History of Birmingham*. Birmingham, 1781.

Hutton, William. *The History of Derby*. London, 1791.

Kames, Henry Home, Lord. *Sketches of the History of Man*, 2 vols. Edinburgh, 1774.

Lyttelton, George, Lord. *The History of the Life of King Henry the Second*, 4 vols. London, 1767–71.

Macaulay, Catharine. *The History of England*, 8 vols. London, 1763–83.

Macpherson, James. *An Introduction to the History of Great Britain and Ireland*. London, 1771.

Middleton, Conyers. *The History of the Life of Marcus Tullius Cicero*, 2 vols. London, 1741.

Millar, John. *Observations concerning the Distinction of Ranks in Society*. London, 1771. Revised as *The Origin of the Distinction of Ranks in Society*. London, 1779.

Montesquieu, Charles de Secondat, Baron de. *Reflections on the Causes of the Grandeur and Declension of the Romans*. London, 1734.

Noble, Mark. *The Lives of the English Regicides*. London, 1798.

Oldmixon, John. *The Critical History of England*, 2 vols. London, 1724–26.

Percy, Thomas. *Northern Antiquities*, 2 vols. London, 1770.

Pinkerton, John. *A Dissertation on the Origin and Progress of the . . . Goths*. London, 1787.

Rapin de Thoyras, Paul. *The History of England*, trans. N. Tindal, 15 vols. London, 1725–31.

Reeve, Clara. *The Progress of Romance*, 2 vols. Colchester, 1785.

Robertson, William. *An Historical Disquisition concerning the Knowledge which the Ancients had of India*. London, 1791.

Robertson, William. *The History of America*, 2 vols. London, 1777.

Robertson, William. *The History of the Reign of the Emperor Charles V*, 3 vols. London, 1769.

Robertson, William. *The History of Scotland*, 2 vols. London, 1759.

Rollin, Charles and Crevier, Jean Baptiste Louis. *The Roman History*, 16 vols. London, 1754.

Russell, William. *The History of Modern Europe*, 4 vols. London, 1779–84.

Sainte-Palaye, Jean Baptiste la Curne de. *Memoirs of Ancient Chivalry*, trans. Susannah Dobson. London, 1784.

Salmon, Thomas. *The History of England*, 13 vols. London, 1735.

Salmon, Thomas. *Modern History, or the Present State of all Nations*, 31 vols. London, 1724–38.

Smith, John. *Galic Antiquities*. Edinburgh, 1780.

Smollett, Tobias. *A Complete History of England*, 4 vols. London, 1757–58.

Smollett, Tobias. *Continuation of the Complete History of England*, 5 vols. London, 1760–65.

Somerville, Thomas. *The History of Great Britain during the Reign of Queen Anne*. London, 1798.

Somerville, Thomas. *The History of the Political Transactions and of Parties, from the Restoration of King Charles II, to the Death of King William*. London, 1792.

Strutt, Joseph. *A Complete View of the Dress and Habits of the People of England*, 2 vols. London, 1796–99.

Strutt, Joseph. *A Complete View of the Manners, Customs, Arms, Habits etc. of the Inhabitants of England*, 3 vols. London, 1775–76.

Strutt, Joseph. *The Regal and Ecclesiastical Antiquities of England from Edward the Confessor to Henry the Eighth*. London, 1773.

Strutt, Joseph. *The Sports and Pastimes of the People of England*. London, 1801.

Stuart, Gilbert. *A View of Society in Europe*. Edinburgh, 1778.

Temple, William. *An Introduction to the History of England*. London, 1695.

Turner, Sharon. *The History of the Anglo-Saxons*, 4 vols. London, 1799–1805.

Tyrrell, James. *The General History of England*, 3 vols. London, 1696–1704.

Universal History. 'Ancient Part', 44 vols. London, 1730–44.

Voltaire, François Marie Arouet de. *The Works of M. de Voltaire. Translated from the*

French. With notes historical and critical. By Dr. Smollett and others, 25 vols. London, 1761–65.

Warton, Thomas. *The History of English Poetry*, 3 vols. London, 1774–81.

Whitaker, John. *The Genuine History of the Britons Asserted*. London, 1772.

Whitaker, John. *The History of Manchester*, 2 vols. London, 1771–75.

Wollstonecraft, Mary. *An Historical and Moral View of the Origin and Progress of the French Revolution*. London, 1794.

Wotton, William. *The History of Rome from the Death of Antoninus Pius*. London, 1701.

Secondary works

Abbattista, Guido. 'The business of Paternoster Row: towards a publishing history of the *Universal History*, (1736–65)', *Publishing History*, 17 (1985): 5–50.

Black, Jeremy. 'Ideology, history, xenophobia and the world of print in eighteenth-century England', in Jeremy Black and Jeremy Gregory (eds), *Culture, Politics and Society in Britain, 1660–1800*. Manchester: Manchester University Press, 1991.

Cochrane, J. A. *Dr Johnson's Printer: The Life of William Strahan*. London: Routledge & Kegan Paul, 1964.

Collins, A. S. *Authorship in the Days of Johnson*. London: Holden, 1927.

Hicks, Philip. *Neoclassical History and English Culture: From Clarendon to Hume*. Basingstoke: Macmillan, 1996.

Hill, Bridget. *The Republican Virago: The Life and Times of Catharine Macaulay, Historian*. Oxford: Clarendon Press, 1992.

Knapp, Lewis. 'The publication of Smollett's *Complete History* and *Continuation*', *The Library*, 16 (1935): 295–308.

Levine, Joseph M. *The Battle of the Books: History and Literature in the Augustan Age*. Ithaca, NY: Cornell University Press, 1991.

Martz, Louis. 'Tobias Smollett and the Universal History', *Modern Language Notes*, 56 (1941): 1–14.

Mossner, E. C. and Ransom, H. 'Hume and the "Conspiracy of the Booksellers": the publication and early fortunes of the history of England', *University of Texas Studies in English*, 29 (1950): 162–82.

Okie, Laird. *Augustan Historical Writing: Histories of England in the English Enlightenment*. Lanham, MD: University Press of America, 1991.

Preston Peardon, Thomas. *The Transition in English Historical Writing, 1760–1830*. New York: Columbia University Press, 1933.

Raven, James. *Judging New Wealth: Popular Publishing and Responses to Commerce in England, 1750–1800*. Oxford: Clarendon Press, 1992.

Rousseau, A. M. 'L'Angleterre et Voltaire', *Studies on Voltaire and the Eighteenth Century*, vols 145–7 (1976).

Sher, Richard B. 'Charles V and the book trade: an episode in enlightenment print culture', in Stewart J. Brown, ed., *William Robertson and the Expansion of Empire*. Cambridge: Cambridge University Press, 1997.

Smith, R. J. *The Gothic Bequest: Medieval Institutions in British Thought, 1688–1863*. Cambridge: Cambridge University Press, 1987.

Sweet, Rosemary. *The Writing of Urban Histories in Eighteenth-Century England*. Oxford: Clarendon Press, 1997.

Woolf, D. R. 'A feminine past? Gender, genre and historical knowledge in England, 1500–1800', *American Historical Review*, 102 (1997): 645–79.

5 Biographical Dictionaries

Primary works: dictionaries

Bayle, Pierre. *Dictionaire Historique et Critique*, 4 vols. Rotterdam, 1697.

Bayle, Pierre. *Dictionaire Historique et Critique . . . Revuë, corrigée & augmentée par l'Auteur*, 2nd edn, 3 vols. Rotterdam, 1702.

Bayle, Pierre. *Dictionaire Historique et Critique, Revue, corrigée & augmentée. Avec la Vie de l'Auteur, par Mr. Des Maizeaux*, 4th edn, 4 vols. Amsterdam and Leiden, 1730.

Bayle, Pierre. *An Historical and Critical Dictionary . . . with many Additions and Corrections, made by the Author himself, that are not in the French Editions*, 4 vols. London, 1710.

Bayle, Pierre. *The Dictionary, Historical and Critical of Mr Peter Bayle. The Second Edition . . . To which is prefixed, the Life of the Author, by Mr Des Maizeaux*, 5 vols. London, 1734–38.

Bayle, Pierre. *Historical and Critical Dictionary: Selections*, trans. with introduction and notes by Richard H. Popkin. Indianapolis: The Library of Liberal Arts, 1965.

Berkenhout, John. *Biographia Literaria: Or a Biographical History of Literature: containing the Lives of English, Scotish, and Irish Authors, from the Dawn of Letters in these Kingdoms to the Present Time, chronologically and classically arranged*, Vol. 1. London, 1777.

Biographia Britannica: Or, The Lives of the Most Eminent Persons who have flourished in Great Britain and Ireland, from the earliest Ages, down to the present Times: Collected from the best Authorities, both Printed and Manuscript, and digested in the Manner of Mr Bayle's Historical and Critical Dictionary, 6 vols in 7. London, 1747–66.

Biographia Britannica: Or, the Lives of the Most Eminent Persons who have flourished in Great Britain and Ireland, from the Earliest Ages, to the Present Times: collected from the Best Authorities, Printed and Manuscript, and digested in the Manner of Mr. Bayle's Historical and Critical Dictionary, 2nd edn., ed. Andrew Kippis, 6 vols. London, 1778–95.

British Biography: Or, An Accurate and Impartial Account of the Lives and Writings of Eminent Persons, In Great Britain and Ireland; From Wickliff, who began the Reformation by his Writings, to the Present Time, 7 vols. London, 1766–72.

The Compact Edition of the Dictionary of National Biography, 2 vols. Oxford: Oxford University Press, 1975.

The General Biographical Dictionary: Containing an Historical and Critical Account of the Lives and Writings of the Most Eminent Persons in Every Nation; Particularly the British and Irish; from the Earliest Accounts to the Present Time. A New Edition, revised and enlarged by Alexander Chalmers, 32 vols. London, 1812–17.

A General Dictionary, Historical and Critical: In which a New and Accurate Translation of that of the Celebrated Mr. Bayle . . . is included, ed. John Peter Bernard, Thomas Birch, John Lockman *et al.*, 10 vols. London, 1734–41.

Granger, J. *A Biographical History of England, from Egbert the Great to the Revolution: Consisting of Characters disposed in different Classes, and adapted to a Methodical Catalogue of Engraved British Heads*, 2 vols and supplement. London, 1769, 1774.

Granger, J. *A Biographical History of England, from Egbert the Great to the Revolution: Consisting of Characters disposed in different Classes, and adapted to a Methodical Catalogue of Engraved British Heads*. 3rd edn, *with large Additions and Improvements*, 4 vols. London, 1779.

The Great Historical, Geographical, Genealogical and Poetical Dictionary; Being A Curious Miscellany of Sacred and Prophane History . . . The Second Edition Revis'd, Corrected and Enlarg'd to the Year 1688, by Jeremy Collier, 2 vols. London, 1701.

Collier, Jeremy. *A Supplement to the Great Historical, Geographical, Genealogical and Poetical Dictionary . . . Together with A Continuation from the Year 1688, to 1705, by another Hand*, 2nd edn. London, 1727.

An Appendix to the Three English Volumes in Folio of Morery's Great Historical, Geographical, Genealogical and Poetical Dictionary. London, 1721.

Moréri, Louis. *Le Grand Dictionaire Historique, ou Le Mélange Curieux de L'Histoire Sainte et Profane*. Lyon, 1674.

A New and General Biographical Dictionary; Containing An Historical and Critical Account of the Lives and Writings of the Most Eminent Persons in every Nation; Particularly the British and Irish; From the Earliest Accounts of Time to the present Period, 11 vols. London, 1761–62.

A New and General Biographical Dictionary; containing An Historical and Critical Account of the Lives and Writings of the Most Eminent Persons in every Nation; Particularly the British and Irish; From the Earliest Accounts of Time to the present Period. New edn, *greatly enlarged and improved*, 15 vols. London, 1798.

[Wood, Anthony]. *Athenae Oxonienses: An Exact History of all the Writers and Bishops who have had their Education in the Most Ancient and Famous University of Oxford, from the fifteenth Year of King Henry the Seventh, Dom. 1500, to the End of the Year 1690 . . . To which are added, The Fasti or Annals, of the said University*, 2 vols. London, 1691–92.

Wood, Anthony. *Athenae Oxonienses. An Exact History of all the Writers and Bishops who have had their Education in the most Ancient and Famous University of Oxford, from the Fifteenth Year of King Henry the Seventh, A.D. 1500, to the Author's Death in*

November 1695 . . . To which are added, The Fasti, or Annals, of the said University, 2nd edn, corrected and enlarged, 2 vols. London, 1721.

Wood, Anthony. *Athenae Oxonienses. An Exact History of all the Writers and Bishops who have had their Education in the University of Oxford. To which are added The Fasti, or Annals of the said University . . . A New Edition, with Additions and a Continuation,* ed. Philip Bliss, 5 vols. London, 1813–15.

Other primary works

Baxter, Richard. *Reliquiae Baxterianae.* London, 1696.

Birch, Thomas. *The Heads of Illustrious Persons of Great Britain, Engraven by Mr. Houbraken, and Mr. Vertue. With their Lives and Characters,* 2 vols. London, 1743, 1751.

Boswell, James. *Boswell's Life of Johnson,* ed. G. B. Hill, rev. L. F. Powell, 2nd edn, 6 vols. Oxford: Clarendon Press, 1964.

Calamy, Edmund. *An Abridgment of Mr. Baxter's History of his Life and Times. With an Account of many others of those worthy Ministers who were ejected after the Restoration of King Charles the Second . . . And a Continuation of their History, till the Year 1691.* London, 1702.

Calamy, Edmund. *An Abridgement of Mr. Baxter's History of his Life and Times. With an Account of the Ministers &c. who were ejected after the Restauration, of King Charles the Second . . . And the continuation of their History, to the passing of the Bill against Occasional Conformity, in 1711,* 2nd edn, 2 vols. London, 1713. Volume 2: *An Account of the Ministers, Lecturers, Masters and Fellows of Colleges and Schoolmasters, who were Ejected or Silenced after the Restoration in 1660. By, or before, the Act for Uniformity. Design'd for the preserving to Posterity, the Memory of their Names, Characters, Writings and Sufferings.*

Calamy, Edmund. *A Continuation of the Account of the Ministers, Lecturers, Masters and Fellows of Colleges, and Schoolmasters, who were Ejected and Silenced after the Restoration in 1660, by or before the Act for Uniformity. To which is added, The Church and Dissenters compar'd, as to Persecution, in some Remarks on Dr. Walker's Attempt to recover the Names and Sufferings of the Clergy that were sequestred, &c. between 1640 and 1660,* 2 vols. London, 1727.

Des Maizeaux, Pierre. *An Historical and Critical Account of the Life and Writings of Wm. Chillingworth, Chancellor of the Church of Sarum.* London, 1725.

Des Maizeaux, Pierre. *An Historical and Critical Account of the Life and Writings of the Ever-Memorable Mr. John Hales, Fellow of Eton College, and Canon of Windsor. Being a Specimen of an Historical and Critical English Dictionary.* London, 1719.

Des Maizeaux, Pierre. *The Life of Mr. Bayle. In a Letter to a Peer of Great Britain.* London, 1708.

Johnson, Samuel. *Lives of the English Poets,* ed. George Birkbeck Hill, 3 vols. Oxford: Clarendon Press, 1905.

Palmer, Samuel. *The Nonconformist's Memorial . . . Originally written by the Reverend and Learned Edmund Calamy, D.D. Now abridged and corrected, and the Author's Additions inserted, with many further Particulars, and new Anecdotes.* 2 vols, London, 1778; 3 vols, London, 1802.

Rees, Abraham. *A Sermon preached . . . upon Occasion of the Much Lamented Death of the Rev. Andrew Kippis.* London, 1795.

Walker, John. *An Attempt towards Recovering an Account of the Numbers and Sufferings of the Clergy of the Church of England . . . who were Sequester'd . . . in the late Times of the Grand Rebellion.* London, 1714.

Walton, Izaac. *The Compleat Angler. The Lives of Donne Wotton Hooker Herbert & Sanderson with Love and Truth & Miscellaneous Writings,* ed. Geoffrey Keynes. London: The Nonesuch Press, 1929.

West, Gilbert. *Education, a Poem. Canto the First.* London, 1751.

Secondary works

Courtines, Léo Pierre. *Bayle's Relations with England and the English.* New York: Columbia University Press, 1938.

Douglas, David C. *English Scholars 1660–1730,* 2nd rev. edn. London: Eyre & Spottiswoode, 1951.

Grafton, Anthony. *The Footnote.* London: Faber and Faber, 1997.

Gunther, A. E. *An Introduction to the Life of the Rev. Thomas Birch D.D., F.R.S. 1705–1766.* Halesworth, Suffolk: The Halesworth Press, 1984.

Lipking, Lawrence. *The Ordering of the Arts in Eighteenth-Century England.* Princeton, NJ: Princeton University Press, 1970.

Osborn, James M. 'Thomas Birch and the *General Dictionary* (1734–41)', *Modern Philology,* 36 (1938–39): 25–46.

Osborn, James M. *John Dryden: Some Biographical Facts and Problems,* rev. edn. Gainesville: University of Florida Press, 1965.

Rogers, Pat. 'Literary Studies', in *The New Cambridge Bibliography of English Literature,* ed. George Watson, vol. 2. *1660–1800.* Cambridge: Cambridge University Press: 1971.

Rogers, Pat. 'Johnson's *Lives of the Poets* and the biographic dictionaries', *Review of English Studies,* NS 31 (1980): 149–71.

Sommerlad, M. J. 'The Continuation of Anthony Wood's *Athenae Oxonienses*', *Bodleian Library Record,* 7 (1966): 264–71.

Stauffer, Donald A. *The Art of Biography in Eighteenth-Century England.* Princeton, NJ: Princeton University Press, 1941.

Stauffer, Donald A. *The Art of Biography in Eighteenth-Century England: Bibliographical Supplement.* Princeton, NJ: Princeton University Press, 1941.

Wykes, David L. *'To Revive the Memory of Some Excellent Men:' Edmund Calamy and the Early Historians of Nonconformity.* London: Dr Williams's Trust, 1997.

6 Review Journals

Primary works: review journals

Analytical Review, 1788–99 (1st ser., 1788–98; 2nd ser., 1799).

Anti-Jacobin Review, 1798–1821.

British Critic, 1793–1843 (1st ser., 1793–1813; 2nd ser., 1814–1825; 3rd ser., 1825–26; 4th ser., 1827–43).

Critical Review, 1756–1817 (1st ser., 1756–90; 2nd ser., 1791–1817).

English Review, 1783–96 (1st ser., 1783–96; incorporated into *Analytical Review*, 1797).

London Review, 1775–80.

Monthly Review, 1749–1844 (1st ser., 1749–89; 2nd ser., 1790–1825; 3rd ser., 1826–30; 4th ser., 1831–44).

Secondary works

Bartolomeo, Joseph F. *A New Species of Criticism: Eighteenth-Century Discourse on the Novel*. Newark: University of Delaware Press, 1994.

Basker, James G. *Tobias Smollett, Critic and Journalist*. Newark: University of Delaware Press, 1988.

Bloom, Edward A. ' "Labors of the Learned": Neoclassic book reviewing techniques', *Studies in Philology*, 54 (1957): 537–63.

Donoghue, Frank. *The Fame Machine: Book Reviewing and Eighteenth-Century Literary Careers*. Stanford, CA: Stanford University Press, 1996.

Forster, Antonia. 'The Griffiths correspondence', *Notes & Queries*, n.s. 42 (June 1995): 173–4.

Forster, Antonia. *Index to Book Reviews in England 1749–1774*. Carbondale: Southern Illinois University Press, 1990.

Forster, Antonia. *Index to Book Reviews in England 1775–1800*. London: The British Library, 1997.

Forster, Antonia. 'Mr. Pope's Maxims', *The Age of Johnson*, 2 (1987): 67–91.

Forster, Antonia. 'Ralph Griffiths', in James K. Bracken and Joel Silver (eds), *British Literary Publishers before 1820* (Vol. 154 of the *Dictionary of Literary Biography*). Detroit: Gale, 1995.

Forster, Antonia. ' "The self–impannelled Jury": the reception of review journals 1749–1760', *Studies in Newspaper and Periodical History* (1993): 27–51.

Graham, Walter. *English Literary Periodicals*. New York: Nelson, 1930.

Jones, Claude E. 'Contributors to the *Critical Review* 1756–1785', *Modern Language Notes*, 61 (1946): 433–41.

Jones, Claude E. 'The *Critical Review* and some major poets', *Notes and Queries*, n.s. 3 (1956): 114–15.

Jones, Claude E. 'The *Critical Review*'s first thirty years', *Notes and Queries*, n.s. 3 (1956): 78–90.

Jones, Claude E. 'Dramatic criticism in the *Critical Review*, 1756–1785', *Modern Language Quarterly*, 20 (1959): 18–26, 133–44.

Jones, Claude E. 'The English novel: a *Critical* view', *Modern Language Quarterly*, 19 (1958): 147–59, 213–24

Jones, Claude E. 'Poetry and the *Critical Review*, 1756–1785', *Modern Language Quarterly*, 9 (1948): 17–36.

Knapp, Lewis M. 'Griffiths's "Monthly Review" as printed by Strahan', *Notes and Queries*, n.s. 5 (1958): 216–17.

Knapp, Lewis M. 'Ralph Griffiths, author and publisher 1746–50', *The Library*, 4th ser., 20 (1939): 197–213.

Knapp, Lewis M. *Tobias Smollett: Doctor of Men and Manners*. Princeton, NJ: Princeton University Press, 1949.

Kuist, James M. *The Nichols File of 'The Gentleman's Magazine'*. Madison: The University of Wisconsin Press, 1992.

McCutcheon, Roger Philip. 'The beginnings of book-reviewing in English periodicals', *PMLA*, 37 (1922): 691–706.

Montluzin, Emily Lorraine de. *The Anti-Jacobins, 1798–1800: The Early Contributors to the Anti-Jacobin Review*. New York: St Martin's Press, 1988.

Nangle, Benjamin Christie. *The Monthly Review First Series 1749–1789: Indexes of Contributors and Articles*. Oxford: Clarendon Press, 1934.

Nangle, Benjamin Christie. *The Monthly Review Second Series 1790–1815: Indexes of Contributors and Articles*. Oxford: Clarendon Press, 1955.

Roper, Derek. 'The politics of the *Critical Review*, 1756–1817', *Durham University Journal*, 53 (1961): 117–22.

Roper, Derek. *Reviewing before the 'Edinburgh' 1788–1802*. Newark: University of Delaware Press, 1979.

Roper, Derek. 'Smollett's "Four Gentlemen": the contributors to the *Critical Review*', *Review of English Studies*, n.s. 10 (1959): 38–44.

Shattuck, Joanne. *Politics and Reviewers: The Edinburgh and the Quarterly in the Early Victorian Age*. Leicester: Leicester University Press, 1989.

Siskin, Clifford. 'Eighteenth-century periodicals and the romantic rise of the novel', *Studies in the Novel*, 26.2 (summer 1994): 26–42.

Spector, Robert D. 'Additional attacks on the *Critical Review*', *Notes and Queries*, n.s. 3 (1956): 425.

Spector, Robert D. 'An attack on the *Critical Review* in *Political Controversy*', *Notes and Queries*, n.s. 22 (1975): 14.

Spector, Robert D. 'Attacks on the *Critical Review*', *Periodical Post Boy* (June 1955): 6–7.

Spector, Robert D. 'Attacks on the *Critical Review* in the *Court Magazine*', *Notes and Queries*, n.s. 5 (1958): 308.

Spector, Robert D. 'Attacks on the *Critical Review* in the *Literary Magazine*', *Notes and Queries*, n.s. 7 (1960): 300–1.

Spector, Robert D. *English Literary Periodicals and the Climate of Opinion during the Seven Years' War*. The Hague: Mouton, 1966.

Spector, Robert D. 'Further attacks on the *Critical Review*', *Notes and Queries*, n.s. 2 (1955): 535.

Spector, Robert D. 'The *Monthly* and its rival', *Bulletin of the New York Public Library*, 64 (1960): 159–61.

Sullivan, Alvin (ed.). *British Literary Magazines: The Augustan Age and the Age of Johnson, 1698–1788*. Westport, CT: Greenwood Press, 1983.

Sullivan, Alvin (ed.). *British Literary Magazines: The Romantic Age, 1789–1836*. Westport, CT: Greenwood Press, 1983.

Zachs, William. *Without Regard to Good Manners: A Biography of Gilbert Stuart, 1743–1786*. Edinburgh: Edinburgh University Press, 1992.

7 Literary Scholarship

Primary works

Bell's Edition of Shakespeare's Plays, As they are now Performed at the Theatres Royal in London, 9 vols. London: John Bell, 1773–74.

Bentley, Richard (ed.). *Milton's Paradise Lost*. London: Tonson, 1732.

Capell, Edward (ed.). *Mr. William Shakespeare his Comedies, Histories, and Tragedies*, 10 vols. London: Tonson, 1768.

Capell, Edward. *Notes and Various Readings to Shakespeare*, 3 vols. London, 1779–83.

Carter, Elizabeth. *All the Works of Epictetus, which are now Extant . . . Translated from the Original Greek*. London: Millar and others, 1758.

Church, Ralph (ed.). *The Faerie Queene, by Edmund Spenser*, 4 vols. London: Faden, 1758–59.

[Cooke, Thomas (ed.)]. *The Works of Andrew Marvell Esq.*, 2 vols. London: Curll, 1726.

Elstob, Elizabeth. *An English-Saxon Homily on the Birth-Day of St. Gregory . . . Translated into Modern English, with Notes, &c*. London: Bowyer, 1709.

Grey, Zachary (ed.). *Hudibras*. London: Innys and others, 1744.

Hanmer, Thomas (ed.). *The Works of Shakespeare*, 6 vols. Oxford: Oxford University Press, 1744.

Hughes, John (ed.). *The Works of Mr Edmund Spenser*, 6 vols. London: Tonson, 1715.

Hughes, John (ed.). *The Works of Spenser*, 6 vols. London: Tonson and Draper, 1750.

Johnson, Samuel (ed.). *The Plays of William Shakespeare*, 8 vols. London: Tonson and others, 1765.

Lennox, Charlotte. *Shakespear Illustrated: Or the Novels and Histories, On which the Plays *of Shakespear are Founded . . . By the Author of the Female Quixote*, 2 vols. London: Millar, 1753.

Malone, Edmond. *A Catalogue of the Greater Portion of the Library of the Late Edmond Malone, Esq.* London: Sotheby, 1818.

Malone, Edmond. *Catalogue of Early English Poetry and other Miscellaneous Works Illustrating the British Drama, Collected by Edmond Malone, Esq. and now Preserved in the Bodleian Library.* Oxford: Oxford University Press, 1836.

Malone, Edmond (ed.). *The Plays and Poems of William Shakspeare*, 10 vols in 11. London: J. Rivington and others, 1790.

Milton, John. *The Poetical Works of Mr. John Milton*, 2 vols. London: Tonson, 1720.

[Montagu, Elizabeth]. *An Essay on the Genius and Writings of Shakespear, Compared with the Greek and French Dramatic Poets. With some Remarks upon the Misrepresentations of Mons. de Voltaire.* London: Dodsley and others, 1769.

Pearce, Zachary. *A Review of the Text of Milton's Paradise Lost, in which the Chief of Dr Bentley's Emendations are Consider'd*, 2 parts. London, 1732, 1733.

Percy, Thomas. *Reliques of Ancient English Poetry*, 3 vols. London: Dodsley, 1765.

Pope, Alexander (ed.). *The Works of Shakespear*, 6 vols. London: Tonson, 1723–25.

Rann, Joseph (ed.). *The Dramatic Works of Shakespeare, In Six Volumes; with Notes.* Oxford, 1786.

Reed, Isaac (ed.). *The Plays of William Shakspeare*, 10 vols. London: C. Bathurst and others, 1785.

Rowe, Nicholas (ed.). *The Works of Mr. William Shakespear*, 6 vols. London: Tonson, 1709.

Shakespeare, William. *Hamlet.* Edinburgh: Donaldson, 1770.

Shakespeare, William. *The Works of Shakespear . . . Collated and Corrected by the former Editions, by Mr. Pope. Printed from his Second Edition*, 8 vols. Glasgow: Foulis, 1766.

Steevens, George (ed.). *Twenty of the Plays of Shakespeare*, 4 vols. London: Tonson, 1766.

Steevens, George (ed.). *The Plays of William Shakspeare*, 15 vols. London: Longman and others, 1793.

Steevens, George and Johnson, Samuel (eds). *The Plays of William Shakespeare*, 10 vols. London, 1773.

Steevens, George and Johnson, Samuel (eds). *The Plays of William Shakespeare*, 2nd edn, 10 vols. London: C. Bathurst and others, 1778.

Theobald, Lewis. *Shakespeare Restored: Or, A Specimen of the Many Errors, as well Committed, as Unamended, by Mr. Pope in his Late Edition of this Poet.* London: Francklin, 1726.

Theobald, Lewis (ed.). *The Works of Shakespeare*, 7 vols. London: Tonson, 1733.

[Tyrwhitt, Thomas (ed.)]. *The Canterbury Tales of Chaucer*, 5 vols. London: Payne, 1775, 1778.

Upton, John (ed.). *Spenser's Faerie Queene*, 2 vols. London: Tonson, 1758.

Urry, John (ed.). *The Works of Geoffrey Chaucer.* London: Lintot, 1721.

Warburton, William (ed.). *The Works of Shakespear*, 8 vols. London: Tonson, 1747.

Warton, Thomas (ed.). *Poems upon Several Occasions, English, Italian, and Latin, by John Milton*. London: Dodsley, 1785.

Warton, Thomas. *Thomas Warton's History of English Poetry*, with a new introduction by David Fairer, 4 vols. London: Routledge/Thoemmes, 1998.

Secondary works

Bonnell, Thomas. 'Bookselling and canon-making: the trade rivalry over the English poets, 1776–1783', *Studies in Eighteenth-Century Culture*, 19 (1989): 53–69.

Brewer, John. *The Pleasures of the Imagination: English Culture in the Eighteenth Century*. London: HarperCollins, 1997.

Crosse, Gordon. 'Charles Jennens as editor of Shakespeare'. *Library*, ser. 4, 16 (1935): 236–40.

Franklin, Colin. *Shakespeare Domesticated: The Eighteenth-Century Editions*. Aldershot: Scolar Press, 1991.

Gondris, Joanna (ed.). *Reading Readings: Essays on Shakespeare Editing in the Eighteenth Century*. Cranbury, NJ: Associated University Presses, 1998.

Groom, Nick. Introduction to *The Johnson–Steevens Edition of the Plays of William Shakespeare*, 12 vols. London: Routledge/Thoemmes, and Tokyo: Kinokuniya, 1995.

Harris, P. R. *A History of the British Museum Library 1753–1973*. London: British Library, 1998.

Jarvis, Simon. *Scholars and Gentlemen: Shakespearian Textual Criticism and Representations of Scholarly Labour, 1725–1765*. Oxford: Oxford University Press, 1995.

Kaminski, Thomas. 'Johnson and Oldys as bibliographers: an introduction to the Harleian catalogue', *Philological Quarterly*, 60 (1981): 439–53.

Kramnick, Jonathan. *Making the English Canon: Print-Capitalism and the Cultural Past, 1700–1770*. Cambridge: Cambridge University Press, 1998.

Lipking, Lawrence. 'The curiosity of William Oldys: an approach to the development of English literary history', *Philological Quarterly*, 46 (1967): 391.

Lipking, Lawrence. *The Ordering of the Arts in Eighteenth-Century England*. Princeton, NJ: Princeton University Press, 1970.

Martin, Peter. *Edmond Malone Shakespearean Scholar: A Literary Biography*. Cambridge: Cambridge University Press, 1995.

Moyles, R. G. *The Text of Paradise Lost: a Study in Editorial Procedure*. Toronto: University of Toronto Press, 1985.

Myers, Sylvia Harcstark. *The Bluestocking Circle: Women, Friendship and the Life of the Mind in Eighteenth-Century England*. Oxford: Oxford University Press, 1990.

Ross, Trevor. 'Copyright and the invention of tradition', *Eighteenth-Century Studies*, 26 (1992): 1–27.

Ross, Trevor. 'Just *when* did British bards begin t'immortalize?', *Studies in Eighteenth-Century Culture*, 19 (1989): 383–93.

Seary, Peter. *Lewis Theobald and the Editing of Shakespeare*. Oxford: Oxford University Press, 1990.

Sutherland, Kathryn. 'Editing for a new century: Elizabeth Elstob's Anglo-Saxon manifesto and Aelfric's St Gregory homily', in D. G. Scragg and Paul E. Szarmach (eds), *The Editing of Old English*. Cambridge: D. S. Brewer, 1994.

Walsh, Marcus. *Shakespeare, Milton and Eighteenth-Century Literary Editing*. Cambridge: Cambridge University Press, 1997.

Wellek, René. *The Rise of English Literary History*. New York: University of North Carolina Press, 1941.

8 Poetic Miscellanies

Primary works: miscellanies and related poetry collections

(Where the editor has not been identified, miscellanies are listed alphabetically by title.)

Caw, George. *The Poetical Museum. Containing Songs and Poems on Almost Every Subject. Mostly from Periodical Publications*. Hawick: G. Caw, 1784.

The Choice Spirit's Chaplet: Or a Posey from Parnassus. Being a Select Collection of Songs, from the Most Approved Authors; many of them Written and the Whole Compiled by George Alexander Stevens, Esq. Whitehaven: J. Dunn, and sold by Messrs Hawes, Clarke, and Collins. London, 1771.

A Collection of Poems by Several Hands. Most of them Written by Persons of Eminent Quality. London: F. Saunders, 1693.

A Collection of Poems. Containing The Minstrel . . . Owen of Charon. Essay on Man. Deserted Village. Traveller. The Grave. The Hermit of Warkworth. Sir Eldred of the Bower and the Bleeding Rock. The Diaboliad . . . By Beattie, Langhorne, Pope, Goldsmith, Blair, Percy, Moore [sic. Hannah More] *and Kenrick*. London: R. [sic. read 'J.'] Dodsley, 1779.

A Collection of Poems: viz. The Temple of Death: By the Marquis of Normanby. An Epistle to the Earl of Dorset: By Charles Montagu, Lord Halifax . . . With Several Original Poems, Never Before Printed, by the E. of Roscommon. The E. of Rochester. The E. of Orrery . . . London: D. Brown; and B. Tooke, 1701.

A Collection of the Most esteemed Pieces of Poetry, that have appeared for several Years. With [a] *Variety of originals, by the late Moses Mendez, Esq; and other Contributors to Dodsley's Collection, to which this is intended as a Supplement*. London: Richardson and Urquhart, 1767.

A Collection of Poems in Two Volumes By Several Hands. Dublin: P. Wilson, J. Exshaw, J. Esdall, R. James, S. Price and M. Williamson, 1751.

A Collection of Poems, Written upon Several Occasions, by Several Persons. Never Before in Print. London: H. Kemp, 1672.

A Collection of Poems, Written upon Several Occasions, by Several Persons. With many Additions, Never before in Print. London: T. Collins and J. Ford; W. Cademan, 1673.

Colman, George and Thornton, Bonnell (eds). *Poems by Eminent Ladies*, 2 vols. London: R. Baldwin, 1755.

Deliciæ Poeticæ; or Parnassus Display'd. London: J. Nutt, 1706.

Dodsley, Robert (ed.). *A Collection of Poems. By Several Hands. In Three Volumes.* London: R. Dodsley, 1748 (4 vols, 1755; 6 vols, 1758).

Dodsley, Robert and Reed, Isaac (eds). *A Collection of Poems in Six Volumes. By Several Hands.* London: J. Dodsley, 1782.

Dryden, John and Tonson, Jacob (eds). *Miscellany Poems. Containing a New Translation of Virgil's Eclogues, Ovid's Love Elegies, Odes of Horace, And Other Authors; With Several Original Poems. By the most Eminent Hands.* London: J. Tonson, 1684.

Dryden, John and Tonson, Jacob (eds). *Sylvæ: Or the Second Part of Poetical Miscellanies.* London: J. Tonson, 1685.

Dryden, John and Tonson, Jacob (eds). *Examen Poeticum: Being the Third Part of Miscellany Poems. Containing Variety of New Translations of the Ancient Poets Together with many Original Copies, By the Most Eminent Hands.* London: J. Tonson, 1693.

Dryden, John and Tonson, Jacob (eds). *The Annual Miscellany: For the Year 1694. Being the Fourth Part of Miscellany Poems. Containing Great Variety of New Translations And Original Copies, By the Most Eminent Hands.* London: J. Tonson, 1694.

Fawkes, Francis and Woty, William (eds). *The Poetical Calendar. Containing a Collection of Scarce and Valuable Pieces of Poetry: With a Variety of Originals and Translations, by the Most Eminent Hands. Intended as A Supplement to Mr. Dodsley's Collection*, 12 vols. London: J. Coote, 1763.

Fenton, Elijah (ed.). *Oxford and Cambridge Miscellany Poems.* London: B. Lintot, [1708].

Gildon, Charles (ed.). *Miscellany Poems on Several Occasions.* London: P. Buck, 1692.

Giles, William (ed.). *A Collection of Poems on Divine and Moral Subjects, Selected from Various Authors.* London: Sold by Buckland; Keith; Vallance and Simmons; and Matthews, 1775.

Harrison, James (ed.). *The Lady's Poetical Magazine, or Beauties of British Poetry*, 4 vols. London: [J.] Harrison & Co., 1781–82.

Husbands, John (ed.). *A Miscellany of Poems by Several Hands. Publish'd by J. Husbands. . . .* Oxford: Printed by Leon Lichfield, 1731.

The Muse in Good Humour: Or, A Collection of Comic Tales, &c. From Chaucer, Prior, Swift, La Fontaine, Dr. King, and other eminent Poets. Together with some Originals, 2 vols. Part I The 4th edn and Part II The 2nd edn. London: J. Noble, 1745.

The Muse in Good Humour: Or, A Collection of the Best Poems, Comic Tales, Choice Fables, Enigmas, &c. From the most Eminent Poets, 2 vols. London: M. Cooper, 1745.

Nichols, John and Reed, Isaac (eds). *A Select Collection of Poems; With Notes, Biographical and Historical*, 8 vols. London: J. Nichols, 1780–82.

Oldmixon, John (ed.). *Poems and Translations. By Several Hands*. London: J. Pemberton, 1714.

Pearch, George (ed.). *A Collection of Poems in Two Volumes. By Several Hands*. London: G. Pearch, 1768.

Pearch, George (ed.). *A Collection of Poems in Four Volumes. By Several Hands*. London: G. Pearch, 1770.

Pearch, George and Reed, Isaac (eds). *A Collection of Poems in Four Volumes*. London: Printed by Assignment from the Executors of G. Pearch, For J. Dodsley, 1783.

Percy, Thomas (ed.). *Reliques of Ancient English Poetry*, 3 vols. London: J. Dodsley, 1765.

Philomel. Being a Small Collection of only the Best British Songs. London: M. Cooper, 1744.

Poems by the most Eminent Ladies of Great Britain and Ireland. Re-Published from the Collection of G. Colman and B. Thornton . . . with considerable Alterations, Additions, and Improvements, 2 vols. London: W. Stafford [1784 or 1785?].

Pope, Alexander (ed.). *Miscellaneous Poems and Translations, By Several Hands*. London: B. Lintot, 1712; 2 vols. 1720.

Pope, Alexander (ed.). *Poems on Several Occasions. By His Grace the Duke of Buckingham, . . . Sir Samuel Garth, . . . Bevil Higgons . . . And other eminent Hands*. London: B. Lintot, 1717.

A Select Collection of Modern Poems, by the Most Eminent Hands. Glasgow: J. Gilmour, 1744.

A Select Collection of Modern Poems, by the Most Eminent Hands, 2nd edn. Glasgow: J. Gilmour, 1750.

A Select Collection of Modern Poems, by the Most Eminent Hands. Edinburgh: A. Donaldson, 1763.

A Select Collection of Poems, From the most approved Authors, 2 vols. Edinburgh: Printed by A. Donaldson, and sold at his Shops in London and Edinburgh, 1768.

Select Poems and Ballads, From Miscellanies Printed Since the Publication of Dodsley's Collection. Glasgow: Printed by R. Chapman and A. Duncan, 1777.

Select Poems, From Dodsley's Collection. Glasgow: Printed by R. Chapman and A. Duncan, 1776.

Select Poems from a Larger Collection. Glasgow: R. & A. Foulis, 1775.

Silver, Samuel (ed.). *The Lover's Manual. Being a Choice Collection of Poems from the most approv'd Modern Authors. With Several Original Pieces*. Sandwich: S. Silver; sold by C. Hitch and L. Hawes [in London], 1753.

A Society of Gentlemen [pseud. John Murdoch]. *The Polyhymnia: Being a Collection of Poetry, Original and Selected. By A Society of Gentlemen*. Glasgow: John Murdoch, [1799].

Steele, Richard (ed.). *Poetical Miscellanies, Consisting of Original Poems and Translations. By the best Hands. Publish'd by Mr. Steele*. London: J. Tonson, 1714.

Tate, Nahum (ed.). *Poems by Several Hands, And on Several Occasions Collected by N[ahum]. Tate*. London: J. Hindmarsh, 1685.

[Theobald, Lewis (ed.)]. *The Grove; Or, A Collection of Original Poems, Translations, &c. By* [double cols] *W. Walsh, Esq; Dr. J. Donne. Mr. Dryden. Mr. Hall of Hereford. The Lady E—— M——[.] Mr. Butler, Author of Hudibras. Mr. Stepeny. Sir John Suckling. Dr. Kendrick. And other Eminent Hands*. London: W. Mears, 1721.

Tonson, Jacob (ed.). *Poetical Miscellanies: The Fifth Part. Containing a Collection of Original Poems, With Several New Translations. By the most Eminent Hands*. London: J. Tonson, 1704.

Tonson, Jacob (ed.). *Poetical Miscellanies: The Sixth Part. Containing a Collection of Original Poems, With Several New Translations. By the most Eminent Hands*. London: J. Tonson, 1709.

Other primary works

Dodsley, Robert. *The Correspondence of Robert Dodsley, 1733–1764*, ed. James E. Tierney. Cambridge: Cambridge University Press, 1988.

Dodsley, Robert and Reed, Isaac (eds). *A Select Collection of Old Plays. In Twelve Volumes. The Second Edition . . . With Notes Critical and Explanatory*. London: J. Dodsley, 1780.

Secondary works

Amory, Hugh. 'Virtual readers: the subscribers to Fielding's *Miscellanies* (1743)', *Studies in Bibliography*, 48 (1995): 94–112.

Ault, Norman. *New Light on Pope: With Some Additions to His Poetry Hitherto Unknown*. London: Methuen, 1949.

Blagden, Cyprian. 'The Stationers' Company in the eighteenth century', *Guildhall Miscellany*, 10 (1959): 36–53.

Blagden, Cyprian. *The Stationers' Company: A History, 1403–1959*. London: George Allen & Unwin, 1960.

Bonnell, Thomas F. 'John Bell's *Poets of Great Britain*: the "Little Trifling Edition" revisited', *Modern Philology*, 85 (1987): 128–52.

Case, Arthur E. *A Bibliography of English Poetical Miscellanies, 1521–1750*. Oxford: Oxford Bibliographical Society, 1935.

Elick, George Baldwin. 'Kind hints to John Nichols, by Joseph Warton and others', *Notes and Queries*, 3 (1956): 76–8.

Forster, Antonia. *Index to Book Reviews in England 1775–1800*. London: The British Library, 1997.

Forster, Harold. *Supplements to Dodsley's Collection of Poems*, Oxford Bibliographical Society Occasional Publication No. 15. Oxford: Oxford Bibliographical Society, 1980.

Gaskell, Philip. *A Bibliography of the Foulis Press*, 2nd edn. Winchester: St Paul's Bibliographies, 1986.

Kahan, Gerald. 'The American career of George Alexander Stevens' lecture on heads', *Theatre Survey: The American Journal of Theatre History*, 18, 2 (1977): 60–71.

Kahan, Gerald. *George Alexander Stevens and the Lecture on Heads*. Athens, GA: University of Georgia Press, 1984.

Lavoie, Chantel. '*Poems by Eminent Ladies*: a study of an eighteenth-century anthology', unpublished PhD Thesis, University of Toronto, 1999.

Lavoie, Chantel. '*Poems by Eminent Ladies*: the encyclopedic anthology of 1755', in *1650–1850: Ideas, Aesthetics, and Inquiries in the Early Modern Era*, 8 forthcoming (2002).

Liebert, Herman W. 'Walpole and Pearch', in Warren Hunting Smith (ed.), *Horace Walpole: Writer, Politician and Connoisseur*. New Haven, CT: Yale University Press, 1967, pp. 296–7.

Lonsdale, Roger (ed.). *The New Oxford Book of Eighteenth-Century Verse*. Oxford: Oxford University Press, 1984.

Lynch, Kathleen M. *Jacob Tonson, Kit-Cat Publisher*. Knoxville: University of Tennessee Press, 1971.

Maslen, Keith. 'Printing for the author: from the Bowyer Printing Ledgers, 1710–1775', *The Library*, 5th ser., 27 (1972): 302–9.

Maslen, Keith. *An Early London Printing House at Work: Studies in the Bowyer Ledgers*. New York: The Bibliographical Society of America, 1993.

Plomer, H. R., Bushnell, G. H. and Dix, E. R. McC. *A Dictionary of the Printers and Booksellers Who Were at Work in England, Scotland, and Ireland from 1726 to 1775*. London: The Bibliographical Society, 1968.

Rose, Mark. *Authors and Owners: The Invention of Copyright*. Cambridge, MA: Harvard University Press, 1993.

Sherbo, Arthur. *Isaac Reed, Editorial Factotum*, University of Victoria English Literary Studies Monograph No. 45. Victoria, BC: University of Victoria Press, 1989.

Suarez, Michael F. 'Dodsley's collection of poems and the ghost of Pope: the politics of literary reputation', *Papers of the Bibliographical Society of America*, 88 (1994): 189–206.

Suarez, Michael F. 'English book sale catalogues as bibliographical evidence: methodological considerations illustrated by a case study in the provenance and distribution of Dodsley's Collection of Poems, 1750–1795', *Library*, 6th ser., 21 (1999): 321–60.

Suarez, Michael F. 'The formation, transmission, and reception of Robert Dodsley's

Collection of Poems by Several Hands' and 'Who's who in Robert Dodsley's *Collection of Poems by Several Hands*', introduction to the facsimile edition of Robert Dodsley and Isaac Reed (eds), *A Collection of Poems by Several Hands (1782)*, 6 vols. London: Routledge/Thoemmes Press, 1997, Vol. 1, pp. 1–230.

Suarez, Michael F. 'Trafficking in the muse: Dodsley's *Collection of Poems* and the question of canon', in Alvaro Ribeiro and James G. Basker (eds), *Tradition in Transition: Women Writers, Marginal Texts, and the Eighteenth-Century Canon*. Oxford: Oxford University Press, 1996.

Tierney, James E. '*The Museum*, the "Super-Excellent Magazine"', *Studies in English Literature*, 13 (1973): 503–15.

Tierney, James E. 'Literary piracy and the eighteenth-century book trade: the cases of George Faulkner and Alexander Donaldson', *Factotum*, 17 (1983): 25–35.

Tierney, James E. 'More on George Faulkner and the London book trade', *Factotum*, 19 (1984): 8–11.

Treadwell, Michael. 'London trade publishers 1675–1750', *The Library*, 6th ser., 4 (1982): 99–134.

Watson, George (gen. ed.). *The New Cambridge Bibliography of English Literature*, 5 vols. Cambridge: Cambridge University Press, 1969–77.

INDEX

Abbattista, Guido   116, 117
Addison, Joseph   210, 230, 231
  Song for St. Cecilia's Day   231
  Spectator   210
advertisements, advertising   25–6, 175, 187
Agitation   180
Ainsworth, Thomas   191
Akenside, Mark   229, 234, 235
Alexander, William
  History of Women   126
Allein, Joseph   145
Allein, Richard   145
Ames, Joseph   62
Amory, Hugh   219
Analytical Review   171, 178, 179, 180
Anderson, Robert
  Works of the British Poets   244
Andrews, John   94
Annesley, Samuel   145
Anstey, Christopher   233
Anti-Jacobin Review   179, 180
Arbuthnot, John   230, 231
Ariosto, Ludovico   199, 200
Aristophanes   85
Arminius   150
Armstrong, John
  A Day   181
Astell, Mary   105–6, 125
Astle, Thomas   156, 165 n. 27
Atterbury, Francis   89, 191, 234, 244

Bacon, Francis, Viscount St Albans   108, 111
Bagford, John   39
Baillie, Hugh   103 n. 82
Baker, Thomas   39
Baldwin, Henry   176
Baldwin, Robert   108, 114, 176
Balfour, John, 120
Balfour, John, Hamilton, Gavin and Neil,
  Patrick, firm of   107, 113
Balguy, Thomas   96, 103 n. 82
Barbauld, Anna Laetitia   225
Barber, Mary   225
Barlow, Thomas   150, 166 n. 45
Barnes, Ernest William   35

Barnes, Joshua   212
Baro, Peter   150
Baron, Richard   95
Barrington, Shute   60, 75 nn. 145 & 146
Basker, J. G.   171
Baskerville, John   7
Baskett, John   51, 52
Baskett, Thomas and Robert   53
Baskett family   52, 58
Bate, James   42
Bate, Julius   42
  Old Testament translated by   41
Bathurst, Allen, first Earl   210
Battle of the Reviews   176
Baxter, Richard
  Reliquiae Baxterianae   146
Bayle, Pierre   137–40, 141–2, 142–3, 144,
  150–1, 152–3, 156, 157, 158, 159, 160,
  162, 163, 166 n. 47
  Dictionaire Historique et Critique   136, 137–9,
    142, 163
  trans. of   137, 139, 142–3, 149–51, 162,
    163
  see also General Dictionary
Beattie, James
  The Minstrel   240
Becket, Thomas   232, 239–40
Behn, Aphra   225
Beinecke Library   177
Belanger, Terry   1, 5, 28
Belke, Edwin   48
Bell, John   10, 12, 17, 23, 210, 211
  Poets of Great Britain   240, 243, 244
Beloe, William   177
Bentham, Joseph   50, 51, 52
Bentley, Richard   41, 205, 211
  Horace, edn of   203–4
  New Testament, planned edn of   41
  Paradise Lost, edn of   196, 200, 203
Berenger, Richard   235
  'Verses to Mr. Dodsley'   235
Berington, Joseph
  History of Henry the Second   129
Berkenhout, John
  Biographia Literaria   146, 154

Bernard, John Peter   136, 149, 150, 163
Berriman, John   69 n. 55
Bible, the   chapter 2 *passim*, 81
  Authorized Version   37–8, 39, 40, 43–4, 51,
    54, 55–60, 61, 62, 64–5, 67 n. 20
  for children   47
  distribution of   47–50
  Geneva   37, 43
  Manx   48, 55
  New Testament, edns and trans. of   41, 43,
    44, 45
  Old Testament, trans. of   41
  printing of   51–3, 54
  Psalms   57
  Septuagint   60
  Vulgate, trans. of   44
  Welsh   48
  Wycliffite   39
Bible Society   54, 63–4
Binns, John   25
Biographia Britannica   95, 135–6, 140, 142,
    145–6, 147, 152–6, 159, 160, 161, 162,
    163, 166 n. 41
Biographia Britannica, 2nd edn   103 n. 80,
    136, 142, 152, 156–8, 159, 161–2, 163,
    167 nn. 65, 72 & 73
  see also Kippis, Andrew
Birch, Thomas   136, 145, 149, 150, 151–2,
    154–5, 157, 161, 162, 166 nn. 41 & 47,
    167 n. 65, 207
  see also General Dictionary
Black, Jeremy   115
Blackburne, Francis   94–6, 157
  Confessional   94, 96
  Memoirs of Thomas Hollis   95
  Remarks on Johnson's Life of Milton   95
Blacklock, Thomas   230, 231
Blair, Hugh
  Sermons   185
Blair, Robert
  The Grave   240
Blake, William   76 n. 153
Blayney, Benjamin   36–7, 58, 60, 61, 64,
    74 n. 138, 75 n. 146
Blount, Charles   154
Bodleian Library   79, 90, 156, 177, 193, 207
Bolingbroke, Henry St John, Viscount   86, 115
  Letters on the Study and Use of History   110,
    117
book auctions   12
book distribution   2, 13, 47–50
book format   23–4
book history   4

book prices   50–1, 209–10, 220–1, 242
book production   2, 4, 5, 21–2
book trades, financing of   9–11
booksellers and bookselling   5, 11–24, 27–30,
    107–8, 111, 218, 222
  see also individual booksellers
Booth, William Bramwell   35
Bossuet, Jacques Bénigne
  Discours sur l'histoire universelle   117
Boston, John   153
Boswell, James   168 n. 82
  Life of Johnson   161, 168 n. 82
Boswell, James jun.   207
Bourdieu, Pierre   80
Bowyer, William, firm of   5, 13
Boydell, John   28
Boyle, Robert   151
Brady, Robert   108
Brandt, Gaspar
  History of the Reformation in the Low Countries
    150
Brett, Thomas   68 n. 51
British Critic   177, 178, 179, 180, 182, 185, 204
British Mercury   7
British Museum   193, 206, 207, 212, 215 n. 29
Brooke, Frances   225
Brooke, Henry   229
Broome, William   206
Brougham, Henry   152
Broughton, Thomas   136, 152, 160, 162, 163,
    167 n. 54
Browne, Sir Thomas   154, 158
  Christian Morals   158
Browne, William   200
Buckingham, George Villiers, second Duke of
    162, 243
Bull, George   89
Bunyan, John   160–1
  Pilgrim's Progress   160, 161
Burke, Edmund   197
Burlington, Richard Boyle, third Earl of   210
Burnet, Gilbert   89, 151, 161
  History of the Reformation   110
Burney, Frances
  Evelina   85
Burrow, J. W.   124–5
Bury, Arthur   79–82, 98
  The Naked Gospel   79, 81, 82, 91
Butler, Alban   215 n. 29
Butler, Joseph
  Analogy of Religion   87, 90
Butler, Samuel   211, 224
  Hudibras   203, 208, 211–12

Cadell, Thomas   10, 16, 18, 19, 28, 29, 96,
      108, 113, 120, 122–3, 156
Calamy, Edmund   136, 137, 146–8, 154,
      166 nn. 38 & 40, 168 n. 88
   Abridgment of Mr. Baxter's History   146–7
   Abridgement of Mr. Baxter's History, 2nd edn
      147
   Account of the Ministers   147
   Continuation   147
   My Own Life   166 n. 38
Callender, John   55
Cambridge University Press   48, 50–3
Camden, William
   Britannia   127
Campbell, John   136, 142, 145–6, 147, 152,
      154, 157, 158, 167 n. 54
   Political Survey of Britain   154
Capell, Edward   196, 204, 205, 206, 214 n. 8
   Notes and Readings   196, 210
   Prolusions   196
   Shakespeare, edn of   196, 201, 203, 204,
      208–9, 209–10
Carte, Thomas   108, 112, 119
   General History of England   108, 112
Carter, Elizabeth   197, 206, 225, 231
   Epictetus, trans. of   197, 211
   Poems   197
Carter, Nicholas   197
Carter, Sally   225
Caslon, William   7
Cave, Edward   197
Caw, George   246 n. 6
   Poetical Museum   220–2
Cawthorn, James   231
   Abelard to Eloisa   231
Cervantes
   Don Quixote   86
Challoner, Richard   44
   Vulgate, trans. of   44–5
Chalmers, Alexander   146, 152, 159–60, 161,
      162
   General Biographical Dictionary   136, 145, 152,
      159–60, 161, 162, 163
   Works of the British Poets   244
Chandos, James Brydges, Duke of   210
Chapone, Hester   225
   Letters on the Improvement of the Mind   125–6
Chatterton, Thomas   222
Chaucer, Geoffrey   199
   edns of   191–3
Chesterfield, Philip Dormer Stanhope, Earl of
      230
Chrysostom, St John   85
Chudleigh, Mary, Lady   225

Church, Ralph
   Faerie Queene, edn of   211
Churchill, Charles
   The Apology   175
Cibber, Colley   211
Cibber, Theophilus   207
   Lives of the Poets   207
Clarendon, Edward Hyde, Earl of   108,
      110–11, 112, 155, 158
   History of the Rebellion   108, 109, 110–11
   Life   111
Clarke, Samuel   56, 89, 94, 151, 162
Cleland, John
   Memoirs of a Woman of Pleasure   174
Cleveland, John   244
Cluer, John   9
Cobb, Samuel   227
Cockburn, Catharine   155, 225
   Works   155
Cole, William   215 n. 29
Collection of Poems, see Dodsley, Robert
Collier, J.
   Parents and Guardians Directory   15
Collier, Jeremy   136, 140–2, 145, 154, 159
   Great Dictionary   136, 140–2
      Appendix to   140
      Supplement to   140, 141, 145, 162
   Short View   140
Collier (or Collyer), Mary   225
Collins, Anthony   152
Collins, Benjamin   25
Collins, William   229, 230, 234, 235, 239
   Poetical Works   239
Collyer, see Collier, Mary
Colman, George, the elder   224, 226
Comparative View of the State and Faculties of Man
      185
Complete History of England   111
Condillac, Etienne Bonnot de   93
Congreve, William   227, 230, 231, 234
   Hymn to Harmony   231
Cooke, Charles   30
   Select British Poets   244
Cooke, John   17, 29, 30
Cooper, John Gilbert   234, 235
Cooper, Mary   226, 227
Cooper, Thomas and Mary   13, 247 n. 17
Cooper, William   12
Coote, John   234
copyright, ownership and sale of   5, 14–17, 20,
      21, 240–1, 248 n. 25
Copyright Act (1710)   16, 17, 18, 228
Cornbury, Henry Hyde, Viscount   117
Cosin, John   89

Cottrell, Thomas   8
Cowley, Abraham   234
Cowley, Charlotte
   The Ladies History of England   126–7
Coxeter, Thomas   207
Craftsman   117
Crevier, Jean Baptiste Louis   122
Critical Review   106, 115, 116, 171, 176, 178,
      179, 180, 181, 182, 184, 185–6, 186–7,
      204, 238
Cromwell, Oliver   154, 155
Crowder, Stanley   28
Cruttwell, Clement   55
Cudworth, Ralph   94, 161
Cumberland, Richard   154
Curll, Edmund   210
   Pope's Miscellany   243

Dalrymple, Sir David, Lord Hailes   157
Daniel, Samuel   111
Darby, Henry   52
Darwall, Mary (*née* Whateley)   225
Davis, Lockyer   156
Dawks, Ichabod
   News-Letter   7
de Hondt, P. A.   239
De la Roche, Michel   142, 151
   Memoirs of Literature   172
De Sallo, Denis   172
Deliciæ Poeticæ   218
Dell, Henry   28
Des Maizeaux, Pierre   142–3, 150, 165 n. 25
   Life of Bayle   139, 164 n. 10
   Life of Chillingworth   143
   Life of Hales   143
Dibdin, Thomas Frognall   30
Dicey, Cluer and William   9, 25
Dictionary of National Biography   145, 163,
      169 n. 107
Diderot, Denis   117
Dilly, Charles   29, 114
Disney, John   87–8
Dobson, Susannah   127
Doddridge, Philip   86
   Family Expositor   87
Dodsley, James   29, 30, 230, 232, 233, 234,
      237–8, 239–42, 244, 249 n. 41
   Collection of Poems   240
Dodsley, Robert   5, 13, 28, 29, 228–9, 230,
      234, 235, 240, 247 n. 17, 248 nn. 19 & 24,
      250 n. 51
   Collection of Poems   217–18, 226, 227–33,
      234–5, 237, 238, 241–2, 244, 247 n. 16

   Dublin edn   228–9
   Scottish edns   230–3
   Melpomene   235
   Select Collection of Old Plays   228, 242
   The Museum   226
Donaldson, Alexander   16, 17, 28, 230, 231,
      232
   Select Collection of Poems   230
   Select Collection of Modern Poems   230–2
Donaldson, John   17
Donne, John   166 n. 41, 224
Donoghue, Frank   171
Dorset, Charles Sackville, Earl of   251 n. 64
Douglas, Gavin   199
Drayton, Michael   200
Dryden, John   160, 162–3, 200, 201, 224, 227,
      230, 231, 243, 244
   Absalom and Achitophel   162
   Aeneid, trans. of   135–6
   Alexander's Feast   231
   Essay of Dramatic Poesy   162
   Miscellanies   243, 250 n. 60
   'Ode on St Cecilia's Day'   162
   'To the memory of Mr Oldham'   162, 163
Dublin booksellers   18, 228–30
Duck, Stephen   229
Dunbar, James
   Essays on the History of Mankind   123
Duncombe, William   244
Dunn, John   236
   Choice Spirit's Chaplet   236
Durrell, David   36, 37, 58, 60, 62, 74 n. 136,
      75 n. 145
Dyer, John   229, 230, 234

Echard, Laurence   108, 111, 112
   History of England   108
   Roman History   122
Edinburgh Review   171, 178
Edwards, Thomas   229
Ellis, John   235
Elstob, Charles   212
Elstob, Elizabeth   126, 212
   English-Saxon Homily, trans. of   212
Elstob, William   212
Enfield, William   185
English Review   177, 179
English Short Title Catalogue   2
engravers and engraving   8–9
Epictetus   166 n.47, 197, 211
Epicurus   166 n. 47
Erasmus   41
Erskine, Sir Harry   222

Etherege, Sir George 251 n. 64
European Magazine 186
Evelyn, John 165 n. 26
Eyre, Charles 51

Farley, Samuel and Felix 25
Farmer, Richard 196, 204, 206, 207, 214 n. 8, 215 n. 29
Essay on the Learning of Shakespeare 196
Faulkner, George 230, 248 n. 24
Fawkes, Francis and Woty, William 233, 234
Poetical Calendar 233–4, 239
Fell, John 145
Felton, Henry 99 n. 14
Fenning, Daniel
Universal Spelling-Book 22
Fenton, Elijah 158, 243, 244
Oxford and Cambridge Miscellany Poems 243
Ferguson, Adam
Essay on the History of Civil Society 123
History of the Roman Republic 122
Fielding, Henry 211
Amelia 22
Joseph Andrews 82–3
Tom Jones 22, 83
Fisher, Samuel 45
Flavel, John 145
Fortescu, Alexander 53, 54
Foster, Sir Michael 167 n. 73
Foulis, Robert and Andrew 210, 232
Select Poems 232–3
Foundling Hospital for Wit 227
Fourdrinier, Henry and Sealy 7
Fowler, Edward 145, 160, 165 n. 26
Foxe, John
Acts and Monuments 80
Frend, William 61
Froude, James Anthony
Nemesis of Faith 79
Fry, Edmund 7
Fry, Joseph 7, 8
The Specimen of Printing-Types 8

Gamble, John 7
Garrick, David 197, 206, 235
Garth, Sir Samuel 243
Gay, John 227, 230, 231, 243
Geddes, Alexander 45, 46, 61, 75 n. 148
General Dictionary 136, 142, 143, 145, 149–52, 153, 154, 155, 159, 160, 161, 162–3, 166 n. 41
see also Birch, Thomas
Gentleman's Magazine 106, 118, 172, 186, 188, 229, 239

Gibbon, Edward 61, 84, 87, 96, 97, 108, 115, 121, 122–3, 124
Autobiographies 84
Decline and Fall 121, 122–3
Gibson, Edmund 38, 46
Camden's *Britannia*, edn of 127
Giles, William
Collection of Poems 250 n. 52
Gill, William 29
Gilmour, John
Select Collection of Modern Poems 230–2
Ginn, Elizabeth 43
Glanvill, Joseph 145–6, 154
Glover, Richard 235
Goadby, Robert 25
Godwin, William 29
Goldsmith, Oliver 112, 119, 120, 181, 230, 235
Deserted Village 240
History of England 119
History of England, in a Series of Letters 125
Roman History 122
The Traveller 119, 240
Gough, Richard 157
Gower, John 199
Grainger, James 235
Granger, James
Biographical History of England 161, 168 n. 91
Graves, Richard
Spiritual Quixote 85–6
Gray, Thomas 91–2, 98, 206, 215 n. 29, 229, 230, 234
Elegy 229
Green, Matthew 229, 230, 231
Greville, Frances 225
Grey, Zachary 197, 211–12
Hudibras, edn of 203, 208, 211–12
Grierson, Constantia 225
Griffiths, George Edward 177
Griffiths, Ralph 28, 171, 172–3, 174, 175, 176, 177, 178, 181, 183, 239
see also Monthly Review
Ascanius 174
Compleat Catalogue 175
Copies of the papers 174
Grove, Henry
System of Moral Philosophy 173
Grover, Thomas 7
Grub Street Journal 203
Gunning, Peter 145
Guthrie, William
General History of England 112, 119

Halifax, Charles Montagu, Earl of
Epistle to Dorset 243

Hallam, Henry　130
Hamilton, Archibald　178
Hamilton, Elizabeth
　　Memoirs of Agrippina　127
Hamilton, William　231
Hammond, Henry　89
Hammond, James　229
Hanmer, Sir Thomas
　　Shakespeare, edn of　201, 208, 209
Hansard, Luke　5
Harington, James, of Christ Church　144
Harley, Robert, Earl of Oxford　210
Harley family　39
Harris, James　161, 168 n. 93
Harris, Mr, contributor to *Biographia Britannica*
　　152
Harrison, James　17, 28
　　Lady's Poetical Magazine　226
Harrison, Thomas　28
Hartley, David　162
Harwood, Edward　43
Haslewood, Joseph　208
Hawkesworth, John　234
Hawkins, Sir John　157
Hays (or Heys), Mary　225
　　Female Biography　127
　　Letters and Essays　127
Hazard, Samuel　25
Hearne, Thomas　212
Heathcote, Ralph　152
Heliodorus　85–6
Henrietta of Gerstenfeld　180
Henry, Philip　145
Henry, Robert
　　History of Great Britain　124
Herbert, George　166 n. 41
Herring, Thomas　56
Hervey, James　155
　　Letters　155
Hervey, John, Baron　210
Heydinger, Carl　28
Heylin, Peter
　　Historia Quinqu-Articularis　150
Heys, *see* Hays, Mary
Hickes, George　145, 165 n. 26, 212
Hicks, Philip　111, 112
Hill, Aaron
　　Gideon　173, 174
Hinton, John　28
Hinton, Revd, contributor to *Biographia*
　　Britannica　152
History of the Works of the Learned　172, 173
Hoadly, Benjamin　89–90, 96
Hoare family　50

Hobbes, Thomas　154
Hogarth, William　211
Hogg, Alexander　17, 23
Holcroft, Thomas　28
Hollis, Thomas　94–6
Hollis, Thomas Brand　95
Holmes, Robert　60
Homer　161, 199, 200
Hooke, Nathaniel
　　Roman History　121
Hookham, Thomas　23
　　and Carpenter, Thomas　12
Hopkins, William　43
Horace　199
Horne, George　41, 166 n. 41
Horsley, Samuel　61
Houbigant, Charles　63
Howe, John　165 n. 26
Hughes, John　195, 230, 231
　　Paradise Lost, edn of　195
　　Spenser, edn of　195
Hume, David　43, 93, 107, 111, 113–14, 115,
　　119, 120, 124, 126, 155
　　History of England　106, 107–8, 109, 112,
　　113–14, 116, 118
　　History of Great Britain　107, 113, 115, 155
　　'Of national characters'　87
Hume, Patrick　200
　　Paradise Lost, edn of　200
Hunt, Thomas　42, 58, 62, 63
Hurd, Richard　83, 84, 85, 92, 93–4,
　　168 n. 82, 212
　　Letters on Chivalry and Romance　129
Husbands, John
　　Miscellany of Poems　220
Hutcheson, Francis　161
Hutchinson, John　41
Hutton, William
　　History of Birmingham　127
　　History of Derby　127

Jacob, Hildebrand　227
James, Thomas　7
Jarvis, Charles
　　Don Quixote, trans. of　86
Jennens, Charles　196, 206
Jervis, Thomas　87–8
Johnson, Anthony　40
Johnson, Jane　46
Johnson, Joseph　29, 179
Johnson, Michael　144
Johnson, Samuel　17, 43, 95, 96, 154, 156,
　　158, 161, 164 n. 12, 165 n. 27,

166 nn. 41 & 44, 179, 197, 204, 206, 207, 220, 229, 234, 235
Dictionary 22
Lives of the Poets 95, 158, 163, 194, 206, 234, 242–3
London 232
'Messiah', trans of 220
Prefaces Biographical and Critical, see Lives of the Poets
Shakespeare, edn of 201, 202, 203, 204, 205, 206, 209, 210
Works of the English Poets 240, 242, 244
Jones, Claude 171
Jones, Mary 183, 225
Jonson, Ben 162, 200, 201
Journal des Sçavans 172

Kames, Henry Home, Lord
Sketches of the History of Man 123
Kennett, White 38, 111, 144
Kennicott, Benjamin 56, 57–8, 59, 60, 62, 63, 75 nn. 145 & 148, 77 n. 167
Kenrick, William 178, 240
A Scrutiny 175
Killigrew, Anne 225
King, William (of Dublin) 166 n. 47
King, William (of Oxford) 244
King's Printer[s], King's Printing House 38, 48, 50, 51, 52, 54
Kipling, Thomas 61
Kippis, Andrew 136, 142, 152, 154, 156–9, 160–1, 161–2, 163, 166 n. 38, 167 n. 72
see also Biographia Britannica, 2nd edn
Kirkpatrick, James 181
Knapp, L. M. 171
Knapton, John 9, 83
Knapton, Paul 9

Lackington, James 19, 23
La Fontaine, Jean de 227
Lane, William 10, 12, 19, 28, 29
Langbaine, William
English Dramatick Poets 207–8
Langhorne, John 249 n. 43
Letters between Theodosius and Constantia 185
Owen of Charon [Carron] 240
Lansdowne, George Granville, Baron 230, 231
Lardner, Nathaniel 97
Credibility of the Gospel History 87, 95
Larpent, Anna 85
Laud, William 145, 155, 167 n. 62
Lavoie, Chantal 226
Law, Edmund 43, 69 n. 57, 166 n. 47
Law, William 84

Christian Perfection 84
Serious Call 84
Leapor, Mary 225
Le Cène, Charles 38, 54, 67 n. 26
Le Clerc, Jean 82, 142
Moréri, edns of 140
Lee, Sidney 145, 163
Leland, Thomas 94
Lennox, Charlotte 206, 225
Lewis, John 38–40, 55, 62, 78 n. 179
History of Translations of the Bible 39
Wyclif, edn of, and life of 39
Lewis, Thomas
History of France 125
Lilburne, John 95, 155
Lintot, Bernard 243
Locke, John 89, 94, 96, 135, 139, 161, 165 n. 26, 234
Essay concerning Human Understanding 89
tracts on toleration 95
Lockman, John 136, 149, 163
History of England 112
London 1, 2, 3, 6, 7, 8, 10, 12–13, 22, 24, 25, 27, 28
London Chronicle 175, 235
London Daily Post 26
London Evening-Post 178
London Magazine 172
London Review 177, 178, 182–3, 184, 185
Long, Thomas 81–2
Longman, George 28
Longman, Thomas II 28, 29, 156
Longmans, firm of 5, 18, 21, 22
and Rees, Owen 16
Lonsdale, Roger 245
Lowndes, Thomas 12
Lowth, Robert 57, 58, 59, 60, 62, 63, 64, 65, 92, 250 n. 57
Lydgate, John 199
Lyttelton, George, Baron 197, 230, 234
King Henry the Second 129

Macaulay, Catharine 109, 112, 113–14, 126
History of England 109, 113–14
Macaulay, Thomas Babington 130
Macpherson, James 128
Introduction to the History of Great Britain 128
Mace, Daniel 40–1, 43
New Testament, edn of 40–1
Macro, Cox 100 n. 27
Madan, Judith 225
M'Gregor, Malcolm 233
Mallet, David 231, 235, 248 n 28
Tyburn to the Marine Society 181

Mallet, Paul
  Introduction à l'histoire de Dannemarc 128
Malone, Edmond 193, 201–3, 204–5, 206, 207, 208–9, 214 n. 8
  Capell, annotations to 208–9
  Shakespeare, edn of 194, 201–3, 204–5, 207, 210
Malthus, Thomas
  Essay on Population 97
Mandeville, Bernard 152
Marcus Aurelius 161
Marsh, Herbert 64
Marvell, Andrew 96, 210
Mason, Monck 207
Mason, William 235
Masters, Mary 225
Mawer, John 69 n. 55
Mayhew, Jonathan 95
Meere, Hugh 7
Mendez, Moses 235–6
  The Seasons 235
Merrick, James 75 n. 139
Middleton, Conyers 91–3, 197
  Letter from Rome 93
  Life of Cicero 91, 92, 122
Mill, John 41
Millar, Andrew 22, 113, 114, 120, 181
Millar, John 108
  Origin of the Distinction of Ranks 123, 126
Milton, John 84, 95, 96, 111, 151, 230, 231, 234
  Comus 200, 231
  Defence of the People of England 95
  edns of 194, 200–1, 202, 210
  Eikonoklastes 95
  Paradise Lost 85, 195, 196, 200–1
  Paradise Regained 201
Monk (or Monck), Mary 225
Montagu, Edward 197
Montagu, Elizabeth 197–8, 206
  Essay on Shakespear 197–8
Montagu, Lady Mary Wortley 225, 229
Montesquieu, Charles Louis Joseph de Secondat, Baron de 93, 117
  Considérations 122
Monthly Epitome 188
Monthly Review 85, 116, 171–88, 238, 239
Montluzin, E. L. de 180
Moore, Edward 235
Morant, Philip 152, 155, 160
More, Hannah 197
  Percy 127
  Sir Eldred of the Bower and the Bleeding Rock 240

More, Henry 161
Moréri, Louis 136, 138, 139–42, 144, 157, 159, 164 n. 12
  Grand Dictionaire 136, 140, 150, 152
  trans. of 140
  see also Collier, Jeremy
Morgan, Thomas 93
Morley, George 166 n. 41
Mortimer, John
  New History of England 128
Mortimer, Thomas
  Universal Director 15
Murdoch, John
  Polyhymnia 222–3
Murray, John I 5, 13, 18, 19, 29, 177
Muse in Good Humour 227

Nangle, B. C. 171
Nares, Robert 177
Nary, Cornelius 69 n. 63
Nayler, James 155
Nelson, Sir Horatio 49–50
Nelson, Robert 89
New Cambridge Bibliography 217
New and General Biographical Dictionary 136, 152, 159, 161
New London Review 179, 185
Newbery, Francis 29
Newbery, John 71 n. 82
Newcastle, Margaret Cavendish, Duchess of 225
Newcome, William 60, 61–2, 75 n. 151
newspapers, news-sheets 1, 24–6
Newton, Sir Isaac 65 n. 4, 94
  Observations upon the Prophecies 35
Newton, Thomas 200
  Paradise Regained, edn of 209
Nichols, John 16, 157, 165 n. 27, 206, 215 n. 29, 242–5
  Select Collection of Poems 242–5
Nichols, Sir Philip 95, 136, 152, 155–6, 161, 162
Noble, John
  Muse in Good Humour 226–7
Noble, John and Francis 12, 13, 23
Noble, Mark
  Lives of the English Regicides 127
Normanby, John Sheffield, Marquis of
  Temple of Death 243
Nutt, John 218

Observator 7
Oldenburg, Henry 151
Oldham, John 163, 227

Oldmixon, John   112, 244
  Critical History of England   112
  Poems and Translations, edn of   243
Oldys, William   136, 152, 155, 207–8
  Langbaine, annotations to   207–8
Orrery, Roger Boyle, Earl of   243
Osborn, James   149
Osborne, Thomas   28, 29–30
Ostervald, J. F.   47
Ovid   163, 200
Owen, John   45
Oxford University Press   38, 48, 50–3, 54, 58,
  108, 201

Paine, Thomas   61
  Age of Reason   97
Palmer, John   25
Palmer, Samuel   43–4, 166 n. 38
paper manufacture   6–7
Parkinson, James
  The Fire's continued at Oxford   80–1
Parnell, Thomas   230, 231, 243
Pearce, Zachary   196
  Review of the Text of Paradise Lost   196, 200
Pearch, George   218, 236–42
  Collection of Poems   237–42, 244, 249 n. 42
Peardon, T. P.   124
Pemberton, John   243
Pennington, Elizabeth   225
Pepusch, John Christopher   211
Percy, Thomas   156, 206, 207, 208, 240, 244,
  250 n. 57
  'The Hermit of Warkworth'   240
  Langbaine, annotations to   207, 208
  Northern Antiquities   128
  Reliques   128, 233, 240, 244
Peters, Richard   46–7
Philips, Ambrose   206, 234, 243
Philips, Katherine   225
Phillips, Halliwell   207
Pilkington, Laetitia   225
Pinkerton, John
  Dissertation on the Goths   128
Pitt, William, Earl of Chatham   114
Poems by the most Eminent Ladies   224–5, 226,
  247 n. 12
Poetical Calendar, see Fawkes, Francis
Pope, Alexander   84, 86, 210, 224, 228, 230,
  231, 234, 240, 243, 244
  Dunciad   86, 94
  Eloisa to Abelard   231
  Essay on Man   86, 240
  Iliad, trans. of   195

Miscellaneous Poems and Translations, edn of
  243, 251 n. 61
Miscellanies, edn of   243
  Ode. . . on St. Cecilia's Day   231
  Poems on Several Occasions, edn of   243
  Shakespeare, edn of   195, 201, 203
prayer-books   46, 49, 52
Priestley, Joseph   43, 61, 87, 108
printers and printing   1, 2, 3, 4, 7–9, 51–3,
  178, 220–1
Prior, Matthew   210, 227, 230, 231
provincial book trade   2, 17, 22
Prynne, William   145
Public Advertiser   26, 115, 187
publishers   4, 14–15, 19, 20, 21, 27
  see also booksellers
Purver, Anthony   45
  Bible, trans. of   45
Pye, Jael Henrietta   225

Quarterly Review   171
Quinn, James   211

Ralegh, Sir Walter   155
  History of the World   155
Ramsay, Alan   222
Randolph, Thomas   36–7, 66 n. 12, 96,
  103 n. 82
Rann, Joseph
  Shakespeare, edn of   204
Rapin de Thoyras, Paul   119
  Histoire d'Angleterre   112
Rawlinson, Richard   144
Raynal, Guillaume Thomas
  Histoire philosophique des deux Indes   117
Reed, Isaac   196, 204, 206, 207, 208, 214 n. 8,
  241, 242
  Shakespeare, edn of   196, 201, 202, 207
Rees, Abraham   158–9
Reeve, Clara
  History of Romance   129
Renwick, William   187
Reynolds, Sir Joshua   197, 225
Rich, John   211
Richardson, Samuel   5, 211
  Clarissa   85
  Pamela   100 n. 27
Richardson, William and Urquhart, Leonard
  234, 235, 237
  Collection of the Most esteemed Pieces   234–5,
  237
Ridley, Glocester   156
Ridley, Nicholas   156
Rivington, Charles and Francis   177

Rivington, James 114, 131 n. 21
Rivington, John 51, 96, 156
Rivingtons, firm of 10, 18, 71 n. 84
Roberts, Rachel 225
Robertson, William 43, 108, 114, 115, 120–1,
    122, 124, 126
  Historical Disquisition 123
  History of America 121
  History of Charles V 106, 110, 120–1
  History of Scotland 120
Robinson, George 10, 16, 28, 156
  and firm of 18
Robinson, Jacob 173
Rochester, John Wilmot, Earl of 227, 243
Rollin, Charles
  Roman History 122
Roper, Derek 171, 178
Roscommon, Wentworth Dillon, Earl of 243
Rose, William 85, 185
Rousseau, A. M. 118
Rousseau, Jean-Jacques
  La Nouvelle Hèloïse 83
  Social Contract 93
Rowe, Elizabeth 225
Rowe, Nicholas 195, 201
  Shakespeare, edn of, Life of 195, 202
Rudd, Sayer 43
Ruffhead, Owen 85
Russell, John 38–9
Russell, William
  History of Modern Europe 125
Russell, William, Lord 151
Rymer, Thomas
  Foedera 110

St. James's Chronicle 176
Saint, Thomas 25
Sainte-Palaye, Jean Baptiste La Curne de 129
  Memoirs of Ancient Chivalry 127
Sale, George 149
sale catalogues 15
Salmon, Thomas 118
  History of England 113
  Modern History 113
Salter, Samuel 155
Sanderson, Robert 148
Saunders, Francis 251 n. 64
Savage, Mary 225
Savage, Richard 220, 227
Scarlett, Nathaniel 44
  New Testament, trans. of 44
Schultens family 63
Scotland
  book trade in 18, 220–3, 230–3

  history in 108, 120, 123
  paper trade in 6
Scott, ? Mary 225
Scott, Sir Walter 130
Secker, Thomas 55–6, 57, 58–9, 60, 62, 63,
    64, 96, 197
Sedley, Sir Charles 227, 251 n. 64
Selden, John 39
Select Poems and Ballads 233
Sellon, William 71 n. 84
Sewell, William 79
Shaftesbury, Anthony Ashley Cooper, first Earl
    of 162
Shaftesbury, Anthony Ashley Cooper, third Earl
    of 139, 160, 161–2, 164 n. 10
  Characteristicks 161
Shaftesbury, Anthony Ashley Cooper, fourth
    Earl of 161
Shakespeare, William 84, 85, 199, 200, 202
  edns of 194, 195, 196, 201–5, 206–7,
    208–9, 209–10, 211
Sharpe, Gregory 42
Shebbeare, John 96, 103 n. 82
Shenstone, William 229, 230
Sher, R. B. 120
Silver, Samuel
  Lover's Manual 223
Simon, Richard 41, 44, 54, 56
  New Testament, edn of 41
Skeat, W. W. 193
Smalridge, George 191
Smart, Christopher 212, 229, 234
  'Solemn Dirge' 229
Smith, George 163
Smith, John
  Galic Antiquities 128
Smollett, Tobias 106, 114–15, 116, 118–19,
    120, 171, 176, 178, 235
  see also Critical Review
  Complete History of England 114–15, 116
  Continuation 108, 114, 115
  Regicide 173
  Voltaire, trans. of 118
Society for Promoting Christian Knowledge
    (SPCK) 47–50, 50–3, 72 n. 94
Somerville, Thomas
  History of Great Britain 124
  History of Political Transactions 124
South, Robert 89, 165 n. 26
Spector, R.D. 171
Spence, Joseph 234, 244
  Polymetis 156
Spenser, Edmund 84, 85, 156, 161, 199, 200
  edns of 195, 199–200, 211

Faerie Queene 199–200, 211
Sprat, Thomas 89, 165 n. 26
Stamp Act 26
Stamp Duty 6
Stationers' Company 5, 13–14, 18, 28, 29, 240
Steele, Sir Richard 211, 243, 244
  Poetical Miscellanies 243
Steevens, George 193, 204, 206–7, 214 n. 8
  Langbaine, annotations to 207–8
  Shakespeare, edn of 201, 202, 203, 204, 205, 207, 208, 210
Stephen, Leslie 145, 163
Sterne, Laurence 83
  Sermons 85
  Tristram Shandy 79, 83, 87, 88
Stevens, George Alexander 236
  Choice Spirit's Feast 236
  Songs, Comic, and Satyrical 236
Stillingfleet, Edward 89
Strahan, Andrew 28
Strahan, William 5, 28, 29, 51, 107, 120, 122, 123, 131 n. 21, 178
Strutt, Joseph 129–30
  Complete View of Dress 129
  Complete View of Manners 129
  Queenhoo Hall 130
  Regal and Ecclesiastical Antiquities 129
  Sports and Pastimes 129
Stuart, Gilbert
  View of Society in Europe 126, 129
subscription, publication by 20, 53–4, 197, 210–12, 219–25, 246 nn. 5 & 8, 250 n. 52
Suckling, Sir John 224
Sunderlin, Lord 207
Sweet, Rosemary 127
Swift, Jonathan 111, 227, 230, 233
Sylvester, Matthew 146

Talbot, Catherine 197
Talbot, William 197
Tanner, Thomas 144, 165 n. 26, 166 n. 45
Tasso, Torquato 199, 200
Temple, Sir William 111, 244
  Introduction to the History of England 110
Theobald, Lewis 195, 196, 205, 206, 214 n. 8, 224
  Shakespeare, edn of 195, 201, 203–4, 208, 209, 210–11
  Shakespeare Restored 195
  The Grove 224
Thirlby, Styan 211
Thomas, Timothy 191, 192

Thomas, William 214 n. 2
Thomson, James 16, 211, 229, 230, 235
Thoresby, Ralph 156
Thornhill, Sir James 211
Thornton, Bonnell 224, 226
Thrale, Hester Lynch 225
Tickell, Thomas 229, 230, 231, 234, 235, 243
Tierney, James 226
Tillotson, John 89
Timperley, C. H. 28, 178
Tindal, Matthew 90–1
  Christianity as Old as the Creation 90–1
Tindal, Nicholas 112
Todd, Henry John 64–5
Tomalin, Claire 171
Tomlins, Elizabeth Sophia 225
Tonson, firm of 194–5, 198, 199, 201, 202
Tonson, Jacob I 28, 194, 210
  Miscellanies 243, 250 n. 60
Tonson, Jacob II 194
Tonson, Jacob III 194
Tooke, Benjamin 243, 251 n. 64
  Collection of Poems 243–4, 251 n. 64
Towers, Joseph 136, 156, 159, 167 n. 55
  British Biography 156, 159
Travis, George 61
Trelawny, Jonathan 81, 82
Trenchard, John 151
Trusler, John 10, 20
Turner, Sharon
  History of the Anglo-Saxons 128
Tyndale, William 62
  New Testament, trans. of 43, 76 n. 159
type manufacture 7–8
Tyrrell, James 112
  General History of England 106
Tyrwhitt, Thomas 191–3, 204, 206
  Canterbury Tales, edn of 192–3, 199, 203
  Observations on Shakespeare 192

Underwood, Thomas 187
Universal History 107, 116–17, 118
Upton, John 199–200, 211
  Faerie Queene, edn of 199–200, 203
Urie, Robert 231–2
Urry, John 191
  Chaucer, edn of 191–2, 202, 208, 214 n. 2
Utterson, Edward 208

Vertue, George 8
Virgil 162, 163, 199, 200
  Aeneid 135–6, 163
Voltaire, François-Marie Arouet 93, 112, 117–19, 197

Voltaire, François-Marie Arouet (*cont.*)
   Candide 118
   Essai sur les moeurs 117–18, 118–19
   Histoire de Charles XII 117
   Histoire de l'empire de Russie 117
   Siècle de Louis XIV 118

Wakefield, Gilbert 43
Walker, John 136, 137, 147–8
   Sufferings of the Clergy 147–8
Walker's Hibernian Magazine 187–8
Waller, Edmund 158
Walpole, Horace 91, 98, 197, 206, 212, 225,
   229, 234, 235
Walton, Brian 64
Walton, Izaac 148
   Lives 166 n. 41
Wanley, Humfrey 39, 144
Warburton, William 63, 83, 84, 85, 86, 88,
   91, 92–4, 98, 196, 205, 206, 208, 211
   Alliance of Church and State 93
   'Charge on the study of theology' 94
   Divine Legation 92, 93, 94
   Doctrine of Grace 85, 94
   Julian 93
   Shakespeare, edn of 196, 201, 208, 209,
   210
   'The true Methodist' 94
Warton, Joseph 206, 250 n. 57
   Essay on Pope 198
Warton, Thomas the elder 243
Warton, Thomas the younger 196, 200–1,
   202, 206, 233, 234
   History of English Poetry 129, 194, 196
   Milton, edn of 200–1
Waterland, Daniel 39, 42, 88–93
   Advice to a Young Student 88–90, 96
   Scripture Vindicated 90, 91
Watson, Richard 88, 96–8
   Anecdotes 97, 98
   Collection of Theological Tracts 96–7, 159
Watts, Isaac 87
   Hymns 22
   Scripture History 90
Wesley, John 55, 83, 94
Wesley, Samuel 229
West, Gilbert 229
   Education 135–6, 154
Wharton, Philip, Baron 50
Whateley, Mary, *see* Darwall

Wheeler, Maurice 52
Whichcote, Benjamin 155, 161
   Aphorisms 155
   Select Sermons, with preface by Shaftesbury
   161, 162
Whitaker, John
   Genuine History of the Britons 128
   History of Manchester 127
Whitefield, George 83, 94
Whitehead, Paul 234, 235
Whitehead, William 229, 235
Whitla, William
   Newton, edn of 35
Wilkes, John
   Essay on Woman 100 n. 33
Wilkins, John 145
Wilson, Alexander 7
Wilson, John 52
Wilson, Thomas 55
Winchilsea, Anne Finch, Countess of 151, 225
Witham, Robert 69 n. 63
Wodrow, Robert 40
Wollaston, William
   Religion of Nature 90
Wollstonecraft, Mary
   Female Reader 126
   *Historical and Moral View of the French
   Revolution* 126
Wood, Anthony 82, 136, 144–6, 148, 150,
   151, 153, 162, 166 n. 45
   Athenae Oxonienses 144–6, 148, 159, 160,
   162, 167 n. 62
Woolf, D. R. 126
Woolston, Thomas 152
Worgan, John 229
Worsley, John 55
Wotton, Sir Henry 166 n. 41
Wotton, William
   History of Rome 122
Woty, William, *see* Fawkes, Francis
Wray, Lady Mary
   Historical Miscellany 126
Wright, R. 208
Wright, Thomas 28, 29
Wright, Thomas, and Gill, firm of 51
Wyclif, John 38–9

Yorke, Charles 94
Young, Edward 211, 243
   Night Thoughts 86